WITHDRAWN
HARVARD LIBRARY
WITHDRAWN

Theology of Hate

UNIVERSITY PRESS OF FLORIDA

Florida A&M University, Tallahassee
Florida Atlantic University, Boca Raton
Florida Gulf Coast University, Ft. Myers
Florida International University, Miami
Florida State University, Tallahassee
New College of Florida, Sarasota
University of Central Florida, Orlando
University of Florida, Gainesville
University of North Florida, Jacksonville
University of South Florida, Tampa
University of West Florida, Pensacola

Theology of Hate
A History of the World Church of the Creator

George Michael

University Press of Florida
Gainesville/Tallahassee/Tampa/Boca Raton
Pensacola/Orlando/Miami/Jacksonville/Ft. Myers/Sarasota

For Suzy

For this book, several persons helped me in different ways. I am thankful to those who granted me interviews, including George Burdi, Matthew F. Hale, and the late Dr. William L. Pierce. I would also like to thank the personnel at the University Press of Florida, especially Eli Bortz and Susan Albury.

Copyright 2009 by George Michael
Printed in the United States of America. This book is printed on Glatfelter Natures Book, a paper certified under the standards of the Forestry Stewardship Council (FSC). It is a recycled stock that contains 30 percent post-consumer waste and is acid-free.
All rights reserved

14 13 12 11 10 09   6 5 4 3 2 1

Library of Congress Cataloging-in-Publication Data
Michael, George, 1961–
Theology of hate : a history of the world Church of the Creator / George Michael.
p. cm.
Includes bibliographical references and index.
ISBN 978-0-8130-3350-1 (alk. paper)
1. Church of the Creator—History. I. Title.
BP605.C55M53 2009
299—dc22   2008055181

The University Press of Florida is the scholarly publishing agency for the State University System of Florida, comprising Florida A&M University, Florida Atlantic University, Florida Gulf Coast University, Florida International University, Florida State University, New College of Florida, University of Central Florida, University of Florida, University of North Florida, University of South Florida, and University of West Florida.

University Press of Florida
15 Northwest 15th Street
Gainesville, FL 32611-2079
www.upf.com

Contents

Introduction vii

1. The Early Life of Ben Klassen 1

2. The Theology and Ideology of Creativity 13

3. The Far Right and the Critique of Christianity 33

4. Reaching Out to the Right 61

5. Groundbreaking in North Carolina 72

6. Disintegration and Collapse 91

7. George Burdi and RAHOWA 108

8. Resurrection: Matt Hale and the World Church of the Creator 120

9. The WCOTC's Women's Frontier 134

10. The Controversy over a Law License 139

11. Benjamin Smith 147

12. Opposition 161

13. Denouement? 170

14. Conclusion: Fragmentation and Beyond 189

Notes 199

Bibliography 253

Index 273

Introduction

Throughout its turbulent history, the Creativity movement has garnered a substantial amount of notoriety. For instance, over the weekend of July 4, 1999, the small racist cult made headlines when a former member embarked on a shooting spree that left two persons dead and nine others injured. Still other sporadic episodes of violence linked to the group preceded and followed that event. In the summer of 1993, the FBI uncovered a plot hatched in California that involved some members of the church who planned to provoke a race war by assassinating prominent Jewish and African American figures. Many of the violence-prone Creators were not church renegades but members in good standing. Under the leadership of Matthew Hale during the late 1990s and early 2000s, the World Church of the Creator was at the center of several free speech controversies that strained communities and divided legal scholars.

Although a marginal movement, Creativity nevertheless exerted a significant influence on the extreme right both in North America and overseas. For example, a band founded by one of its members—RAHOWA—did much to popularize the "white power" music genre in the skinhead subculture. Although the Creativity movement has attracted only a small following, it has had an influence far beyond what its relatively small membership would suggest. In particular, it contributed to the radicalization of the extreme right and its movement away from Christianity.

Unlike the extreme right in Europe, Christianity in the United States has featured prominently in the American extreme right. From the Anti-Masonic Party of the early nineteenth century to the contemporary Christian Identity movement, Christianity has served as an inspiration and organizing principle in the far-right movements that have punctuated American history. However, over the past decade or so, one can discern a shift in attitude toward Christianity in the American far right, most notably, among its younger affiliates. Some segments are now highly critical of Christianity and see it not as a path to salvation, but rather as a road to spiritual alienation and racial oblivion. How did this new sentiment come about? Some "traditionalists" in the movement sought to resurrect paganism and encouraged whites to rediscover their native spirituality. The influence of the Norse neopagan religion, Odinism, or Asatru, on the far right is now well documented.[1] Arguably, nearly as important in "de-Christianizing" the far right has been the Creativity movement, which developed a critique of Christianity that influenced subsequent pagan racialists.

The Creativity movement began with the late Ben Klassen who founded the organization in 1973 with the release of his book *Nature's Eternal Religion*. The creed he formulated—"Creativity"—rejects all metaphysical beliefs and supernatural deities. Instead, it offers an all-encompassing *Weltanschauung* based on the veneration of the white race. In a nutshell, Creativity posits that the white race is nature's most gifted creation. Therefore "Creators" espouse "racial loyalty" and seek to unite the white race in a single global community devoid of all other races. For this objective to be achieved, certain measures are advanced to enhance the health (eugenics) and survival of white people as a distinct racial group (thus there are strictures against miscegenation and whites are encouraged to have large families). Although its critics often dismiss Creativity as a "pseudo-religion," its followers maintain that their creed is an authentic and appropriate belief system for racial activists, who seek an alternative to the "Jewish-inspired" faith of Christianity. Moreover, Klassen believed a religious movement was far more potent and enduring than a political party. Therefore, he explicitly sought to fashion his ideology as a religion.

Despite the church's influence on the far right and the notoriety stemming from sporadic violence, a definitive history of the organization has yet to be written. The propensity of Creator members to commit acts of violence is remarkable even among the most radical elements of the extreme right. Furthermore, the organization attracted some of the most dysfunctional personalities, even by far-right standards. Thus the group's small size notwithstanding, it managed to attain a considerable amount of publicity in the mainstream media.

This book chronicles the history of the Creativity movement, which has gone by several names during its tumultuous history, including the Church of the Creator, the New Church of the Creator, the World Church of the Creator, the Creativity Movement, the Church of the RaHoWa, the White Crusaders of RaHoWa!, and the Church of Creativity. Thus throughout the book, when referring to a specific incarnation, the corresponding title is used. "Creativity movement" will be used to designate Creativity over the course of its entire history. Chapter 1 explores the early life of the church's founder, Ben Klassen. The theology that he formulated—Creativity—is the subject of chapter 2. Creativity did not rise in a vacuum but emerged in a political subculture that had grown increasingly disenchanted with mainstream Christianity. Chapter 3 examines the far right's disillusionment with Christianity, which originally commenced in Germany and Austria in the early part of the twentieth century, but later spread to America after World War II. After founding his church, Klassen sought to promote his religion among other activists in the extreme right. These efforts are detailed in chapter 4. Chapter 5 discusses the early history of the first incarnation of the Church of the Creator, which was established in North Carolina in 1982. Although it experienced moderate growth, by the early 1990s the church was in disarray and nearly collapsed after the death of Ben Klassen in 1993. These events are covered in chapter 6.

Despite these setbacks, the Creativity message, which survived in the skinhead scene in large part because of George Burdi, is introduced in chapter 7. Chapter 8 looks at Matthew Hale, who was principally responsible for resurrecting the organization in 1995. The church also reached out to females through its Women's Frontier, which is discussed in chapter 9. Chapter 10 examines the controversy surrounding Hale's quest to receive a law license after he graduated from law school and passed the Illinois Bar examination. Arguably, the controversy surrounding this issue sparked the rampage of a former church member, Benjamin Smith, who embarked on a shooting spree during the July fourth weekend in 1999. These and other episodes of Creativity-related violence are covered in chapter 11. Not surprisingly, such violence has occasioned opposition from both the government and private monitoring groups—the subject of chapter 12. Faced with such formidable opposition, the World Church of the Creator was dealt a serious blow with the arrest and imprisonment of its leader, Matthew Hale. His many legal troubles are recounted in chapter 13. Finally, the conclusion discusses the influence of the Creativity movement on the extreme right and speculates on its future direction.

1

The Early Life of Ben Klassen

Childhood

Bernhardt Klassen, who was named after his father, was born into a Mennonite family on February 7, 1918. His family lived for many generations in a colony in the village of Rudnerwiede, located on the Molotschna River in southern Ukraine. The Mennonite community in that country was established near the end of the eighteenth century at the invitation of Catherine II.[1] According to Klassen, his ancestors migrated from either Holland or the Danzig area of Prussia sometime around the sixteenth century. In addition to himself and his parents, Klassen's family included two brothers, Henry and Korni, twelve years and ten years his senior, respectively; and two sisters, Sarah and Katie, six years and four years his senior, respectively.[2]

As an infant, Klassen was subjected to the turmoil of the Russian Civil War, as his village was frequently ravaged by the Red Revolutionary Army and assorted brigands that were released from the Russian penitentiaries following the Bolshevik Revolution. In April of 1918, occupying German troops established a semblance of order in the colony. After the armistice was signed in November 1918, however, the German troops retreated, thus leaving the colony exposed to renewed depredations. One nemesis in particular, was the anarchist, Nestor Ivanovich Makhno (1889–1934), whose marauders plundered the Mennonite villages. Makhno was an anarcho-communist Ukrainian, who refused to align with the Bolsheviks after the Revolution. He sought to implement a form of anarchism in the Ukraine territory, which the struggling Bolshevik government had ceded and recognized its independence with the signing of the Brest-Litovsk Treaty of 1918. Not wanting to live under the rule of the Central Powers, the Ukrainian people revolted. Eventually, the rebellion turned into an anarchist revolution of which Makhno was one of the main organizers. He joined a coalition of revolutionary groups—the Revolutionary Insurrectionary Army of Ukraine (RIAU), or the Black

Army—which fought against the counterrevolutionary White Army. By doing so, Makhno played an important part in saving the newly installed Bolshevik government from collapse. Nevertheless, he had a falling out with Trotsky and the Bolsheviks and was eventually driven into exile. He first fled to Romania, then Poland, and finally settled in France, where he set up an organization of Russian exiles in Paris known as the Cause of Labor. He died in 1934.[3]

Their pacifist orientation notwithstanding, the Mennonites, upon discovering that Makhno and the Bolsheviks had joined forces, finally defended themselves in an action known as *Selbstschutz*, which lasted from November 1918 to March 1919. Understandably, the early experiences left the young Klassen with a disdain for Bolshevism. Moreover, these experiences seemed to have triggered his anti-Semitic worldview, as he attributed Bolshevism to Jews, whom he claimed had never assimilated and constituted a fiercely hostile and revolutionary element in Russian society. Later in life, he attributed the feeble self-defense efforts of the Mennonites to the passivity engendered by Christianity. To make matters worse, a famine beset the area as well, resulting in the deaths of some six million people over a two-year period. Faced with such grim prospects for the future, the Klassen family fled the fledging Soviet Republic in 1924, when young Ben was six years old. They first settled in the state of Chihuahua in Mexico with four other Mennonite families. Together, they all lived in one flat-roofed adobe building that contained exactly five rooms with dirt floors. For about a year and a half, the settlers grew beans, corn, and potatoes, but the project was deemed a failure and thus disbanded.[4]

Growing up in Canada

Next, in 1925, the Klassen family moved to Canada and settled in Herschel, Saskatchewan, an area to which some of Klassen senior's relatives had already moved the prior year. The travels took a toll on the young Ben Klassen, who picked up intestinal worms somewhere which left his body thin and vulnerable to the cold weather in Canada. On one Christmas morning, he examined the meager gifts he received, which was constituted of hand-me-downs and makeshift items. As he recalled, it slowly dawned on him that there was no Santa Claus. The turbulent years of his early life impressed upon him that he and his family were on their own without assistance from any benevolent creator.[5] Nevertheless, by pooling resources and borrowing from other Mennonites, his father arranged to purchase a 640-acre wheat farm. With the help of his industrious family, Bernhard senior was on the road to renewed prosperity.[6] One of the first things that the approximately forty Mennonite families did was to build a communal church which was completed in 1927.[7]

According to his autobiography, Klassen was a bright student. Although English was not his native language, he claimed to have jumped grades because of his academic aptitude.[8] The first school he attended was a one-room structure in Oskaloosa. For a short period of time, he actually had a black friend named Earl Lafayette with whom he played baseball. But for the most part, the young Klassen excelled in solitary accomplishments. In 1931, his father sent him to a small Mennonite school called the German-English Academy at Saskatchewan, located 150 miles northeast of Hershel. In the classroom, the young Klassen occasionally sought to outsmart his teachers and make them look foolish. At the end of the school year, he came in second in his class.[9] He then attended the Saskatoon Normal School in Saskatchewan, where he first became interested in girls. A handsome young man, he was said to have judged girls on a superficial level according to how they served his interest and needs.[10]

About a year after completing Normal school, Klassen enrolled in the University of Saskatchewan in 1935. While in college, he developed an intense interest in history. After learning about the multitude of religions in human history, Klassen came to the conclusion that they were all contrived and, hence, without any basis in fact. He left college in 1937 and soon thereafter returned to the Saskatoon Normal School, where he took a position as a schoolteacher and janitor with a salary of fifty dollars per month.[11] Before long, however, he found that he was not cut out for this career. He was frequently at odds with his pupils and actually had fistfights with two of them.[12]

In the summer of 1938, Klassen returned to the University of Saskatchewan and took a six-week course in child psychology so that he might "unlock the secret of what made those little brats tick."[13] Next, he transferred to the University of Manitoba from which he received a degree in engineering. He acquired enough academic credits to receive a degree in arts and sciences from the University of Saskatchewan as well.

As events in Europe in the late 1930s heated up, there ensued a political polarization between some of the pro-German Mennonites and the pro-British Canadians, especially the Canadian Legion veterans of World War I.[14] Fluent in German, Klassen read *Mein Kampf*, which had a profound influence on the development of his *Weltanschauung*. Increasingly, he identified with the new German Reich and he made plans to study engineering at the University of Heidelberg. His plans were dashed, however, when World War II commenced in Europe in September 1939. Not long after the German invasion of Poland, Canada stood by England and declared war on Germany, thus rendering Klassen's plans to study in Germany unfeasible. While in college, Klassen enlisted in the Canadian Officers Training Corps, but he still maintained dreams of moving to Germany to "help build the New Order" and even entertained the notion of joining the air force so that he could somehow drop into Germany and join the Axis cause. With his sympathies lying with Germany, Klassen had no interest in serving in the Canadian military. When he first heard of Hitler's invasion of the Soviet Union on June 22, 1941, he recalled that he felt "exhilarated." Electrified by the *Wehrmacht's* stunning early battle victories, Klassen saw them as retribution for all the destruction and agony the communists had inflicted on his family and Mennonite community.[15] With the defeat of the Third Reich in the spring of 1945, Klassen lost interest in politics and devoted his energies to establishing a career in engineering in the United States.

On to California

In late 1945, Klassen made his way to in California. The next year, he married Henrie Etta McWilliams, an attractive woman with blonde hair and Nordic features, which were the physical attributes that he preferred in women. While in California, he went though some odd jobs. First, in September of 1946, he went to work for Bardwell McAllister, a lighting company. After about two months, he left that job to work as a technical sales representative for a man named Jerry Miller, who sold oscillographs (i.e., instruments for measuring alternating or varying electric current in terms of current and voltage) equipment. He did not stay long, however, soon leaving that position to work for another manufacturer's representative called the W. Bert Knight Company, a firm which represented about a dozen national manufacturers in the field of electronics. Despite receiving a good salary, Klassen longed to work for himself.

An ambitious man, Klassen dreamed of being his own boss. While in Los Angeles, he established a real estate firm in partnership with a man named Ben Burke. It was not long, however, before he found fault in his partner, who, according to Klassen, was prone to gambling and drunken binges. In consequence, Klassen decided to buy him out and go into business exclusively on his own. He rented a larger office and hired four or five salesmen to help him with his real estate business. One of them, Merle Stanley Peek, encouraged Klassen to buy into large land development projects in Nevada. Together, they went into partnership and established the Silver Spring Land Company.[16] Eventually, Klassen decided to end his partnership with Peek, whom he increasingly found to be a contemptible character. So in 1952, he sold his share of the company to another investor, Phillip Hess, and came away with $150,000—a substantial amount of money at that time. From then on, Klassen decided to live the life of a retired gentleman.[17]

In 1951, his only child and daughter, Kim Anita, was born. His atheism notwithstanding, in 1955 Klassen, along with his family, joined a Presbyterian church in Glenmore Gardens, California, and together, they were baptized. However, Klassen found the sermons boring and even suspected that the church leader, Pastor Tom Fuhr, did not believe in Christian theology but rather went along with it out of force of habit.[18] By 1967, Klassen decided that he had finally "had enough of this religious garbage and [would] never set foot in [a] church again."[19]

A moderately successful inventor and businessman, Klassen invested in a company called the Commercial Tobacco Corporation that sought to market a self-lighting cigarette. His most successful invention, though, was an electric can opener, which he marketed as Canolectric. In March 1956, Klassen filed an application with the U.S. Patent Office for a patent on his invention. Ironically, two Jewish attorneys by the name of Gardner and Zimmerman handled his application. To market his product, Klassen teamed-up with a firm called Robbins & Myers and together they created a partnership called Klassen Enterprises, Inc., and Robbins & Meyers. At one point, they even received a call from Sears Roebuck. The prominent retailer was interested in discussing a major purchasing contract; however, the deal was never realized.[20] Furthermore, Klassen's product soon faced stiff competition from the more established manufacturers, such as General Electric, Sunbeam, Oster, and Nu-Tone, which could provide similar products at a lower price. In Klassen's words, they "were outclassed and outmaneuvered by the giants."[21] Finally, in 1962, Klassen and his partners dissolved the company.[22]

His most lucrative endeavors, though, were in the area of real estate, which effectively enabled him to retire at a fairly young age. Florida, in particular, was the state in which Klassen concentrated his real estate investments. With more time on his hands, Klassen devoted more energy to politics and vacationing, as he made numerous trips to Europe, Egypt, Mexico, and Hawaii. While there, he paid acute attention to the racial dynamics of populations. By the late 1950s, he and his family relocated to Florida from California.

Entering Politics

The specter of communism and the civil rights movement rekindled Klassen's interest in politics. In particular, it was the vehement opposition to Senator Joseph McCarthy's anti-communist crusade that made Klassen suspect that something was "rotten" in the American political system. Still, he later made it clear that he had no sympathy for McCarthy. After all, as he pointed out, the Wisconsin senator had Jews on his staff, including Roy Cohn and David Schine. What is more, his failure to identify the "real enemy" (Jews), instead of focusing on a nebulous communist conspiracy, undercut Klassen's respect for McCarthy as well. Nevertheless, he believed that McCarthy was on to something and consequently was killed by Jews.[23]

Like so many other prominent figures in the radical right, Klassen sojourned through the John Birch Society (JBS). At one time, he even operated an American Opinion bookstore. For two years, he served as the chairman of the John Birch Society's Fact Finder's Forum and promoted speakers from the American Opinion Speakers Bureau. The origins of the JBS can be traced to 1958, when a successful candy manufacturer, Robert H. W. Welch, Jr., convoked a meeting of like-minded friends in Indianapolis, Indiana, to create an organization to counter the communist subversion they saw throughout the U.S. government.[24] The Society was named after John Birch—a young fundamentalist Baptist preacher and intelligence officer, who served in China during World War II.[25]

Welch developed a relatively tight-knit and disciplined organization, which at its peak in the mid-1960s, reached a membership of approximately 50,000–60,000 members—an astronomical figure by far right standards.[26] Through his dissemination of conspiracy theories, Welch made significant contributions to the worldview of the radical right. This caused some consternation for Jewish defense organizations, such as the Anti-Defamation League, which closely monitored the JBS. Earlier research suggested that these seemingly innocuous conspiracy theories propounded by the Birch Society could potentially be transformed into anti-Semitic narratives.[27] The Birch Society was an important nexus and gateway to the radical right during that period. There were several examples of JBS members who were, or went on to become, leading anti-Semites.[28]

One of Klassen's more notable efforts for the JBS was his promotion of a book written by John Stormer called *None Dare Call It Treason*, which he sold through his American Opinion bookstore. A popular book in rightist circles, it explored the history of communism in the United States and its putative penetration of government, education, organized labor, and tax-exempt foundations.[29] In later years, Klassen corresponded with Stormer and encouraged him to read Klassen's book, *Nature's Eternal Religion*, explaining, that after all, he had sold 80,000 copies of *None Dare Call It Treason* and that Stormer should at least read it out of gratitude for Klassen's previous efforts.[30] In particular, Klassen implored Stormer to consider his critique of Christianity.

Proceeds from the 80,000 copies of the book that he supposedly sold were contributed to the presidential campaign of Barry Goldwater in 1964. But by the time of the general election in November, Klassen had become thoroughly disenchanted with the Arizona senator. In fact, he went so far as to accuse him of deliberately losing the election to discredit and undermine the conservative movement. As Klassen saw it, although Goldwater was only half Jewish, "underneath his phony veneer, his true loyalty [lay] with the Jewish cause."[31]

In 1966, running as a Republican and an openly avowed Birch Society member, Klassen was elected a state representative of Broward County in Florida, which at the time had a population of approximately 750,000 residents. He ran his campaign on an anti- busing and anti-UN platform.[32] A month after his victory, Robert Welch introduced Klassen at the John Birch Society's Eighth Annual Birthday Dinner in New York.[33]

Not long after the election, however, the Supreme Court ordered redistricting of Florida, which necessitated a new round of elections. Klassen decided to run for the state senate but was defeated in his bid in 1967. He was still active in the Birch Society but became increasingly disillusioned because of its tolerant position on Jews.

His final assessment of the organization was characteristic of so many of his counterparts; that is, the Birch Society was directed by Jews to deliberately lead the white man down a blind alley. To buttress his claim, Klassen pointed out that Birch Society leaders were always skittish when discussing the topic of Jews. As Klassen saw it, the Birchers did not have the temerity to identify the Jews as the true enemy of the white race. Rather, the Birch Society confused its members with Byzantine conspiracy theories that essentially nullified any meaningful activism. In August 1969, Klassen formally resigned from the Society by sending a letter to the chairman, Robert Welch, from whom he demanded a $1,000 refund for a lifetime membership for which he had previously paid. In the letter, he castigated Welch for confusing American conservatives by keeping them focused on a nebulous communist conspiracy, when, Klassen argued, the real problem was a Jewish conspiracy of which the former was just one small part. According to Klassen, Welch responded with a letter that sought to whitewash the "Jewish issue." He never did get his $1,000 back.[34] For its part, the Birch Society excoriated the "collectivist tendencies" of the racialist and anti-Semitic right. Welch went so far as to release a tape-recorded speech to his followers—"the Neutralizers"— in which he claimed that communists had planted anti-Semites in his organization in an effort to discredit it.[35]

The presidential candidacy of George Wallace attracted elements of the racist right. Klassen first met Wallace in 1968 and went on to serve as the Florida state chairman of the American Independent Party.[36] To support Wallace, Klassen established a Florida chapter of the Citizens Council of America, which had its national headquarters in Jackson, Mississippi. As vice-chairman of the Florida state committee for Wallace, Klassen staged a number of pro-Wallace rallies, one of which was organized jointly with the Ku Klux Klan.[37] However, his anti-Semitism unsettled the state party leadership and they eventually requested his resignation, which Klassen gave them in 1969. Not one to leave quietly, he sent a number of angry letters to the party leaders excoriating them for their failure to identify Jews as the primary culprits of America's malaise.[38] Wallace, though, was careful enough not to openly affiliate with certain segments of the extreme right. Although he harbored prejudice against blacks and is believed to have actually had two Klan leaders on his payroll—Asa Carter and Robert K. Shelton—he knew that anti-Semitism could have a devastating effect on his credibility.[39] Therefore, he sought to distance himself from those rightists too closely associated with any anti-Jewish animus. By 1969, Klassen had become disenchanted with conservative politics and he and his colleague, Austin C. Davis, Jr., began looking for more radical organizations to which they could devote their efforts.

For a short time, Klassen flirted with openly avowed Nazi parties. Initially impressed by their forthrightness on the Jewish issue, Klassen considered aligning himself with various neo-Nazi groups, including Matt Koehl's National Socialist White People's Party (the successor of George Lincoln Rockwell's American Nazi Party). Prior to Rockwell's creation of the American Nazi Party in 1958, there were a few organizations, such as the Columbians and the National Renaissance Party (NRP), which adopted some of the symbolic and stylistic trappings and ideology of Nazism. However, the Columbians quickly ran afoul of the law and were effectively shut down while the NRP remained a small cult until its dissolution in 1979.[40] Rockwell's American Nazi Party (ANP) was the first explicitly neo-Nazi party to gain widespread notoriety in the United States. Flamboyant and articulate, Rockwell captured much publicity for his National Socialist cause with his provocative antics. Along with his stormtroopers, Rockwell would visit racial hot spots around the country. His "in your face" tactics provoked angry opposition and brought much attention to his organization, which gave observers the perception that it was much larger than it really was (estimates are that it never exceeded fifty members at any given time).[41] Rockwell tirelessly set about creating a viable party and established links with like-minded activists, which culminated in the creation of the World Union of National Socialists in the village of Cotswold in England in 1960.[42] Deliberately provocative, Rockwell's approach occasioned fierce opposition. The Anti-Defamation League—a Jewish defense organization that monitors threats to the Jewish community—once persuaded the FBI to open an investigation of Rockwell.[43] At one time, his party was a target of the FBI's COINTELPRO program (which will be discussed in greater detail in chapter 12). It was not easy for Rockwell to hold his followers together, as his organization attracted more than its share of the mentally unstable and provocateurs. In 1967 a disgruntled member, John Patler, assassinated Rockwell as he left a Laundromat in a shopping center located near the ANP headquarters in Arlington, Virginia. In the extreme right subculture, Rockwell is an iconic figure and influenced several individuals in the movement. His organization actually continues to this day under the name New Order in Wisconsin, but it is essentially a book distributor.

Klassen looked at the National Socialist White People's Party (the immediate successor to the ANP), but was not impressed with its leader, Matt Koehl, whom he once met and described as a "poor speaker."[44] Moreover, he even suspected that Koehl was a "controlled stooge" in service of the Jewish conspiracy to neutralize "the most aggressive elements of [the white] race."[45] Tactically, Klassen did not believe that an openly Hitlerian approach was viable in America. In his estimation, the shrill approach of the explicitly National Socialist organizations merely served the interests of Jewish groups in their fund-raising.[46] In the realm of religion, he criticized Koehl's organization for failing to come to grips with Christianity, of which Klassen was becoming increasingly critical.[47] Nevertheless, over the years, he corresponded with some of the most radical elements of the neo-Nazi movement, including David Rust, who once led the National Socialist Liberation Front in California.[48] Yet, he maintained a nagging suspicion that the explicitly Nazi organizations were, in effect, an "organized opposition" under false leadership.[49]

Klassen also explored the National States' Rights Party, which was led by J. B. Stoner and Dr. Edward R. Fields.[50] Initially impressed by the organization, he seriously contemplated joining it.[51] He personally knew both Stoner and Fields and, at first, was on relatively good terms with them. However, he was put off by the organization's failure to take a position against Christianity, which it favorably promoted. In later years, Klassen suspected that Stoner and Fields were not genuine.[52]

As he distanced himself from conservative politics, Klassen bitterly criticized the more respectable figures of the far right, especially those who did not openly express criticism of Jews. In particular, he was critical of Christian conservatives, such as Billy James Hargis, the leader of the Christian Crusade. The retired USMC Lieutenant General P. A. del Valle, who championed traditionalist rightist themes including Constitutionalism, Christianity, patriotism, and opposition to the Federal Reserve System, did not escape Klassen's acerbic pen. In 1971, he reproached the general for not openly identifying Jews as the principal enemy. Furthermore, Klassen advised that basing a patriotic movement on a Christian foundation was misguided insofar as the "suicidal teachings" contained in the New Testament were not an effective foundation for resistance. For his part, del Valle defended his position and would not countenance Klassen's critique of Christianity. Klassen later explained that there was no other experience that convinced him so strongly than his exchange with del Valle that the white race needed a completely new religion.[53]

In November 1970, Klassen and his associate, Austin Davis, eventually decided to create their own organization, which they called the Nationalist White Party (NWP). The new party received a charter as a nonprofit corporation from the state of Florida in that same year.[54] Interestingly, the party actually evoked mildly Christian themes, as it described itself as a movement of "white Christian people who conquered America [and] don't intend to be relegated to second class citizenship."[55] The party platform included "fourteen points," which were explicitly racialist in character.[56] With this party, Klassen abandoned more respectable, conservative politics once and for all. A logo—consisting of the letter "W" with a crown and a halo above it—was also created for the new party, which would later be carried over to the Church of the Creator.[57]

During the earlier days of his conservative political activism, Klassen actually accused Jews of attacking Christianity, his in-the-closet atheism notwithstanding. Echoing the Identity Christians (who will be covered in chapter 3), in a letter to the *Sun Sentinel* written in 1970, Klassen even claimed that Jesus was not a Jew.[58] By 1971, however, Klassen began expressing serious apprehensions about Christianity. He was dismayed that the religion seemed to temper the radicalism of his followers. As he saw it, Christianity was inherently philo-Semitic, and as such, undermined any serious efforts to oppose Jews. Moreover, the liberal churches, Klassen believed, were preaching racial "mongrelization." During this period, he became increasingly strident in his critique of Christianity. His first notable exegesis on this topic was a letter that he wrote to John R. Adams, a college professor, who entered into an exchange with him on the topics of race, religion, and politics. In the letter, Klassen lambasted Christianity, arguing that it was counterproductive to the white race. To Klassen, the West was great in spite, not because, of Christianity. He wrote to the professor that he planned to expand his ideas into a book. Evidently, Klassen thought much of his letter and even sent copies of it to party members on the west coast. The letter was not well received, however, and as a consequence, all NWP activity in that area came to an end.[59] The fact that his detractors did not adequately refute his arguments assured him all the more that he was correct in his critique of Christianity.[60]

By 1971, Klassen decided to take a closer look at the Christian Bible to "see what all the fuss was about." After a close rereading of the Bible, he concluded that the Sermon on the Mount, as preached by Jesus Christ, was full of "suicidal advice" (e.g., "turn the other cheek," "resist not evil"). In fact, according to Klassen, the New Testament was intended by design to diminish the effectiveness of whites in conflicts with Jews. With this new perspective, Klassen began to reinterpret history and observed that Christianity had been responsible for some of the worst fratricidal conflicts in Europe. Further, he believed that the egalitarian message of Christianity laid the groundwork for communism in the twentieth century.[61] What was needed was a new paradigm, a comprehensive worldview to lead the white man out of the wilderness. He decided that he would look to the laws of nature for guidance in his effort to create a creed for the salvation of the white race.

2

The Theology and Ideology of Creativity

Ben Klassen designated 1973 as the first year in the history of the Church of the Creator.[1] In that year, he published *Nature's Eternal Religion*, which outlined his new religion—Creativity—and applied for incorporation papers to establish his church as a legally recognized religious institution. At this time, Klassen was living in Lighthouse, Florida.

The Critique of Christianity

In a sense, Klassen offered a critique of Christianity reminiscent of Nietzsche's *Twilight of the Gods* and *The Anti-Christ* but much more scathing. Not unlike Nietzsche, Klassen described Christianity as a "slave religion" that originally appealed to the dregs of society. According to Klassen's theory, Jews and whites have been involved in a struggle extending back several millennia. Klassen argued that Christianity, far from being the white man's salvation, was concocted by Jews to confuse him and thus weaken his sense of tribal identity. Thus, the universalistic tendencies of Christianity have caused whites to misplace their altruism away from their racial comrades. Christianity, according to Klassen, was woefully inadequate as a guiding mythos for the white race and could no longer be ignored. If whites were to survive, it was absolutely imperative that they overcome their affiliation with Christianity and recognize it for what it is—a Jewish-contrived theology deliberately designed to "confuse" them. He described the Christian faith as the Jews' "Maginot Line," which must be surmounted before the enemy could be destroyed.[2] As he explained, Christianity had, in effect, left whites rudderless with no sense of direction:

> In Prov. 29:18 is spelled out the idea of a long term [Jewish] program, "where there is no vision, a people perish." If contrast this with the advice the Jews foisted on the White Race in the New Testament: for instance, Matt. 6:34 where it says, "take therefore no thought for the morrow: for the morrow shall take thought for the

things of itself." Here we see clearly spelled out that it is essential for the Jews to have vision for the long term, a long-term plan. In reality, their religion is a perpetual conspiracy which is essential for their survival as a parasitic race. But in order to weaken and soften their victim for aggression, conquest and slavery, the White Race has had its brains polluted with all kinds of bad Jewish advice. . . . The Jews have laid their long term plans, going back thousands of years, for the mastery and enslavement of the world.

The White Race, in contrast has no plan, no program for survival. It has no religion to rally around or to unite its White Brothers. It is just fumbling, bumbling and stumbling along with absolutely no defense against the Jew, whose historical mission it has been over thousands of years to destroy or enslave the White Race.[3]

Nature's Eternal Religion advanced a thoroughgoing deconstruction of Christianity. Virtually every story in both the Old and New Testaments came under Klassen's scathing scrutiny. He expounded on the historical unlikelihood of events such as the story of Adam and Eve, the Great Flood, Jonah and the whale, Joshua and the Battle of Jericho, and the resurrection of Jesus Christ. The Book of Revelations was derided as "a Jewish nightmare in Technicolor." Not only did Klassen find the biblical parables ridiculous, but he also believed that Christianity stymied initiative insofar as it encouraged believers to place their trust in what he thought was a nonexistent God rather than take responsibility for themselves. To Klassen, Christianity was a self-imposed handicap as it encouraged whites to recognize Jews as "God's chosen people." Moreover, it instructed whites to love their enemies, which he reasoned amounted to a suicidal demand.[4] Finally, he posited that the religion imposed a substantial psychological toll on its followers as well. Inasmuch as Christianity often makes contradictory demands, it could ultimately lead to frustration and even mental breakdown:

> When people are continuously threatened with a no-win situation it produces despair, depression, frustration, schizophrenia and in severe cases, mental breakdown. The number of Christians that have been driven to insanity by the fear of hell has never been recorded, but undoubtedly runs into the millions.
>
> The list is endless of how Christianity cripples the mind and reduces its subjects to self-destructive, self-incriminating victims,

standing naked and defenseless before the rapacious Jew, who wrote the script, but will have none of that nonsense himself.[5]

His critique of the Christian afterlife was not unlike that of Hitler, who also spoke scornfully of the Christian concept of hell, as he once commented that "even a child of three can be made to acquire a terror of mind which will remain with him for the whole of his life." Like Klassen, Hitler blamed the Catholic Church for impressing this fear of hell into its adherents. The German führer found the concept ridiculous, commenting that "a man possessed of a minimum of intelligence who [took] the trouble to ponder over [it would] have no difficulty realizing how nonsensical these doctrines of the church are."[6] More recently, a similar critique can be found in some mainstream academic quarters as well. For example, writing in *The God Delusion*, the esteemed Oxford biologist, Richard Dawkins castigated Christianity for psychologically abusing people with the fear of eternal damnation.[7]

Explicitly rejecting any of the assumptions of Christian theology, Klassen asked, If the Christian God is infallible, why has he made so many mistakes? For example, why the struggle between God and the Devil, when the former could eliminate the latter anytime he wanted? If God is really so concerned about the human race, why did He create hell with the intention of sending so many poor souls there in the afterlife? How could God have planned every minute detail of history yet at the same time accorded free will to humans?

In the Christian God, Klassen saw nothing redeeming, as He evinced some of the worst traits including vindictiveness, jealousy, cruelty, and vainglory. Furthermore, inasmuch as Klassen saw the Jews of the Old Testament as "reprobates," he wondered what kind of God would select them as His chosen people. He referred to the biblical prophets Judah, Abraham, Isaac, Lot, David, Solomon, and others as "the most reprehensible bunch of murderers, whoremongers, and moral lepers that you could possibly all get together in one book."[8]

According to Klassen, those who professed a belief in Christianity never really bothered to seriously question the religion's tenets and plausibility. For example, he questioned the historicity of Jesus and found no real corroborative evidence of his existence:

> [I]t is highly strange that despite the great commotion and fanfare that supposedly heralded the birth of Christ and also his crucifixion

(according to the bible), we find not a single historian nor a single writer of the era who found time to take note of it in their writings. Outside the fabricated biblical writings, no Roman historian, no Roman writer, and no Roman play-writer, has left the slightest hint that he had the faintest awareness that his supposedly greatest of all greats was in their very midst and preaching what is claimed the greatest of all gospels.

. . . Christ himself, who had supposedly the greatest message to deliver to posterity that the world has ever known, left not the slightest scrap of paper on which he had written a single word.[9]

To his claim, Klassen pointed out that no historical record could be found that King Herod ordered the slaughter of children who were under two years of age in the town of Bethlehem. Moreover, according to recorded chronology, by the time Christ was supposed to have been born in A.D. 1, Herod had already been dead for four years.[10] As he pointed out, the "Christ" myth could be found in numerous religious sagas and legends.[11] As far as spirituality was concerned, he found nothing uplifting about the "Good News" offered in the New Testament, which consisted mainly of threats of damnation. Christianity, according to Klassen, was highly divisive, as sectarian differences had often provoked wars in the history of Christendom. In his reading of history, Christianity had been responsible for many fratricidal conflicts in Europe, most notably, the Thirty Years' War, which decimated the population of Germany.[12] According to his reasoning, this was deliberate, as he believed that Jews systematically instigated wars between the white nations of the world to weaken them and diminish their populations. Like those who embraced classic anti-Semitic narratives, Klassen believed that Jews were masters at the strategy of divide and conquer.

After reviewing the scriptures, Klassen came to the conclusion that Christianity was a Jewish concoction that ultimately is extremely harmful to the welfare of the white race. He theorized that Christianity was originally based on the Essenes' cult that prevailed around the first century A.D. According to Klassen's thesis, Jews had observed this cult and come to the conclusion that it was highly destructive. Saul of Tarsus—the Saint Paul of Christianity—later repackaged the Essenes' cult as the religion of Christianity and sold it to the Romans. Thus Christianity was deliberately crafted as a weapon with which to subvert the Roman conquerors.[13]

After contributing to the downfall of the Roman Empire, Christianity plunged Europe into the Dark Ages in which it wallowed for a thousand years of ignorance, poverty, superstition, and disintegration. Klassen, of course, was not the first observer to blame Christianity for the downfall of the Roman Empire. For example, in the eighteenth century, the British historian and member of Parliament Edward Gibbon propounded the same thesis in his opus *The History of the Decline and Fall of the Roman Empire*. Likewise, Adolf Hitler expressed similar sentiments that were published in his so-called *Table Talk* after the Second World War. Klassen claimed to have reached his conclusion on his own and read those books only after he had already written *Nature's Eternal Religion*.[14] Other researchers have questioned the motives of Saul as well. For example, in an interesting spin, a Dutch researcher, Thijs Voskuilen, theorized that Paul the Apostle, rather than acting as a Jewish agent to subvert Rome, was actually a Roman agent who attempted to proffer Christianity to the Jews and thus deflect their temporal political activities to otherworldly aspirations.[15]

A glaring omission in Klassen's historiography is his failure to acknowledge episodes of anti-Semitism associated with Christianity. In fact, anti-Semitism first appeared in a significant incarnation in the West with the establishment of the Christian Church. According to the controversial research of Kevin MacDonald, by the third century, Jews had come to be seen as a powerful competitor of the Gentiles. The Church sought to counter the influence of Judaism, and anti-Semitism was given an official imprimatur. For example, Jews were accused of deicide and eventually were barred from certain influential professions and government service. Moreover, they incurred legal and civil liabilities as well. These anti-Semitic overtones in Christendom carried over to later centuries, as anti-Semitism experienced a revival during the medieval period when the Church worked vigorously to exclude Jews from economic and political influence. By the thirteenth century, the Church's position toward Jews had become even more hostile, and anti-Semitism figured prominently in the Spanish Inquisition.[16] As the historian of anti-Semitism, Robert S. Wistrich, observed, during the medieval period, Jews in Christendom were often portrayed as agents of Satan. On occasion, the Church even postulated that both the Anti-Christ and his main supporters would be Jews.[17]

Not only did Klassen reject the Christian Bible but he also denounced all supernatural claims such as reincarnation and the existence of spirits and ghosts. His disdain for superstition notwithstanding, he realized fully the power of religion. According to his reading of the history of Western civilization, the white man had been shortchanged in this regard. In his estimation, religion was like fire in that it could be used for good or bad purposes. Ultimately, Klassen judged religions by how well they served their followers on earth—and not in the hereafter. In this respect, Klassen frequently characterized Judaism as a powerful racial religion that had worked wonders for its people.

Likewise, Klassen thought Islam (which he usually referred to as Mohamedism) an appropriate religion for the Arabs. Mohammed was dismayed at the lack of unity among the Arab peoples as they were divided into many clans and tribes. Thus Islam proved to be a very potent vehicle for uniting the disparate peoples of the Middle East into a cohesive collectivity centered on religion. Illustrative of his conspiratorial worldview, Klassen even theorized that Jews created Islam for the sole purpose of launching an attack on the white race when it was at its most vulnerable position in relation to its neighbors. As he noted, when inspired by the religion of Islam, the Arabs penetrated deep into Europe until they were halted by Charles Martel at the Battle of Tours in 732. To Klassen, this advance was all the more remarkable in that it was composed of people whom he saw as racially inferior to whites.[18] The fact that Islam could mobilize nonwhites into a serious conquering threat to whites was stark proof of the power of religion. In his mind, religion was "the most powerful and dynamic force in the world in capturing the minds of men."[19] Klassen believed that the divine revelations of Islam were spurious, as they were in all religions. Nonetheless, the Islamic faith had a profound effect on shaping Arab culture, language, and politics. Viewing Islam from a utilitarian perspective, Klassen believed that through it Mohammed achieved his objectives, which included unifying the scattered desert tribes into a cohesive religious body and creating a powerful empire with Mohamed as its leader.[20] What began as a small following among members of Bedouin tribes ultimately established the foundation for an Arabic empire. Commenting on more recent history, Klassen spoke admiringly of the late Ayatollah Khomeini, who had a great advantage over Mohammed Reza Pahlavi, the Shah of Iran, in that Khomeini had a powerful ideological weapon in Islam, which ultimately enabled him to prevail over the shah.[21]

Why were Jews able to persevere for so long as a distinct group? The principal reason, Klassen argued, was because of their religion, which he regarded as the most powerful ever created. More than two decades later, the evolutionary psychologist Kevin MacDonald propounded a more scholarly and sophisticated rendition of this same theory. Published in 1994, MacDonald's book, *A People that Shall Dwell Alone: An Evolutionary Theory of Judaism,* posits that Judaism can be viewed as an evolutionary strategy that features such characteristics as endogamy, ethnic exclusivity, and in-group altruism. According to MacDonald, Judaism has been a highly adaptable strategy, and this trait has enabled the religion to endure in numerous environments throughout history; note that Judaism, as it is known today, has survived at least since the period of Babylonian captivity. In his estimation, the strategy has been largely successful, despite periodic reversals of fortune as a result of anti-Semitic actions.[22]

Rejecting the principle of faith, Klassen believed that it was important for beliefs to be supported by evidence. In this regard, he found the laws of nature to be far more predictable and reliable than beliefs based on superstition or metaphysics. To Klassen, man was not above nature but, rather, an integral part of it. Ultimately, survival is the foremost imperative of nature, as perpetuating the species is the principal objective of life. Furthermore, he believed that conflict inhered in nature and was thus unavoidable: "Eternal struggle is the price of survival." He drew parallels with the animal kingdom to illustrate that tenacity was a common trait among those higher animals that have persevered.[23]

Expanding on the Creativity theology, Klassen published *The White Man's Bible* in 1981. To support his critique of Christianity, Klassen reprinted in the book an old article originally published in the now-defunct *Century* magazine by a Jewish writer named Marcus Eli Ravage. In "A Real Case against the Jews," Ravage claimed in a sardonic tenor that the true reason for anti-Semitism was not that the Jews had killed Jesus Christ but, rather, that they had given birth to him in the first place. According to Ravage, the apostle Paul bolstered the stature of Jews by introducing Christianity to the Gentiles. This had a deleterious effect on the European Gentiles as Christianity was a religion incompatible with their natural pagan ethos. As a result, whites no longer looked to their own racial heritage but identified instead with the tribal history of Jews, as evidenced by the centrality of the study of theology among the West's most learned men for centuries. In that sense, the European man had become disconnected from his true heritage and instead had absorbed an alien culture that was totally incongruent with his own spiritual constitution. The Jewish national homeland became the Gentiles' holy land and the Jewish national literature became the Christians' Holy Bible. Moreover, according to Ravage, Christianity was divisive insofar as half the wars in Europe from the sixteenth to the seventeenth century were fought over religion or interpretation of various Jewish teachings. Although animosity toward Jews in the form of anti-Semitism may linger, Ravage stated that gentiles could not explain why:

> In your hearts you still are pagans. . . . We have merely divided your soul, confused your impulses and paralyzed your desires. . . . You Christians have never become Christianized. To that extent we [Jews] have failed with you. But we have forever spoiled the fun of paganism for you. . . . Your real quarrel with us is not that we have rejected Christianity, but that we have imposed it upon you.[24]

Unlike other extreme right critics who have accused Jews of undermining Christianity, Klassen argued that such surface appearances were merely a smokescreen. Rather, Jews worked to preserve Christianity because it vitiated collective white resistance. To cite an example, Klassen pointed out that Christian Bibles could be found in every room in any chain of motels and hotels owned by Jews anywhere in the country.[25]

Klassen identified several key books in the arsenal of Jews in their putative struggle against whites: the Old Testament, the New Testament, the Talmud, *The Protocols of the Elders of Zion*, and Karl Marx's *Das Kapital* and *The Communist Manifesto*.[26] The principal purpose of the Old Testament was to emphasize that God had a special covenant with the Jews. Klassen found the Ten Commandments to be so elementary and primitive that they could not be credibly compared to Roman law. He impugned the historicity of the personages in the Old Testament but, nevertheless, conceded that as folklore, they served Jews well by developing a shared sense of history and destiny for them. The New Testament, by contrast, was intended for a Gentile audience. Whereas Judaism was designed to foster Jewish tribal solidarity, Christianity was designed to divide, confuse, and ultimately destroy the white Roman race.

Klassen identified the Talmud as the true foundation of Judaism. Compiled around A.D.500 in Babylon, the sixty-three-volume Talmud serves as an encyclopedic guide for the Jewish people containing many laws and strictures on relationships between each other and also with Gentiles. The Talmud emphasized class harmony among Jews and a strong sense of collective economic responsibility.[27] Furthermore, Talmudic regulations encouraged high fecundity, as Jews, especially the most intelligent, were encouraged to have many children.[28] Although relatively few far rightists have actually read the Talmud, it has long come under criticism as an expression of alleged Jewish hostility toward Gentiles.[29]

The Protocols of the Elders of Zion purports to be the minutes of an alleged meeting of Zionist leaders who have devised a fantastic plot to conquer the world and enslave Gentiles.[30] Methodically, the plot is advanced with the unwitting assistance of Freemasons and other "shabbez goy" dupes. The plot culminates with the enthronement of a Jew as king of the world. The small but influential tract has long been a staple in the literature of the extreme right and more recently, among anti-Zionists in the Muslim World as well.[31]

Finally, Klassen believed that Karl Marx formulated his ideology so that it could be used by the international Jewish community as a weapon with which to fight Gentiles. The far right has long embraced as an article of faith the idea that Jews were the driving force behind communism. Klassen was quick to note that Marx, although he was raised a Lutheran, descended from a family of rabbis. Allegedly, there were ulterior motives to his communist theory in that his ideas were inherently nihilistic and supposedly designed to destabilize the Western world and mobilize the nonwhite world against it.[32] Also, the fact that American Jewish capitalists such as Jacob Schiff would contribute a huge amount of money to the Bolsheviks was adduced as further evidence of Jewish complicity in the communist conspiracy.[33] According to Klassen, the real power behind communism was the Jewish Kehilla and Jewish bankers who sought to overthrow the hated Romanov dynasty in Russia. The use of such seemingly high-minded slogans as "empowering the workers," Klassen averred, was only a ruse to enable Jews to gain control of the country and implement a systematic program of genocide that resulted in the deaths of 20 to 30 million white Russians.

Although Jews may be extremely clever, Klassen did not believe that they had the capacity to create any meaningful culture or civilization. Rather, their evolutionary specialization was parasitism, which historically had been directed toward the white race because, as Klassen argued, that race was the most productive and exploitable. Klassen catalogued a long chronology of Jewish expulsions that have punctuated the history of the Diaspora as proof of Jewish malfeasance and treachery.[34] Jews were depicted as the destroyers of civilizations. He accused them of controlling the slave trade, not only for profit, but also to dilute the racial homogeneity of the host population, thus ultimately producing a mongrelized and pliable population. To Klassen, blacks occupied the bottom of the racial hierarchy. The chief threat they posed was their mere presence. Even the most stringent attempts at segregation would allow for some miscegenation, which would ultimately mongrelize the white gene pool over successive generations. Reminiscent of Hitler, Klassen argued that all civilizations of antiquity that whites had created were eventually destroyed by miscegenation. For example, Klassen believed that the ancient Egyptian civilization ultimately perished due to an influx of Nubians. Likewise, the ancient Aryan culture of the Indian subcontinent had been "degraded" by admixture with nonwhites, the rigid caste system notwithstanding. Left to their own devices, blacks really did not pose an immediate, existential threat. However, when mobilized by Jews—for example, in the American civil rights movement—blacks could pose a serious peril, according to Klassen.

Not unlike Lothrop Stoddard, who wrote decades before him, Klassen warned that whites faced certain annihilation if they allowed nonwhites to cohabit with them indefinitely.[35] To illustrate his point, he cited significant differences in population growth, which demographically favored nonwhites. The slaughter of whites by blacks and mulattos in the French colony of San Domingo (present-day Haiti) in the early eighteenth century was invoked as a harbinger of what whites could expect in the future if they did not attain racial separation.[36] Although Klassen stopped short of advocating genocide for blacks, he called for their expulsion to Africa, the logistical cost of which he believed would be a small price to pay considering how much public money had been spent on welfare programs for the largely black underclass.

In a historical analysis reminiscent of Joseph Arthur Comte de Gobineau, Klassen credited the white race with history's most important creative and civilizational achievements. Written in the late nineteenth century, Gobineau's book, *An Essay on the Inequality of Human Races*, popularized the notion of white racial superiority and postulated that whites were the sole builders of civilizations.[37] The French aristocrat and conservative grouped the races of the world into three broad categories: white, yellow, and black. For Gobineu, race was the primary factor accounting for the rise and fall of civilizations. Once miscegenation destroyed the racial integrity of an Aryan population, chaos resulted.[38] Like Gobineau, Klassen maintained that all of the major civilizations of history were founded and developed by whites. However, Klassen believed that whites were extremely credulous in certain areas—most notably, superstition—and gullibility constituted the Achilles' heel of the white race.[39] For example, he considered the ancient Egyptians as an early exemplar of white civilization; however, their principal weakness was their obsession with religion and a supposed afterlife, which manifested in fruitless projects such as the construction of the pyramids.[40]

Despite his admiration for the technological genius of Western civilization, Klassen believed that perhaps technology had gotten out of control and should be reined in. For example, he argued that the space exploration program—seemingly the marvel of white genius—was a monumental waste of effort, as he saw nothing in space worth exploring.[41] The ulterior motive was not some Faustian spirit to "seek out and explore new worlds" but rather to generate huge profits for "Jew-owned corporations."[42] Such an endeavor, Klassen reasoned, was about as meaningful as the construction of the pyramids in ancient Egypt. He also expressed concern for the environment, which he believed was endangered in large part by "greed and the Jewish monetary system that feeds it."[43] Rather than an inordinate preoccupation with technology, he believed that whites would be better served by expending more effort on improving their gene pool. Although the white race had achieved many great civilizational accomplishments, Klassen felt that it was naively unaware of the group dynamics of race, which were of the most vital importance:

> In this respect no creature has ever taken such a dumb stance as has the White Race. It may be the most creative, the most intelligent creature in technology, science, literature, arts and many other fields of endeavor that go to make up civilization—but when it comes to looking to its own survival, its own upgrading of its species, keeping its own genetic health, to the recognition of its

natural enemies—in all these most vital aspects the White Race has most flagrantly flouted all of Nature's laws and is more stupid than the lowly mud hen I observed on our slough in Canada.[44]

The Creativity Creed

After deconstructing Christianity, Klassen outlined the foundation of his new religion. In a sense, he sought to create a creed that contained the functionalist features that the French sociologist Emile Durkheim saw as the underpinnings of religion—that is, beliefs and rituals that enhance solidarity in the community. Durkheim believed that the origins of religion were social and not supernatural. Without commitment to a shared belief system, members would tend to pursue private interests without regard for the group to which they belong.[45] Essentially, Klassen sought to develop a religion in the Durkheimian sense shorn of all supernatural elements. Creativity presents itself as a totalistic religion in that it seeks to answer all of the important questions of the white race's predicament. As Klassen explained, the creed consisted of four dimensions: "a sound mind in a sound body in a sound society in a sound environment."[46] Toward this end, Klassen advocated "salubrious living," which encompassed occasional fasting, exercise, a clean environment, and a vegetarian diet. Not unlike his mentor, Adolf Hitler, Klassen believed that meat eating was harmful to humans. Instead, he recommended a "frugivorian" diet, which emphasized uncooked fruits, vegetables, and nuts.[47]

To ensure white racial survival, Klassen exhorted whites to recognize their group interests. To illustrate this point, he wrote a parable titled "Never Again through the Serpent's Eyes" to explain what he saw as misplaced altruism on the part of the white race. The story begins with a young pioneer mother living in a cabin in the days of the early American West. She shares the cabin with her husband and their three children. To her horror, one night she discovers under her child's bed, a rattlesnake with newly delivered baby snakes. Immediately, she removes her children from the area and searches for a club in the woodpile with which to club to death the rattlesnake and her brood. At first, it seems commonsensical to assume that the pioneer mother has a justifiable right to protect her family by killing the snakes. As Klassen explained, however, viewed from the perspective of the snake, its right to survival and habitation could also be defended on the grounds that she and her ancestors had roamed the prairies for centuries before the white settlers and therefore for the snake to attack the settlers would be justified. Klassen used the parable to illustrate the Darwinian aspect of his new religion. In his mind, Christianity has led the white race to see things through the eyes of the serpent (i.e., Jews and nonwhites) rather than from the perspective of their own racial self-interest.[48] As he saw it, nature "played no favorites." Therefore, it was incumbent upon each species to look after its own welfare. Moreover, Klassen saw nothing morally wrong with the emotion of hate. In fact, he believed that it was the flip side of love. Hate had great mobilizing power and enabled people to better confront their enemies.[49]

Ironically, Klassen contended that Creativity owed much to Judaism. In fact, he admitted that he got the idea of creating a racial religion from his reading of Jewish history and religion. He credited Jews with creating a powerful racial religion that worked wonders for them. Klassen conceded that he "never invented the wheel"; rather, he sought to apply exclusivist and ethnocentric principles to a religion geared toward whites. Ultimately, Klassen judged a religion not so much by the veracity of its theology, but by how well it served its people. In this respect, he considered Judaism the paragon of religions and an approach worthy of emulation:

> There is not a scintilla of historical evidence that there ever were any Jewish characters such as Jesus Christ, Abraham, Isaac, Jacob, or even Moses, for that matter. All we have is an immense collection of confused, helter-skelter propaganda dumped on us like a load of manure, but little else. Since their stories are so outrageously bizarre, only the most naïve yokel could swallow such idiotic tall tales. . . .
> One of the greatest accomplishments of the Jews is the fact that they have fashioned a religion that has proved to be completely in tune with their innately parasitic nature, and consequently, tremendously effective in enhancing those characteristics with which Nature has endowed them. . . .
> We will state up front that in structuring a racial religion for the White Race we have learned more from Judaism than all the other religions combined, and we make no bones about it. The reason

is simple: if a racial religion such as Judaism can sustain a scurvy race of parasites for 50 centuries and propel them upward to gain control of the world, then just think what a similar racial religion can do for the White Race.[50]

Ben Klassen was the first major far-right figure to explicitly recognize the religion of Judaism as an organizing model to be emulated. He wanted to create a counterpart that could mobilize whites as a monolithic entity. In recent years, a more scholarly and sophisticated version of Klassen's proscriptions has been propounded by Kevin MacDonald, a professor of psychology at the University of California at Long Beach.[51] His scholarship draws heavily on social identity theory to explain the dynamics of Gentile and Jewish interactions.[52]

Klassen exhorted whites to unify and put aside the differences that have historically divided them. To that end, he advocated racial solidarity over nationalism and sought to proselytize all whites to accept Creativity as their common religion. To Klassen, a religious movement was far more powerful and enduring than a political party. To foster unity, he recommended Latin as a universal language for the white race.[53] Latin, he believed, was phonetically perfect. Moreover, it had the advantage of tradition and the status of neutrality, as no nation speaks it today.[54]

For Klassen, it was absolutely essential to "identify" the enemy. And once Creativity was launched, he never shirked from that position. He often invoked the term "Delenda est Judaica!" or "Death to Judaism!" Although he expressed doubts about the mainstream version of the Holocaust, Klassen was generally unconcerned with the matter. He thought it was folly to judge Jews as individuals, a sentiment echoed by other far-right ideologists as well.[55] Rather, it behooved whites to take no chances and therefore assume that Jews, as a group, constituted the most serious threat to their survival and act accordingly to mitigate this predicament. As Klassen explained, whether the white race was aware of it or not, it was involved in a race war with either racial oblivion or complete victory as the only two possible outcomes. To effect the latter, Klassen propounded "the Sixteen Commandments" of Creativity:

> 1. It is the avowed duty and the holy responsibility of each generation to assure and secure for all time the existence of the White Race upon the face of this planet.

2. Be fruitful and multiply. Do your part in helping to populate the world with your own kind. It is our sacred goal to populate the lands of this earth with White people exclusively.

3. Remember that the inferior colored races are our deadly enemies, and the most dangerous of all is the Jewish race. It is our immediate objective to relentlessly expand the White race, and keep shrinking our enemies.

4. The guiding principle of all your actions shall be: What is best for the White Race?

5. You shall keep your race pure. Pollution of the White Race is a heinous crime against Nature and against your own race.

6. Your first loyalty belongs to the White Race.

7. Show your preferential treatment in business dealings to members of your own race. Phase out all dealings with Jews as soon as possible. Do not employ niggers or other coloreds. Have social contact only with members of your own racial family.

8. Destroy and banish all Jewish thought and influence from society. Work hard to bring about a White world as soon as possible.

9. Work and creativity are our genius. We regard work as a noble pursuit and our willingness to work as a blessing to our race.

10. Decide early in youth that during your lifetime you will make at least one major lasting contribution to the White Race.

11. Uphold the honor of your race at all time.

12. It is our duty and privilege to further Nature's plan by striving toward the advancement and improvement of our future generations.

13. You shall honor, protect and venerate the sanctity of the family unit, and hold it sacred. It is the present link in the long golden chain of our White Race.

14. Throughout your life you shall faithfully uphold our pivotal creed of Blood, Soil and Honor. Practice it diligently, for it is the heart of our faith.

15. Be a proud member of the White Race, think and act positively. Be courageous, confident and aggressive. Utilize constructively your creative ability.

16. We, the Racial Comrades of the White Race, are determined

to regain complete and unconditional control of our own destiny.[56]

The Creativity theology seeks to synthesize disparate themes in history including Roman classicism, German National Socialism, and the spirit of the American western frontier. Klassen drew much inspiration from ancient Rome, which he recognized as the most exemplary and enduring of white civilizations. He was especially fond of Roman law and the Latin language as well as Roman architecture, government, pragmatism, and military prowess. However, he criticized the Romans for failing to recognize the importance of race. Furthermore, he believed that they failed to appreciate the power of ideas, propaganda, and religion, which ultimately made them vulnerable to the blandishments of Christianity.[57] Adding a conspiratorial spin, Klassen asserted that Julius Caesar was a pawn of the Jews. Brutus and a group of patriotic senators assassinated him and in doing so, ended Rome's experiment with democracy. His successor, Emperor Augustus, ushered in *Pax Romana*, a period of grandeur, which according to Klassen, was finally brought down by Christianity.[58]

To Klassen, "Adolf Hitler was the greatest leader the White Race ever had." Despite this admiration, he emphasized that Creativity was not just another variant of neo-Nazism, as he pointed out several key differences between his creed and National Socialism. First, whereas, National Socialism championed the German nation, Creativity recognized the entire white race as its prime concern. Repeatedly, Klassen emphasized that nationalism had been a divisive feature in the history of the West. Creativity exhorted whites all over the world to put aside their national affinities and instead accept a racial basis for identity. Creativity was also superior to National Socialism insofar as National Socialism was basically a political movement while Creativity was a religious movement. Religion was far more potent and enduring. Klassen was also highly critical of Hitler's alliance with the Japanese, whom he saw as just another "mud race."[59] Finally, Klassen criticized Hitler for not attacking Christianity head-on. By contrast, Creativity was explicitly and vehemently anti-Christian. All of that said, Klassen believed that Hitler was worthy of reverence; however, white racialists should not try to reproduce his Nazi movement or develop a cult based on his political philosophy.[60] Although Klassen greatly admired Hitler and saw in him a great orator, tactician, and strategist, he once described him as only a mediocre philosopher.[61]

Nevertheless, several themes in Hitler's tome, *Mein Kampf*, are evident in Klassen's writings. For example, Hitler argued that the psyche of the great masses was not receptive to weak, half-hearted measures.[62] Similarly, Klassen patterned Creativity on many of the precepts of National Socialism and sought to reach potential recruits in a visceral way. Democracy came under Hitler's caustic criticism as well: "Sooner will a camel pass through a needle's eye than a great man be 'discovered' by an election."[63] Klassen also had a critique of democracy yet added that his religious philosophy was not dogmatic about government structure as long as government did diverge from the precepts of Creativity.[64] Like Klassen, Hitler observed that religion was far more potent than a state or a political party.[65] Both men shared an evolutionary approach to their readings of history. Only through eternal struggle, Hitler believed, had mankind attained preeminence over other species.[66] Hitler, like Klassen, disdained class struggle, seeing it as a divisive force that undermined the solidarity of the nation. Hitler packaged his socialism in what he saw as a dynamic ideology that appealed to all strata of German society. Regarding propaganda, Hitler recommended that the proper technique should emphasize one fundamental principle repeated with unrelenting consistency.[67] Similarly, Klassen maintained that ideology without action was sterile and in his various writings, he stressed a few major themes with repetition and reinforcement. In the Jews, Hitler, like Klassen, saw an implacable enemy with whom there could be no compromise. Both gave the highest priority to the preservation of the race. They also shared a similar conception of the neutrality of nature, as Hitler commented, "the race which cannot stand the test will simply die out, making place for healthier or tougher and more resisting races."[68] Hitler believed that the Germans were a "chosen race" only so long as they used ruthlessness and superior intelligence combined with a very strong will to hold power.[69] Both saw the white race as the sole species capable of creating any worthwhile accomplishment, whether in science, art, technology, or civilization. Furthermore, they saw the results of miscegenation as catastrophic, the root cause of the downfall of once-great civilizations. Both advocated eugenics as a way of improving the race. But in the case of Hitler, he went much further, suggesting sterilization of the "defective."[70] Klassen made no reference to a Naziesque "life unworthy of life program" but instead advocated a system in which the most desirable elements of the race would be encouraged to have the most offspring. Hitler, like Klassen, believed in the authenticity of *The Protocols of the Learned Elders of Zion*.[71] With regard to politics, both rejected an unwavering worship of the state, which they saw as merely an instrument whose principal purpose was to safeguard the race. Finally, both drew upon similar imagery for the design of their movements' flags.[72]

Although Klassen greatly admired and was inspired by Hitler, he believed that the legacy of World War II presented a serious challenge to white racial survival. Like many other commentators in the postwar far right, Klassen believed that World War II was an important watershed in the history of the West. That epic conflict set in motion the direction of cultural and political events in the postwar era, which Klassen saw as a drastic course for the worse. In short, the war was a tragic fratricidal conflict between the various peoples of the West. Moreover, according to Klassen, the defeat of the Third Reich represented a monumental victory for Jews and the opportunity to influence the future course of history. Severely stigmatized in the postwar era, "Nazi" became a term of opprobrium with which to smear those who sought to preserve the white racial heritage.[73]

For Klassen, the settlement of the western frontier was the apogee of American history. The Mexican-American War was a fine example of white martial prowess against nonwhites. At the Alamo, a small band of frontiersmen held out against a much greater number of Mexican soldiers. He regarded James Polk, who led the American nation during the Mexican-American War, as the greatest American president. In that conflict, Klassen found a paradigm for white expansion all over the world. Foreshadowing contemporary immigration restriction activists, Klassen argued that it was imperative for white America to secure its border with Mexico and halt migration. He contended that the only "good" wars America ever had were the Indian wars and the Mexican-American War. Viewed from this perspective, even the American Revolution was not really that important. Even worse, contemporary historians did no favors by dwelling on the American Civil War, which according to Klassen, was a tragic internecine conflict that divided America's white population.[74]

The strident and explicit racism of the Creator creed notwithstanding, Klassen rejected the label "white supremacist." Rather, he preferred no social intercourse between whites and nonwhites. Without total geographic separation, eventually miscegenation would take place, even within a very rigid caste system such as that of ancient India. Slavery was a disaster insofar as it had introduced into North America millions of blacks who would later be emancipated and allowed to live among whites. Furthermore, he believed that modern technology had obviated the need for human slavery. Therefore, Klassen believed that racial separatism better characterized his creed insofar as Creativity did not seek to rule over nonwhites but to stay apart from them. That said, Klassen frequently emphasized that the white race should not be retreatist and settle for a rump state in North America in the style of the Northwest Imperative.[75] Rather, Klassen believed it was the destiny of whites to exclusively inhabit all the desirable areas of the planet. He conceded that this would not happen overnight but articulated it as a long-term goal to be systematically pursued through a program of settlement into new territories and expulsion of nonwhites who resided therein. Not unlike Hitler, Klassen viewed history as a saga of racial migrations and movement. For Klassen, there could be no middle ground. Either the white race must establish dominion over the entire planet or face inundation and ultimately oblivion from the nonwhite races. Whites were approaching the eleventh hour in the struggle for their racial survival and must act quickly or face oblivion:

> The White Race is now in grave danger of extinction and only a miracle can save it. The White people of the world are now facing the most critical and precarious time they have ever been confronted with in their long, chaotic and tumultuous history....
>
> Unless we drastically change course and do it now, we, many of whom are living today, are about to witness the greatest most abysmal tragedy that has ever befallen mankind.[76]

Despite his dire tone, Klassen believed that the white race could still avoid a racial conflict of apocalyptic proportions if it "straightened out its thinking." According to his line of reasoning, whites were their own worst enemy insofar as Western nations provided foreign aid, financial assistance, and technology transfers to destitute third world countries. Once this ceased, Klassen believed that the nonwhite races would "wither on the vine" and hence no genocidal program would be necessary as "nature would take its course." Despite the seemingly perilous demographic situation, Klassen maintained that with a worldwide population of roughly 500 million, the white race still had enough people to prevail.[77] When left to their own devices, other races posed no serious threat to the white race. According to Klassen, the only meaningful weapons that nonwhites have are those that whites have given to them.[78] What is more, Klassen believed that whites had a decisive advantage in a racial conflict with nonwhites. He believed that nonwhites need whites to provide them subsistence but the white race could do just fine without the nonwhite peoples.[79]

Explicitly rejecting the atheist label, which Klassen argued implied the absence of belief, the Creativity creed offered a comprehensive worldview and, as such, qualified for the status of a religion. It was futile, Klassen suggested, to attack a religion without offering an attractive alternative.[80] Nevertheless, he reached out to atheists but had little to no success.[81] To his detractors, who charged that Creativity was a pseudo-religion, Klassen countered, "Our religious beliefs are not based on silly and untenable myths or fairy tales that have no basis in fact, nor are such myths even logical. Our beliefs are well founded and well grounded in the Eternal Laws of Nature."[82]

Klassen's worldview and critique of Christianity did not develop in a vacuum. Rather, they were indicative of a broad trend in the extreme right over the past several decades.

3

The Far Right and the Critique of Christianity

The seemingly nihilistic orientation of Creativity notwithstanding, its creed did not emerge de novo. Over the past few decades, other non-Christian religions have also gained currency. Increasingly, Aryan revolutionaries in both North America and Europe are adopting neopaganism as their new religion. This development is suggestive of a trend in which the far right has moved away from mainstream Christianity. As the mainstream became more inclusive and tolerant, it lost much of its appeal for the extreme right. Arguably, there is an inherent tension between contemporary Christianity and some variants of right-wing extremism. According to its original message, the Christian faith espouses universalism, tolerance, and humility. By contrast, fascism, for example, espouses particularism, heroism, and often a cult of violence. Moreover, that fact that Christianity is a Jewish-inspired religion does not lend itself well to the anti-Semitism that looms so large in the contemporary extreme right. To better understand the influence of non-Christian religions on the contemporary extreme right, we need to look back at the events surrounding the rise of the Third Reich. Not only did various neopagan and nature cults influence National Socialism but the historical period of the Third Reich looms large in the mythos of contemporary rightist pagans and Creators as well.

The Religion of Nature

The roots of the "religion of nature" can be traced back to the nineteenth century. The Enlightenment ideas of positivism, rationalism, universalism, and democracy that swept over Europe eventually spawned a counter movement known as German Romanticism. A relative latecomer among the modern European states, Germany did not achieve unity until 1871. Older nation-states, such as France and England, had a long history of nationhood on which they could look back and from which they could draw inspiration. Although Italy was a latecomer, it nevertheless had as its nationalist myth the grandeur that was Rome. Thus, German nationalists had something of an identity crisis, a feeling of national historic inferiority compared with their neighbors. This spawned a search for an authentic German national identity and a mythic Germanic golden age extending back to antiquity, which crystallized in the *völkish* movement.

Charles Darwin's *The Origin of Species*, which was published in 1859, added a scientific veneer to this development. His theory of evolution was later applied to the social sciences and transformed into social Darwinism, which became popular in the second half of the nineteenth century. In Britain, its chief proponent, Herbert Spencer, used the concept to buttress laissez-faire economics and politics. By contrast, in Germany it tended to take the form of nature worship and racial mysticism. The German zoologist, Ernst Haeckel, for example, saw in evolution a unifying force that explained the cosmos as an all-embracing whole. In 1904, he founded a group called the German Monist League that stressed the oneness and unity of reality. A "world soul" was conceptualized as a phenomenon in which all forms of life evolved in an upward direction. Nature was seen as a neutral force, not favoring any particular race or species. Rather, the "survival of the fittest" maxim applied to all creatures without favor. Out of this struggle, a higher grade of perfection would result. When applied to race theory, proponents postulated that each race had its own unique nature and innate characteristics beyond the mere surface appearances, such as skin color and phenotypical features. Inasmuch as the white race was seen as the apogee of the evolutionary process, miscegenation was anathema. Inherent in the religion of nature was a strident critique of Christianity, which was attacked for turning people away from the strictures of nature. Lacking a belief in an anthropomorphic god, nature worship emphasized a pantheistic worship of nature. Monism gained popularity with the fledging neopagan movement as well as proto-Nazi groups, which shared a desire for the creation of a new Germanic faith as a substitute for traditional Christianity, whether Catholic or Protestant. Not unlike Klassen, the Nazi race theorists saw existence as an eternal struggle with only those having the requisite will surviving. Integral to the Nazi mission was restoring the "natural order," which would result in a "new man." Although Jews were often characterized as parasitic and uncreative, they were nevertheless designated as formidable enemies, who threatened the very physical existence of Aryans through chicanery, most notably, promoting racial admixture.[1]

The high priest of Germandom, the composer Richard Wagner (1813–1883), contributed to the pagan revival by resurrecting the old Germanic myths and legends through his operas, including *Parsifal* and the *Ring of the Nibelungs*. He endeavored to Germanize the Christ figure and cast doubts on his Semitic origins. In essence, Wagner syncretized the mythos of the old Norse religion with Christianity. His refusal to abandon Christianity ruptured his friendship with Frederich Nietzsche, who despised the Christian faith and derided it as a "slave religion." Wagner's operas evidently exerted an abiding influence on Hitler. A longtime friend, August Kubizek, recalled one incident from their youth in which the two attended a Wagnerian opera. After the performance, Hitler appeared transfixed and gave an impassioned speech to his friend in the early hours of the morning. Decades later, when the man became reacquainted with the German führer, Hitler solemnly recalled the incident and remarked that "in that hour it began."[2]

The Völkisch Movement

German ethnic nationalism was most pronounced in Austria, the citadel of the *völkisch* movement, and it is there where the roots of modern Norse paganism lie. Many ethnic Germans felt besieged in the multi-ethnic Austro-Hungarian Empire. The pan-German movement was born in the scattered university fraternities in Austria during the 1860s, and in the late 1870s where Georg von Schoenerer launched his Pan-German Party, which sought to unite all German-speaking peoples into one union. The pan-German phrase "blood knows no borders" implied that German ethnicity would be the primary criterion for inclusion in the new German *Volksgemeinschaft*. The upheaval of World War I put a halt to Schoenerer's Pan-German party, but its ideas would resonate with many German nationalists, including Adolf Hitler.

It was a Russian, however, who would provide the final impetus for the pagan renaissance. Madame Helena Blavatsky spearheaded the nineteenth-century occult revival with the creation of her Theosophical Society and her two-volume *Secret Doctrine*, which propounded a cyclical theory of history in which various root races emerged and disappeared. She believed in a hierarchy of races in which the fifth root race, the Aryans, occupied the top position.³ Blavatsky's themes would figure prominently in the writings of subsequent occultists and racial mystics.

These developments effectively laid the groundwork for the revival of Germanic paganism; the father of this movement is recognized as Guido von List, who was born in 1848 and raised in an Austrian Catholic family. As a youth, List once visited the catacombs under St. Stephen's Cathedral. The visit left a lasting impression on him, as he came to believe that the labyrinth tunnels were remnants of a pre-Christian shrine dedicated to a pagan deity.⁴ Soon afterward, he vowed to revive the worship of Wotan⁵—the all-father of the Norse pantheon—and build a shrine in his honor. In the 1890s, he began lecturing and publishing articles on the subject of the ancient holy priesthood of the Wotan cult. An advocate of eugenics, he outlined a program for ensuring German racial purity that bore much resemblance to the Nuremberg racial laws (which proscribed marriage and extramarital sexual intercourse between Germans and Jews) that were subsequently promulgated in 1935.⁶ In the early part of his career, List concentrated on the exoteric aspects of Germanic mythology; however, in 1902, after undergoing an eye operation and nine months of blindness, List began concentrating on more esoteric occult themes, including the meanings of the runes. The runes not only comprised an alphabet known as the *futhark* but were also used for magical purposes, including divination. For the most part, organized Odinism disintegrated after List's death in 1919, although individual followers, including Hitler's fellow putschist, General Erich Ludendorff, continued to worship the old gods.

Nevertheless, List's ideas would continue to influence other occultists partly through his List Society, which became an important conduit for racial mystical ideas. His pan-Germanism would find its way into the nationalist lodges scattered throughout Germany and Austria. Many occultists including Jorg Lanz von Liebenfels⁷ and members of the *Thule Gesellschaft* were inspired by his writings. The latter was officially a study group composed of leading members of Munich high society; it blended numerous themes, including racial mysticism, occultism, German nationalism, and anti-Semitism. As the organization was elitist in orientation, prospective members were required to prove German lineage going back at least 200 years. In an effort to win the support of the broad masses, the Thule Society launched the German Workers' Party (DAP) in 1919. That same year, an obscure Army corporal investigating nationalist groups attended a meeting of the nascent political party. Adolf Hitler would eventually assume leadership and change the name of the party to the German National Socialist German Workers Party (NSDAP). Several figures, who would go on to high positions in the NSDAP, were once Thulists, including Dietrich Eckart, Julius Streicher, Rudolf Hess, and Alfred Rosenberg.[8]

National Socialism

Some scholars have sought to depict National Socialism as political religion—that is, a totalizing political ideology that substitutes for traditional religion. The National Socialist movement created a historiography that contained several religious and metaphysical elements. For example, the success of the small, fledging NSDAP was depicted as a miracle in which the original seven members grew to include the entire German *Volk*. In German textbooks during the Nazi period, the emergence of Hitler was portrayed as a providential event replete with biblical connotations. Apocalyptic themes figured prominently as well. For example, the Third Reich faced a Satanic foe—the Jew—who was depicted as the antithesis of all that was noble in the German. In order for the German to surmount his challenge, extreme sacrifice was called for in a struggle that attained apocalyptic proportions.[9] Once in power, the Nazi regime implemented policies that were intended to regenerate man and transform German life, and these included the sacralization of politics. The Nuremberg rallies were replete with quasi-religious symbolism, including the consecration of the flags, which bore semblance to the Catholic mass. In fact, Hitler acknowledged that his own Catholic upbringing inspired his subsequent political pageantry.[10] Moreover, Hitler organized his NSDAP not unlike the Catholic hierarchy in which he stood as a kind of pope whose word was infallible.[11] Despite these surface resemblances to religion, the scholar Richard Steigmann-Gall argued that German National Socialism could more aptly be described as a form of "religious politics" in the sense that it sought to defend and restore Christianity rather than destroy it. Although several of the top Nazi leaders expressed anti-Christian sentiments, Steigmann-Gall observes that they were not given any kind of official imprimatur from the party.[12]

Still, uneasiness with Christianity remained. To the historian Robert Pois, the philosophy of National Socialism was a revolt against the Judeo-Christian tradition. As he explained, National Socialism was symptomatic of a "largely unconscious, discomfiture with the Judeo-Christian tradition."[13] Although National Socialism explicitly ignored supernaturalism, it nevertheless retained a strong sense of mysticism in the sense that it asserted the ultimate unity of man and the divine.[14] The Nazi movement was frequently billed as a "revolution of the spirit." Through pageantry and an all-encompassing philosophy, National Socialism presented itself as a quasi-religion. Hitler believed that he had rediscovered long-forgotten truths concerning the relationship between man and nature. He repeatedly stressed that man was not above nature but rather an integral part of it receiving no special preference.[15]

It comes as no surprise that the struggle between fascism and Christianity was most pronounced in the Third Reich. German National Socialism was the most totalizing of all the variants of fascism. The historian Peter Viereck once described the ideology as a meta-political doctrine insofar as it encompassed a comprehensive *Weltanschauung* that sought the total allegiance of its adherents.[16] Furthermore, some of the top Nazi leaders, including Hitler, Martin Bormann, and Heinrich Himmler, considered National Socialism and Christianity incompatible. Some alternatives to mainstream Christianity emerged during the Third Reich, including the German Christian Movement.

The German Christian Movement

The so-called German Christian movement (*Glaugenbewegung Deutsche Christen*) sought to harmonize the two seemingly irreconcilable creeds. As the German Christians saw it, Christianity, in its modified form, and National Socialism were actually mutually reinforcing. Not an insignificant movement, the German Christian movement sustained a membership of over half a million followers in branches in all parts of Germany for more than a decade. Essentially Protestant in congregational composition, it was disapproved of by the mainstream clergy. What is more, the movement never really found itself in the good graces of the Nazi Party, whose leaders resented its attempt to combine National Socialism with Christianity, and by doing so, alter the ideology. Some Nazi critics derided Christianity as a Jewish-inspired faith and as such, incompatible with National Socialism.

The German Christian movement worked to develop a brand of Christianity that would be more consistent with the precepts of National Socialism. For instance, there were efforts to de-Judaize Christianity. The German Christians Aryanized the Christ figure and sought to expurgate all Jewish references in the Bible. The Jew, Saul of Tarsus—the Saint Paul of the New Testament—was blamed for corrupting the true message of Christianity. Inasmuch as the contemporary biblical text was suspect, the German Christian movement was fundamentally anti-doctrinal. Moreover, it blended in themes from the religion of nature, suggesting that God revealed himself not only through Jesus but also in nature and history.[17] Finally, the German Christians sought to reposition Christianity as a warrior ethos in which the Sermon on the Mount was minimized or cast away completely. Some leading Nazi Party officials sought to modify Christianity as well.

Alfred Rosenberg and *The Myth of the Twentieth Century*

Alfred Rosenberg, the heralded Nazi Party ideologist, also sought to revitalize religion in the new Germany. Some historians have interpreted his book, *The Myth of the Twentieth Century*, as the definitive expression of the Nazi philosophy. An important influence on his philosophy was Meister Eckhart (1260–1327) whom Rosenberg saw as a progenitor of a new German national Christianity. Rosenberg found both "positive" and "negative" aspects of Christianity and was highly critical of the Hebrew and Roman influences, which he believed impose an excessive legalism on the religion. According to Rosenberg, Christianity had become corrupted through St. Paul. Failing to stamp out the fledging movement, Rosenberg argued that Paul, a grand conspirator, sought to Judaize the religion and transform the original message of Christ. After its transformation, Rosenberg contended, the religion was foisted upon Rome with the intention of subverting its civilization. In a sense, Rosenberg argued, Paul was a forerunner of Karl Marx. By uniting the poorer classes, Paul sought to destroy Rome. With that task accomplished, an independent Jewish state could be reestablished in Palestine. In later years, this Jewish conspiracy through religion, posited Rosenberg, sought to destroy the nationalistic spirits of Gentile nations while strengthening the Jewish people's sense of uniqueness and nationhood. The Old Testament, in his estimation, was nothing more than a highly nationalistic account of the Hebrew peoples cast against a religious background. The Catholic Church, Rosenberg lamented, had failed to rescue Christianity. Instead of fostering an original Germanic faith that emphasized pride and self-reliance within the Church, Christianity promoted a faith that encouraged its followers to become defensive and unsure of themselves thus rendering them "spiritual cripples." Lutheranism came under Rosenberg's criticism as well. Although the German theologian harbored anti-Semitic tendencies, Rosenberg criticized Martin Luther for not going far enough in condemning Judaism. Moreover, inasmuch as Luther popularized the Old Testament, Rosenberg concluded that he turned Christians into "spiritual Jews."

To help Germans regain their sense of nationhood, Rosenberg proffered a new German national religion that would make no appeals to universal brotherhood but, rather, concentrate exclusively on Germans and related kinsmen. The crucible of World War I would serve as the myth of national regeneration in which a new sense of German peoplehood would emerge. Like Richard Wagner and Houston Stewart Chamberlain, Rosenberg claimed that Christ was an Aryan, not a Hebrew. The Nordic Christian Church, envisaged by Rosenberg, would be based on Western, rather than Eastern, values. Jesus would be recast as a Nordic hero worthy of Europeans. Although he evinced sympathy for the old Norse gods and myths, Rosenberg thought that resurrecting them would be a futile exercise, as he exclaimed "Wotan is dead."[18]

Not surprisingly, Rosenberg's book was not well received by the established churches. In 1934, Pope Pius XI went so far as to place *The Myth of the Twentieth Century* in the Roman Index of Forbidden Books; Catholics who read these books were committing a mortal sin. The reaction to Rosenberg's book in Nazi circles was mixed. Although some of his ideas were taken up by the German Christians, many others found the book heretical or uninspiring. Apparently, Hitler was not favorably impressed with the book and did not regard it as an expression of the official doctrine of the NSDAP.[19] What is more, Hitler did not endorse the book's latent paganism.

Klassen also found little merit in the book and criticized Rosenberg for seeking to build his new Nordic religion on the foundation of Christianity. He saw as misguided Rosenberg's efforts to selectively cull out the parts of the New Testament attributed to St. Paul. Furthermore, Klassen saw nothing worthwhile in the philosophy of Meister Eckhart that was of pertinence to the white race today. Finally, Klassen took issue with Rosenberg's narrowly focused nationalistic approach in creating a religion exclusively for Germanic peoples. The only really redeeming quality he found in his work was its emphasis on racial values.[20] Klassen was a much greater admirer of Adolf Hitler whose religious outlook is worth examining.

The Religiosity of Hitler

There is much speculation over the religiosity of Hitler. Some observers have characterized him as a Christian while others have labeled him a practitioner of the black arts.[21] By examining his pronouncements and private conversations, we can gain a clearer picture of his religious outlook.

Although Hitler was raised a Catholic, he appears to have lost his Christianity at an early age. Not unlike the adherents of Christian Identity, Hitler once claimed that Christ was an Aryan. However, St. Paul, claimed Hitler, "used his doctrine to mobilize the criminal underworld and thus organize a proto-Bolshevism."[22] Whatever the origins of Christianity may have been, Hitler believed that ultimately it was incompatible with National Socialism.[23] In later years, he developed a strident critique of the religion, which he once described as "a rebellion against natural law, a protest against nature" and "an enemy to beauty."[24] In an analysis almost identical to that of Klassen, Hitler viewed Christianity as a contrived plot to enslave the world:

> The heaviest blow that ever struck humanity was the coming of Christianity. Bolshevism is Christianity's illegitimate child. Both are inventions of the Jews. . . . In the ancient world, the relations between men and gods were founded on an instinctive respect. It was a world enlightened by the idea of tolerance. Christianity was the first creed in the world to exterminate its enemies in the name of love. Its key-note is intolerance.[25]

Communism, Hitler maintained, was nothing but an updated variant of Christianity.[26] According to Hitler, Jews used Christianity to mobilize the masses of slaves against Roman society in much the same way that the proletariat was used to undermine the traditional order in Europe.[27]

Hitler, like Klassen, attributed the fall of the Roman Empire to Christianity.[28]

Despite his contempt for Christianity, Hitler nevertheless evinced a spiritual side. He often invoked the term "Providence" to suggest that he was guided by some higher calling and once assured the German people that he followed the dictates thereof with the "assurance of a sleepwalker." In some ways, his autobiography, *Mein Kampf*, reads like the story of a man who has undergone a religious conversion. As he explains in the book, as a youth, he initially recoiled when he first encountered discussion of Jews and anti-Semitism. For the young Hitler, Jews were nothing more than another religious group. He found the endemic anti-Semitism of Vienna to be crude and "unworthy of the cultural tradition of a great nation." Over time, however, he began to view Judaism as a conspiracy whose followers were locked in an epic struggle to subjugate and defile the German people, and by extension, the Aryan race. Thus his animus against Jews was not based on a Christian variant of anti-Semitism but, rather, on what he believed was a sound reading of history.[29] To be sure, Hitler's worldview did not develop in a vacuum. A common theme in the anti-Semitic literature during and leading up to the Nazi period was that Jews were eclipsing Germans in a racial struggle. This theme had its most persuasive expression in Houston Stewart Chamberlain's *Foundations of the Nineteenth Century*, which would have a major influence on the development of Hitler's worldview. In Jews, Hitler saw a formidable adversary, one that posed an existential threat to Aryans. Despite his belief in Aryan racial superiority, Hitler believed that Jews threatened the German nation through subversion and the promotion of racial admixture.

For Hitler, Jews were first and foremost members of a particular race—"the Mosaic religion is nothing other than a doctrine for the preservation of the Jewish race."[30] The Jewish Holy text, the Talmud, was not a book to prepare man for the hereafter but only a practical guide for a profitable life in the terrestrial world.[31] His crusade against the Jews was often couched in religious terms—"Hence today I believe that I am acting in accordance with the Creator: *by defending myself against the Jew, I am fighting for the work of the Lord* [italics in original]."[32] Finally, he described his decision to enter politics as an epiphany. In late October 1918, Hitler was convalescing at a military hospital after he was subjected to a gas attack in which he was temporarily blinded; on regaining his sight,

Hitler had an inner vision in which he discovered his true mission—he decided that he would go into politics.[33]

Although Hitler was basically anti-Christian at heart, he was able to portray himself as the guardian of Christianity against the atheistic communism of the East. He skillfully sought to allay the fears of those Germans who thought that his fledging NSDAP held anti-Christian positions. In a 1923 speech he exclaimed, "This symbol [the swastika] is not directed against the Christian cross. On the contrary it is a political manifestation of what the Cross attends or must attend."[34] In his public pronouncements, Hitler occasionally defended Christianity, but more in a cultural than a pious way; as he remarked in June 1944, "I might not be a sanctimonious church-goer, that is not what I am. But, still deep down I am a religious person."[35] On occasion, he would invoke the name of Christ. Even devout Christians could be moved by his religious pronouncements and his seeming spirituality. For example, Leon Degrelle, a Belgian, who led the Waffen-SS Wallonian Legion in World War II, met with Hitler on numerous occasions and had long conversations with him.[36] Degrelle once commented that Hitler exhibited an abiding spirituality:

> Propagandists portrayed Hitler as an atheist. He was not. . . . No one in the world has spoken to me so eloquently about the existence of God. Hitler's faith transcended formulas and contingencies. God was for him the basis of everything, the ordainer of all things, of his Destiny and that of all others.[37]

His surface spirituality notwithstanding, historians have had difficulty identifying Hitler's precise religious outlook. Some observers believe that he was sympathetic to neopaganism. After all, much Nazi ritual and pageantry at the Nuremberg rallies was replete with pagan undertones, as some of the symbols employed once held sacred significance for the pre-Christian Germanic tribes of Europe. Nevertheless, Hitler had no desire to resurrect the old Norse gods. Furthermore, in *Mein Kampf*, he wrote derisively of the "völkish" traditionalists:

> The characteristic thing about these people is that they rave about old Germanic heroism, about dim prehistory, stone axes, spear and shield, but in reality are the greatest cowards that can be imagined.

For the same who brandish scholarly imitations of old German tin swords, and wear a dressed bearskin with bull's horn over their bearded heads, preach for the present nothing but struggle with spiritual weapons, and run away as fast as they can from every Communist blackjack. . . .

[Moreover] they make a ridiculous impression on the broad masses, and the Jew has every reason to spare these folkish comedians, even to prefer them to the true fighters for a coming German state. . . .

[T]heir whole activity leads the people away from the common struggle against the common enemy, the Jews, and instead lets them waste their strength on inner religious squabbles as senseless as they are disastrous.[38]

Nevertheless, Hitler did seem to believe that the martial qualities of some pagan religions made them superior to Christianity. In one of the "table talks" (numerous discussions between Hitler and his intimate associates that Martin Bormann persuaded Hitler to be taken down by a shorthand writers)Hitler praised the Shinto religion of the Japanese for its cult of heroism.[39] Still, he was not interested in reviving paganism in Germany. There is some evidence that Hitler was interested in the old Norse legends and the occult; however, he remained contemptuous of the individual occultists and their esoteric elitism.[40] The only high-ranking person within the Nazi hierarchy who seriously considered making paganism a mass movement was SS-Reichsführer Heinrich Himmler.[41] However, Hitler was dismissive of Himmler's mysticism and rejected his idea for establishing a new religion. Even the party's other pagans considered Himmler's views bizarre.[42] Unlike the neopagans, Hitler was not particularly enthusiastic about dramatizing the early Germanic period in Europe. Although Himmler was eager to underwrite such projects, Hitler was not interested in such endeavors, much to Himmler's despair.[43] In a conversation he once had with Albert Speer, Hitler stressed that the excavations in search of ancient artifacts of the Aryan race sponsored by the Ahnerbe[44] division of the SS were misguided:

Why do we force the whole world to know that we have no past? As if it were not enough that the Romans were already constructing great edifices while our ancestors were still living in clay huts, Himmler is now starting to dig up those clay villages and becomes enthusiastic about every clay potsherd and every stone axe he finds. The only thing he proves is that we still threw stone hatchets and squatted by open fires at a time when Greece and Rome had reached the highest cultural level. We really have every reason to be quiet about that age.[45]

Although many of the neopagans welcomed the rise of the Third Reich as the fulfillment of their millennial fantasies, the Nazi regime did not reciprocate such sentiments and never considered giving its imprimatur to such a movement. On the contrary, many of the occultists, including the Germanic neopagans, had their activities curtailed, though some continued underground. And even that became dangerous, when in early 1941, the former Thulist, Rudolf Hess, flew to Scotland in a bizarre attempt to broker a peace agreement between Germany and England. Not all the details leading to his decision are clear, but there are some indications that he made the trip at the behest of some of his associates in the occult underground. This was the last straw for the occultists. In *Aktion Hess*, Hitler ordered the roundup of the neopagans and occultists, many of whom were sent to concentration camps and even executed.[46]

His lack of piety notwithstanding, Hitler rejected outright atheism, contending that such an approach amounted to "a return to the state of the animal." He preferred a policy that kept his party aloof from religious questions so that sectarian divisions would not undermine its cohesion. Rather than confront the churches directly, Hitler believed that a more expedient approach would be to allow Christianity to die a natural death. The advances of science, Hitler predicted, would eventually wear away religion and its myths would crumble.[47] Hitler, like Klassen, built his *Weltanschauung* on what he perceived as the precepts of nature. In essence, Hitler conjoined a scientific view of the universe with a form of pantheistic mysticism that conformed to natural laws.[48] Hitler believed that he had unraveled history's ultimate secret—the primacy of race.[49] Instead of faith, Hitler believed in the primacy of the will and took the idea to a metaphysical extreme. As he once remarked, as long as a few thousand individuals were willing to go to prison for an idea, the cause was not lost.[50]

The Nazi regime never really had a consistent approach to the issue of religion. In the end, Christianity, not paganism, would gain the state's grudging acceptance. Even those Nazis who were involved with pagan and esoteric societies evinced little interest in paganizing the masses.

Rather, they preferred to maintain exclusive orders, not unlike the Freemasons, with an emphasis on racial mysticism instead of Enlightenment ideas. Although there were trappings of the old Norse heathenism in Nazi rituals and symbols, there was no serious effort to resurrect paganism as a national religion. For the most part, the Nazi regime preferred a policy of separation of church and state. Hitler respected power; the established churches still had the support of most Germans, and neither the German Christian movement nor the neopagans had comparable support. Furthermore, Hitler was a pragmatist and treated the churches carefully. For the most part, the Nazi regime stayed away from doctrinal disputes with both the Catholic and Lutheran churches. Hitler resisted efforts by the more anti-Christian elements in his party, such as Martin Bormann, to declare a "war" on Christianity.[51] Publicly, Hitler consistently maintained that he was only concerned with matters of state and not religion. If, however, Germany had won the war, it is conceivable that Hitler might have eventually taken a harsher position toward the churches.

Despite the failure of the neopagan movement to take hold in the seemingly fertile ground that was Nazi Germany, non-Christian religions would continue to influence the extreme right in the postwar era. An important bridge between historical fascism and neofascism was the Italian aristocrat Julius Evola.

Julius Evola

The scion of a noble Sicilian family, Julius Evola was born on May 19, 1898, in Rome. During World War I, he served as a mountain artillery officer at the Austrian front on the Asiago plateau in northern Italy. After the war, he became interested in oriental studies as well as the occult. Later, he immersed himself in the Western esoteric tradition as well. His philosophy was significantly influenced by the political thought of Plato, Nietzsche, and Oswald Spengler. In 1934, his magnum opus, *The Revolt against the Modern World*, was first published. In it, Evola defended what he referred to as "Tradition" against the leveling effects of egalitarianism.[52] Like Klassen, Evola had a very strong critique of Christianity and imputed the decline of the West to religion. A staunch defender of aristocratic principles, Evola extolled the Hindu-Aryan caste system as the ideal society. He subscribed to a Hindu-influenced cyclical view of history and equated the modern world with the dark age of Kali Yuga in which virtually all tradition is forgotten and chaos reigns. An element of anti-Semitism was evident in Evola's writings, as he accused Jews of having a corrosive effect on the West.

Although he never joined the Italian Fascist Party, Evola nevertheless exerted a certain influence over its ideology, which he sought to transform into a more aristocratic and monarchical orientation. Mussolini actually adopted some of Evola's ideas on race in his official fascist racial theory in 1938, when Italy enacted its own version of race laws that were distinct from Germany's Nuremberg Laws. For a while, Evola was involved in the short-lived Republic of Saló—the rump Italian state in the north established in 1943—which continued to resist the Allies after the Italian government in Rome had pulled out of the war.

In National Socialist Germany, Evola found a better model of his vision of an aristocratic European state. He saw Himmler's SS as an exemplar of the new warrior elite. However, in marked contrast to the Nazi racial theorists, Evola held a more spiritual, rather than biological, conception of race.[53] During an air raid while in Austria near the war's end, he suffered a serous spinal injury that permanently paralyzed him in both legs. Despite this debilitation, he continued to inspire neofascists after the war. In 1953, he wrote *Men among the Ruins* as an analysis of the postwar period in which he hoped for the creation of a united Europe based on aristocratic, rather than democratic, principles.[54] Later losing hope for such a project, in 1961, he wrote *Ride the Tiger* as a guide to help the remaining dispirited elites attain inner fulfillment amid what he saw as a rapidly deteriorating world in the final throes of the dark age.[55] In his later years, he contributed to the corpus of esoteric extreme right thought that focused primarily on the Indo-Aryan tradition; he was an important bridge between historical fascism and postwar fascism, and his writings inspired Aryan revolutionaries in both Europe and North America.[56]

The American Far Right

At first blush it seems surprising that non-Christian religions would take hold in the American far right. After all, Christianity has been an enduring theme in the history of the American far right from the Anti-Masonic Party of the early nineteenth century to the contemporary Christian Identity movement.[57] Furthermore, the American religious tradition would seem to work against this development as well. As Robert Bellah observed, an "American civil religion," which blended Christianity with themes from the American political tradition, took on the significance of a quasi-religion. The Declaration of Independence and the Constitution are regarded as semisacred scriptures. George Washington is often seen as a more recent incarnation of Moses who led his people out of the hands of tyranny. The Civil War can be viewed as a period of great tribulation in which themes of life, death, and rebirth feature prominently and the country gains redemption after the scourge of slavery.[58] In short, this national creed, as it is currently construed, does not dovetail well with the exclusionary worldview of the extreme right. Be that as it may, certain trends would contribute to the extreme right's movement away from mainstream Christianity.

After World War II the various Christian denominations began to distance themselves from racial bigotry. Moreover, the fundamentalist congregations adopted a more philo-Semitic attitude toward Jews, as they saw in the creation of the state of Israel the fulfillment of biblical prophecy. In his study of the history of anti-Semitism in America, Leonard Dinnerstein observed that one of the most far-reaching breakthroughs in the post-World War II era has been the enormous change in Christian beliefs and behaviors concerning Jews. Not only the Catholic Church but also leading academic theologians reexamined Christian perspectives and teachings about Jews in a much more favorable light.[59] Rather than anti-Semitism, philo-Semitism has come to characterize the attitude toward Jews in many American Christian churches—most notably, the evangelical denominations. What is more, the legacy of World War II and the Holocaust severely stigmatized the far right, which came to be associated with wartime fascism. Finally, monitoring groups, such as the Anti-Defamation League and the Southern Poverty Law Center, have effectively delegitimized the views of the extreme right in contemporary political and social discourse.[60] All of these factors discouraged many would-be followers from joining far-right movements or at least encouraged some to choose more respectable conservative vehicles for their political activism. As a result, the small numbers of radicals and true believers that remained were more amenable to fringe movements, such as neopaganism, Creativity, and Christian Identity.

Christian Identity

Reluctant to jettison Christianity, some denizens of the extreme right have found solace in Christian Identity, an obscure religious theology that does much to bind the movement together. Christian Identity has no central body but is a very loose network of individual believers and small congregations. The religion has its origins in England's "British Israelism," which first gained popularity in the nineteenth century. The creed posited that the peoples of Northwestern Europe were the true descendants of the ten lost tribes of Israel. Originally, the British version was philo-Semitic in character, seeking to identify the British as a kindred people of the Jews. In the early twentieth century, the sect found its way to America and later metamorphosed into Christian Identity. Although there are several variations in beliefs and not all are anti-Semitic, many variants of this religion demonize Jews and reject their ancestral claim to the Israel of the biblical era.[61]

There is no single book or document that is accepted as the authoritative doctrine of the Christian Identity theology. Some followers subscribe to the so-called two seeds doctrine, which posits that the biblical character of Adam in the Garden of Eden was preceded by inferior races designated as "pre-Adamic." According to this doctrine, Eve was seduced by the snake (Satan) and procreated with a representative of the pre-Adamic race. Hence was born Cain, the progenitor of the Jews, who would go on to procreate with other pre-Adamic races. The nonwhite races of today are considered to be the descendents of these pre-Adamic races and are derisively referred to as "mud people." By contrast, Abel was putatively born a pure offspring and was the progenitor of the Aryan or "white seed." Thus Identity believers trace their conflict with Jews back to the Book of Genesis in the Bible. Other variants of Christian Identity see contemporary Jews as impostors and claim that they are actually the descendants of a long-lost Eurasian tribe, the Khazars.[62]

According to several versions of Christian Identity, the victory of the righteous and faithful is not assured. Thus it is conceivable that Satan and his minions could actually triumph in Armageddon. This eventuality instills a sense of desperation among some Christian Identity believers. Hence, the shrill calls for political violence suffused with millennialism. Several observers argue that a millennial ethos is conducive to terrorism as it loosens the moral and ethical constraints that would normally curb the more secularly inspired terrorists.[63] This thought is consistent with the results of previous studies, which indicate that a disproportionate number of those arrested for right-wing terrorism were followers of this sect.[64]

That said, it is important not to overstate the significance of the Christian Identity theology. Although observers of this movement like to expound on its rather convoluted theology, it appears often to be more of a rationalization for followers' racism than an actual belief of the heart.[65] Thus, Christian Identity is in large part an attempt to provide a theological justification for a political ideology. In this way, religion adds a sense of legitimacy and purpose to the mission of Christian Identity followers.[66]

The late Wesley Swift is considered the single most significant figure in the history of the Christian Identity movement in America. He introduced the theology to Richard Butler, who went on to found the Church of Jesus Christ Christian and its political arm, the Aryan Nations. Some of its more notable leaders today include Thomm Robb, Pete Peters, Dan Gayman, Charles A. Weisman, and Richard Kelly Hoskins. Its influence also reaches beyond the confines of the revolutionary radical right as it has gained adherents in the Christian Patriot movement as well.[67]

Christian Identity has gained much attention from law enforcement authorities, monitoring groups, and even the academic community. It is often referred to as a pseudo-religion by it detractors. Although the theology has served as an important commonality in the far-right underground, its influence appears to be waning. Many of its followers are older, and there are not enough new converts to replace those who are dying.[68] Increasingly, the younger affiliates of the extreme right have been attracted to Odinism.

Odinism and the Far Right

The most popular variant of neopaganism in the extreme right is Odinism, which looks to the old Norse gods for inspiration. In recent years, one can discern a noticeable shift in attitude toward Christianity in the American extreme right, most notably among its younger activists. Some segments of the movement are now highly critical of Christianity. What is needed, they argue, is a religion that speaks to their racial interests. To many of the younger affiliates of the far right, Christian Identity stretches the bounds of credulity. In its stead, they prefer Odinism, a reconstructed neopagan religion that fits well into the Zeitgeist of contemporary identity politics. Thus, Odinism appears in many ways to be a manifestation of a white ethnic variant of multiculturalism not unlike black nationalists' embrace of Islam. Moreover, in a milieu in which anti-Semitism looms so large, it is not surprising that some of its affiliates would seek an alternative to Christianity, which has its roots in Judaism. A cursory review of its myths and development is in order.

Odinism is a reconstructed religion. There is no evidence of an unbroken chain of followers extending back to the pre-Christian era, despite some claims to the contrary.[69] The new Odinists have created a syncretic blend of Norse mythology, millennialism, and a modern warrior cult. The Odinist religion is polytheistic. At the center of the pantheon is the all-father Odin. His son, Thor, the god of thunder, was the most popular of the gods among the pre-Christian Germanic Tribes. Other gods and goddesses include Frey, Freya, Frigga, Baldur, and Braggi. Odinism stresses loyalty to the tribe, as the emphasis is more on honor than on any Manichean notion of good and evil. The greatest honor is to die in battle after which Valkyries take the slain to Valhalla to enjoy an afterlife of blissful battling in the day and feasting at night. Ragnarok is the endtimes apocalypse in which the gods battle Loki, and are destroyed. Out of the ruins, a new epoch is ushered in with a new pantheon of gods led by the sole survivor, Baldur.

Just when American far rightists discovered Odinism is difficult to determine with precision. One thing is certain: individual Odinists emerged before the advent of organized Odinism.[70] In the 1950s and 1960s Norse neopagan motifs appeared in right-wing literature. Perhaps more important, references to Viking themes appeared in the popular culture, which helped set the stage for the Odinist revival.[71] Ironically, it was an Australian who actually planted the seeds of the Odinist movement in America.

In the 1930s, Hitler's Third Reich, with its pagan symbology, captured the imagination of an eccentric Australian, A. Rud Mills, who sought to develop an Anglo-Saxon brand of Odinism. In his 1930 tract, *The Odinist Religion: Overcoming Judeo-Christianity*, he posited that ancient Europe was the original fount for all of the world's civilizations and claimed that the white race had a single distant common ancestor named either

George or Sigge. In the 1950s, he launched the First Church of Odin. Mills called upon whites to recognize Odin as their true god. Arguing that Christianity had been an unmitigated disaster for the West, Mills castigated the religion for disconnecting divinity from the natural world. Instead, he encouraged white people to rediscover their pagan roots. As he explained, by losing their authentic Norse God, whites had also lost their true source of strength. His analysis was not unlike the Marxian notion of "false consciousness," as he argued that whites recognized followers of another religion—Judaism—as the "Chosen People."[72] His efforts never really got off the ground, but in the 1960s, one American couple, Else Christenson and her husband, discovered his writings and helped establish the nascent Odinist movement in North America.

With the creation of the Odinist Fellowship in 1971, Else Christensen is generally considered to have founded the first organized Odinist group in America. In doing so, she offered a religious alternative to Christianity for people of European ethnic background. Her brand of Odinism kept ritual to a minimum and concentrated instead on fostering Nordic awareness and pride. It was not long before some neo-Nazis groups noticed and began integrating Odinist motifs into their literature. Moreover, some Odinists also began founding their own kindreds, or small pagan congregations. For over two decades, Christensen promoted Odinism, and in the early 1980s, she established a prison-outreach ministry. However, her activism effectively came to an end in 1993, when she was sentenced to five years in prison for involvement in a drug-trafficking scheme.[73] Perhaps her negative experience with the law caused Christensen to call for a more tempered approach to Odinist activism, which stressed cultural, rather than political, themes. Nevertheless, her spadework would inspire other Odinist organizations that followed.

By the early 1970s Odinist groups began to spring up spontaneously and independently of one another in several countries including England, Iceland, Germany, and the United States. Some Odinists wanted to develop a form of the old religion that would not be besmirched with Nazism, with which their reconstructed religion was increasingly being identified. They wanted a brand of Odinism that could gain acceptance with a large congregation with no social stigma attached. Moreover, they wanted to avoid the harassment of watchdog groups and state authorities. They called their brand of Odinism Asatru. Its first organization in

America is believed to be the Asatru Free Assembly (AFA), which was founded by Stephen McNallen in 1972.

McNallen significantly contributed to contemporary Odinist thought, most notably through his theory of "metagenetics," which posits that tradition and culture are a matter of genetic inheritance. Borrowing heavily from the Swiss psychologist Carl Gustav Jung's archetypes and theory of the collective unconscious, metagenetics claims that the old pagan gods inhered in the hearts and souls of generations of European folk but lay dormant until they deemed it propitious for their resurrection. In his 1936 essay "Wotan," Jung discussed the "archetype" Wotan which punctuated German history. Periodically, Wotan would stir the peoples of Central Europe into a frenzy and lead them into a hunt. The archetype's most recent manifestation, according to Jung, was German National Socialism with Hitler as the Wotanic *Ergreifer* (one who seizes) incarnate.[74] Metagenetics is now a common theme and a justification for the exclusivity of Odinism—that is, only people of European ethnic background can be adherents. This tenet would prove to be a bone of contention between the racially oriented Odinists and the more ritually based Asatruars.[75] Doctrinal differences divided the AFA, as it was later replaced by two rival Asatru groups, the Asatru Alliance and the Ring of Troth.[76]

Race is the main issue that causes the most friction between the Odinist and Asatru factions of the Norse neopagan movement. The followers of Asatru worry that the more racially inclined Odinists will undercut the legitimacy of their religion before it even gets a chance to take root. The Odinists tend to be less organized and often seem to be more concerned with effecting the political goals of the white separatist movement. By contrast, Asatruars seek to develop a legitimate niche in the religious constellation in America. Many neo-Nazis and other far rightists have appropriated the Norse symbols as a backdrop for the mythos behind which they organize. But even within these ranks, there are still those who are very serious about their new religious faith. For instance, David Lane emerged as perhaps the most important voice of racialist Odinists. The most celebrated of the imprisoned members of the Order (which will be discussed in chapter 5), Lane, ironically, came to be seen as a Nelson Mandela of sorts to those in the white separatist movement. He was best known for coining the "14 Words" credo—"We must secure the existence of our people and a future for White children"—which is a popular salutation in the discourse of the movement. After his incarceration in 1985 for his involvement in the terrorist campaign of the Order, Lane immersed himself in reading and has devoted much energy to writing tracts on revolutionary tactics from his prison cell. Most notable in this regard was his contribution to "leaderless resistance"—a theoretical approach to terrorism that favors violence by individuals or small cohesive groups.[77]

Despite his imprisonment, Lane married Katja née Maddox in 1994, and together with Ron McVan, founded Wotansvolk around that same time. Lane died in May 2007, and the future of the organization is uncertain. Previously, McVan was involved in the Church of the Creator. In 1990, he moved to the headquarters in Otto, North Carolina, and became the editor of *Racial Loyalty* and commander of the White Berets.[78] Wotansvolk published a newsletter *Focus Fourteen*, which was usually written by David Lane. One effort on which the organization has expended significant energy is a prison outreach program that as of 2001 was reported to have worked with more than 5,000 prisoners. Still, other related religions gained followers in the extreme right as well.

Cosmotheism

A scion of the white supremacist movement, William Pierce created his own unique religion, Cosmotheism. By the 1990s, Pierce was regarded as the elder statesman of the American extreme. Obviously a man of considerable intelligence, he was once employed as part of a research team at the Los Alamos Scientific Laboratory in New Mexico as well as a scientist at a jet propulsion laboratory in California. Later, he earned a Ph.D. in physics from the University of Colorado and became a tenured professor at the University of Oregon. However, he soon tired of academe, and in 1966, went to work as the editor of *National Socialist World*—a journal published by George Lincoln Rockwell's American Nazi Party. After Rockwell's death, the American Nazi Party soon fell into disarray. By 1970, Pierce broke with that organization to join the National Youth Alliance under the tutelage of Willis Carto. Eventually, the two split and Pierce formed a new corporation under the title National Youth Alliance in Virginia and rented office space for it in Arlington, Virginia. In 1974, Pierce discontinued the National Youth Alliance and created a new organization called the National Alliance, which was formally incorporated in Virginia and which he would continue to lead until his death in 2002.[79]

To add a religious dimension to his political philosophy, Pierce founded the Cosmotheist Community, an esoteric branch of the National Alliance available for those who were most receptive to his message. Reminiscent of Ernst Haeckel's German Monist League, Cosmotheism is based essentially on the notion that the white race should willfully seek an evolutionary path that will enable it to reach divinity. According to a racialist version of evolutionary theory, the harsh conditions of the Ice Age in particular resulted in a more rigorous selection process for those people who lived in Northern Europe during that period. Over the centuries, the various European-derived peoples developed a unique genetic makeup that has greatly influenced Western civilization. Cosmotheism is essentially pantheistic in orientation, which essentially means that it views everything in nature as interrelated. Humans are not independent and self-contained but are an integral part of nature. Unlike the theistic conception of God, in which the Creator is viewed as a commanding father to whom followers have a deferential and devotional relationship, the pantheistic conception does not view God as an anthropomorphic deity. God is not otherworldly but is immanent in this world. Rather than a deferential relationship to God, pantheists have a sense of respect and awe for God's creation. Usually, pantheists reject the notion of life after death in some sort of conscious form. Nevertheless, Pierce sees the white race as a chain extending backward and forward in time in which each individual is viewed as an important link in an evolutionary process.

Despite his efforts to create a religion, Pierce once admitted that the project never really went anywhere. What is more, the IRS did not recognize it as a church, thus rejecting it claim of tax-exempt status. Although some of his critics have questioned the sincerity of his commitment to spirituality, a fair reading of his writings and lectures would indicate otherwise. Pierce occasionally invoked the "Faustian spirit" as the guiding ethos of the "Western man." Furthermore, he frequently argued that the malaise of Western civilization was principally neither political nor economic but, rather, spiritual in nature.[80] Hitler, in particular, had an abiding influence on Pierce. National Socialism features prominently in the mythos of the extreme right. Some have even gone so far as to depict the German führer as a demigod.

Hitler as Demigod

A woman, Savitri Devi, also made significant contributions to postwar National Socialism. Born in France to a Greek father and an English mother, Devi was well educated and received a Ph.D. in chemistry in 1931, though she quickly lost interest in science and turned her attention to mysticism. An avid Germanophile and admirer of Hitler, she traveled to Germany soon after World War II and began propagandizing for a rebirth of National Socialism. These efforts landed her in an allied prison. Upon her release in 1956, she wrote her most important book, *The Lighting and the Sun*—a bizarre hagiography of Hitler, which syncretized National Socialism with Hindu mysticism. According to Devi, Hitler was the "man against time," a figure of demigod stature sent by providence to lead the Aryan man out of the dark ages and into a new golden age. Although few read her book, it was well received by several leading figures in the postwar National Socialist movement and had a profound influence on the development of their worldviews. German National Socialism was henceforth recast as a universalistic ideology, indeed a quasi-religion, under which all European-derived peoples could work to create a "new order" based on the "eternal laws of nature."[81] Despite her efforts, her writings did not extend much beyond a handful of fanatics.[82] However, in recent years, there has been a revival in the extreme right of interest in her writings.

Still more rightists eulogized Hitler and held him up as a model for emulation. James Larratt Battersby, a member of the British Union of Fascists who was interned during World War II, wrote a short book titled *The Holy Book of Adolf Hitler* in 1951; in it he described the German führer as a god sent to Earth to lead the Aryans—God's chosen race. According to Battersby, Hitler's National Socialist movement sought to create a union of heaven and earth by the joining of the flesh and spirit. Although not explicitly rejecting Christianity *in toto*, Battersby argued that it had become hopelessly corrupted and that the original gospel of the Aryan Jesus had been "vitiated and twisted out of all recognition." In its stead, Battersby put forth a program of Aryan racial renewal based on the precepts of Hitlerism but with a more socialist spin in which communal ownership would be promoted over private ownership and benefit when possible. He also advocated using old Germanic sacred symbols, such as the swastika and the sun wheel, in religious festivals.[83]

George Lincoln Rockwell, the founder of the American Nazi Party, also looked upon the German führer as a figure of spiritual significance. While still in high school, Rockwell lost faith in Christianity, an experience that initially troubled him. An intellectually curious youth, he claimed to have "read and re-read" the Bible but was appalled by some of the more violent exhortations of the Hebrew God in the Old Testament. Like Hitler, he rejected explicit atheism, commenting that without religious guidance, civilization would collapse.[84] Despite his seeming agnosticism, Rockwell asserted a belief in some higher entity but not in the anthropomorphic sense of Christianity.[85] Inasmuch as Christianity was by and large the religion of most whites, Rockwell declared himself a defender of the religion. His American Nazi Party was left open to men of all Christian denominations as well as atheists and agnostics.[86] As for himself, Rockwell pledged his fealty to the German führer. He recalled that particular moment of decision in a style of religious prose. In the midst of a personal crisis in 1958, he once recounted how the example of Hitler had given him inspiration to persist with his political activism:

> I went home, drew the living room blinds closed and hung the beautiful banner completely across the wall. In the center I mounted a plaque of Adolf Hitler. Then I placed a small bookcase under it and set three lighted candles in front. I stood before my holy altar to Adolf Hitler, alone in the silent house, without a single soul knowing what I was doing—or caring. Then, for the first time since I had lost my Christian religion, I experienced the soul-thrilling upsurge of emotion which is denied our modern, sterile, atheist "intellectuals," but nevertheless remains the force which has moved the human race for countless centuries: religious experience. As I looked at the stern face of the greatest mind in twenty centuries, I felt the unbelievable flood of "religious" power pouring into me which would be easily understood by any savage Indian standing on a mountain top at sunrise and communing with the Great Spirit before battle. The very power which the so-called intellectuals have denied themselves because of their conceit that they can "know" everything. . . .
>
> I was moved beyond the power of words to describe. Goose-pimples rose all over me, my hair stood on end, my eyes filled with tears of love and gratitude for this greatest of all conquerors of hu-

man misery and shame, and my breath came in little gasps. If I had not known that the Leader would have scorned such adulation, I might have fallen to my knees in unashamed worship, but instead, I drew myself to attention, raised my arm in the eternal salute of the ancient Roman legions and repeated the holy words, "Heil Hitler!"—meaning every syllable with all my heart, mind and soul.[87]

To Rockwell, National Socialism was a form of religion based on the tenets of nature in which all living things should pursue a higher level of existence and move "toward God." In that sense, National Socialism was far more than a mere political ideology in that it entailed a "worshipful attitude toward Nature and a religious love of the Great gifts of an Unkown Creator."[88]

Rockwell's successor, Matt Koehl, went even further in sacralizing Hitler. In his tract, *Faith of the Future*, Koehl sought to establish Hitler as an object of religious veneration. The book contained a critique of Christianity, arguing that it created an "inner tension," an angst that distorted Western culture from its inception. Echoing Klassen, Koehl argued that the West was great in spite of Christianity, not because of it. With the onset of the age of reason, the credence of Christianity began to wane, and consequently, the faith lost "the emotional, polarizing force necessary to direct the spiritual life of a culture." Without a guiding mythos, the West was rudderless and slipped into decline. However, the arrival of Hitler heralded the "start of the second half of human history." Far from perfect, the Third Reich, "the provisional state" of the new order, was nevertheless infected by ideas and elements of the old order. The cataclysm of the Second World War set in motion the total end of the old order that could not be rescued. Although the National Socialist movement suffered utter military defeat, its spiritual ideas lived on. To the faithful, Koehl exclaimed, National Socialism endeavored to "restore the natural laws to their rightful place in human affairs—thus reforging the sacred link between man and Nature, a link that was shattered by a "Semitic ideology." Although Hitler may have died in the physical sense in his Bunker on April 30, 1945, Koehl maintains that the führer continues to "articulate our deepest, most heartfelt feelings and longings as Aryans." In Hitler, Koehl finds more than just a mere historical phenomenon—"something which is eternal and infinite" whom Providence endowed with a special mission. Thus, by following the dictates of Hitler, Koehl avers, Aryans possess the potential to transcend "the limitations of [their] own mortal existence."[89]

Conclusion

Klassen's worldview did not rise in a vacuum but came into being in a subculture in which mainstream Christianity had lost much appeal. With neopaganism and Christian Identity, members of the extreme right appropriated a religion that was consistent with their preexisting political beliefs. As Hitler, Evola, Rockwell, Klassen, and others have counseled, a political ideology is strengthened when it has a theological justification.

Although Christian Identity probably still has more followers than does Odinism, it does not seem to hold much popularity with far rightists outside of North America. Moreover, even in America, Identity's following appears to be limited to persons with a Christian fundamentalist background.[90] In an effort to capture the dynamism of Odinism and appeal to the youthful segment of the movement, some Christian Identity sects have sought to incorporate the Norse gods and goddesses as "Israelite heroes" or identify elements of Odinism as basically Christian.[91]

Since the end of World War II, some elements of the extreme right have come to eschew nationalism in favor of a broader pan-Aryan identity that transcends national borders. Increasingly, they view their individual nationalist movements as part of a larger struggle for white racial survival against a rising tide of nonwhite demographic expansion, said to be orchestrated by the forces of globalization and international Judaism. Here, the Internet has been important, allowing disparate groups to spread their message and exchange ideas. Pagan motifs, with their emphasis on warrior values, are popular with younger affiliates of the movement. In this regard Odinism travels well across different countries, linking together many disparate groups and individuals. Odinists, on past occasions, have been able to collaborate with Christian Identity members despite holding beliefs that in theory would offend them. Various far-right groups have no trouble finding common cause with them. According to one estimate, Norse neopaganism has been appropriated by Aryan revolutionaries in up to forty countries.[92] Nicholas Goodrick-

Clarke argued that the rise of Odinism and related Aryan cults may be symptomatic of a divisive direction in the course of multiculturalism in Western democracies. The popularity of neopaganism, Christian Identity, and other unconventional religions suggests a movement toward a more radical direction of the extreme right. Klassen would seek to reach out to some of these elements for his Creativity movement.

4

Reaching Out to the Right

After creating his religious creed, Klassen set about finding followers for his new belief system. Right from the beginning, he experienced resistance. By the summer of 1972, he was so far into writing *Nature's Eternal Religion* that he decided to look for a printer for his book. Given its controversial content, Klassen decided to self-publish the book. He initially struck a deal with Universal Printing Company in Hialeah, Florida. Two weeks after submitting his manuscript, however, the firm returned the manuscript along with an uncashed check. The Bechtel family, who owned the firm, were devout Christians and thus not willing to do the job after they discovered the contents of the book.[1] Eventually, he found a printer and the book was self-published. He invested a considerable amount of his own money to promote Creativity and spent much time corresponding with prospective recruits. His abrasive personality, however, often strained his relations with other rightists.

Despite his misgivings about the open Hitlerian approach, Klassen continued to interface with neo-Nazi groups. Inasmuch as Klassen greatly admired Adolf Hitler, he believed that neo-Nazis would be amenable to the Creativity message. Klassen unapologetically praised the German führer and even referred to him as "the greatest white man who ever lived." Although there may have been some disagreements over religion, he emphasized that there was no conflict between the Nazi philosophy and Creativity. However, he added that Creativity was much more comprehensive than the Nazi philosophy.[2]

Nevertheless, National Socialism came under Klassen's criticism for its narrow nationalistic focus. Rather than nationality, Klassen sought to make race the organizing principle of his church. What Klassen failed to notice was the perceptional transformation of National Socialism in the postwar era. In fact, even during the war, especially when the *Wehrmacht* was locked in a death struggle against Bolshevism in the east, National Socialism increasingly exhibited less of a narrow, chauvinistic pan-German quality and took on a more inclusive pan-European quality, in large measure out of practicality in order to enlist the support of more people in Europe. Most notable in this regard was the Waffen-SS, the military arm of the infamous *Schuzstaffen*. As the regular German Army, or *Wehrmacht*, was reluctant to release enough Germans from its manpower pool to the SS, Heinrich Himmler created foreign legions to fill out his Waffen-SS divisions. At its height, the Waffen-SS grew to 950,000 men organized into thirty-eight divisions. By war's end, over half the remaining 600,000 soldiers were of foreign origin.[3] In his study of nationalism, *The Wrath of Nations*, William Pfaff argued that Nazism could be conceptualized as a universalistic ideology rather than just another narrow variant of nationalism. As he explained, the National Socialist program envisaged a united Europe primarily under the Nordic people comprising Germany, the Scandinavians, the Dutch, and even the English.[4]

In reaching out to neo-Nazis, Klassen had only limited success. He established a correspondence with the leading neo-Nazi activists in America, including William Pierce, Matt Koehl, James H. Madole, Tom Metzger, Frank Collin, and Harold Covington.[5] He even sought to enlist Allen Vincent, who led the National Socialist Movement, a fringe group even by neo-Nazi standards, which had about thirty members, in the San Francisco Bay area. James Mason was affiliated with the group as well. The group was the subject of a documentary called *California Reich*. According to Klassen, for a while James Madole, the leader of the National Renaissance Party, was interested in Creativity but later reverted to his esoteric brand of Nazism, which included the Atlantis myth and elements of eastern mysticism.[6]

One of the few neo-Nazi figures with whom Klassen established an amiable rapport was William L. Pierce, the founder of the National Alliance. Still, Klassen criticized Pierce's religion, Cosmotheism, as being too vague for ordinary white people to understand. As Klassen explained to Pierce, "In short, Bill, I am as confused as ever as to where you stand about Christianity, gods, demons, spooks in the sky and the whole bit about the world of the unreal and supernatural."[7] In later years, Pierce would sporadically deride the more fundamentalist variants of Christianity but refrained from public criticism because he did not want a war with Christianity.[8] He once commented that he "faile[d] to see anything that [was] good or useful in Christianity." Although not an Odinist,

Pierce believed that the "European spirit" was much better expressed in the pagan traditions of Northern Europe. Be that as it may, Pierce acknowledged that many Christians were decent and reasonable people.[9] As such, he did not want to offend them by attacking Christianity in a strident and open way in the style of Klassen.

Essentially, the two only disagreed over tactics. For example, Klassen criticized Pierce's opus, *The Turner Diaries*, as an unrealistic blueprint for white racial revolution. It is perhaps the most widely read book in the subterranean world of the far right and has sold approximately 350,000 copies—an amazing figure for an underground book.[10] Cleverly written as a novel, it tells the story of a cellular white-supremacist revolutionary group—the Organization—which conducts a terrorist campaign against the U.S. government that is controlled by a Jewish cabal working from behind the scenes. A struggle of apocalyptic proportions ensues and American society implodes under the weight of racial strife. Eventually, the organization acquires nuclear weapons and a global atomic war ensues involving America, the Soviet Union, and Israel. For his service, the protagonist Earl Turner is inducted into a quasi-monastic inner circle of the organization known as the Order. His final mission is to fly a small crop duster plane equipped with a nuclear bomb on a Kamikaze mission to destroy the Pentagon. Turner selflessly agrees to fly the mission and succeeds, thus dealing the system its fatal blow. After victory in America, the revolution spreads throughout the rest of the world. The book closes with a millennial tone. Out of the ashes of devastation the countries of the West experience a civilizational renewal and are once again master of their own destinies.[11] For his part, Klassen thought the scenario was unrealistic and impractical. How, he asked, could a small revolutionary group restore order and seize power once a stage of anarchy had been reached?[12]

Despite their differences in tactics and strategy, Klassen and Pierce remained on good terms. Although he rejected metaphysical doctrines, Klassen nevertheless found some merit in Pierce's Cosmotheism insofar as it searched "for a meaningful purpose in life and a coherent, realistic philosophy of bringing it about." Still, he criticized Pierce's Cosmotheist scriptures for invoking such terms and phrases as the "Divine Spark," "God's purpose," and "up-toward the Creator" as obfuscating the critical issue of white racial survival.[13] In correspondence between the two, Klassen expressed gratification that Pierce eschewed any part in the "spooks in the sky" story. Furthermore, he commended Pierce for his work in *Attack!* magazine.[14]

Not surprisingly, Klassen took issue with the Christian fundamentalists, especially the Identity Christians who figure prominently in the American far right. According to Klassen, the Christian Identity religion was hopelessly misguided. Creativity fully acknowledges the Jewish origins of Christianity. At first, Klassen sought to reach out to some Identity preachers, such as Dan Gayman, and convert them to his creed.[15] However, over the years, Klassen became increasingly hostile to Identity Christians and characterized them as "enemies." Moreover, he described Christian Identity as a form of mental pathology whose followers suffer from an extreme credulity:

> Some of these Christians, those who have discovered what skillful and congenital liars the Jews are, how obnoxious and repugnant they have been throughout history, found themselves in a serious dilemma. Since most of their precious bible is Jewish from cover to cover and keeps gushing repeatedly about Yahweh's endless and palpitating love affair with these despicable reprobates, they found this hard to take. So some ingenious inventor came up with a brilliant new twist. Why not claim that the Jews are not at all the real Israelites, but children of the Devil, and we, the White Race, are the genuine article. Why with a sleight of hand, some clever juxtapositioning and a lot of gullibility, we can claim that the "Ten Lost Tribes of Israel" wandered into an uninhabited Europe sometime in the first millennium B.C.E and rapidly populated it from one end to the other . . . Ipso facto, the problem is solved.[16]

For their part, Identity Christians were deeply offended by Klassen's derisory remarks about "Jewish Christianity." Nevertheless, Klassen did find some common ground with them insofar as he did not consider Jews to be whites. Rather, he maintained that roughly 90 percent of contemporary Jews were actually descendants of a long-lost Eurasian tribe, the Khazars.

With the Norse neopagans, Klassen developed a somewhat more amicable relationship. Although, he commended Odinists for rejecting Christianity, he chided them for seeking to resurrect "Aryan" gods. As he liked to remind them, "We do not have time for games." What is more,

Klassen thought it was odd that white racialists would seek to revive the Norse variant of paganism when other variants, such as the Greek or the Roman, would be more intellectually appealing.[17] On occasion, he lamented on the lack of explicit racialism in Odinism. For example, he criticized the long-time Odinist activist, Stephen McNallen, for not revering Adolf Hitler.[18] He maintained a more cordial correspondence with the founder of the Odinist Fellowship, Else Christensen, but in the main, Klassen believed that Odinism was sorely lacking as a vehicle to mobilize the white race, as history had proven that this religion had not survived the test of time:

> If Odinism did not have the intellectual and spiritual strength to hold its own against Jewish Christianity a thousand years ago when the Vikings had Europe at its mercy, what would lead any reasonable person to believe it can now reverse the situation under conditions that are a thousand times more unfavorable than they were then? Why would anyone want to resurrect an ancient failure from the scrap heap of history?[19]

For Klassen, it was folly to follow the religions of the Druids, Viking, Celts, and others insofar as their cultures were less intellectually advanced than that of contemporary society. Inasmuch as modern man knew more about science and the world around him, why would he look for guidance to those who were comparatively primitive?[20] Also, he thought that it was delusional to expect some kind of intervention from the old gods in the struggle for white racial survival; as he once explained to an Odinist: "the spooks won't cut the grass for you nor will they give us any help in the impending battle."[21]

Nevertheless, on occasion, there have been episodes of cooperation between Odinism and Creativity. For example, the Creator newspaper, *Racial Loyalty*, once published an article by David Lane, an imprisoned member of the Order (which will be discussed in chapter 5).[22] David Lane also invoked the laws of nature as guiding principles of his brand of Odinism, similar to their importance in Creativity. In fact, Lane found his version of Odinism, with its emphasis on the laws of nature and the precepts of Creativity so striking that he actually felt compelled at times to explicitly distance himself from any official connection to Creativity in order to maintain his distinctiveness.[23] Nevertheless, at one time, Lane actually praised Creativity, referring to it as the apex of the racialist movement, and counseled that "eventually all will have to recognize the ultimate and purest of hard truths which Creativity espouses."[24] Some Creators also identified with Odinism, including Tom Padgett.[25]

His disdain for traditional Americanism notwithstanding, Klassen reached out to numerous "patriot" activists including Robert De Pugh, who once led the far-right underground group, the Minutemen. Founded in Missouri in 1960, this anticommunist group ironically modeled its organizational structure on a cell system reminiscent of the communist revolutionary models of Lenin and Mao.[26] Eventually, governmental authorities, including then Attorney General Robert Kennedy, took notice of the organization.[27] Consequently, in the late 1960s, the organization was infiltrated and effectively neutralized.[28]

In 1977, Klassen attended a conference organized by De Pugh that sought to unite various elements of the far right. Many right-wing notables attended the event. At the conference, Klassen was most impressed by John R. Harrell, a former U.S. senator, who then led the Christian-Patriots Defense League. The master of ceremonies was Ardie McBreary who, years later, was convicted for his part in the campaign of the Order, a terrorist group that was active in the Pacific Northwest. Another attendee was Robert K. Shelton, the leader of the United Klans of America, who organized a lie detector program—so-called stress analyzers—to ferret out potential informants in his organization. The leader of the Odinist Fellowship, Else Christensen, and Allen Vincent, the leader of a small neo-Nazi group in San Francisco, attended as well. Gerda Koch, a Christian Identity activist, lectured on the influence of Christianity on the U.S. Constitution. Klassen described her as "a real battle-axe of a woman" who "represented the epitome of the narrow-minded 'born-again' spook-chasers." In his speech, Klassen argued that such matters as country, flag, and the Constitution were minor side issues compared to the race problem, which, if it was not solved, would lead to their collective doom. He surprised the audience by telling them that Christianity was counterproductive and that they should seek a new racial religion, namely Creativity. His speech was not well received; as he recalled, after he finished, a stunned silence greeted him.[29] For his part, Klassen was unimpressed by the traditional conservative approach promoted by the attendees and lamented that far-right activists were always going off on meaningless tangents.

In a letter to De Pugh, Klassen criticized him for failing to identify the race issue and the "perfidious Jew," in particular, as the root cause of the white race's predicament. Without clearly identifying the enemy, Klassen argued, it was impossible to mount meaningful resistance. He found it impractical to try to unite a disparate collection of rightist groups and individuals. Instead, Klassen counseled, they must follow the example of Hitler and not water down their ideology.[30] He asked what good American patriotism was if it meant "laying down your life . . . if you are only safeguarding real estate for the niggers to breed and multiply and the Jews to control and make billions."[31] He urged De Pugh to forget about traditional staples in the far right's litany of complaints—big government, communism, the IRS, the UN, and Christianity—and instead concentrate on Jews as the focus of attention and the root cause toward whom he should direct his animus.[32] What was needed, he counseled, was a common ideology around which the racialist movement could "polarize." Be that as it may, Klassen still espoused some traditional patriot themes. For example, he dabbled in tax rebellion and claimed not to have filed a tax return to the IRS since 1980. In 1981, he went so far as to send the IRS an angry letter, explaining why he believed the personal income tax was unconstitutional, along with a number of legal briefs supporting his position.[33]

With his irreverent critique of Christianity, Klassen alienated many like-minded persons who basically shared his racialist philosophy but rejected the atheism of Creativity. Furthermore, Klassen was highly critical of some aspects of Americanism. He was particularly vitriolic toward traditional American "patriots," as he mockingly referred to them as "Kosher Konservatives." In his estimation, their loyalties had been terribly misplaced insofar as they were devoted to such "superficial" affinities as Christianity, country, flag, and the Constitution. The notion of a country, he maintained, was a totally man-made concept, consisting of basically a particular part of real estate, whose boundaries were artificial and subject to change.[34] Furthermore, Klassen believed that whites should not devote their allegiance to a particular type of government such as democracy but, rather, to their race, which he believed was more enduring and significant when judged by the long view of history. For Klassen, it was the eleventh hour for the white race. As such, whites did not have the luxury of indulging in fantasies or unrealistic propositions.

Arguably, no other man has had more influence on the postwar American radical right than Willis Carto, the founder of the Liberty Lobby, which was one of the most significant and enduring institutions in the far-right constellation until its dissolution in 2001. The central figure in the movement, Carto has been involved in nearly every major enterprise of the American far right in the postwar era.[35] Although a reclusive figure unknown to most Americans, he has reached out to figures from both the mainstream and the fringes of the political right. Liberty Lobby published a weekly newspaper, *The Spotlight*, which was the most read organ of the far right. In addition, Carto is credited with establishing an institutional basis for Holocaust denial with the founding of the Institute for Historical Review in 1978. Carto has occasionally ventured into electoral politics as evidenced by his involvement with the Populist Party in the mid-1980s.

Klassen had a brief correspondence with Carto, who actually complimented him on his book *Nature's Eternal Religion*.[36] In a letter to Carto associate John Tiffany in 1978, Klassen remarked that it would be great to have Carto's network behind Creativity.[37] Years later, however, Klassen criticized Carto for not taking a stand against Christianity. Moreover, he ridiculed his circumlocutions toward Jews, as Carto's organ—*The Spotlight*—did not attack Jews qua Jews, but rather Jews as Zionists, dual loyalists, communists, and so on.[38] For his part, Carto did not seem concerned about Klassen's criticism. In fact, Carto's publications would occasionally carry advertisements for Klassen's books long after Klassen's death in 1993.

Given his somewhat elitist self-image, it is not surprising that Klassen preferred to seek out intellectuals in the far right and persuade them to support Creativity. But in this area, he seemed to alienate more than build bridges. Not even the erudite professor of classics, Revilo P. Oliver, escaped his caustic pen. Klassen criticized Oliver's tract, *Christianity and the Survival of the West*, in which he lamented the decline of Christianity as a unifying principle for Western civilization. Oliver defended Christianity on cultural, rather than spiritual, grounds. The Christian faith was also important, observed Oliver, insofar as the "pro-American" movement was composed mainly of Christians—in much higher proportion than were found in the general population. Rejecting conspiratorial explanations for the decline of the Christian faith, he imputed its retreat to the advances in science that undercut the credibility of its religious myths. As a result of its decline, a spiritual vacuum emerged, which he viewed as a catastrophe in that it left the West rudderless without any sense of direction. Oliver exhorted believers and nonbelievers alike to base their hope on science, technology, and the white race's capacity for objective thought. Only through that approach, suggested Oliver, could the white race hope to ensure a place on the planet for its progeny.[39] Klassen's response to the tract was basically, good riddance. While conceding that Christianity was part of the historical and cultural tradition of the West, Klassen pointed out that so were smallpox, leprosy, and the plague.[40]

In later years, Oliver seemed to come around to Klassen's critique of Christianity. Writing under the pseudonym Ralph Perier, he argued in the style of Klassen that Christianity was a "Jewish invention, devised for the specific purpose of enfeebling and paralyzing the civilized peoples of the world." Anti-Semitic policies in the Catholic Church's history were dismissed as a ruse so as not to raise the suspicion of the gullible church members of the true intentions of the religion. Like Klassen, Oliver derided the Christian Identity theology as "preposterous" and "demoralizing."[41] Despite their disagreements, Klassen respected Oliver, whom he once characterized as an erudite scholar.

Wilmont Robertson's *The Dispossessed Majority*—one of the most esteemed books in the literature of the far right—came under Klassen's sharp criticism as well.[42] The book laments the declining influence of the white majority in the United States, which, according to Robertson, commenced with the U.S. Civil War. This trend accelerated in the twentieth century as a result of two fratricidal world wars, the New Deal, the rise of liberalism, the secularization of religion, and massive nonwhite immigration.[43] Klassen took issue with Robertson's relatively milquetoast approach, which sought to organize whites around the nebulous concept of the "majority" and offered only an oblique critique of Jews. Moreover, he found the tone of the book to be defeatist. Finally, he took issue with Robertson over Christianity, which Robertson defended on cultural grounds.[44]

Despite his disdain for what he saw as an over-intellectualizing of the predicament of the white race in contemporary society, he nevertheless held some of the movement intellectuals in high esteem, most notably, William Gayley Simpson, author of the 750-page turgid tome titled *Which Way Western Man?* Written in the 1970s, the book chronicles

Simpson's religious and ideological evolution. Born in 1892, Simpson had a significant influence on William Pierce, who first published Simpson's book in 1978. Initially a Christian, Simpson lived for nine years in a Franciscan community. The service/reform message of Christianity was a major attraction to him during his younger years. He later concluded, however, that he was misguided during this phase of his life. After reading Nietzsche, Simpson's worldview changed dramatically as he came to reject the universalistic and egalitarian aspects of Christianity. Further, he posited that Christianity was at odds with the spiritual makeup of Western man. The Christian religion, he bemoaned, separated man from nature, which led to a sense of alienation and the spiritual demoralization of the West. In its stead, Simpson adopted an evolutionary outlook that called for the ennoblement of man. Beyond all of the rarified discussion on spirituality, Simpson also devoted much attention to standard rightist themes, such as race, eugenics, Jews, and a critique of democracy.[45]

Klassen believed that there was little utility in constantly rehashing the predicament of the white race. Defeatism, he argued, kept the movement hamstrung without the will to fight. As he once pointed out, an overweening "fear of the Jews" paralyzed the movement into inaction.[46] Furthermore, as he explained, at a certain point one must stop frittering away time with planning and take concrete action. Although he admired some of the intellectuals, Klassen believed that they were of little use in the struggle for white racial survival as they tended to focus their attention on problems rather than solutions. Without offering any practical advice, Klassen believed that such intellectuals actually committed a disservice to the racialist movement.

> We Creators are not interested in hearing a rehash of the problem for the hundredth time no matter how intellectual, how cleverly it might be rephrased. Nor are we interested in witnessing a brilliant display of some writer's intricate knowledge of past details, if in all of this there is no answer toward solving the problem that overwhelms all other issues, and that is—the survival, expansion and advancement of the White Race.
>
> In one way such intellectual armchair strategists do a great deal of harm, other than taking the White Man's money and wasting his time in rehashing the same old problem, and that damage is this: The average yokel, who does not consider himself an expert by any

means, upon reading such "expert" analysis, is greatly depressed and discouraged. He comes to the logical conclusion that if such a knowledgeable expert has no answer, has no solution, and thinks there is no hope, how can he be expected to know what do? He concludes that it is hopeless and throws in the towel.[47]

To establish a more solid institutional basis for his religion, Klassen ordered the construction of a church in North Carolina. By the early 1980s, Klassen decided to wind down his active management in real estate to devote all of his energy to Creativity.[48] After several years of disseminating *Nature's Eternal Religion* and corresponding with rightists around the country, Klassen decided that his religious movement needed a headquarters. To that end, in 1982, he established the first Creator church in North Carolina.

5
Groundbreaking in North Carolina

By the early 1980s, Klassen had decided that his church needed a fully functioning headquarters so that its message could be spread to a larger audience. Previously, Creativity had been, in the main, a mail-order ministry. Klassen had no illusions that establishing Creativity as a durable religion would be an easy task. After all, as he pointed out, the most successful religions, including Christianity, Islam, and Mormonism, had had to endure severe tribulations on their way to widespread acceptance.[1] Toward this goal, in 1982, construction began for the headquarters of the Church of the Creator (COTC) in the town of Otto located in the Appalachian mountains of North Carolina, just three miles from the Georgia state line. Klassen sought out the longtime far right activist, Emory Burke, for assistance in designing the church with a western frontier motif.[2] Billy Sanders was the actual contractor for the church building.[3] The COTC center officially opened on March 10, 1982.[4] After residing in Florida for over twenty years, Klassen felt that it was time to move. The Mariel Boatlift, which had commenced in April 1980, occasioned substantial Hispanic immigration into Florida, thus making the sunshine state an uncongenial locale for his church. As he put it, "South Florida is due for a lot of turmoil when the bloody fighting breaks out."[5]

In some ways, North Carolina was a poor choice as the Appalachian region is in the heart of the southern Bible Belt. Klassen once commented that his "fiercest and most vocal opposition came from the local little preachers of the numerous fundamental churches in the county."[6] On several occasions, locals vandalized the church's property. The most notable incident occurred on June 15, 1983, at 1:45 a.m. when a Molotov cocktail was hurled at the corner of the church. During that same incident a shotgun blast damaged the logo sign in front of the church.[7]

Ensconced in the new headquarters, Klassen launched several new initiatives. In 1983, the church began the publication of its monthly organ, *Racial Loyalty*, which, according to Klassen's memoirs, reached a circulation of 15,000.⁸ In 1984, *Racial Loyalty* started a column called Cupid's Corner, which encouraged correspondence between prospective couples. To groom future leaders, Klassen sought to establish a school for gifted boys that would inculcate youngsters with the Creativity program. A flag was created to symbolize the church. The color red was chosen in that it symbolized the struggle for the survival of the white race. A white-colored end-side triangle was meant to signify the "whiter and brighter" world that will emerge out of the racial struggle. The COTC logo adorns the center of the flag.⁹

Efforts were made to build a solid organizational infrastructure as well. To effect his racial revolution, Klassen propounded a plan in which every Creator would form a Primary Group or join an existing one. The Primary Group was to be the basic cell of the COTC, with two persons minimum, five persons optimum, and ten persons maximum. This arrangement would make it more difficult for enemy agents to penetrate. From there, five Primary Groups would organize into Secondary Groups. After that, five Secondary Groups would create a COTC Unit. Next, five COTC units would constitute a Section. Finally, five Sections would compose a Legion whose leader would be appointed by the Pontifex Maximus, the supreme leadership position held by Klassen.¹⁰ The term, Klassen explained, derived from Roman history. Originally, the title referred to the head of state religion in the Roman Empire. After the empire fell, the term was appropriated by the Catholic Church. Klassen was adamant that his use of the term referred to the historical Roman usage and not that of the Catholic Church.¹¹

Klassen published several books during the 1980s and early 1990s, mostly compilations of reprinted articles from *Racial Loyalty* but two autobiographies as well.¹² In the area of health, Klassen expanded on his regimen for salubrious living. In 1983, he published an eponymously titled book as a guide for proper nutrition. The main author was Arnold DeVries, who wrote twenty-one of the book's twenty-two chapters. Klassen contributed a short introduction and a conclusion that discussed eugenics. DeVries, who was born in 1921, attended the University of Iowa and there he became fascinated with nature and the lifestyles of primitive cultures. In 1952, he published his first book titled *Primitive Man and His Foods*. A self-styled amateur researcher of nutrition, DeVries worked as a bus driver in Los Angeles where he drove on the famed route of Hollywood and Vine. In his later years, he moved back to Iowa, where he died in 1996. Following his marriage to his first wife, he became an ordained minister of the Universal Church of the Master, a religious organization that blends Christianity with New Age spiritualism.[13] Today, his nutritional regimen is cited by numerous authors and Web sites on raw food.[14] It is somewhat surprising that DeVries would collaborate with Klassen with whom he seemingly disagreed on many issues. What is more, DeVries's chapters in *Salubrious Living* extol the lifestyles of many non-Western cultures in the Pacific who are described as paragons of health. Pacific Islanders are lauded for their physical beauty and carefree attitude toward life. By contrast, the lifestyles and dietary habits of Western cultures come under intense criticism. Their populations are depicted as sickly and decrepit, beset with physical and facial deformities. A regimen consisting of periodic fasting, plenty of sunshine (heliotherapy), and a diet of uncooked foods, primarily nonstarch vegetables, fruits, and nuts, is advocated as the path to mental and physical well-being. Cooking foods, DeVries argued, deprived them of their vitamins and minerals, thus lessening their nutritional value. Even meat, he counseled, was better eaten raw than cooked. Conventional medical treatments are cast aside, as fasting is seen as an effective treatment to cure most ailments.[15] Both DeVries and Klassen were very critical of the medical establishment. Klassen often complained that it was dominated by Jews and did not improve public health. Despite his advocacy of healthy nutrition, some of his associates claimed that in practice Klassen did not actually follow the "salubrious living" regimen, as he often ate red meat and ice cream.[16]

A small primer on Creativity was published under the title *The Little White Book* which was meant to serve as a kind of prayer and rudimentary guide book for Creators. It succinctly explained, among other things, how Creators should comport themselves, the proper attitude that they should take, the proper relations with other people, how they should practice salubrious living, and the basic program of the religion.[17] In the style of Islam, Klassen propounded "five fundamental beliefs of Creativity" that are supposed to be memorized and repeated as a sacred religious ritual five times a day:

1. WE BELIEVE that our Race is our Religion.
2. WE BELIEVE that the White Race is Nature's Finest.

3. WE BELIEVE that Racial Loyalty is the greatest of all honors, and racial treason is the worst of all crimes.

4. WE BELIEVE that what is good for the White Race is the highest virtue, and what is bad for the White Race is the ultimate sin.

5. WE BELIEVE that the one and only, true and revolutionary White Racial Religion—Creativity—is the only salvation for the White Race.[18]

A principal aim of the new church was to convert elements of the far right to Creativity. Klassen frequently emphasized the importance of "polarization" in the racialist movement. According to his analysis, the numerous racialist groups were stymied by hubris in that they all wanted their small niche without ever really presenting any serious opposition to "the system." Only through "polarizing" around the religion of Creativity could the racialist movement forge a strong battering ram with which to smash its enemies. Along with polarization, Klassen also advocated dispersion, that is, the spread of the Creativity creed throughout the world with activists establishing deep roots that would enable the larger religious movement to persist if leaders were eliminated through arrest or assassination.[19]

Klassen thought that it was imperative to establish multiple strongholds for the COTC in the event that the headquarters in North Carolina was "wiped off the map," hence the imperative of dispersion.[20] The term did not, however, imply the fragmentation of the racialist movement. In fact, he frequently criticized the proposition that a fraction consisting of small groups and individuals would be able to establish order in the event of a societal breakdown, which he believed was on the horizon. Although he did not explicitly mention the term "leaderless resistance" (it would gain much greater currency after Klassen's death), Klassen was highly critical of the concept, as he concluded such efforts would ultimately prove to be ineffectual in the absence of a strong, monolithic, revolutionary movement embodied in a single organization.

Only a powerful movement built around a single ideology could provide the proper cement for a movement that could withstand such tribulation.[21] To make his point, Klassen frequently invoked the example of Hitler, who successfully persuaded the disparate nationalist groups extant during the Weimar era, to rally behind his National Socialist party, which refused to compromise its program. Rather, the ideology should be totalistic and out of it a monolithic movement would spring forth. The Creativity movement, according to Klassen, contained the "whole package" necessary for the white man's redemption and survival in an increasingly hostile world. In Creativity, Klassen exclaimed, he had "the TOTAL PROGRAM, the FINAL SOLUTION, the ULTIMATE CREED."

To be expected, Klassen was highly critical of democracy. Reminiscent of the führer principle, he believed that only strong leadership personified in a highly effective organizer could direct an effective movement against the white race's enemies. Therefore, Klassen exhorted the other racialist organizations to put their "hubris" aside and join the Creativity movement. The religious approach, Klassen averred, had several advantages over the political approach in that it entailed greater zeal, fanaticism, loyalty, and totality of thought.[22] Furthermore, by presenting their struggle as a religious, rather than a solely political, movement they could avail themselves of special tax advantages and enjoy greater legal protection. Finally, given the special status of religious groups in America, authorities would be more reluctant to harass them if they were organized on that basis.[23]

Not unlike the corporatism of fascism, Klassen advocated "racial socialism" in which whites would work together toward common goals but without the massive economic planning in the style of the Soviet GOSPLAN. Socialism, in theory, was not ipso facto malicious; rather, it merely implied "organized society."[24] Such organization was absolutely necessary in a world of racial competition. Nevertheless, Klassen supported the notion of a free-enterprise economy, but with limitations. He did not fetishize the market in the style of contemporary mainstream conservatives. As he once explained, the free market can result in monopolization, which would allow an unscrupulous monopolist to wipe out competition. Klassen also took issue with the notions of liberty, freedom, and individualism, all of which have had a long tradition in the history of American conservatism. Although whites as individuals may still accomplish noteworthy achievements, Klassen believed that as a race, they were being left behind, due to the superior racial and ethnic organizing of Jews and nonwhites. As long as whites adhered to the hubris of individualism, they could mount no serious opposition to Jews.[25]

Nevertheless, he took issue with some of the more anticapitalist "Third Positionists" in the white racialist movement, including Tom Metzger, who founded the White Aryan Resistance, or WAR as it is more popularly known, in 1983. His political odyssey included stints in the John Birch Society, the tax rebellion movement, Second Amendment organizations, the Knights of the Ku Klux Klan, and the Christian Identity movement; at one time in the early 1960s, Metzger was a campaign worker for one of Ronald Reagan's gubernatorial bids. However, he eventually became weary of all these projects and thought they were too mild for his political tastes. Instead, he has promoted a "third way" variant of National Socialism that is highly critical of capitalism. In that sense, Metzger is heir to the Strasser brothers of the Nazi period in Germany, who sought to steer Hitler in a more socialistic and anticapitalist direction. What is more, Metzger actually draws much inspiration from such left-wing icons as Vladimir Lenin and Jack London. Once when visiting Metzger's home, Klassen was flabbergasted that his library contained most of Lenin's works. In an article titled "Bashing the Rich," Klassen took issue with the "Strasserite" segment of the contemporary extreme right, such as Tom Metzger, Wyatt Kaldenberg, and Gary Gallo, who excoriated capitalism.[26] He criticized the leftist proclivities of Metzger and his efforts to recruit primarily from the white working class. This approach, he argued, was misguided in that he found the affluent to be generally better material to recruit. In his estimation, as a group, the rich had more to offer to the white racialist movement than any other segment. To be sure, that segment included its share of opportunistic "race traitors." Nevertheless, generally speaking, the wealthy were more likely to be highly energetic, imaginative, intelligent, and interesting than the "average yokels." Were they any worse, Klassen mused, than the "average blue collar worker, who is content watching the boob tube while guzzling his beer[?]" Such class politics, Klassen insisted, was divisive to the white community. He reminded these "deviationists" that the "real enemy . . . is not the rich White, but the goddamn sinister worldwide Jewish network."[27]

Still, Klassen maintained that whites of all classes should be mobilized and were welcome to join the COTC.[28] Not unlike the corporatism of German National Socialism and Italian Fascism, all members of the national or racial community were thought to have had an important role to play. One of the tenets of the Creativity program was that each person should set out to make at least one lasting contribution to his race during his lifetime.

Perhaps the anticapitalist ethos is one reason the extreme right is chronically strapped for cash. Mike German, a former Federal Bureau of Investigation (FBI) undercover agent who infiltrated extremist groups, observed that an intense antimaterialism pervades the movement and stems from a crass stereotypical notion that Jews control the world's financial institutions and currency markets. Such attitudes, German noticed, impede the movement's effectiveness and contribute to its marginalization:

> They feel the quest for financial gain beyond what is necessary to support the family distracts from the movement and creates a quiet form of slavery that uses false promises of future wealth to keep white people toiling in a rat race instead of working with the resistance. They seek to end dependence of any sort of government services or reliance on anyone outside the movement. If recruits' employment requires them to interact with other races, they are encouraged to quit and find other work. They are taught it is better to be poor than to compromise their beliefs.[29]

The mid-1980s was a dramatic period in the history of the American extreme right. In 1983, Gordon Kahl, a member of a radical antitax, militia-style organization known as the Posse Comitatus, was killed in a standoff with authorities in Arkansas. Earlier that year, he fatally shot two U.S. Marshals and wounded four other in a confrontation in North Dakota.[30] In the summer of 1983, shortly after his death, an annual Aryan Nations Congress was held at the compound in Hayden Lake, Idaho. At the meeting, a young charismatic member of the National Alliance, Robert Jay Mathews, hatched the idea of creating an underground resistance group to avenge the death of Kahl. Mathews had considerable powers of persuasion and was able to ultimately draw nearly fifty members into his clandestine terrorist group, the Order.[31]

Mathews drew much inspiration for the formation of his organization from the novel, *The Turner Diaries*, written by his ideological mentor Dr. William Pierce (under the pseudonym Andrew Macdonald), the chairman of the National Alliance. So enamored of the novel was Mathews that he made it required reading for all members. Abandoning all hope of legal political action, Mathews built a clandestine resistance group, which went on a crime spree and a terrorist campaign that gained nationwide notoriety and included counterfeiting, armored car heists, bank robberies, and four homicides.[32] One armored car heist took in a whopping $3.6 million, which at that time in 1984, set the record for the highest amount of money ever stolen in such a robbery. In a milieu in which terrorists more often resemble the gang that couldn't shoot straight than professional terrorists, the exploits of the Order were—in a word—electrifying.

Although the Order was racist and anti-Semitic in orientation, it gave its highest priority to targets, such as the state and other prominent institutions. Mathews instructed members to avoid petty conflicts with racial minorities, as that would only distract the group from its primary mission. A list of prominent enemies marked for assassination was compiled, which included the leader of the Southern Poverty Law Center, Morris Dees; the former secretary of state, Henry Kissinger; the banker, David Rockefeller; the television producer, Norman Lear; and the international financier, Baron Elie de Rothschild.[33] These high-value targets notwithstanding, the Order settled for a Denver-based Jewish disk jockey, Alan Berg, as its first target of assassination. An acerbic talk radio host, Berg frequently berated far-right callers on his radio program.

To be expected, the Order's exploits soon caught the attention of authorities, and the FBI identified the group as the most serious domestic terrorist threat in the country.[34] Ultimately, a counterfeiting operation led to the group's demise One of its recruits, though not an official member, Tom Martinez, agreed to become an informant for the FBI after his arrest for passing counterfeit money that the Order had printed. He set up two of his colleagues, including Mathews, in a sting operation at a hotel. A shootout ensued, but amazingly, Mathews escaped after wounding an officer. On the lam, he remained undaunted and issued a "Declaration of War" against the United States government, which he sent to several newspapers. Finally, authorities caught up with him at Whidbey Island in Washington State. Refusing to be taken alive, he resisted in a standoff that lasted two days and included several shootouts with SWAT teams. Eventually, the authorities lost their patience and on December 8, 1984, dropped white phosphorous illumination flares onto the roof of the house in which Mathews had barricaded himself. This action set off a fire that engulfed the structure and Mathews perished in dramatic fashion. A concerted effort by federal, state, and local law enforcement agencies eventually crushed the Order and many of its members are now serving lengthy prison sentences.[35] The Order has been lionized and its incarcerated members are regarded as prisoners of war (POWs) by others in the movement.[36]

Although the Order tactically did not really achieve much, it was significant in marking a change in the orientation of the extreme right. The U.S. government was now seen as the enemy and the extreme right began to take on a more revolutionary posture. No longer did it seek to preserve the status quo. Rather, it sought the overthrow of the U.S. government, which it reasoned was now under the heel of ZOG, or the Zionist Occupation Government. Whereas previously the far right had been characterized by ultra patriotism, after the campaign of the Order, the movement became increasingly nihilistic. Thus, on a symbolic level, the Order's campaign was important, as explained by George Eric Hawthorne, a one-time leading figure in the skinhead movement and member of the COTC:

> Although their precise actions mean little in the greater scheme of things, the fact that they ACTED [emphasis in original]—acted with unprecedented selflessness and sacrifice—means everything to this movement today.[37]
>
> Tactically speaking, Alan Berg was a bad choice . . . The physical act of killing Alan Berg was about as meaningless as assassinating the White House gardener. . . . But historically speaking, in the wider context of things, it was of unfathomable significance. It marked the transition from conservatism to radicalism. It marks the beginning of the Second American Revolution, a revolution that shall strike into the heart of everything diseased that America has become.[38]

On a more instrumental level, the Order was believed to have distributed much of its stolen money to "above ground" far-right organizations around the country. It was hoped that the stolen money could be used as "mortar" to cement the fragmented elements of the racialist right.[39] For example, Robert Jay Matthews disbursed $200,000 to Glen Miller for his White Patriots Party that was active in North Carolina during the 1980s.[40] It was strongly suspected that Matthews gave Dr. William Pierce of the National Alliance a substantial amount of money as well.[41]

For his part, Klassen was somewhat dismissive of the Order. Although he lauded their motives, he counseled that other activists should not emulate such a reckless course of action. Instead, would-be terrorists, Klassen suggested, should be more calculating in their planning and would be more effective in emulating their counterparts in the Middle East:

> They [the Order] launched into a program of criminal activities such as armed robbery and even managed to assassinate a filthy Jewish talk-show host by the name of Alan Berg. The end result of all this was that these brave young racial fighters, some thirty-five of them, are now behind bars, their energetic activities neutralized and thwarted, probably for the rest of their lives. Bob Matthews is dead, having died heroically in a fiery shoot-out against the overwhelming odds of a massive swat team launched against him by the Jewish establishment.
>
> I believe this is an unduly heavy price to pay in terms of our young activists for the killing of one lousy Jew. If, instead, they had gone their own quiet separate ways, secretly planned and planned well a number of attacks on groups of Jews, they could, for the same price, have killed probably as many as twenty, or fifty or a hundred Jews each. The sum total price exacted for the thirty-five now behind bars could have been several hundred dead Jews, instead of one filthy talk-show host. . . .
>
> Let's take a look at some of the strikes the Arabs, who generally are none too bright, have successfully executed. A classic example is the bombing of the U.S. Marine compound in Lebanon on October 23, 1983. There we find one lone truck driver (presumably an Arab) who willingly went to his death with a big smile on his face. But as he did so, he took with him 240 [sic][42] of his enemies (dead) as well as hundreds of wounded. Now if we compare that maneuver to the effectiveness of what The Order episode accomplished, we find that the lone Arab was approximately 35 X 240, or more than 8000 times as effective as were each of the 35 some members of The Order. Now that, my fellow White Racial Comrades, is one

hell of a difference. Let's give this effectiveness a name. Let's call it the Enemy Toll Effectiveness Factor (E.T.E.F.). . . . The quality of the enemy destroyed also enters in. We must remember those killed and wounded were U.S. Marines, fighting men in the prime of their manhood, a much more meaningful action than merely killing an equal number of random riff-raff.[43]

In *Racial Loyalty*, Klassen sometimes ran a column called "Best E.T.E.F. Award" in which he listed examples of racist lone wolves and how many victims they took down. Generally, he saw these episodes as counterproductive and argued that such terrorists would be able to better channel their frustration into more constructive measures by propagandizing rather than engaging in random acts of violence. As he explained, in 1989, the white race was outnumbered in the world by a ratio of somewhere between 12 or 13 to 1. Consequently, the sporadic killing of nonwhites that would usually result in the imprisonment and/or death of the white perpetrators would do little to bring about a successful white racial revolution.[44]

During the 1980s, the COTC established a presence in several countries. The most notable was in Sweden due to the efforts of a young activist, Tommy Rydén, who was born in Linköping, Sweden, on January 5, 1966, and raised in a revivalist Baptist family, something of an oddity in a country with a strong tradition of state-supported Protestantism. Rydén worked hard to establish a Creativity presence in Sweden. Before discovering Creativity in 1983, he sojourned through numerous conservative and far-right groups and corresponded with such luminaries as Jerry Falwell and Cal Thomas. At that time, he followed Christian Identity and was at first affronted by Klassen's anti-Christian approach. However, after a four-month stay in South Africa in 1988, he became disillusioned with Christianity, as he explained:

> In South Africa I met a lot of people that were telling me that Jesus was going to save them. Well, somehow I found this strange that their Jewish messiah were [*sic*] going to save neo-Nazi-looking white militants in South Africa. . . . [I]t was just a little too much. Even if I try to be understanding, that's nonsense.[45]

While in South Africa, Rydén made contact with the Afrikaner Resistance Movement (AWB) and similar groups. Despite his racism, he was emphatic that he never supported the system of apartheid, which relied on cheap black labor for menial work that he believed whites should have done for themselves. He counseled white South Africans that Christianity played a destructive role in their country, but they were not receptive. The South Africans he met thought racial segregation was viable, but he maintained that only an all-white area could survive in the long run.[46]

In 1988, Rydén founded an offshoot of the COTC, which he called *Kreativistens Kyrka*. He proved to be an avid promoter of the church, and Swedish authorities even arrested him for distributing copies of the church's newspaper, *Racial Loyalty*. A Swedish court convicted him of incitement of racial hatred in October 1990, and he served a four-month sentence in 1991.[47] Despite these occasional obstacles, Rydén soldiered on, but by late autumn 1992, he split with the parent organization—but not for long—to establish the Ben Klassen Academy. He briefly returned in April 1993 but left again not long after the death of Ben Klassen in August 1993, after which he transformed his movement into *DeVries Institutet* (DeVries Institute), which recommended self-healing, a vegetarian diet, breast feeding for children as long as possible, abstention from drugs and alcohol, and regular exercise.[48] Still not satisfied, he founded *Den Reorganiserade Kreativisten Kyrka* (the Reorganized COTC) in the summer of 1994. Ironically, he sought to model the new organization on the Catholic Jesuit Order, as members were to form a priestly caste.[49] All of these efforts notwithstanding, Rydén was never able to attract more than a handful of recruits in Sweden. He officially resigned from the COTC in 1995.[50]

Looking back on his involvement with the church, Rydén believes that Klassen was too intelligent for the American people. The crux of Klassen's problem, according to Rydén, was his inability to find a charismatic leader who could turn the Creativity movement into a truly religious movement.[51] After his departure from the COTC, Rydén moved on to similar projects. He dabbled in Odinism and sought to establish a Cosmotheist Church (*Cosmotistkyrkan*) modeled on William Pierce's religious movement.[52] In the mid-1990s, Rydén devoted his efforts to the *Hembygdspartiet* (Homeland Party) in Sweden which he led. The party blended rightist themes with environmental and animal protection issues.[53]

Despite the arduous travails on which his activism had led him, Rydén remains a committed racialist and holds an anti-Semitic worldview.[54] After years of activism, Rydén decided to concentrate on earning a living and raising a family, which includes a wife and five children, as he feels at this juncture of his life that he is not in a strong position to make a contribution to the white racialist cause if he remains economically marginal.[55] Despite his departure from the church, Rydén remains a staunch advocate of Klassen's "salubrious living" regimen.

The influence of the COTC even reached as far as South Africa, where some members, who also happened to belong to an undercover police unit called the Civil Cooperation Bureau, sought to recruit their countrymen into a race war against the African National Congress (ANC). Allegedly, the two had ties with the ANC's rival, the Zulu Inkatha Party, with whom they shared weapons for an armed campaign against the ANC.[56] In another incident, two other South African COTC members, Jurgen Matthews and Johannes Jurgens Grobbelaar, were killed in a gun battle with South African police while attempting to smuggle weapons to a survivalist compound in Namibia. The two were arrested, and while on their way to a nearby police station, they detonated a smoke bomb and attempted to escape. The police later caught up with the suspects and a gunfight ensued during which two officers were shot, one fatally. The two COTC members were killed when the officers returned fire.[57]

The first recognized "martyr" of the church was Brian Kozel, a member of the White Berets—the security detail of the COTC. Previously, Kozel had belonged to a chapter of the Northern Hammer Skinheads called United White Youth in the Milwaukee area. Accounts differ on the events surrounding his death. According to the COTC's version, he was shot dead on September 15, 1990, by a carload of Mexicans following an earlier altercation between the same group and several members of the White Berets. Kozel was supposed to have been distributing leaflets on the street. After the incident, the Mexicans later spotted him and shot him in the back; the bullet passed through his heart and killed him. The church eulogized Kozel in a style reminiscent of the way Horst Wessel had been memorialized, as a memorial picture of Kozel appears on the first page of two Creativity books.[58] According to the police version of events, Kozel was shot dead shortly after leaving a bar. He and some buddies were allegedly kicking in the sides of passing cars at which point somebody pulled over and fatally shot him.[59]

While in North Carolina, Klassen expended a considerable amount of effort in finding an adequate Hasta Primus (Latin for spearhead), who could serve as his assistant. His first recruit for the position was Timothy J. Gaffney, whom he appointed in October 1982. A twenty-seven-year-old college graduate, Gaffney had previously worked as an accountant for the state of New York. Before coming to North Carolina, he led a small group called the National Force and Order. He did not last long, however, and was gone by January 1983. His wife was a devout Catholic, and a priest discouraged her from having anything to do with promoting the Creativity creed.[60]

Shortly thereafter, Richard F. Becker, a graduate of the Citadel in South Carolina and resident of Greenville, North Carolina, replaced Gaffney, but he did not impress Klassen, who described him as a former patient of an insane asylum and a coward. Furthermore, Klassen resented the fact that Gaffney brought along a "mangy dog" and a "dissolute and uncouth slob of a companion," who had been an associate of his while he was in the mental institution.[61]

After Becker's departure, Klassen sought to recruit Duke McCoy, from Rossville, Georgia, for the position. He invited him and his wife to tour the Otto area in North Carolina. Klassen estimated that McCoy was in his mid-thirties at the time and described his wife as a "beautiful young blonde." Still, Klassen was disappointed in McCoy, who seemed to disagree with Klassen's plans on the editorial direction of *Racial Loyalty*. McCoy suggested that it should take a more subtle slant in the style of *The Spotlight*—an unreasonable compromise for the strident Klassen. Finally, Klassen came to the conclusion that McCoy was a JOG (Jewish Occupation Government) agent, and as a result, sent him and his wife packing.[62]

Richard Becker then recommended Tyler Thompson, also from Greenville, North Carolina, for the Hasta Primus position. Klassen considered him despite some character flaws that he detected in the new candidate—a drinking problem and a defensive attitude. Nevertheless, after interviewing him, Klassen found him to be reasonably intelligent, with the proper racialist leanings for the position. Thompson was destitute and told Klassen that he needed an advance of $200 for some new clothes and bus fare. However, Thompson reneged on the offer and never returned to Otto. To his dismay, Klassen later learned that Thompson spent the $200 advance "on a grand drunk."[63]

Getting more desperate, Klassen called Tim Gaffney again in the hope of finding another suitable candidate. Gaffney recommended Bill Tucker whom Klassen invited to Otto. He arrived with his wife, whom Klassen described as "the dominant factor in the equation," on April 9, 1983, but they left that same evening.[64]

Changing his mind, Klassen decided to reconsider Richard Becker for the Hasta Primus position. Becker had written Klassen back in 1981, after reading *Nature's Eternal Religion*, which had a profound effect on him. Describing him as a man about forty years of age who regularly jogged and lifted weights, Klassen found him also to be a good typist. Later, Klassen discovered that Becker's father, a college professor, had actually temporarily committed his son to a mental institution. In the end, Klassen found Becker's behavior odd and unnerving and thus let him go once again.[65]

Next to fill the position was Keith Williams, a radio announcer and disk jockey from Roseburg, Oregon. Expecting "a suave, polished radio pitchman," Klassen was disappointed when he met Williams whom he described as "a big fat slob, in his early fifties, unshaven and unwashed [that] would take any job on any terms."[66] The Secret Service later investigated Williams for allegedly threatening Democratic presidential candidate Gary Hart and former president Jimmy Carter.[67]

Still another Hasta Primus prospect, Carl Messick, took over in April 1984, arriving in North Carolina in "a jalopy, trailer, and all his belongings."[68] Messick proved to be much more reliable and competent than his predecessors and finally brought a sense of stability to the position. Klassen considered him to be a great asset to the church. However, Messick got enmeshed in a legal problem when he fired a number of shots at a vehicle whose occupants had trespassed on the church's property in North Carolina in the early morning of June 14, 1986. According to Klassen's version of the story, Messick had overheard the occupants in the car parked outside the headquarters building talking about blowing up the church and claimed that they even threatened to shoot him if he came out of the building. He duly called Klassen at 3:10 a.m., and Klassen immediately attempted to call the sheriff, but the line was busy. Quickly, he threw on some clothes, grabbed his gun, and called again. He then jumped in his car and drove toward the headquarters. While en route, Klassen saw the car coming up the road; it stopped at an intersection, turned around, and headed back toward the headquarters. As he chased the car, Klassen heard the sound of faint gunfire. As the car approached the headquarters, Messick stepped into the road, and when the car kept coming, fired a warning shot. Still the car moved toward him at which point Messick fired off more than a dozen shots trying to shoot out the tires. The car roared past him, missing him by no more than two feet and headed south on the highway. Finally, at 4:05 a.m., forty-five minutes after Klassen had called them, the sheriff's deputies arrived—a long period of time considering they only had to travel thirteen miles to get to the destination. On previous occasions, the church property had been vandalized, firebombed, and shot at, but the authorities showed little interest.[69]

Not far away from where the incident occurred, two sheriff's deputies found the car in question with some thirty bullet holes in it. They soon learned that the car belonged to William and Patricia Trusty, who told the deputies they had been driving with some friends and inadvertently turned down a wrong road. They claimed that they turned out their lights at which point someone began shooting at them.[70] The next evening, shortly after 6:00 p.m., six men in three squad cars came to the headquarters to arrest Messick. Claiming to have a search warrant, the investigators went through the building thoroughly and took numerous photographs. Klassen conjectured that the Anti-Defamation League had orchestrated the incident in the first place.[71] After a brief trial in December 1986, Messick was convicted and sentenced to seven years in prison. Eventually, he was released after serving twenty months, but he did not return to the Hasta Primus position.[72]

Don Johnson from Houston replaced Messick, and Klassen's bad luck returned. A paralegal by profession, he offered to develop a program to help church members deal with legal harassment. He offered to represent Messick in his legal battles as well. Johnson persuaded Klassen to invest almost a half a million dollars of his and the church's money in the Chilton Private Bank, which became insolvent soon thereafter.[73] The scheme had interested Klassen as he distributed his money among numerous banks hoping that if the government raided one account for back taxes he would have enough time to transfer funds into another account.[74] After six months of desperate effort, Klassen recovered only twenty-eight cents for every dollar of the half million he had deposited in the Chilton Private Bank.[75] As a result of that fiasco, Klassen concluded that Johnson had instigated the affair to "help JOG wreck [his] movement."[76]

To make things worse, on November 3, 1987, Johnson's wife, Bobbi, called Klassen and notified him that her husband had stopped breathing. The fifty-two-year-old Johnson died and Klassen suspected foul play. About a year earlier, the husband of Bobbi's mother, a seemingly healthy man of sixty-eight, had died under very similar circumstances—a sudden heart attack. Soon thereafter, Klassen gave notice to Bobbi that he was evicting her from the premises. She complied two weeks before the deadline.[77]

Will White Williams, a Vietnam veteran and moderately talented cartoonist, took over the reins as Hasta Primus in May 1988. Described by some of his critics as a con man, he did not last long. He brought along his girlfriend Lucinda, whom Klassen required him to marry if they were to live together. Klassen did not appreciate the fact that the couple brought their dog onto the premises. Unlike his mentor Hitler, Klassen was not fond of canines. According to Klassen, Williams's experiences in Vietnam had left him with deep psychological scars.[78] Allegedly, Will began physically abusing his wife and separately they left.[79]

In 1989, Klassen was joined by Victor Wolf, who was next to take over the Hasta Primus position. Born in Lithuania in 1955 and an accountant by profession, Wolf helped compile publications for the church, including *Portfolio One* and *The Little White Book*. He also wrote an important article for *Racial Loyalty* titled "The Basis of Organization." The essay propounded a multistage plan that included first establishing an ideology and then building a solid organization that would implement a strategy of propaganda and proselytization.[80]

In order to reach the white masses, Klassen searched desperately for a "financial angel," that is, a wealthy individual who would underwrite the promotion of Creativity to a larger audience. To this end, he sought out prospective donors for his cause. In January 1989, he visited Prescott Rathborne in New Orleans. A fifty-year-old bachelor, Rathborne was the heir to a large fortune and intensely interested in the Creativity movement. Previously, he had visited the COTC headquarters and spent four days with Will Williams discussing plans for the organization. However, on meeting him, Klassen found Rathborne to be "a very spoiled, opinionated and stubborn man." Furthermore, the two quibbled over stylistic approaches that the church should take. Rathborne preferred the use of the term "species" instead of "race." Exasperated by his pushing, Klassen finally retorted, "I don't care how much money you have. The creed and program as laid down in our books is inviolable at any price. Whether you offered me ten million dollars, or one hundred million dollars, I wouldn't change one word of it. I don't need your money."[81]

Klassen also contacted the now deceased DeWest Hooker, a shadowy far-right figure, who was a close confidant of George Lincoln Rockwell. Born into a wealthy family, Hooker was a graduate of Cornell University and a veteran of World War II—a conflict that he believed then and until the end of his life should not have been fought. In another career, Hooker had worked as an advertising model and a Broadway actor. He was also a personal friend of Joseph P. Kennedy from whom he unsuccessfully sought to solicit funding to create a "fourth" television network. Later, in the 1950s, he worked as a talent agent for the Music Corporation of America (MCA). Hooker claimed to have been working behind the scenes on brokering a deal with Arabs to ship oil to Israel on which he would receive a commission. With the proceeds, he supposedly intended to fund the white nationalist movement in the United States. However, the plan never came to fruition.[82] Hooker expressed support for Klassen, but he never gave any financial assistance. For his part, Klassen was suspicious of Hooker, who, according to Klassen, kept a mistress who was both Jewish and a member of the ADL. Furthermore, Klassen was not keen on the idea of collaborating with Muslims. He was especially put off by Hooker's dalliance with Minister Louis T. Farrakhan, the leader of the Nation of Islam, and maintained that it was folly to enter into alliances with "mud races."[83] Nevertheless, Klassen consistently took the Arab side in conflicts with Israel in the Middle East. Hooker died of cancer on September 22, 1999.

By the late 1980s the church had experienced moderate growth. However, it attracted an inordinate number of dysfunctional personalities and this would plague the organization and contribute to its demise.

6

Disintegration and Collapse

The Search for a Successor

In the final years of his life, Klassen looked in earnest for a successor to replace him as Pontifex Maximus, the title he created to signify the leader of his church. He did not see himself as a natural leader or an orator. Rather, he felt his main purpose was that of a philosopher who would establish a creed for the redemption of the white race.[1] Only a "great promoter" could take Creativity to the white masses. For this position, he preferred an energetic man in his mid-thirties. Klassen searched far and wide for a candidate to be his successor but lamented that in doing so he "ran into a variety of strange, twisted characters, probably half of whom were Jewish stooges and/or government agents."[2] His personal wealth attracted a number of unscrupulous individuals, who caused considerable dissension in the church.[3]

In April 1986, Klassen traveled to Mississippi to meet with Richard Barrett, a lawyer and leader of the Nationalist Movement. The previous year, Barrett had sent Klassen a copy of his autobiography and political testament, *The Commission*. Looking into his background, Klassen noticed that Barrett had run for various state and federal offices but always lost by a large margin. Nevertheless, he was impressed by the fact that in his book, Barrett appeared in photographs with a number of political notables—including Alabama governor George Wallace, Phyllis Schlafly, New Hampshire governor Meldrim Thomson, Georgia governor Lester Maddox, and U.S. senator James O. Eastland—and thus might be a good promoter.[4] In a private conversation, Klassen alleged that Barrett was on the same wavelength with him concerning Christianity. However, inasmuch as he was always running for office, out of practicality, he could not take an openly anti-Christian position. When Klassen broached the topic of the Pontifex Maximus position, Barrett proposed making the COTC into a subsidiary of the Nationalist Movement. Unwilling to compromise, Klassen looked askance at Barrett's brand of nationalism, which he saw as inherently divisive. Furthermore, he was not impressed by Barrett's espousal of traditional patriotic themes, such as the flag, Christianity, and the Constitution. In sum, Klassen concluded that Barrett was of no use to the Creativity movement and speculated that he might even be a JOG agent.[5] The next year, Barrett worked briefly with David Duke to organize a demonstration in Forsyth County, Georgia, which received nationwide recognition. However, the two soon had a falling out over money.[6]

Tom Metzger, the founder of White Aryan Resistance (WAR), was the next person Klassen considered to lead the COTC. Perhaps more than any figure, Metzger exemplifies the revolutionary orientation of the racialist right. He has been in the forefront of the extreme right's multimedia efforts to disseminate its propaganda to a larger audience. Toward that end, he produced a monthly newspaper, *WAR* (later renamed *The Insurgent*), which is one of the most provocative underground publications in the movement and contains articles that advocate the "leaderless resistance" approach to right-wing terrorism. He also maintains a prison outreach program and he lists the names and prison addresses of various "POW" white racists who are currently incarcerated. In the late 1980s, Metzger was quite adept at attracting media attention. He was one of the first far-right activists to take advantage of computer technology and, in 1981, created a computer bulletin board that linked like-minded activists. Other projects included a Web site, recorded messages on a telephone line, and a TV program, *Race and Reason*, which aired on cable public access stations in scattered towns and cities across America. Articulate and well attired, Metzger, often with his son John at his side, appeared on several major network talk shows, such as *Geraldo*, *Oprah*, the *Whoopi Goldberg Show*, and the *Morton Downey Show*. This exposure made Metzger among the most visible figures in the movement.[7] Inasmuch as Metzger garnered so much publicity, Klassen viewed him as a "great promoter" who could be a huge asset to his organization. Furthermore, he admired his ability to get on many talk shows and passionately promote the white racialist cause.

Although they had some philosophical differences, Klassen was impressed with Metzger's indefatigable activism. Moreover, the fact that he was twenty years younger than Klassen would make him a good candidate physically to be the "great promoter" that Klassen had long sought.

Shortly after appearing as a guest on Metzger's *Race and Reason* program in December 1984, Klassen sent him a letter urging him to form a Church of the Creator group in Fallbrook, California, where Metzger resided at the time. As he explained, Metzger could operate both his WAR organization and the COTC contemporaneously in that Klassen saw nothing incompatible between the two entities. He offered to ordain Metzger as a minister and would even create for him a higher title, equivalent to a bishop or cardinal in the Catholic Church, one of the advantages of which was that it would provide some legal protection from the IRS. Inasmuch as Metzger, a former Identity minister, had abandoned Christianity and was a zealous advocate of white racialism, Klassen saw in him a suitable representative of the Creativity creed. Metzger's son, John, actually became an ordained minister of the Church of the Creator at age sixteen. Eventually, Klassen soured on the idea of Tom Metzger as his replacement as the former seemed interested only in absorbing the COTC into WAR.[8] Furthermore, Klassen was unimpressed by some of Metzger's associates, in particular, Mike Brown, a former bodyguard for George Lincoln Rockwell, who was once convicted for possession of explosives that he allegedly planned to use to blow up the United Nations building.[9]

In 1990, Metzger and his son John were the targets of a civil suit filed by the Southern Poverty Law Center. This suit arose out of the 1988 assault and death of a young Ethiopian immigrant, Mulageta Seraw, who, with two friends, was attacked by three skinheads in Portland, Oregon. The skinheads responsible had never met either one of the Metzgers; however, they occasionally consorted with Daniel Mazella, a loose associate of the Metzgers' who was neither involved in nor present at the assault. Dees argued that the Metzgers were responsible for the conduct of their associate Mazella who had allegedly influenced the racist beliefs of the skinheads involved in the assault. A jury agreed with Dees, and in 1990 Seraw's family was awarded $12.5 million in damages.[10] However, the Metzgers remain undeterred, as WAR continues its operations to this day.

Dr. William L. Pierce, the founder and chairman of the National Alliance, was considered for the Pontifex Maximus position as well. He and Klassen corresponded and shared similar ideological views. In an interview with this author, Pierce recounted that Klassen occasionally visited him when he traveled through the Washington, D.C., area. Although

Klassen did not explicitly offer the church to him, Pierce said he knew that was Klassen's aim. Klassen hoped that Pierce would be interested in the church, but he had his hands full with the National Alliance.[11] Pierce recalled his experiences with Klassen:

> I knew Ben Klassen slightly. He had stopped in my office a couple of times on his way through Washington. And we had maybe exchanged ten letters over a period of ten years. Klassen and I agreed on some fundamental things. We disagreed on tactics. His was an in your face, very abrasive, anti-Christian stance. And my attitude was, well, you know I agree with you a lot on a lot of these things about Christianity, but I don't think it's good, because there are many good people who are Christians, or think of themselves as Christians. And I don't see the need to alienate all of these people. I think a lot of them can be won over. . . .
>
> I thought that his whole approach was seriously flawed. The type of people that he attracted was a lower grade of people. His newspaper, *Racial Loyalty*, had very crude stuff in it. Klassen was a sincere guy, but he was not an intellectual. He took a sort of plebian approach to this problem as reflected in the cartoons in *Racial Loyalty* [the cartoons often crudely lampooned both Christianity and Judaism]. He basically had the right ideas, but he expressed himself in fairly crude form and it was guaranteed to appeal to mostly rednecks and skinheads and other people on the bottom of the socio-economic ladder who felt immediately threatened by the racial changes that were taking place in the country. . . .
>
> Klassen's position was that unless you can cure the white race of its Christian fixation you can't win. And I agree with that in the long run. . . . You got to get people away from that, but we have a lot of other things to do too [before then].[12]

The next candidate slated to become the church's Pontifex Maximus was Rudy "Butch" Stanko whose family had been involved in the meatpacking business since 1912. His two companies—Cattle King and Nebraska Beef Packer—had grown into large operations, employing more than 600 employees with $200,000,000 in business. By the early 1980s, his company had become the largest manufacturer of ground beef for both a federal school lunch program and the U.S. military.[13] At one time, his companies had contracts worth over $20,000,000 to supply over 18,000,000 pounds of ground beef to public school cafeterias.[14] Although the business had been successful, he found himself in legal trouble in the early 1980s. Unfortunately for Stanko, there were allegations of improprieties in his meat-packing operation. He alleged that a Jewish conspiracy was launched against his companies because of their success and not any supposed wrongdoing. According to Stanko, an NBC media outlet had planted a story that was intended to discredit his enterprise. A Canadian news program patterned after *60 Minutes—First Camera—* aired a story charging that Cattle King/Nebraska Beef sold unsanitary beef and engaged in unfair labor practices along with other illegal operations. Soon thereafter, the United States Department of Agriculture (USDA) suspended government contracts with his company. A congressional hearing on the matter followed. Several months later, the USDA, working with the Department of Justice, handed down indictments against Stanko.[15] Behind all of these machinations, insisted Stanko, was the Kehilla—a committee of powerful Jews that sought to take over his meat-packing business and had colluded with the Anti-Defamation League of B'nai Brith to bring about his downfall.[16] Convicted in 1984, Stanko received a $140,000 fine and a six-year prison sentence, which he began serving later that same year. Another indictment followed in 1985; however, charges were later dropped. Stanko wrote a book about his ordeal called *The Score*, which, ironically, he dedicated to Jesus Christ. Stanko later wrote a tract titled "Slavery! Survives in America!" in which he decried the practice of prison industries, describing it as a system of exploitation in which companies took advantage of very cheap prison labor, thus attaining an unfair advantage over their competitors.[17]

While in prison, Stanko proved to be an effective racial activist who quickly organized white inmates wherever he went. In one particular incident, he was said to have had fifty white inmates shouting "Sieg Heil" in the yard. A Klassen associate, Roger Elletson, sent Klassen a copy of Stanko's book, *The Score*. Impressed, Klassen first contacted Stanko on the telephone on January 25, 1989. Thereafter, he made numerous long trips to visit him in prison, but Stanko was frequently transferred to different facilities in a practice known as "dieseling." Finally, in December 1991, he was released from federal prison. In March 1992, he and a Creator associate, Paul Jackson, made their way to Otto, North Carolina; however, they did not stay long. After just a few days, Stanko told Klassen that he was returning to Scottsbluff, Nebraska, and had no intention of taking over the church. Losing interest in the Pontifex Maximus position, he severed his association with Klassen. During their meeting, Stanko suggested to Klassen that he sell the church, commenting that it was just another piece of real estate. This proposition infuriated Klassen who also felt a tremendous sense of betrayal after visiting Stanko over the past two years in prison and lauding him to the COTC's membership in the pages of *Racial Loyalty*.[18] To add insult to injury, according to Klassen, Stanko made off with his mailing lists and a large supply of his books, as Stanko would later advertise them for sale in *Resistance* magazine (which will be discussed in chapter 7).

Despite his rupture with Klassen, Stanko continued to promote Creativity. In 1990, he was reported to have placed copies of *Racial Loyalty* under windshield wipers of cars in Denver. Not long after his release from prison, Stanko was charged with obstructing a police operation, criminal mischief, and driving with an expired license.[19] In 1992, he moved to Nebraska and told a local newspaper that he was no longer a reverend in the church. In 1995, though, he moved to Montana, where he operated Creator Publishing in Billings, which distributed Church of the Creator books. During his time in Montana, Stanko had numerous brushes with the law. For example, he was once charged with unlawful restraint for handcuffing a woman to a staircase. In another incident, he was charged with a misdemeanor for reckless boating on the Yellowstone River. Once, he allegedly sought to use his position in the COTC to gain access to female inmates in the Montana prison system. The Montana Supreme Court, however, denied him this access.[20] He later moved to Wyoming, and in 2002, filed a suit to be allowed to kill grizzly bears and wolves on federal grazing land.[21]

In the spring of 1992, Klassen chose Charles Altvater from Baltimore, Maryland, to be his heir apparent. In Klassen's own words, Altvater "was by no means the ideal candidate." Nevertheless, he admired his enthusiasm and dedication to the Creativity creed. On May 8, Altvater arrived at the headquarters; however, it was not long before Klassen determined that he was not the man for the job. Thus he was dismissed after spending less than a month at the headquarters. According to Klassen, Altvater lacked the intellectual capacity for the Pontifex Maximus position; moreover, he seemed unduly paranoid.[22] Later that same year, Altvater was arrested and convicted for placing a bomb on the porch of a Baltimore policeman's home. The bomb exploded, but no one was injured. Altvater was also accused of bombing a state police car on the same day.[23] Later convicted, he received a five-year sentence for reckless endangerment and a twenty-year sentence (seven years of which were suspended) related to the bombing charges.[24]

At this stage of his life, at the age of seventy-four, Klassen described himself as "tired, burned out" and without "the energy to propel [his] great movement forward at the increasing momentum that it deserved." Compounding his misery, his wife of many years, Henrie Etta, became seriously ill around this time. She was first diagnosed with cancer in the spring of 1991. Despite his disdain for the medical establishment and conventional treatments for cancer, Ben Klassen submitted to the judgment of her physicians and approved her surgery, in marked contrast to the regimen he advocated in *Salubrious Living*. Finally, at 8:30 a.m. on January 24, 1992, she succumbed to the disease, with Klassen at her bedside. In accordance with her wishes, her body was cremated shortly thereafter.[25]

Considering all the bad fortune that had befallen him, Klassen believed that now was the appropriate time to move the COTC's headquarters from the isolated rural area of Otto to an urban area where larger groups could assemble and meet on a regular basis. Mark Wilson, the leader of the Skinhead Army of Milwaukee (AKA Northern Hammerskins), was the next candidate chosen to replace Klassen. Wilson's organizing efforts in Milwaukee impressed Klassen.[26] He arranged to transfer his quarter-million dollar inventory of Creativity books for shipping costs alone. After selling the property in Otto, Klassen sent a check for $95,000 to the Milwaukee COTC. Despite these gestures, Wilson never formally acknowledged accepting the position of Pontifex Maximus.[27] Soon, rumors abounded that Wilson and his skinhead friends were squandering the church's money and behaving recklessly. Moreover, Wilson never even bothered to thank Klassen for the financial support. Against Klassen's advice, Wilson hired Steve Thomas as his office manager. Thomas, a convicted felon, had spent four years at Fort Leavenworth for the 1966 rape and murder of a Vietnamese woman, Phan Thi Mao, when he was in Vietnam. The episode formed the basis of Brian De Palma's 1989 film, *Casualties of War*. To make matters worse, Thomas was still on parole and Klassen suspected that threatened with the prospect of returning to prison, he would "report to his JOG superiors regularly" on information concerning the COTC. Klassen ordered Wilson to fire Thomas, but he did not comply.[28] Wilson's leadership, Klassen complained, alienated many COTC members and caused some of the more capable activists—for example, Tommy Rydén of Sweden—to resign. One policy Wilson sought to implement required each prospective Creator reverend to personally appear before him and seek approval, a measure that Klassen thought was foolhardy.[29]

As a result of Wilson's indiscretion and mismanagement, Klassen dismissed him after only six months and in his stead, appointed Dr. Rick McCarty as the next Pontifex Maximus. Wilson though, did not take his dismissal lightly and he and his loyalists attempted a last-minute coup against McCarty during a meeting with him that took place in a Milwaukee hotel. Luckily for McCarty, the police arrested three members of Wilson's faction on concealed weapons charges before they could threaten him.[30] McCarty, armed with a written power of attorney from Klassen, met Wilson and worked out a deal whereby the Milwaukee faction returned $50,000, the COTC mailing list, and all but 5 percent of the remaining Creativity books.[31]

At last, Klassen thought he had found a suitable successor in Dr. McCarty, a psychologist who practiced in Florida. Back in 1985, he was been accused of operating a telemarketing scam selling soft drink distributorships in Birmingham, Alabama, but the charges were later dropped.[32] Despite some minor peccadilloes in McCarty's past, Klassen saw him as a man of many talents. Furthermore, his background in psychology, Klassen believed, would be useful in attracting recruits to the church. Previously, McCarty claimed to have doubled the membership of a Klan group led by Thomm Robb. However, McCarty disapproved of the Christian orientation of Robb's group and thus found a more suitable organizational fit in Creativity. In a formal letter to McCarty, Klassen transferred his leadership to him effective January 25, 1993. McCarty was to serve the remainder of a ten-year term that would end in 2000. Klassen indicated that he would still remain the president of the Church of the Creator, Inc., which was registered in North Carolina. The letter also instructed McCarty to create a twelve-member body called the Guardians of the Faith Committee, whose duty it would be to maintain the Creativity creed and "prevent it from ever being altered, adulterated or tampered with." Further, McCarty was instructed to develop a leadership school to train future leaders. Finally, he was requested to set up a college of electors whose duty would be to select the best-trained and most capable leader when the time came for the selection of McCarty's successor.³³ Klassen was pleased that McCarty quickly responded and graciously accepted the offer. In a letter, McCarty vowed to carry on Klassen's mission and even declare a special holiday in his honor.³⁴

To establish a solid legal basis after his departure, Klassen decided to change the structure of his organization to a trusteeship. His daughter Kim and her husband Walt volunteered to serve as trustees.³⁵ To assist him in this transition, Klassen enlisted the help of Sam Dickson, an attorney sympathetic to his cause who completed the necessary paperwork for Klassen for $1,500.³⁶

Not long after assuming leadership, McCarty moved the church headquarters to Niceville, Florida.³⁷ Klassen was pleased with the direction of the COTC under McCarty's stewardship. Quickly, McCarty revived *Racial Loyalty* with articles Klassen found to be well written. Moreover, he began production of more of Klassen's books. Finally, McCarty appeared on the Sally Jessy Raphael talk show in which he expounded on Creativity to a nationwide audience.³⁸ At last, a semblance of stability seemed to settle over the COTC. However, around this same time, numerous COTC members were implicated in sporadic acts of violence and criminality, which once again jeopardized the future of the church.

First, on May 17, 1991, George Loeb shot and killed Harold Mansfield Jr., a black Gulf War veteran, in a parking lot altercation that took place in Neptune Beach, Florida, near the Mayport Naval Station. The incident began when the two almost collided in their vehicles in the parking lot of a shopping center. An argument ensued and angry words were exchanged after which the Loebs entered the store and purchased groceries. Mansfield left the lot but soon returned with a friend. When the Loebs departed the store, Mansfield confronted George Loeb with a brick. Loeb produced a .25 caliber semiautomatic handgun and fired one shot into Mansfield's chest. He then fired several shots at Mansfield's companion who ran to the grocery store for help.³⁹ Loeb and his wife Barbara immediately left the state to evade authorities, but were arrested on June 6 in Poughkeepsie, New York. Authorities in Florida arrested Steve Cabott Thomas as an accessory after the fact of the crime insofar as he allegedly helped the Loebs leave town. In exchange for information, which indirectly led to the whereabouts of the Loebs, Thomas received a light sentence.⁴⁰ Barbara Loeb was convicted on a weapons possession charge and was sentenced to a one-year term to be served in a New York state prison. George Loeb was extradited to Florida, where he was convicted of first-degree murder and sentenced to life in prison on July 29, 1992, with no chance of parole for twenty-five years. Before the killing, Loeb was reportedly involved in two previous altercations with African Americans, both of which resulted in arrests.[41] Despite the negative publicity surrounding the episode in Florida, the August 1991 issue of *Racial Loyalty* hailed Loeb as a hero and a martyr, who killed Mansfield in self-defense. The Loeb affair would go on to haunt the Church of the Creator in the years ahead.

One of the most ambitious terrorist plots in which COTC members were implicated transpired in July of 1993. COTC members, along with elements of White Aryan Resistance and the Fourth Reich Skinheads, were arrested for their involvement in a bizarre plot to bomb the First African Methodist Episcopal Church in Los Angeles and kill its pastor, the Reverend Cecil Murray.[42] Allegedly, the conspirators planned to foment a race war and targeted for assassination Rodney King, Al Sharpton, Louis Farrakhan, Urban League president John Mack, members of the prominent black rap bands, Public Enemy and NWA (Niggaz with Attitude), and unspecified Jewish leaders.[43] The putative ringleader was Christopher David Fisher, who led other suspects from a variety of backgrounds, including Geremy C. Von Rineman, a twenty-two-year-old skinhead who was paralyzed as a result of a violent encounter between skinheads and minority group members. He was joined by his common-law wife, Jill Scarborough, a financially strapped, single mother. Previously, the couple had written articles for *Racial Loyalty*. Unwittingly, the couple was responsible for bringing into their circle an informant working for the Federal Bureau of Investigation (FBI), who presented himself as "Rev. Joe Allen" and had written articles for *Racial Loyalty* as well. Also arrested were Josh Lee and two unidentified juveniles. Uncharacteristic were Doris Nadal and her husband Christian, both of whom were affluent young professionals. The couple was arrested on weapons charges related to the conspiracy. Doris Nadal worked as an accounting manager for Century 21 while her husband worked as a flight engineer for Continental Airlines. They owned a private plane and displayed a Nazi flag and a poster of Hitler at their home in a ritzy neighborhood in the San Fernando Valley.[44] Another suspect, Christopher Berwick, was arrested later and pleaded guilty to conspiring to manufacture and sell approximately sixteen machine gun receiver tubes for gun kits provided by

Christian Nadal.[45] Authorities made the arrest after an eighteen-month FBI investigation. Terree A. Bowers, the U.S. attorney for the Central District of California, called it "one of the most successful infiltrations of white supremacist groups."[46] Interestingly, the Anti-Defamation League (ADL) had released a survey on the growth of the skinhead movement just days before the arrests.[47]

An undercover FBI agent, Mike German, was responsible for thwarting the plot. An Army brat, he had received a bachelor's degree from Wake Forest University and a juris doctorate from Northwestern University. Immediately after graduation in 1988, German joined the FBI, where he spent sixteen years as a special agent. His first assignment dealt with white-collar crime, but one day, an agent assigned to the Los Angeles Joint Terrorism Task Force walked through his office and announced, "I need a young Nazi." Although in his late twenties, the youthful-looking German, with blond hair and blue eyes, made a good fit for the investigation into violent skinhead activity in Los Angeles. German spent a year infiltrating the skinhead scene in California in 1992. Race relations at that time were strained in Los Angeles; the Rodney King beating trial had resulted in acquittal for the officers charged in the incident, and that spring, riots of protest had convulsed the city. Working with cooperating witnesses, German was able to ingratiate himself into the inner circle of those involved in the more serious criminal activities. He discovered that some of them were involved in procuring illegal weapons.[48] For his efforts, the FBI awarded him a medal of valor. In the mid-1990s, German infiltrated the Washington State Militia; his activity led to the arrest of several members on various weapons charges, including the production of pipe bombs.[49] German left the FBI in 2004 after he reported several instances of mismanagement in the agency.[50]

Just eleven days after the arrests in Los Angeles, the police in Salinas, California, arrested two skinheads on shoplifting charges—Wayne Paul Wooten and Jeremiah Gordon Knesal, the Washington state director of the COTC. During a search of their car, police discovered weapons, extremist literature, and a page from a telephone book that listed various Jewish agencies and synagogues. Knesal later confessed to federal agents that he was involved in the July 20, 1993, bombing of an NAACP office in Tacoma, Washington. Authorities alleged that the bombing was part of a larger conspiracy to attack Jewish and African American institutions, military installations, gay and lesbian meeting places, and television stations.[51] The police later arrested Mark Frank Kowaalski, a twenty-four-year-old ex-convict in connection with the alleged plot.[52]

As the authors Dave and Neta Jackson observed, many of the violence-prone Creators were not church renegades. Rather, they were usually members in good standing. Some were even ministers and honored by the organization for their activities.[53] As evidenced by Klassen's desperate attempt to find a suitable successor, by the early 1990s, the church had fallen on hard times. During this period, Klassen became involved in a particularly vicious feud with Harold Covington.

Over the years, Covington has earned a very controversial reputation in the far right. Highly literate and articulate, he has done a significant amount of writing and theorizing on strategy.[54] However, he has also been involved in several very bitter internecine feuds that have led some activists to impugn his movement credentials. Covington attained notoriety for his connection to the so-called Greensboro Massacre. On November 3, 1979, members of a neo-Nazi party, the National Socialist Party of America (NSPA), and a local Ku Klux Klan organization clashed with demonstrators led by members of the Communist Workers Party in a "Death to the Klan" rally. The confrontation was the culmination of a series of disputes between the two sides. At the demonstration, a shootout between the two sides ensued in which five members of the Communist Workers Party were fatally wounded. The Klansmen and neo-Nazis suffered no serious casualties.[55] At that time, Covington was the leader of the NSPA and a principal organizer of the demonstration, but he was conspicuously absent from the actual event. Rumors surfaced among both left- and right-wing representatives that he was an informant and agent provocateur for the FBI, the Bureau of Alcohol, Tobacco, and Firearms (BATF), and the Central Intelligence Agency (CIA). Covington denies these allegations.[56]

Covington had actually maintained a correspondence with Klassen since the early 1970s, but the two often disagreed over religion and strategy. Klassen criticized Covington for not taking a position against Christianity.[57] Covington was an abiding advocate of separatism as a temporary measure by which whites in North America could establish and consolidate an independent state before embarking on an eventual campaign of reconquest. In the late 1980s, Covington dallied with the idea of southern nationalism or the creation of a separate white southern state. He counseled Klassen that for such a plan, an anti-Christian program in the style of Creativity would amount to "total political hara-kiri." As Covington saw it, Southern Nationalism was essentially a Christian movement. Although he originally admired certain aspects of Creativity, Covington argued that the movement had to establish roots in the common people and their communities, which meant that it must refrain from bashing Christianity.[58] By the late 1990s, Covington had shifted his separatist strategy to establishing a white nation in the Pacific Northwest. To that end, he wrote a trilogy of novels in which a white guerilla organization wages war against the federal government and establishes a separate white republic.[59]

According to Covington, he first came into contact with Klassen while in Florida in the early 1970s. At the time, Covington worked as an editor of Matt Koehl's newspaper, *White Power*, which was published in Arlington, Virginia. Covington claimed that Klassen first attempted to enlist him in the COTC in 1972, but he was not interested because he found Klassen's anti-Christian approach impractical in a movement in which Christianity figured so prominently, especially in the American South. In the summer of 1987, Covington claimed that he met Klassen's associate, Will Williams, for the first time; he described Williams as a forty-five-year-old man "with a distinct disinclination to get a job." At first, the two got along fairly well. A fellow native of North Carolina, Williams had collaborated with Covington in earlier ventures, including an effort to utilize public access television to broadcast Tom Metzger's *Race and Reason* Program. Covington claimed that Williams told Klassen he could promote Creativity in North Carolina and reach out in particular to members of Glenn Miller's White Patriot Party, which, at the time, was the most prominent racialist organization in the state. Very skeptical, Covington thought that this idea was doomed to fail insofar as the area was a stronghold for evangelical Christianity. When Williams failed to deliver, Covington claimed that Klassen decided to let him go. Williams's ulterior motive, according to Covington, was to get his hands on Klassen's money. Expecting that Klassen did not have much longer to live, Williams hoped to inherit the Pontifex Maximus position and Klassen's assets as well.

The relationship between Covington and Williams eventually soured. The vitriol against Covington in the pages of *Racial Loyalty* was so strong that in 1989 he filed a libel suit against the paper, Williams, and Klassen. The paper alleged, among other things, that Covington was a government agent, a closet rabbi, an agent provocateur of the Greensboro Massacre, an ADL informant, and a Mossad agent. For his part, Covington categorically denied the allegations but nonetheless, he later dropped the suit.[60] In retaliation for the suit, Klassen and Williams contacted Covington's employer, who subsequently fired him.[61] Covington complained that as a result of the defamation campaign, donations to his Confederate National Congress had fallen considerably.[62]

Striking back, Covington later accused Klassen of being a Jew and a homosexual. He characterized the COTC as a "sodomy cult" and alleged that Klassen had attempted to sodomize young skinheads who frequented the church's headquarters in North Carolina. According to Covington, in 1987, a seventeen-year-old skinhead from Cincinnati named Dennis Witherspoon went to Otto, North Carolina, to work at the COTC headquarters and in one incident, Klassen attempted to sodomize the young Witherspoon while he slept. Awakened by the sexual assault, Witherspoon was supposed to have "beat[en] the crap of Klassen while the wretched old faggot screamed for mercy."[63] In order to buy his silence, Covington claimed that Klassen paid Witherspoon $10,000 and provided him with a used car with which to leave North Carolina. Further, Covington alleged that Witherspoon would not keep quiet about the incident; finally, he was found dead in October 1990 in Dade County, Florida, bound and gagged and with five .22 caliber hollow-point bullets in his head. Supposedly, Covington had received confirmation of the story from correspondence with George Loeb as he sat in prison. So notorious was Klassen's reputation, said Covington, that skinheads referred to him as "Old Benny Buttfuck."[64] According to the Miami-Dade County Police Department, as of April 2008 the case of Witherspoon's murder is still regarded as unsolved. The opinion of the investigating officer is that the homicide was consistent with other drug-related killings. This leads the department to believe that the case was drug related though it has not yet been officially solved.[65]

Allegations such as the ones that Covington made are not uncommon in the extreme right and must be taken with skepticism. In the late 1980s, a young skinhead musician, George Burdi (who will be covered in greater detail in chapter 7) spent three months at the COTC headquarters in North Carolina. As he recalled, on most days, he saw Klassen, who would come down from his hilltop home to visit the COTC staff. Usually, he would say a few words of encouragement and then leave. On a few occasions, Klassen invited Burdi to his home to talk. Burdi was emphatic that at no time did he sense anything weird about Klassen. Never did he offer Burdi alcohol, say anything suggestive, or do anything else untoward in the style of Covington's allegations. In his estimation, Covington had a personal axe to grind against Klassen.[66] According to Burdi, he spent many hours listening to Klassen, time that he described as a great learning experience.[67]

With the death of his wife and the failure of his church, Klassen slipped into a deep depression. On August 6, 1993, Klassen took a number of boxes of documents to a local recycling center and probably between late August 6 and early August 7, he consumed four bottles of sleeping pills, which resulted in his death. Two days later, his daughter Kim discovered his body. He left a suicide note, which invoked a section of *The White Man's Bible* asserting that suicide was an honorable way to end a life that was no longer worth living.[68] As he pointed out in the book, if a person is wracked with suffering, then prolonging life in such a situation is not a compassionate act.[69] At Klassen's request, Kim and her family had his remains buried on his property in North Carolina on a spot designated as the Ben Klassen Memorial Park. Inscribed on his gravestone are the words "He gave white people of the world a powerful racial religion of their own."[70]

Writing under the nom du guerre Winston Smith, Covington mockingly dismissed Klassen and his legacy. The passage illustrates the enmity between the two men:

> Benny Klassen is dead, and it's a Whiter and Brighter world without him. The Founder of the "Church of the Creator" sodomy cult, the man whose deviate [sic] sexual lifestyle was so notorious that American Skinheads named him "Old Benny Buttfuck," the self-proclaimed greatest Aryan genius who ever lived—most probably a rabbi's son from Vilna—came crawling back to the cult's ashram in Otto, North Carolina in the early weeks of July. Over a year ago he had fled into hiding, in fear of prosecution for a cult-related killing in Florida.
>
> In the early morning hours of August 7th, Klassen swallowed the contents of four bottles of sleeping pills. The Macon County sheriff reports that the quondam Maximum Pontoon left a rambling and incoherent suicide note on a yellow legal pad by his bedside. Con-

sidering Klassen's wonted verbosity, the sheriff was lucky he didn't decide to turn it into another lengthy, excruciatingly boring book.

. . .

For twenty years, Benny Klassen performed one gigantic act of psychological and political sodomy on us all. He never had any real religion or political message. It was all gull, warmed-over classical anti-clericalism framed in the manner of Talmudic response, mixed with crude race baiting and pseudo-scholarship, garnished with soft core pornography and served up on a bed of crap.

Yet the turgid, gibberish in his interminable books was reverenced as inspired wisdom; the most arrant nonsense in his so-called theology was seriously debated; and flaming bird-brained idiots that we are, all but a few of us accepted the liver-lipped old baboon at his own estimation of himself. The reason is simple and shameful: money. Klassen was a millionaire, and with pitifully few exceptions Movement people and Movement leaders in particular genuflect in the presence of wealth. . . .

Given the general depravity of our so-called leaders, I can understand why many of them kept their lips firmly pressed against Klassen's withered buttocks in hope of catching some of the dribble from his overflowing bank accounts. But you'd think they might at least have managed a mumble or two of protest when the vile monster started killing kids. . . .

We sank low during the Klassen years. Now let us see how high we can rise.[71]

Writing in his organization's newsletter, Pierce defended Klassen against attacks by Covington and categorically denied that he was a Jew, homosexual, and a murderer. He accused Covington of attempting to sabotage the COTC by sending many letters to members of the group that cast aspersions on Klassen.[72]

Klassen's appointed successor, Rick McCarty officially notified COTC members of their leader's death in a letter dated August 12, 1993:

In the early hours of Sunday, August the 8th [sic] our beloved founder and friend Mr. Ben Klassen passed away. I learned this from Klassen's daughter Monday morning. She told me that his last thoughts were about you. How important and significant each one of you are in the survival of our race and religion. The faith he has in each of you to continue with the courage you have always shown. To make a stand and not to back down. To take up the banner of the COTC and to carry it to victory.[73]

In addition to the death of Klassen, other mounting troubles took their toll on McCarty. He later complained in a 1993 issue of *Racial Loyalty* that Klassen's daughter refused to continue her father's financial support for the organization.[74] In July 1993, McCarty was arrested in Niceville for driving under the influence of alcohol.[75] In addition, the whole Los Angeles matter in which some COTC members were implicated in a terrorist conspiracy was an embarrassment for the new Pontifex Maximus, who sought to dissociate himself and the COTC from the affair. In an effort at damage control, McCarty began issuing press releases attempting to distance himself from these incidents, claiming that he disavowed violence.[76] But the last straw came in March 1994, when a Florida court ruled that the COTC bore responsibility for George Loeb's murder of Mansfield, whose family won a $1,000,000 lawsuit initiated by Morris Dees of the Southern Poverty Law Center (which will be covered in chapter 13). McCarty did not contest the suit. Seeking to extricate himself from the mess, he disbursed the Creativity books and other church assets and terminated his leadership. He has not been publicly involved in the movement since.[77]

With Klassen's demise, the church entered a phase of rapid decline. However, a young Canadian would spread the message of Creativity to skinheads through the emerging genre of "white power" music.

7
George Burdi and RAHOWA

Not long after Klassen's death, the Church of the Creator began to implode. Klassen's successor, Dr. Rick McCarty, voluntarily dissolved the organization as a result of a civil suit initiated by the Southern Poverty Law Center stemming from the homicide committed by a church member, George Loeb. However, George Eric Burdi, a young Canadian musician from Canada, drew inspiration from Creativity and formed a band called RAHOWA named after an acronym Klassen had coined that stands for RAcial HOly WAr. It is meant to be a call to arms not unlike the Arabic word jihad used by Islamic militants.[1] With Burdi's rise to prominence in the 1990s, some observers saw in him the potential to be the seminal figure of the white nationalist movement of the decade.[2]

Born in June 1970 in a Toronto suburb, Burdi was raised as a Roman Catholic and once served as an altar boy. The son of an insurance salesman, Burdi described his childhood as happy.[3] As a youth, he demonstrated high intelligence and intellectual curiosity; he claims to have completely read the Bible while still in early adolescence.[4] By age sixteen, he discovered Frederich Nietzsche and was mesmerized by his philosophy. As he recalled, the German philosopher awakened his "racial soul." Taken not only by the "will to power," Burdi also absorbed some of the anti-Semitic and anti-Christian themes culled from Nietzsche's writings. In *Anti-Christ*, he found an anti-Christian manifesto for white power activists in America and Europe.[5] A life of genteel upper-middle class existence would prove too boring for the young Burdi and he began to seek out what he referred to as the "truly potent" elements of Western culture including Plato, Thucydides, Cicero, Shakespeare, Poe, Bacon, Dostoyevsky, and Shaw.[6]

While still in high school, Burdi did not exhibit any overtly hostile racist inclinations; he described himself as basically a popular student who played on the football team and was president of the student council. He even belonged to a multicultural group composed of blacks and whites called the Chocolate Cake Club. An avid fitness enthusiast, the six-foot-tall Burdi began regularly working out and reached a weight of about 200 pounds. At age eighteen, he began a romance with a girl whose German father was involved in the racialist movement; Burdi once described him as a "unique personality, a complicated man, and extremely well read." For the intellectually curious Burdi, the man's political outlook represented a radical departure from the way he had previously viewed the world.[7] Burdi went to work for him at his moving company. One day while in his home, he discovered a copy of George Lincoln Rockwell's book, *White Power* and was fascinated by his exhortations of white racial solidarity.[8]

After graduating from De La Salle College (the Canadian equivalent of a high school) in 1989, Burdi enrolled in the University of Guelph to study political science. Around that same time he discovered Ben Klassen's *Nature's Eternal Religion* and *The White Man's Bible*. At first, he was turned off by the extreme racism of Creativity. Nevertheless, the nihilistic tenor of Klassen's writing left an indelible impression on him; as Burdi once remarked, "*The White Man's Bible* [made] Rockwell's *White Power* look like an Aesop fable."[9] Just as he was contemplating taking an active part in the movement, Burdi was also going through a period in which he began to reject Christianity. In fact, Klassen's writings on the subject were the single most attractive feature of the COTC for him.[10] Soon thereafter, he contacted Klassen and made such an impression on him that Klassen agreed to pay Burdi's expenses to travel to and from North Carolina. Burdi described Klassen as an avuncular figure, a "kind, friendly, generous, egoistic but not intolerable, old school Republican, reclusive, logically oriented, [and] unemotional."[11] He worked at the church for two months but found the organ, *Racial Loyalty*, to be disappointing, believing it to be a poor representation of Creativity.

Back in Toronto, Burdi assisted Ernst Zündel at his Samisdat offices. Since the mid-1970s, Zündel has gained notoriety as Canada's largest purveyor of Holocaust denial and has been involved in several high-profile free speech controversies stemming from his activities.[12] Burdi recalled Zündel as a very intelligent man who expressed himself eloquently. Through him, he began to understand National Socialism "as a creative, positive force and ideology."[13] On one opportunity, Burdi even had the chance to meet David Irving, the prominent British historian on the Third Reich whose controversial historiography has frequently come under fire.[14]

After completing only one year of university studies, Burdi dropped out of school and decided to devote all of his time and energy to the racialist movement. Eventually, Burdi would come to agree with Klassen that Christianity was a serious impediment to the white racialist revolution. As he explained, white people would not be able to "act with the necessary ruthlessness while still saddled with the Christian baggage."[15] Later, Burdi even once went so far as to advocate the inclusion of Satanists in the white racialist movement and was eager to foster links between so-called black metal and white power music.[16]

Upon returning to Toronto, Burdi began consorting with skinheads in the downtown area. Music is what seemed to finally impel him to become a true believer of the racialist movement. Sometime earlier, Zündel had sent Burdi a white power music tape for his review. Burdi recounted what happened next as an almost "road to Damascus" experience:

> Much later that night, I almost forgot that I had the tape in my pocket when I started my drive home with the post bar-closing traffic. I was fatigued, and stared wearily at the road, thinking about the struggle I was deeply attracted to. More than half-way home, I remembered that the "White Power" tape was in my pocket. Almost immediately, my speakers hissed with white noise, and my woofers buzzed from being over-bassed as the first song kicked in. It was Hail The New Dawn by Skrewdriver, and it sent shockwaves through my body. I mean, here I was, in a movement that surrounded me with middle-aged and elderly men, and suddenly I heard this voice—this amazing, soulful, mighty voice—that was from a young man, like myself. Thirty minutes of listening later, I was hooked on Skrewdriver. . . . I still remember today how much that first experience impacted my life.[17]

Growing up, Burdi's musical tastes were varied, as he listened to a variety of bands, including Meatloaf, the Beatles, and Led Zeppelin. Musically eclectic, he enjoyed listening to new wave and Motown as well.[18] Spearheading the "white power" musical genre in North America, in 1989, he, Jon Latvis, and other local COTC members formed a white power musical band called RAHOWA, based on a formula of similar bands based overseas, most notably, Skrewdriver in England. Burdi assumed the surname Hawthorne while he was a member of the band. Their most famous CD recording, *Cult of the Holy War*, was released in 1995 and supposedly sold 45,000 copies.[19] The music was once described as a "stunning mix of hard rock, the heaviest of metal, and Goth, with strains of neo classicism throughout."[20] The band played occasional concerts, the most memorable of which was on Adolf Hitler's birthday in 1993 and was filmed by MTV. Burdi found that it was much easier to draw a crowd to a skinhead concert than it was to a traditional political meeting. The concerts were often rowdy; Burdi once estimated that he was involved in at least fifteen riot situations with the police and antiracist groups.[21]

In order to disseminate their music, in 1993, Burdi and Mark Wilson (Klassen's former heir apparent) launched their most successful enterprise—Resistance Records—a recording company that produced CDs for white power bands. They chose Detroit, Michigan, as their location because it was an equal distance between Milwaukee and Toronto. Furthermore, by operating in the United States, Resistance Records enjoyed First Amendment protection and could thus avoid the more restrictive speech codes in Canada.[22] In just a few short years, Resistance Records established itself as a major producer of white power music and had assumed the role in America that Ian Stuart had played earlier in England.[23] Where the seed money for the project came from is not certain; some believe that the Swedish skinhead movement provided the initial funding.[24] The enterprise proved to be quite successful; Burdi estimated that between 1994 and early 1997, the company sold over 60,000 CDs and tapes, and perhaps as many as 100,000.[25] Under his stewardship, the company maintained contact with about forty European recording labels in a number of countries including, Poland, the Czech Republic, Yugoslavia, Sweden, Italy, Germany, Switzerland, France, England, Denmark, Finland, Norway, Lithuania, Russia, Bulgaria, Hungary, South Africa, Australia, and even Japan.[26]

As Burdi saw it, white power music gave the youthful segment of the racialist movement a tremendous boost of confidence:

> There is a bold new force on the horizon—and you guessed right—it is Resistance Records. . . .
>
> The most important emotion that you can feel is not hatred, nor love. It is empowerment. Empowerment is the feeling of strength that results from positive influences, be they actions or ideas. The revolution—any revolution—begins in the hearts and minds of the

most heroic elements of a population: the revolution begins with you....

So I implore you to believe stronger than you have ever believed. Believe that you can make history instead of just reading it.... Believe that we shall win, and do what must be done to realize our dream.[27]

According to Burdi, the American racialist right had pursued a wrong approach. In many ways the far right is a tract society in that it has produced a multitude of books and pamphlets to "expose" the various conspiracies and machinations against the white race. Instead, Burdi believed that what the far right needed was raw emotion, not more learned treatises rehashing the problems the white race faced:

> Adolf Hitler is considered one of the best orators in human history, by people that do not even understand German. I for one can understand very little, yet I love to sit and listen to him speak, because it makes me feel alive.
>
> Our music, especially the best songs, has that effect on the listener. It operates on an entirely different level than the cold, dry, rational approach of our predecessors. Music can chill you to the bone, raise up your spirit, and make you want to explode with energy and vibrancy. It has the power to reach you on the deepest emotional level. Probably the two most successful pieces of literature ever produced by our movement are Dr. William Pierce's masterpieces *Hunter* and *The Turner Diaries*. I believe that the reason for their success is the same as for music—they reach the reader on an emotional, rather than a rational, level.[28]

Echoing Hitler's dictum of the power of the spoken over the written word, Hawthorne (Burdi) counseled that the movement must reach potential recruits in a visceral, not an intellectual, way:

> Anyone who feels that he or she is going to write *the* book that will awaken the slumbering White masses is a fool that does not understand political and psychological reality. How many Christians have read the bible? How many of the National Socialist soldiers that bled the Danube red with their sacrifices had even read *Mein Kampf* or Rosenberg's *Mythos*? How many pseudo-Marxists have read *Das Kapital*? The list goes on and on. Many people are

strongly influenced by books they read, but on average, most are not.[29]

This visceral approach appealed to the fledging skinhead scene in the United States. The skinheads first emerged in America in the early 1980s. The subculture was largely imported from Great Britain and revolved around a style of music known as "Oi." A British musician Ian Stuart and his band Skrewdriver did much to popularize the skinhead scene with this style of music. Soon skinhead bands emerged throughout North America and Europe. Although their numbers are estimated to have reached only a few thousand in the United States, the emergence of the skinheads in the extreme right was significant for a number of reasons.[30] First, they injected an element of youth into a movement that was aging. Through their music, the skinheads helped spread their message, not only throughout a portion of the extreme right, but also to rebellious youths who would otherwise not be interested in radical politics. In this sense, their music served as a recruiting mechanism. Second, the skinheads had a radicalizing effect on the rest of the movement. They tended to eschew the more conservative approaches and preferred more direct action. Third, this orientation often led to violence. Skinheads were frequently involved in confrontations with minorities, law enforcement, and rival antiracist skinhead gangs. Unlike the elderly denizens of the movement, who were often staunch Christians, the skinheads were more likely to look toward unconventional sources for religious inspiration, such as neopaganism and Creativity.

At one time, Burdi saw the skinheads as the vanguard of the racialist movement. Their lack of finesse only added to their authenticity. Eventually, he predicted, the embattled white masses would be drawn to their raw dynamism and energy:

> As primitive a form of culture as it may be, White Power concerts, and the mechanisms that surround it, are the breeding ground for a new identity. In this age of war, we are not afforded the luxury of contemplating the cosmos in peace and security. Instead, we live in a world that bloodlusts for our annihilation, and our music reflects the aggression and anger of a generation forced into war by powers beyond our scope of understanding. . . . When a cat is cornered, it does not think about the "morality" of its reaction. It will lash out, teeth bared, claws slashing wildly, and hair standing on end to

create an illusion of great mass. It is concerned only with its survival, not looking "nice" or "pretty" or "friendly." Much like that cat, Skinheads are not elements of conservatism or stability. They are symptoms of a social disease called egalitarianism, and they react with vengeance and extreme dissension. Once the masses of White people have exhausted hope in the Pat Buchanans and David Dukes of America, regardless of how noble their intentions might be, they will turn in droves for a radical solution to a radical problem. And Skinheads will be waiting in the wings, trained in maximum ferocity, each man worth ten sheeple[31] in fighting ability—tough, tenacious, and indefatigable. We are the manifestation of a survival mechanism programmed into our most primal instincts from the age of barbarism.[32]

Despite the exhortatory tone of his writing, Burdi counseled the movement's youth to avoid recklessness, arguing that assaults against nonwhites accomplished nothing and were actually counterproductive: "Beating some worthless mud to death is not an act of revolution, it is an act of poor judgment. . . . Remember, this is a war and you are living behind enemy lines. Act accordingly."[33] The bombastic rhetoric of his musical lyrics notwithstanding, Burdi cautioned that the time was not appropriate to strike at the system in a physical sense. Rather, he counseled that the racialist movement must first attain the solid support of the majority of the white population. Every effort had to be made to reach the white masses, and the youth in particular.[34]

To that end, in the spring of 1994, *Resistance* magazine was launched with an impressive initial circulation of 5,000. The second issue reached 10,000 in circulation. In the glossy magazine, Burdi combined hard-hitting editorials on white revolution with music reviews, color photos, interviews with activists, and articles on related interests.[35] Resistance Records also operated a Web site, which featured downloadable samples of music and articles. An automated e-mail newsletter—*Resistlist*—claimed several thousand subscribers.[36]

Burdi did not confine his activism to Resistance Records and his band. He also organized paramilitary training for his COTC faction in Canada. The group conducted weekly training led by Eric Fisher, a former member of the elite Canadian Forces Airborne Regiment. In one incident in 1992, his training regimen was so rigorous that one COTC recruit collapsed and died. Authorities declined to file any charges in connection with the incident. However, Fisher, along with his brother Elkar Fisher and Drew Maynard, were later arrested in connection with the kidnapping and beating of a member of the Heritage Front, whom they suspected had stolen a computer.[37]

In the political arena, Burdi was also affiliated with the Heritage Front based in Canada and was a close confidant of its leader Wolfgang Droege.[38] Through their exploits, Burdi and Droege had become the most recognized racial activists in Canada by the early 1990s. On December 8, 1990, RAHOWA, played at an event that marked the first-ever Heritage Front public rally. The date was significant in that it was meant to mark the sixth anniversary of the death of Robert Jay Mathews of the Order, who died at Whidbey Island in 1984. Paul Fromm, a prominent immigration restrictionist activist, delivered a speech at the event, exclaiming, "We're all on the same side. We know who we are, but we must also know who the enemy is."[39] Through these various efforts, Burdi garnered considerable publicity for his cause, as he was interviewed on major media venues, including CNN and MTV. The *New York Times* once referred to him as a "Neo-Nazi Mogul."[40] According to Devin Burghardt of the Center for New Community, by around 2002, there were over 100 white power bands in the United States, with still others in Europe.[41] Perhaps more than any other figure, Burdi was responsible for giving white power music an institutional basis.

It was not long, however, before he began experiencing setbacks. In the fall of 1993, a series of arrests severely damaged the Heritage Front. After a RAHOWA concert that was held in Ottawa on May 29, 1993, Burdi got involved in a fracas with antiracist counterprotesters and was subsequently arrested for assaulting a woman, Alicia Reckzin, a member of Anti-Racist Action, after he gave a speech. His case became a cause célébre for the COTC, as members in Los Angeles organized a legal defense fund on his behalf. In connection to that incident, in 1995, he was convicted of assault and sentenced to a year in prison.[42] Although he was released on appeal after one month, in 1997, his conviction was upheld and he was ordered to return to prison to serve the remainder of his sentence. Around this time, he and the other members of his band decided to split up.

Still other problems followed. In April 1997, Michigan authorities raided the offices of Resistance Records near Detroit to execute a warrant as part of an investigation for nonpayment of taxes. Supposedly, the Anti-Defamation League (ADL) brought pressure on the authorities to take action against the company.[43] In Ontario, just across the border, Canadian authorities raided Burdi's home as part of an investigation on whether the company was using the U.S. address to circumvent Canada's stringent hate speech laws.[44] The Canadian authorities seized Nazi paraphernalia and arrested Burdi along with two of his aides.[45] The tax case in the United States turned out to be minor insofar as most customers of Resistance Records were out of state and thus not required to pay state sales taxes on purchases through the mail. Eventually, the matter was settled with a fine, but the management of Resistance Records was shaken.[46]

Soon after this incident, Burdi left Resistance Records at which time the company was in shambles, with no real management to speak of. The operation, according to Burdi, was chronically strapped for cash, yet the skinhead musicians expected lucrative royalties as they thought it was a very profitable enterprise. Inasmuch as Burdi's chief priority was getting his ideological message out, profit was not his primary concern. *Resistance* magazine was often distributed free to prison inmates. The CDs were marketed to Eastern Europe often below the cost of production. Furthermore, the company at times even encouraged piracy so that more listeners could hear the music and its attendant message.[47]

With the company in free fall, Willis Carto, the head of the Liberty Lobby, acquired the Resistance Records label but soon sold it to Todd Blodgett, a former low-level staffer in the Reagan White House and protégée of Lee Atwater. Blodgett once worked on projects with Carto, but the two eventually split, presumably over finances. In 1996, Carto sold a copy of Liberty Lobby's mailing list to Blodgett for $85,000. By 1998, however, relations between the two became strained and Carto banned Blodgett from the offices of Liberty Lobby.[48] After acquiring Resistance Records, Blodgett did not really seem interested in rebuilding the company. Therefore, he soon sold it to Dr. William L. Pierce, chairman of the National Alliance. Under Pierce's, and later, Eric Gliebe's, direction, Resistance Records appears to have rebounded and has potential to be a substantial moneymaker for the organization.[49]

During his incarceration, Burdi had much time for contemplation and would often stay up all night thinking. As he explained, he was surrounded by "white trash" who "blamed everybody but themselves for the sorry state of their lives." To his chagrin, Burdi recalled that he began to see himself in them. They were not unlike the skinheads with whom he associated on the outside except that they lacked the "thin veneer of idealism."[50] Eventually, Burdi tired of the movement and decided to leave. As he recalled, three factors figured prominently in his decision. First, he regretted the great pain that his activism had caused his family. His father, who once held white-collar positions, had been dismissed by several employers. As a result, his family was forced to leave Toronto; his father could not find employment due to his son's notoriety. A second factor that influenced Burdi's decision was what he perceived as the futility of the white racialist cause. Despite his years of activism, he felt that little had been accomplished. Finally, Burdi seemed dismayed by the fact that the jury at his trial consisted of all whites and believed that they convicted him not on the facts of the case but because of his political views. All these factors engendered a "paradigm shift" in Burdi's thinking. Seeking a new direction in life, he immersed himself in fasting, meditation, and a quest for spiritual discovery. No longer could the racialist movement provide the purpose that he so desperately searched for in life.[51] In his estimation, the movement was terminally flawed and had to be entirely rebuilt if it was to ever be effectual.[52] Eventually, Burdi came to believe that his whole approach had been wrong:

> Mark Wilson and I knew right from the outset that the chest-beating machismo of the "movement's" music wasn't going to accomplish anything, except to reaffirm the public's fear of us, and arouse the wrath of the system. What the positively-oriented members of the "movement" must understand is that as long as they are carrying all of these dead-weights, then they will continue to be marginalized and viewed as losers and misfits. If you think that you'll succeed on such a massive revolutionary challenge by taking behavioral cues from WWF Wrestling and The Jerry Springer Show, then you are a fool.... Many times I was the ringleader, so I have no one to blame but myself. But in retrospect, I wish I had the maturity to find a better circus.[53]

Looking back, Burdi explained to this author what he thought was the major shortcoming of the white racialist movement:

The principal weakness of the ideology is the lack of strong examples of the higher culture and conduct that the movement pretends to champion. This weakness springs from an over-emphasis on biological materiality, i.e., race, which puffs up its members with false pride based on vicarious association with greatness and high achievement.[54]

After his release from prison in 1998, Burdi cut off all his ties to the movement. However, in 2000, he gave an interview to *Resistance* magazine to explain his decision. Despite his public departure from the movement, Burdi claims that most of his former colleagues have been polite to him and respected his decision, although on occasion, he receives "some nasty emails."[55] At the present time, Burdi lives in Toronto and is married to an East Indian woman whom he described as "very well educated" and having once worked for antiracist groups.[56] Continuing with his musical pursuits, he plays in a band called Novacosm, which includes two black members. Looking back on his activism, Burdi realizes that the white power movement never suited his true nature or his higher goals in life. In retrospect, he believes that it imbued him with a negative mind-set. In the racialist movement, Burdi saw a tremendous gap between theory and practice. Although many activists may have claimed to be fighting for European culture and values, he often found them to be the most ignorant of what this means. Furthermore, increasingly, he was put off by their boorish and loutish behavior. Burdi now rejects the material/biological self as a primary basis of identity as he exclaimed, "I AM NOT MY DNA [emphasis in original]"[57] Buddhism, especially the teachings of S. N. Goenka, now inspire him. Furthermore, he now finds the extreme secular view of Creativity's spirituality, based on racial and tribal ancestral worship, to be devoid of metaphysics which now interests him as he seeks to turn his efforts inward to become a better person.[58] Nevertheless, Burdi still maintains a somewhat contemptuous attitude toward the masses reminiscent of his racialist past. Yet he rejects conspiracy theories that suggest some "Dr. Evil [is] hiding behind levers of control." Instead, Burdi explains, "corporations are the will of the people, and the masses want to be amused."[59] Although he has repudiated his racialist past, Burdi is unapologetic for the part he played in Resistance Records:

While I feel it is unfortunate that Resistance Records released so much negative music, and continues to do so, I wouldn't undo my past. I said what I needed to say at that time, and I will always defend a person's right to do so. With the work I do now, including Novacosm, I work to counteract the negativity spread during my younger years.[60]

Despite Burdi's departure and the demise of his band, the Creativity idea would not die. Just a couple of years before Burdi left the movement, a young law student would set out to revive the Church of the Creator.

8

Resurrection

Matt Hale and the World Church of the Creator

The Church of the Creator languished for a few years after Ben Klassen committed suicide in 1993. After the resignation of Rick McCarty, the organization split into factions and lost membership. Yet Klassen's ideas still remained potent in the extreme right subculture and small splinter groups soldiered on. During the mid-1990s, the Milwaukee faction referred to itself as the Worldwide Church of the Creator and issued a newsletter called *RaHoWa News*, which was edited by Frank Martin. Around that same time, another faction in New York under the leadership of the Reverend Carl Hess called itself the First International Church of the Creator (FICOTC). Although not affiliated with that group, the Milwaukee faction supported the FICOTC insofar as there was concern that a single Creativity organization led by a single individual would be vulnerable to a decapitation strategy by JOG.[1]

In 1995, the Church of the Creator once again emerged as a unified movement. In that year, an enterprising young law student, Matt Hale, revived the church and became the movement's recognized leader. Not long before his death, Klassen had designated a small group of followers known as the Guardians of the Faith to carry on the religion. The reconstituted church was supposed to have held its first service on July 2, 1995, in Washington, Illinois.[2] Although Matt Hale had not sought the leadership position, in October 1995, COTC Reverend Brian Kachikis endorsed him as a candidate for Pontifex Maximus, just four months after Hale's public declaration of support for Creativity. Kachikis cited Hale's previous support for the church, which included putting out a Creativity newsletter and running Creativity shows on cable public access channels.[3] Moreover, Hale had experience in running for public office and was an able public speaker. The body unanimously confirmed Hale's appointment as Pontifex Maximus at Reverend Slim Deardorf's ranch in Missoula, Montana, on July 27, 1996.[4] Approximately thirty-five persons attended the event.⁵ Jonathan Viktor, a Klassen loyalist who was educated at this "School for Boys" at the former COTC headquarters in North Carolina, was elected Hasta Primus.⁶

In the following months, numerous Creativity branches united under Hale's leadership.⁷ Some observers contend that for all practical purposes, the church was defunct and Hale merely revived it, as no other person sought the mantle of leadership.⁸ The organization was first rechristened the New Church of the Creator but soon thereafter the name was changed to the World Church of the Creator.⁹ Since assuming control, Hale has demonstrated an almost single-minded commitment to his leadership of the church.

The last of four sons, Matthew F. Hale was born on July 27, 1971, to Russell Hale Jr. and Evelyn Anderson Hale. According to Hale, he grew up in a liberal household where both of his parents supported government affirmative action programs. Despite ideological differences between him and his parents, they encouraged him to think for himself.¹⁰ His father, now a retired police officer, raised Hale and his three brothers alone after a bitter divorce in 1980, when Hale was only nine years old.¹¹ During the year of his divorce, Russell Hale was deemed mentally unfit for work; he was once accused of abandoning his duties by visiting his wife and threatening to kill himself while on duty. Although he was temporarily fired, he was later rehired after his case went all the way to the Illinois Supreme Court, which ruled in his favor. During this turbulent period of his life, Matt Hale's worldview crystallized.¹² For a year or two, he lived with his mother, but then he returned to his father to live in the old family home,¹³ a two-story frame house that Hale's grandfather, a German immigrant, had built in 1909.¹⁴

Although he played sports, including Little League baseball, the young Hale seemed to prefer solitary pursuits, most notably music and reading. He began studying the violin and later played in a Chicago-area symphony. At the age of twelve, Hale came across a copy of William Shire's opus, *The Rise and Fall of the Third Reich*. After reading the 1,200-page book in just one month, he was fascinated with the National Socialist movement. Although Shirer was critical of the Nazi regime, Hale nevertheless was awed by what he had read. Soon afterward, he obtained a copy of *Mein Kampf* and was intrigued by Hitler's worldview. As he later recalled, he read the book so many times that it began falling apart.¹⁵ Around that same time, one incident in particular awakened Hale's incipient racism. One day while he was in a local eatery—Shakey's Pizza Parlor—where an after-hours dance for teenagers was held, he saw white girls kissing black boys. The experience, according to Hale, left him feeling "nauseous." He once described interracial marriage as a "form of bestiality."[16] By the time he reached eighth grade, he began forming racialist clubs, the first of which was called New Reich. Fascinated by Hitler, Hale would on occasion dominate discussions in his history class when the topic came up.[17] He discussed his "racial awakening" with this author:

> I first became racially conscious at the age of twelve. In fact, maybe even eleven when I was doing a lot of reading and studying of the world. And one thing I realized fairly quickly was that if all the races were truly equal as I've been taught, they should have contributed to the world equally.... Here I was learning all the time and hearing it all the time that the races are equal to one another and yet here I read in the encyclopedia that 99 percent of accomplishments are from white people.... These things definitely came to my attention.[18]

When he was fifteen, Hale read the philosophy of Friedrich Nietzsche, whose strident critique of Christianity piqued his interest. To Hale, Nietzsche's philosophy dovetailed well with Hitler's ideology. At the time, he was still a nominal Christian, albeit with a racial bent, who believed that God wanted to keep the races separate. Hale claimed to have read the Bible three times but didn't find much with which he agreed. He shared with this author his critique of Christianity:

> Christianity from its very inception was a Jewish creed, a Jewish philosophy. And we believe that Christianity was fed, so to speak, to the white Romans in an effort to destroy the white Roman Empire, and has been fed to white people ever since in general to destroy them and to damage their interests worldwide. And we can see it readily by the fact that today you can walk into any Christian church and hear a talk about how all people are equal and God loves us all and racial intermarriage is okay and things of this nature....
>
> I think that any religion that has a Jew as a savior, is doomed. I think that it is a very troubled religion when you have a Jew as your savior. Now, Christian Identity people say that he was not a Jew af-

ter all. But I think that is ridiculous. I mean, Jesus Christ obviously is not from our people—if he even existed, which we don't believe he did. Even assuming he did exist, he came from Palestine, of Jewish background. So, basically, Christianity has a seed of destruction for white people within it by virtue of having a Jewish savior.[19]

Seeing himself as more mature than his peers, as Hale recalled, in a sense he was never a teenager. By the age of twelve he began to "think like an adult" and sought activities to exercise his intellect. A former high school classmate described him as "competitive."[20] Some of his peers were put off by his seeming narcissism and aloofness. As a result of their rejection, he developed something of a persecution complex. On some occasions, he was beaten up in school and subjected to ridicule. Nevertheless, the charismatic Hale attracted a circle of followers. Calling themselves the "White Guard," they distributed crudely written white supremacist literature in school, an activity for which the dean threatened to expel the young Hale. All of this unsettled Hale's father, the local policeman. To placate his father and the school administrators, He curtailed his political activities until his senior year in high school when a new and more permissive dean took over. Throughout his senior year, he remained serious minded and did not date, drink, smoke, or take drugs.[21]

After graduating from high school, Hale gained admittance into the selective Bradley University, a private school, where he received a partial scholarship for his violin talent. In May 1993, he graduated with a bachelor of arts degree in political science. During his college days, Hale remained politically active. A pattern emerged in which Hale eschewed existing racialist organizations and instead focused on forming his own, presumably so that he could direct them. While at Bradley, he attempted unsuccessfully to create a White Student Union. In 1990, he sought to attach himself to the National Association for the Advancement of White People—an organization founded by David Duke. That same year, he founded the American White Supremacist Party, which received press coverage. At first, he recalled, he was petrified at having to speak in public. After his public activism at Bradley, however, he began to relish the opportunity and his previous shyness quickly dissipated. Before long, he was giving interviews to NBC, CNN, and the Associated Press.[22] In one event on April 20 (Hitler's birthday), 1991, Hale spoke on the state capitol steps in Denver at a white supremacist rally. In August 1992, he founded yet another group, the National Socialist White Americans Party.

On at least one occasion, Hale dabbled in electoral politics. In April 1995, he ran for a seat on the East Peoria, Illinois, city council. At that time, Hale estimated that the demographic composition of Peoria was 98 percent white. During his campaign, he stated that he wanted to create more jobs for whites and make sure that the children were receiving a proper education.[23] The local economy, which at the time was dominated by the Caterpillar Tractor Company, experienced a downturn when the firm cut back significantly in the mid-1980s. Today, the town is better known for its riverboat casino industry.[24] Although he lost the election, he received a respectable 14 percent of the vote.[25] For a while, Hale considered electoral politics as an appropriate vehicle for attaining political power. When prominent white nationalists, such as David Duke, ran for office, Hale publicly supported their candidacies.[26] In later years, however, he condemned the "foolishness of voting" and preferred a more antisystem, revolutionary approach to politics.

In the early 1990s, Hale stumbled on a copy of *Racial Loyalty*, which exposed him to Creativity. Borrowing a copy of *Nature's Eternal Religion*, he found the idea of combining a political program with a militant religion a brilliant idea.[27] Enthusiastic over the creed, he began distributing hundreds of copies of *Racial Loyalty* and maintained close contact with the church headquarters in Otto.[28] After five years of public activism and moving from one organization to another, in 1995, Hale finally decided to dedicate his life to Creativity.[29] He jettisoned the political approach for the more religious orientation of Creativity, believing that a religious movement was more potent than a political party; as he explained, "running for office does not permeate the psyche of people like religion does."[30] He established his headquarters in East Peoria, which was in actuality his bedroom in his father's house.[31] An Israeli flag served as a doormat in the entrance.

After assuming leadership of the resurrected church, Hale set out to reorganize the group. He replaced *Racial Loyalty* with a newsletter called *The Struggle*. Also, he wrote *The Creator Membership Manual*, in which he suggested ways in which members could spread the church's message, deal with law enforcement, and handle the media. The manual details the requirements for becoming an ordained minister in the church. Prospective candidates are supposed to read and study *Nature's Eternal Religion* and the *White Man's Bible* after which an open-book exam on these tests is required.[32] In the manual, Hale also outlined the theoretical organizational structure of the church. At the apex is the Pontifex Maximus, the supreme leader, who serves a ten-year term. At the expiration of this term, a successor is chosen by the Guardians of the Faith Committee—a body "composed of twelve of the most tried, true and tested church ministers."[33] Below the Pontifex Maximus, the church is organized first on a national basis, with subordinate subnational units below as illustrated in Table 8.1.[34]

Table. 8.1. Organizational Hierarchy of the World Church of the Creator

			Pontifex Maximus					
		National Director			National Director			
State Director		State Director		State Director			State Director	
County Dir.	County Dir.	County Dir.	County Dir.	County Dir.	County Dir.	County Dir.	County Dir.
City D.	City D.	City D.	City D.	City D.	City D.	City D.	City D.	City D.

Adding to the robust corpus of Creativity literature, Hale later produced a *Festum Album*, which contained suggestions for Creativity holiday ceremonies to be held in lieu of Christmas from December 26 to January 1. Creators are instructed on how to burn candles in an appropriately ordered arrangement—black, white, white, red, white, white, and black (the colors of the Creator flag). Each day of the week represents a separate theme: Day 1—History, Day 2—Destiny, Day 3—Unity, Day 4—Ingenuity, Day 5—Memorial, Day 6—Law, and Day 7—Purity. Creators are encouraged to have discussions with friends and family members on topics related to these themes.[35] Ben Klassen's birthday, February 20, is regarded as a church holiday called Klassen Day. February 21—Founding Day—is designated as a church holiday as well.[36]

The WCOTC also made contributions in the area of literature. In the extreme right underground, several novels—most notably, *The Turner Diaries* and *Hunter*—have attained popularity. These novels are often cited as blueprints for revolution. Continuing in this genre, the Reverend Kenneth Molyneaux authored two novels based on Creativity themes. *White Empire* is a novel set in the year 2050, thirty years after the great revolution that ushered in the global hegemony of Creativity. The period prior to this is referred to as the Doom Age. Animated and inspired by Creativity, the white race regained control over much of the world. Through Creativity, whites have established a virtual hegemony over most regions of the world, including Europe, North and South America, the Middle East, and Africa. However, Asia has not yet been fully conquered, although their opposing military forces are no match for the superior technology and martial prowess of the (Creativity) Empire's armed forces.

The protagonist of the story is Captain Wolfgang Gerhard, a native of Germany and a member of an elite military force called the Holy Legions—a multinational unit that includes members from a variety of European ethnic backgrounds. Gerhard is described as physically strong and of stoic, heroic character. He is happily married to a beautiful, loving wife, Isabelle, with long flowing blonde hair and the couple has five healthy children. As a result of "salubrious living," the average life-span has increased to 100 years. The Empire is described as grand in scale, surpassing any preceding civilization. Its leader, Magnus, exudes supreme confidence and is adored by all of the Empire's citizens whom he greets with the salutation "RAHOWA." The Empire's capital is Klassengrad, where a special boulevard was constructed so that victory celebrations could be held in the style of the Nuremburg rallies of Nazi Germany. A grand coliseum—The Megabowl—holds a maximum capacity of 500,000 persons and massive Creativity flags adorn the top of the structure. At one ceremony, Gerhard is awarded the Empire's highest honor—the Klassen medal—for his military service in Africa.

Shortly thereafter, the proud Gerhard joins an old friend, John Granger, whom he introduces to his sister-in-law, Marie, a beautiful, intelligent, and thoughtful history teacher. The two quickly fall in love and announce their plans to marry. However, tragedy soon befalls the couple. While visiting a popular site known as Salubrious Park, the two die in an attack by a suicide bomber, appearing as a disheveled man, who screams "Death to the Empire!" just before detonating his explosive device which he wears under his trench coat. Devastated by the loss, Gerhard vows to avenge their deaths. He requests a transfer from the Holy Legions to a clandestine intelligence division known as the Shadow Corps in the hope of penetrating the group responsible for the terrorist attack in Salubrious Park. After rigorous training, Gerhard is accepted into the unit and sets out to infiltrate a group of renegade whites, who consort with nonwhites, take drugs, and listen to cacophonic music reminiscent of the "gangsta rap" of the Doom Age. On his first mission, he gains entry into an underground club that operates in the style of a speakeasy. Inside, whites and nonwhites mingle together. Appalled by their licentiousness, Gerhard eventually loses his temper, at which point a melee breaks out and many of the patrons and a few Shadow Corps agents are killed in a shootout. Intelligence reports reveal that a secret compound is operating in newly conquered territory that was once China. Directed by Jews, kidnapped whites, captured at the outskirts of the Empire, are held captive and subjected to mind control drugs that turn them into docile zombies. They were described as not unlike Christians from the Doom Age in that their minds were befuddled with "suicidal, contradictory, and farcical beliefs." Once brainwashed, these whites were programmed to conduct terrorist missions like the one that occurred at Salubrious Park. Others were used to crush any dissent against the government in China, which was secretly controlled by the Jews. After careful planning, Gerhard leads a commando mission that destroys the compound. By doing so, he removes virtually all obstacles for the Empire's final conquest of Asia.[37]

Molyneaux's second novel, *Klassen*, is a fantasy in the style of J. R. R. Tolkien's *Lord of the Rings*. The protagonist Klassen rebels against his father, Ubelig, a contemptible figure who willfully collaborates with the Universal Church to encourage immigration into their land. Klassen and his family belong to the Nobilis race, which is solely responsible for creating civilization. However, in recent years, their idyllic land—Teramon—has been beset by an immigration invasion of hideously ugly ogres—an ignorant and parasitic race that contributes nothing to the community except filth, vice, and crime. Klassen's people are subjected to a "Nobilis tax" in order to subsidize the welfare of the ogres. All of this is aided and abetted by the Universal Church, which promotes superstition and ignorance to the Nobilis race. Recently, the church has been promoting intermarriage between the two races. Intuitively, Klassen rejects the church's creed. Once, while riding on his horse in the forest, Klassen happens upon two ogres that are in the process of violating a fair Nobilis maiden named Alianna. Klassen slays the two ogres and saves the damsel in distress. Later, Klassen travels in search of the famed Honor Brigade—a chivalric order determined to redeem the Nobilis race. Members follow "The Ten Laws of Honor Brigade," which are essentially an abridged rehashing of Klassen's "Sixteen Commandments." Eventually, Klassen reaches the brigade's headquarters, a massive, colossal structure known as the Imperium Castle. While there, he undergoes a rigorous training regimen that includes learning how to use a sword—the order's weapon of choice. Furthermore, he is subjected to a program of ideological indoctrination in which he discovers that the main source of their woes is a race known as the orc, who are responsible for running the hated Universal Church as well as mobilizing the ogres against the Nobilis race. After a long trial period, Klassen is inducted as a paladin of the order. Shortly thereafter, he heads back to his town of Utgart to organize resistance against the enemies of his people. To his dismay, he discovers that members of his family, led by his father Ubelig, are among the most egregious collaborators against the Nobilis. Ubelig, who had been thoroughly corrupted by the orcs, now serves as a high priest in the Universal Church and locals refer to him as "Savior." In a final battle, Klassen's brother, Grausen, slays Klassen's beloved Alianna on orders from Ubelig, who plans to execute his rebellious son as well. Before he can carry out this task, however, members of the Honor Brigade storm the building and overcome the guards. Once freed, Klassen gleefully kills both of his traitorous parents with a dagger, which he raises in the air before his fellow paladins at which point he roars, "Victory is inevitable!" Thus concludes the story.[38]

In 2001, Molyneaux was the first person ever prosecuted under the city of Akron's litter statute, which prohibits placing unsolicited fliers on car windshields. He was also charged with criminal trespassing after refusing police orders to remove the handbills he had placed on an estimated 150 cars. The Ohio Ninth District Court of Appeals overruled Molyneaux's conviction, concluding that the statute was too broad and infringed on protected speech. The appellate court, however, let the criminal trespassing conviction stand.[39]

In preparation for his street activism, Hale revived the two WCOTC security details collectively known as the Security Legions: the White Berets and the White Rangers. The principal purpose of the legions is to provide security services for church members and church property. Their secondary purpose is to prepare members of the church for "active and effective self-defense." Members of the legions are supposed to be physically fit, practice martial arts, and learn first-aid techniques and police communications. Furthermore, each member is supposed to own at least one handgun and become proficient through target practice. The difference between the two security details is basically stylistic. Whereas the White Rangers' uniform is in the tradition of the American West and includes cowboy hats and cowboy boots, the White Berets' uniform includes a white beret and paratrooper boots. For a while, Guy Lombardi, the group's Southeast regional director, served as commander of the White Berets, who, along with Hale, once appeared on the *Jerry Springer Show* to present the views of the WCOTC. Lombardi later left the church and Tony Evola assumed the position in the early 2000s. Matt Hale served as the interim leader of the White Rangers until a suitable candidate could be found.[40]

By conducting numerous "literature drops" in communities around the country, the WCOTC garnered much local publicity. Members frequently distributed a pamphlet titled *Facts That the Government and the Media Don't Want You to Know* in shopping malls, schools, and other venues. The pamphlet contains a number of reprinted articles concerning racial issues including the peril of black-on-white crime, the consequences of U.S. support for Israel in the Middle East, Third World immigration, race and IQ, the "Kosher racket," the role of Israel in the "sex slave" industry, and the putative control of the media by Jews.[41] In 1998, one member, Benjamin Smith, claimed responsibility for placing hundreds of WCOTC fliers under car windshields throughout the city of Bloomington in Indiana. To counteract Smith and the WCOTC, in early August 1998 various concerned citizens coalesced in a group christened Bloomington United Campaign against Hate Speech and Hate Crimes, which organized numerous rallies in the area.

The new WCOTC also established a noticeable presence in cyberspace. By doing so, it amplified the group's real size. The site suggested numerous methods by which people could interact and become more informed on Creativity. Furthermore, an e-commerce section offered books, videos, clothing, and other items for sale.[42] The Web site even featured a section called "Creativity for Children," which sought to appeal to younger recruits.

The medium of television was exploited as well. In 1984, the U.S. Congress mandated that cable companies create public access channels for public, educational, or governmental use. Current federal law prohibits cable companies from interfering with the editorial content of such programs unless the material is obscene or of a commercial nature.[43] Using this avenue, Hale introduced a half-hour program titled *White Revolution*, which was broadcast on some public access channels by cable companies.

In many ways, Hale exhibits the characteristics of the "great promoter" that Klassen sought for so long. A rather slightly built man, Hale is said to weigh 145 pounds.[44] Nevertheless, he was not one to shy away from the media spotlight. He has interfaced considerably with the media, appearing on such programs as *Montel Williams*, the *Jane Whitney Show*, *Jerry Springer, Ricki Lake, Leeza Gibbons, Today, Politically Incorrect*, and *Geraldo*; he appeared on a news special with Tom Brokaw titled "Web of Hate" and was included on an MSNBC panel called "Race in America." In 2000, this author asked Matt Hale for his thoughts on how Ben Klassen might perceive his leadership if he were alive today:

> Well I think he would be pleased. Definitely, we have disappointed our critics immensely. They said that the Church of Creator was dead when Ben Klassen died. They're now eating their words. The World Church of Creator is stronger than ever. The religion is stronger than ever. We have more supporters than ever. And I think that Ben Klassen would be very proud. And I am very proud to lead and stand in his shoes today.[45]

Hale never met Klassen but once had the chance. In retrospect, he regrets that he missed the opportunity and did not realize that the situation was so pressing at that time in North Carolina, when the group began to unravel in the early 1990s.[46] Heeding the advice of his mentor, Hale claims to live a Spartan life, eschewing alcohol and drugs, and prefers raw natural foods—a diet consistent with Klassen's *Salubrious Living*.[47] For a brief period in 1997, Hale was married to Terra Herron, but they divorced after only three months of marriage. Their divorce occasioned a departure from the church of some members, including the Hasta Primus, Jonathan Viktor.[48]

Unabashedly identifying himself as a racist, Hale considers the epithet a "badge of honor." However, he adds that his organization is no more a hate group than are mainstream minority advocacy groups, such as the NAACP. Furthermore, he rejects the characterization of "white supremacist," arguing that he and his organization have no desire to reign over other races. Rather, they endeavor to establish a regime of racial separation.[49] Racism, Hale contends, is a natural part of the human condition.

Struggle inheres in nature, and in that sense, humans are no different from other species in the animal kingdom that must compete against their "natural enemies."[50] Multiculturalism, asserts Hale, invariably leads to racial strife and violence. The only way to avoid such a predicament, he counsels, is racial separation. However, he believes that America is too far gone and is already ineluctably on a course of racial cataclysm. In his estimation, the white middle and upper classes are "seeing the handwriting on the wall" and more and more are coming to realize that a multiethnic society is a "mistake."[51]

On several occasions, Hale found himself in trouble with the law. At age nineteen, he was found guilty of violating an open burning ordinance in East Peoria as a result of torching an Israeli flag at a demonstration. A year later, he distributed pamphlets in an East Peoria mall, for which he received a fine for littering. In May 1991, he was arrested for mob action after he and his brother allegedly threatened three blacks with a firearm. He was also charged with felony obstruction related to the incident for refusing to cooperate with police when they asked for information to help the authorities locate Hale's brother.[52] The mob action charge was later dropped. In 1992, Hale was charged with criminal trespass, resisting arrest, aggravated battery, and carrying a concealed weapon after allegedly attacking a security guard in a shopping mall. He received thirty months of intensive probation for the various charges stemming from the incident. And in 1998 he was once again arrested for littering after throwing pamphlets on lawns.[53] In light of his experiences, Hale saw the courtroom as an important venue for political activism, which may have influenced his decision to go to law school.

After graduating from college, Hale entered law school at Southern Illinois University at Carbondale and graduated on May 9, 1998. One of the principal factors that encouraged Hale to pursue a law degree was his desire to prepare himself for legal battles involving the racialist movement. Hale further advised racial activists who aspired to go to law school to keep a low profile and "stay out of trouble," "remain silent, work hard, and get the license." Hale believed that the courtroom would prove to be one of the most important battlefields for his movement:

> Make no mistake! It is in the courtroom where social change begins. Whether one is talking about the Dred Scott decision, school integration, or the "right to choose," courtroom battles have largely

shaped our society. The outcomes of these battles spell either good or evil for our people. In order that these battles may be shaped to our good, it is necessary that our side be represented in the court of law.[54]

The exact membership of the World Church of the Creator is difficult to estimate. During its height under Klassen's leadership, membership may have reached up to 3,000 with perhaps 100 ordained ministers.[55] A report released by the Center for New Community identified seventy-six chapters in twenty-five states and five foreign countries as of 2000. Estimates of the membership of the WCOTC vary considerably. Hale claimed that Benjamin Smith's shooting spree (which is covered in chapter 11) gave the organization tremendous publicity and by doing so greatly increased membership. By 2002, he claimed that membership had reached 70,000–80,000, but that figure was undoubtedly wildly inflated.[56] The Anti-Defamation League estimated that a more accurate figure was probably around 2,000.[57] Mark Potok of the Southern Poverty Law Center estimated that the group probably had no more than "200 hard core activists."[58] But as Carolyn Swain noted, membership numbers are not always the best guide for assessing the potential influence of a movement insofar as some groups avoid membership lists and place much recruitment effort on the Internet. Through that medium, one can become a true believer of the ideology without any formal organizational nexus.[59] At one time or another, the WCOTC sites representing chapters in Austria, Belgium, Ireland, Poland, Russia, and South Africa have operated on the World Wide Web.[60] By the early 2000s, Hale claimed that the northeastern United States was probably his strongest region for support.[61] According to the Southern Poverty Law Center, the real strength of the WCOTC was in the states of California, Florida, and Illinois.[62]

Although solid demographic data are hard to come by, anecdotal evidence suggests that members are overwhelmingly white males between the ages of twenty and thirty.[63] According to Hale, Creativity's radical program appeals to the rebelliousness of young whites, who often feel alienated by issues such as affirmative action and multiculturalism.[64] The nihilistic creed of Creativity proved a magnet for violent skinheads across the United States. Consequently, the movement became largely an urban-based phenomenon.[65] In fact, a WCOTC initiative dubbed "Operation Skinhead," sought to recruit white youths in the cities.[66]

The WCOTC appears to appeal to some disaffected youths. Hale observed that members of the working class comprise a disproportionately large share of the white racialist movement.[67] Yet, he added, the WCOTC attracted "a lot of people of higher financial status" as well. College students, Hale claimed, represented "the vanguard of [his] church" whom he recruited mainly through the Internet. Some of them were supposedly from the most elite private universities, including Princeton, Harvard, Yale, and Northwestern. WCOTC literature has appeared on bulletin boards at Harvard Square and at Northwestern University.[68] Hale claimed that it has been relatively easy to recruit college students at elite institutions and conjectured that they tend to be open-minded and thus more receptive to the Creativity message.

The membership composition of the WCOTC has drawn criticism in some quarters of the extreme right. Dr. William L. Pierce, the founder of the National Alliance, once stated at a National Alliance leadership conference that the WCOTC fulfilled a useful function in that it siphoned away the more dysfunctional activists from the National Alliance.[69] The WCOTC has been described as a "poor man's rival" to the National Alliance.[70] For his part, Hale maintains that he is more approachable and is thus able to reach out to some elements that might not make the grade in other extreme right organizations.[71] On that note, the WCOTC has made efforts to reach out to like-minded persons behind bars. In fact, the COTC even allowed prison inmates to be ordained as ministers in its church, and a Creativity Prison Ministries operated in California. Hale even assisted some inmates in preparing legal paperwork.[72] Despite the number of Creators with criminal histories, Hale once claimed that the WCOTC did not welcome people who were prone to criminality.[73] Besides prisoners, there have also been efforts to reach out to women, a demographic group that has traditionally been underrepresented in the American extreme right.

9
The WCOTC's Women's Frontier

Women are playing an increasingly prominent role in the white racialist movement. In fact, the movement has long been concerned with women, as they are seen as vital for the future of the race. In movement literature, women are often depicted as the weak link in that they are susceptible to miscegenation, thus threatening the long-term survival of the race. For many years, women tended to play supportive roles in the movement. Recently, however, women are encouraged in some quarters to fight alongside the men.[1]

Several COTC leaders, including Ben Klassen and Tommy Rydén, were concerned that the church was not attracting enough women.[2] To ameliorate this gender distortion, Lisa Turner founded the World Church of the Creator's Women Frontier in the late 1990s. What was needed, she counseled, were women, who could bring a "nurturing" and "loving" influence to the racialist cause. Turner, who lives near Sacramento, California, attended law school but did not complete her legal studies. Somewhat reclusive, she does not allow her picture to be taken, but once described herself as a petite, reddish-blonde-haired, blue-eyed woman of German and Swedish ethnic ancestry. While growing up in California, Turner recalled that she had her "racial awakening" when her neighborhood received a massive influx of illegal Mexican aliens. This experience quickly transformed her and her family's previously liberal views on race.[3] Like Hale, Turner believes that a race war is inevitable in the United States, although she would prefer that it not happen. In fact, she cites the violence perpetrated by nonwhites on whites as a form of low-level race war that has already begun.[4]

Through the Internet, Turner established contact with Hale, who encouraged her to take up a leadership role.[5] She once described him as a "magnetic person" who impressed her with his charisma and leadership ability. Prior to this encounter, she had loose affiliations with groups such as David Duke's National Association for the Advancement of White People (NAAWP) and Tom Metzger's White Aryan Resistance (WAR).

She did not formally join these organizations but read their newsletters and literature. *Mein Kampf*, in particular, left a lasting impression on her as it did on Hale. Turner was not interested in the Christian Identity movement, as she had a very negative critique of Christianity.[6] Once Hale introduced her to Creativity, she began reading the organization's primary books, including *Nature's Eternal Religion* and *The White Man's Bible*. She formally joined the WCOTC in March 1998.[7]

According to Turner, a leadership vacuum existed in the white racialist movement. Faced with its perilous predicament, Turner reasoned that the white race must enjoin all of its members—men, women, young, and old—to contribute their part to white racial survival. Indeed, it would be folly to think that the church "could win the battle with only 50% of the White population as active participants in the struggle!" Thus a "People's Revolution" was necessary to succeed. The Frontier conceded that men and women were not "equal" and not "alike." Nevertheless, women had vital roles to play in the struggle, including that of mother, leader, activist, supporter, and friend. After the revolution, women could go back to the more "natural rhythm of birth, family life, marriage, home, [and] hearth."[8] As Turner explained, she felt that it was counterproductive for white women to stand on the sidelines and not fight side by side with their male counterparts. By exclusively relying upon men, the movement was, in effect, trying to "run a race with one leg."[9]

According to Professor Kathleen Blee, by the late 1990s, women composed roughly 25 percent of the membership of white nationalist organizations. Furthermore, in her estimation, that proportion is growing, as she believes that they account for roughly 50 percent of all new recruits.[10] According to Turner, by 2000, her monthly newsletter, *The Women's Frontier*, had roughly 700 to 800 subscribers.[11] She claimed that her efforts have been very well received by men in the movement and approximated that roughly 80 percent of the subscribers to her e-mail list were men.[12] Most of the women affiliated with her organization, she estimated, fell within the eighteen- to twenty-five-year-old age group and came from a variety of professional backgrounds.[13] By 2000, there were six chapters of the Sisterhood of the WCOTC and four chapters of the Women's Frontier.[14]

Critical of mainstream activists, such as Betty Friedan and Gloria Steinem, Turner has sought to reorient feminism away from what she believes is an antiwhite orientation and decries the fact that women are conflated with other social "misfits" as part of a scheme to co-opt the former in a broad antiwhite coalition:

> The fact is—women have been "co-opted" by the corrupt Liberal Establishment in order to make a tenuous (and of course, politically advantageous) link between women and "people of color" (or gays, druggies, and any other creep they happen to want to include in "THE LIST"). The media has "elected" women to be the fellow members and "colleagues" of an unsavory group which usually feature law-breakers, homos, the "culturally diverse," bums, and ill, dysfunctional individuals from every walk of life....
>
> The connection between White women and these societal horrors is as spurious as the black/jew connection. It's a media invention designed to create links where there are none—to forge bonds where none, in reality, exist.... And, of course, the unspoken media "truth" buried within these human laundry lists is that all of us: bums and gays, illegal aliens, and dope-heads and ... WOMEN are united against the WHITE MALE as the ultimate oppressor who must be destroyed.
>
> What we must understand, as White women, is that we are being USED as pawns in a dirty game. The callous, game-playing jewish feminists like Gloria Steinem and Betty Friedan have been more than happy to see women lumped in with human garbage for the last 30 years....
>
> The only thing that you, as a White woman, are ever going to get from a deal like this is: USED—by a sophisticated, slick, minority-loving, White-hating machine. Then, you'll be dumped with a resounding thud on the side of the road when this crew has gotten their media mileage out of you.... Make no mistake: these media moguls do not "care" about women. Women's welfare and well-being is the last thing on their mind. If they truly cared, they'd be writing stories about the daily hell that White women deal with in their minority infested schools, jobs and on the street.
>
> ... White women are not losers, illegals, faggots, or scum. We are not professional victims. We are sick of being identified AS A GROUP with crud. Make it clear: We want it stopped! And we want it stopped NOW![15]

Turner's message to white women was that their solidarity belonged to their race and not any rarified notion of universal womanhood. She encouraged them to reject the feminist caricature of the white male oppressor.[16] For Turner, a woman's primary role is still that of mother and wife.[17] To further the latter role, on her Web site, Turner offered tips on how women can find good Aryan husbands. Nevertheless, she lauds various women who have demonstrated leadership. Her Women's Frontier Web site carried a "Women's Hall of Fame," which included such right-wing luminaries as Pauline Hanson of Australia, Pir Kjaersgaard of Denmark, Alessandra Mussolini of Italy, and Catherine Megret of France.[18] Further, she noted that Ben Klassen admired Queen Isabella of Spain for expelling Jews and Muslims from that country.[19] Defending Creativity, Turner also pointed out that the WCOTC allowed women to be ordained as ministers and lead local churches and chapters. Although the Pontifex Maximus position is reserved for a man, the Hasta Primus position is open to women.[20]

Insofar as the Women's Frontier sought to increase white fecundity, the organization strongly opposed abortion. Turner wrote, "The killing of a healthy white child through abortion is the ultimate sin against our race and against nature and any white woman who commits the crime of abortion is a race traitor of the highest order."[21] Abortion was permissible, however, in the event that a woman was impregnated by someone of a "mud race."[22] In opposing only white abortions, the WCOTC parted company with the mainstream conservative right wing. Sharing the view of Hitler's Third Reich, which bestowed upon child-bearing women the Honor Cross of the German Mother, Turner sees in motherhood a vitally important and noble role for white women.[23]

Closely related to the Women's Frontier was the WCOTC's Sisterhood. While the Women's Frontier purportedly concentrated more on direct racial activism (e.g., distributing WCOTC literature), the Sisterhood served primarily as an outlet for white women to express feelings of racial loyalty in a positive way, such as writing poetry and providing support for fellow sisters. The Sisterhood also had a Prisoner Support Group through which one member, Erica Chase, met Leo Felton, a biracial convict and fanatical white supremacist. Chase belonged to the WCOTC and Felton was a member of the White Order of Thule. The couple met when Chase corresponded with Felton while he was serving a sentence for attempting to murder a black taxi cab driver. After his release, the two were later arrested for allegedly planning to blow up Jewish and black targets in Boston, Massachusetts, in an effort to ignite a race war.[24] The couple was arrested after they were caught passing a counterfeit $20 bill at a doughnut shop in Boston. An off-duty police officer spotted the couple and apprehended them. The two were convicted on a variety of charges, including conspiring to make a bomb, conspiring to make counterfeit money, obstruction of justice, and firearms violation. Chase was sentenced to nearly five years in prison for her role in the plot, while Felton received a nearly twenty-two-year sentence.[25]

Despite the success of her ventures, differences eventually arose between Turner and the parent organization. In December 2001, Lisa Turner and Melody La Rue publicly left the WCOTC citing disagreements over its leadership. Together, Turner and La Rue ran the Sisterhood. The departure of La Rue and her husband Jason was said to have crippled the WCOTC in the Pacific Northwest.[26] The couple still runs a Creativity-related Web site called Hypatia Publishing.

Still other hardships would bedevil the organization, as the Reverend Hale and his church faced numerous battles both in and out of the courtroom. One conflict in particular over Hale's pursuit of a law license would set in motion a chain of events that would have far-reaching repercussions for the church.

10

The Controversy over a Law License

Shortly after graduating from Southern Illinois University's School of Law at Carbondale, Hale passed the bar exam on his first attempt in July of 1998. Typically, once an applicant has passed the exam, the certification process is pro forma. When Hale first applied to the Illinois bar, his application was reviewed by a single member of the state bar's Committee on Character and Fitness of the Third Judicial District, Gregory K. McClintock, associate judge of the Ninth Circuit. McClintock decided not to recommend Hale's application to the Board of Admissions and the Committee on Character and Fitness. He based his decision on the grounds that Hale's character rendered him unfit to practice law due to his unconventional political beliefs and thus he should not be granted a law license.

Pursuant to the rules of procedure, Hale's application was then forwarded to a three-person inquiry panel composed of McClintock and attorneys Stuart R. Lefstein and Lawrence W. Baxter. On November 25, 1998, the inquiry panel interviewed Hale at which time he did not attempt to conceal his racist views; in fact, when questioned about his moral character, he remarked that "his frank and open admission of the advocacy of racism show[ed] greater moral character than do lawyers and others who [were] in fact racist but who utter[ed] such thoughts only in privacy." When asked if he could obey a ruling prohibiting discriminatory treatment of litigants, lawyers, witnesses, jurors, and others based on race, sex, religion, or national origin, Hale answered that he would follow such rules and laws until such time that they could be changed by peaceful means.[1] He reaffirmed previous statements that he would uphold both the U.S. Constitution and the Illinois State Constitution.[2] Relevant to this case, in a previous decision, the U.S. Supreme Court ruled that states could not penalize applicants solely on grounds that they might espouse illegal aims.[3]

On December 16, 1998, the inquiry panel denied Hale certification, with McClintock and Lefstein voting against him. Baxter, a lawyer, who practices in Ottawa, Illinois, voted to grant Hale a license based on his belief that Hale could "hold racist views and practice law in accordance with his oath as attorney." The majority felt otherwise, and although they conceded that Hale had not yet threatened to exterminate anyone, writing for the majority, Judge McClintock argued that history suggested that extermination is not far behind when governmental power is held by persons who hold such racial views.[4]

After the inquiry panel handed down its decision, the Illinois State Bar Committee created a five-member hearing panel to determine whether Hale should be certified to practice law. Gordon L. Lustfeldt, a judge from the Twenty-first Judicial Circuit, chaired the panel. The other panel members included Associate Judge Thomas Dunn of the Twelfth Judicial Circuit; Judge Clark Erickson of the Twenty-first Judicial Circuit; Charles Marshall, a retired judge of the Thirteenth Judicial District; and L. Lee Perrington, the sole practitioner.[5] On April 10, 1999, this panel held a five-hour hearing at which numerous witnesses testified about Hale's character. Several witnesses stated that despite Hale's racist beliefs, he nonetheless possessed the requisite character and fitness to practice law.[6] For example, Brian McPheeters, a respected Illinois lawyer who had once employed Hale, testified that he had worked courteously with minority co-workers and clients, his racist beliefs notwithstanding. McPheeters believed that Hale was able to adequately separate his personal convictions from his professional responsibilities. In fact, while he was a legal intern at McPheeters's office, Hale worked with a secretary who was married to an African American with whom she shared a biracial child. According to McPheeters, Hale treated her in a courteous and professional manner.[7] When questioned about the church and the appropriateness of violence, WCOTC member Benjamin Smith replied that he had considered violence at one time, "but Reverend Hale had talked him out of it."[8]

In a unanimous decision, on June 30, 1999, the hearing panel announced that Hale lacked the requisite moral character to possess a law license. The panel reasoned that his belief in private sector discrimination was inconsistent with the letter and spirit of the state bar's rules of professional conduct. The panel cited Hale's racist beliefs as evidence that he would not be able to adequately serve the court. Conceivably, he would not be able to fairly represent minority clients. Moreover, the committee concluded that Hale was not sufficiently open with the panel during the hearing.⁹ The members pointed out that Hale failed to mention on his bar application previous convictions for some minor crimes, including the violation of an ordinance that prohibited the distribution of hand bills. Although these incidents stemmed from his advocacy of white supremacy activities and may have been constitutionally protected, he was still required to disclose them in his bar application and their omission was significant.[10]

More seriously, the panel cited another incident in which Hale, along with his brother, was carrying placards and chanting racist slogans near the University of Peoria; later they were threatened in their car by a group of African Americans. Hale's brother used a handgun to threaten the blacks and then fled the scene. When Matt Hale was apprehended by the police, he refused to cooperate and instead lied about the event which, in the estimation of the panel, cast doubt on his truthfulness. For this offense, he was convicted of felony obstruction of justice, but the conviction was later overturned by the Illinois Supreme Court on Miranda grounds.[11] In 1992, he was arrested again, this time for assault and battery on a mall security guard after he allegedly pushed and threatened to punch the guard during an argument over Hale's beliefs. The charges were later dropped. Still, more troubles followed. Shortly after that incident, Hale was nearly placed on academic probation at Bradley University after calling a fellow student a "Jew Boy." Finally, he was given a citation for littering after he threw Creator materials from his car. Despite these brushes with the law, the only crime for which he was convicted (and the conviction was upheld on appeal) was the public ordinance violation for littering, and Hale could arguably claim First Amendment protection for that. In fact, every instance of misconduct cited by the inquiry panel fell into the category of political speech.[12] Previous Supreme Court rulings—for example, *Chaplinsky v. New Hampshire* (1942)—have held that offensive speech could not be penalized consistent with the current interpretation of the First Amendment.[13]

Still other evidence cited by the hearing panel was a letter that Hale had written in 1995 and which was published in the *Peoria Star Journal*. In it, Hale responded to statements that a woman had made with respect to her support of affirmative action. Hale took issue with her position and chastised her for clinging "to the misbegotten equality myth." Further he asked, "Is it going to take your rape at the hands of a nigger beast or your murder before you become aware of the problem? . . . I'm looking forward to the day when our people's eyes are opened and when people who believe in the equality myth no longer have any power to promote this garbage to others." Offended by the vitriol of his writing, the panel surmised that the statement demonstrated a "monumental lack of judgment" on the part of Hale. The opinion of the majority concluded that it could not "certify as having good moral character and fitness to practice law a person who has dedicated his life to inciting racial hatred."[14]

The decision divided legal scholars, some of whom interpreted the precedent to mean that state bars could deny a law license to an applicant solely because that person held repugnant views. Such a basis, they argued, was insufficient for withholding a license. Moreover, by denying Hale's application on the grounds that he might likely commit misconduct if admitted to the bar, the fitness committee implied that the state bar would not fulfill its duty to police misconduct.[15] Others argued that Hale's personal views were diametrically opposed to the professional standards established by the Illinois State Bar Association and, as such, were sufficient reason to deny him a license.[16]

Other scholars asserted that the Illinois Bar's decision was a flagrant violation of rules of law established by U.S. Supreme Court jurisprudence. As the high court ruled in the *Baird v. Board of Bar Examiners* (1971) decision: "It is sufficient to say we hold that views and beliefs are immune from bar association inquisitions designed to lay a foundation barring an applicant from the practice of law."[17] Furthermore, some scholars interpreted the decision as a violation of Hale's First Amendment rights of free speech and association. Previously, in a similar case—*Law Students Research Council v. Wadmond* (1971)—the U.S. Supreme Court had ruled that an applicant could be denied admission to the bar for advocating the overthrow of the U.S. government, but only if such advocacy was coupled with the specific intent to achieve that end.[18] Critics argued that the Illinois Bar's decision went too far in equating the repugnance of Hale's political beliefs with a lack of moral character. The former amounted to political speech and would thus be protected by the First Amendment.[19]

The fitness committee's decision was highly controversial insofar as Hale, the petitioner, had not engaged in any specific conduct that would have violated the disciplinary rules of the state bar. Some legal observers feared that the case presented a slippery slope and conceivably, once the standard was set, lawyers could be disbarred for controversial and/

or offensive speech.[20] According to one standard, for immoral behavior to become relevant to bar authorities, there must be a nexus between the immoral behavior and the practice of law. For instance, adultery, although immoral, would not disqualify a candidate from bar admission because such behavior would not adversely affect his fitness to practice law.[21]

Defenders of the bar's decision pointed out that Hale's racist ideology sought to overturn the Fourteenth Amendment's equal protection clause. Although Hale maintained that his movement would endeavor to bring about such goals in a lawful manner, he also made clear that his Creativity ideology put race above other affiliations, including the Constitution and even America.[22] Moreover, racist beliefs, some legal scholars argued, could undermine a lawyer's ability to practice law. For example, a white racist might not provide competent representation to a nonwhite client. Furthermore, an attorney who is an avowed racist could have a detrimental effect on the public image of the profession. Minority members of the population, in particular, could perceive the justice system as less than fair. Applying this standard to law enforcement, it was argued that the racist views of Mark Fuhrman, a detective and key witness in the murder trial of O. J. Simpson, arguably contributed to Simpson's acquittal despite the very strong circumstantial evidence implicating the defendant. Finally, once a lawyer receives a law license, he or she becomes an officer of the court. Possibly, such a person could aspire to become a prosecutor. Prosecutors often have broad discretion in deciding which cases to bring to trial. Thus a prosecutor harboring racist inclinations might exercise race-based discretion in the charging function, plea bargaining process, and sentencing recommendations.[23]

Still other legal scholars argued that lawyers should be given broad First Amendment discretion so they would be free to represent "unpopular clients, dissenters, and those who oppose powerful state and private institutions." Consequently, the Hale precedent could potentially be used to prohibit other prospective lawyers, who are members of marginalized groups, from obtaining law licenses.[24] Although applicants to the bar are not required to disclose mere membership in "subversive" organizations, they are required to reveal whether they belong to a group that advocates the overthrow of the government by force and whether they share that specific intent.[25] Although Hale might be controversial, his pronouncements arguably fall in the realm of "pure speech" and not illicit conduct;

as such, they warrant First Amendment protection. By denying him a license, the Illinois bar risked establishing a principle that an applicant could be denied admission for espousing viewpoints that are at odds with the mores of the time. Could this standard then be applied, for example, to those who believe that the death penalty is unconstitutional, that sodomy statutes are immoral, or that the decision in *Roe v. Wade* is incorrect? As W. Bradley Wendel persuasively argued, "lawyers are sometimes the voices of the powerless, and . . . these voices may not always be pleasant to hear."[26] Furthermore, some legal scholars took issue with the inquiry panel's speculation that Hale's beliefs might incline him to future misconduct. As the U.S. Supreme Court ruled in the *Bond v. Floyd* (1966) decision, the attempt to prognosticate future bad acts from previous advocacy and punish a public official based on such a prediction did not pass constitutional muster.[27] The American Civil Liberties Union (ACLU) of Illinois invoked that precedent when it filed an amicus curiae brief with the Illinois Supreme Court on Hale's behalf.[28]

The extreme right has played an important part in the development of free speech law in the United States.[29] This country is exceptional in comparison to other Western democratic governments in allowing right-wing extremists such a great degree of latitude to express their views. Over the past few decades, many democratic states have taken measures to restrict the speech and activities of the far right by creating laws against group defamation, incitement to violence, and propagation of false history, all of which have often been labeled "hate speech." What is surprising from an American perspective is the ease with which these laws have been enacted, as their supporters experienced very little opposition.

The American model of free speech was most poignantly expressed by Justice Oliver Wendell Holmes's "market place of ideas" metaphor. The argument goes that people should have unfettered access to a variety of ideas, even those that are very unpopular. Open debate inclusive of all views will determine which ideas have merit. This argument assumes that government should be neutral to all ideas and only ensure a level playing field, or to use the economics metaphor, a nonmonopolistic, perfectly competitive marketplace of ideas. Any government sanction of speech, even if unpopular, runs the risk of a slide down a slippery slope in which more and more abridgments of expression could be made.

Critics of the American model occasionally cite the example of Weimar Germany as paradigmatic of what can happen if there are no prohibitions against certain forms of speech—especially speech that denigrates and scapegoats minorities.[30] The fledging National Socialist German Workers Party (NSDAP) had several organs to propagate its views including the *Völkish Beobachter*, and Julius Streicher's *Der Stürmer*. The NSDAP eventually won a plurality in the Reichstag, and the aging Reich president Hindenburg appointed Adolf Hitler as chancellor. All of this was achieved by legal means. This experience may well have influenced the limits of free speech protection in many of the post-Holocaust constitutions, including Canada's and those of many countries in Europe.

The First Amendment scholar Samuel Walker argued that the strong tradition of free speech in America came about from a series of choices and was not predetermined by the original Constitution. What he sees as determinative in shaping free speech law is the influence of advocacy groups. In his view, free speech has triumphed in large part because it has had an effective advocate. Conversely, as he sees it, there has never been a strong advocate for restricting free speech. Hence, the free speech battle has been "terribly one-sided."[31] Walker points out that several of the Jewish defense organizations including the American Jewish Congress and the National Jewish Community Relations Advisory Council have usually pursued a strategy of education and "quarantine" to deal with right-wing extremists.[32] What's more, these organizations made common cause on the free speech issue with both libertarian and civil rights groups. The major civil rights groups abandoned the idea of restrictive speech laws, such as group libel, because they believed such laws could pose a threat to their efforts to attain equal rights. They calculated that their principal strategy for advancing group rights could best be achieved through the expansion of constitutionally protected individual rights.[33] As Walker points out, "provocative speech was a crucial weapon for the civil rights movement and the struggle for racial equality."[34]

According to Hale, the hearing panel based their decision on part on information received from the Southern Poverty Law Center and Hatewatch Web sites.[35] In a rare meeting of the minds, the Anti-Defamation League (ADL) originally came out in favor of granting Hale a law license and issued a press release that criticized the panel's decision.[36] The story took another strange twist when Alan Dershowitz, a high-profile attorney and outspoken member of the Jewish American community, represented Hale for a short time. Dershowitz expressed concern over such a precedent. Consistent with the pragmatism of the Creativity doctrine, Hale saw no compromise of his principles in his choice of counsel:

> As far as whether or not my dealings with him were in some ways contradictory to our message, I don't think so. We Creators have always realized that the end justifies the means and whatever tool we have to use in order to accomplish the particular goal at hand, well, why not use it? It's kind of like this. If you hand a slingshot or Uzi gun to someone, which should he choose? It is true that one comes from the Jews and one came from white people probably thousands, and thousands, and thousands of years ago. But which is more effective? You have to use the tool that is most effective at that time.[37]

Although Dershowitz deplored Hale's philosophy, he nevertheless feared that refusing to grant him a law license set a dangerous precedent:

> I always said, if he were struck by lightning, I would shed no tears. But he wasn't struck by lightning, he was struck by a character committee. To me it was always the principle of whether or not we want to resurrect character committees, which were started in Pennsylvania explicitly to keep Jews out of the bar. My fear was that if he was kept out of the bar, members of the Jewish Defense League, or radical black activists, or radical feminists could be kept out of the bar too on the basis of ideology.[38]

Dershowitz said that he would donate all the fees he earned from the case to antiracist groups.[39]

The controversy over Hale's law license would go on for a few more years and will be discussed further in chapter 12. One of Hale's most trusted followers was so enraged by the Illinois Bar's decision that he embarked on a murderous shooting spree that brought unprecedented attention and notoriety to the WCOTC.

11

Benjamin Smith

The tone of Creativity's literature has most probably contributed to the sporadic violence perpetrated by some of the organization's members. The vehement rhetoric of Creativity notwithstanding, Klassen emphasized that a violent revolution was not really necessary to redeem the white man. Rather, all that was needed was to "straighten out" the white man's befuddled thinking. Once, this was achieved—through the distribution of 10 million copies of *Nature's Eternal Religion*—Klassen believed that the battle would basically be won. As he often reminded his readers, "Organized, informed and aroused, the White Race is ten times more powerful than all its enemies combined."[1] Be that as it may, he left open the possibility that physical violence may be necessary at some juncture in the future.

> Now we come to the crux of our position. Should the Jewish government use force to violate our Constitutional rights to freely practice our religion; to peacefully assemble; to peacefully organize; to distribute our White Man's Bible; to use the mails and any other prerogative in promoting and expanding our legal religious organization and the full practice of our religion, then we have every right to declare them as open criminals violating the Constitution and the highest law of the land. They then obviously are the criminals, and we can treat them like the criminal dogs they are and take the law into our own hands. This is the obvious, logical thing to do. We must then meet force with force and open warfare exists. It will then be open season on the Jews.[2]

As Jeffrey Kaplan observed, the violent fringes of the extreme right "no longer make the distinction between the government, the dominant culture, and the 'other.' They have effectively become inextricably interconnected, and thus to strike at one is to strike at them all."[3] Over the years, several members and former members of the church have been involved in random violence against Jews and nonwhites. The case of George Loeb was documented earlier. Still more incidents followed.

A reputed member, Joshua Mark Gilmore, was accused of attempting two racially motivated murders in California. A resident of Fair Oaks, he supposedly carried out the crimes to benefit a local chapter of the WCOTC. Gilmore was convicted of the July 3, 1997, beating of Jeff Almon, whom Gilmore and others had mistaken as a member of an antiracist skinhead gang. The sixteen-year-old Almon lay in a coma for five days after the beating. Gilmore was also convicted for his part in a mob attack of Andrew Harris. Ten men, including Gilmore, swarmed Harris whom they had mistaken as a member of an antiracist rival skinhead group. Convicted under a special enhancement used for street gangs, Gilmore received two life sentences.[4]

In August 1997, members of the WCOTC allegedly assaulted an African American and his son after they left a rock concert in Sunrise, Florida. In April 1998, the WCOTC Florida state director Jules Fettu and fellow members Donald Hansard and Raymond Leone were arrested and charged with the attack.[5] They were also charged as a result of another incident, which included two other members, Angela King and Dawn Witherspoon. The four were indicted on a hate crime conspiracy charge for the March 29, 1998, armed robbery and assault of the owner of an adult video store in Hollywood, Florida. They allegedly planned on donating a portion of the proceeds to the national headquarters of WCOTC. All of the defendants pleaded guilty. Witherspoon received a thirteen-month prison sentence, Hansard received a four-and-a-half year sentence, King received a six-year sentence, and Leone received a sentence of more than eight years.[6] Another member and leader of the White Berets security legion, Guy Lombardi, pleaded guilty to charges that he attempted to intimidate a witness in the case.[7] He spent four months in jail for the offense and was then released and placed under house arrest. As a result of the prosecutions, the WCOTC in Florida began to disintegrate. Lombardi renounced his ties to the group but later returned. The handful of remaining members bickered among themselves, with some of them leaving to join other white power organizations.[8]

In the summer of 1999, two brothers, Benjamin Matthew and James Tyler Williams, heightened fears in California. They were accused of the double murder of a gay couple—Gary Matson and Winfield Scott Mowder. The bodies of Matson and Mowder, who were murdered in a grisly fashion, were found with multiple gunshot wounds on their platform bed in their Redding home. As part of a nationwide probe, the FBI sought to determine whether these murders were connected to a larger conspiracy involving the WCOTC and other extremist groups.[9] The two brothers were also accused of arson in connection with fires at three Sacramento-area synagogues that caused an estimated $3 million in damages. Not long after they purchased ammunition loaders with a credit card belonging to one of the victims in the Redding murder, the two suspects were arrested. Authorities suspected that there might be a link between the arson incidents and the WCOTC as the organization's literature was distributed in the area around the synagogues.[10] When investigators went through the suspects' personal effects, they discovered ammunition, WCOTC literature, and a notebook that contained a list of thirty-two Sacramento-area Jewish and civil leaders.[11]

Seemingly ordinary, the two brothers had grown up in a religiously devout family; they operated a landscaping and lawn service out of their parents' home in Palo Cedro, California. Mathew was supposedly the leader of the two and convinced his younger brother to go along with his plans. Described as a searcher, Matthew drifted from one fad to the next. Prior to the incidents related above, the Williams brothers had no criminal records. In the courtroom, Matthew's remarks suggested that he was a follower of Christian Identity. He invoked the term "Yahweh" and described himself of "Brittanic-Nordic" racial extraction.[12] While in jail, Benjamin committed suicide after which James pleaded guilty to the murders.[13]

Benjamin Smith

The most notable instance of violence occurred during the weekend of July 4, 1999, when Benjamin Smith, a former member of the WCOTC who had recently resigned from the organization, embarked on a shooting spree in Illinois and Indiana that left two dead and nine injured.[14] Smith was born on March 22, 1978, to an affluent family and raised in a posh neighborhood in suburban Wilmette. The eldest of three sons, he seemed to have an ordinary upbringing. His father, Kenneth Smith, was a physician in internal medicine at Northwestern Memorial Hospital; he left that position in 1996 to sell real estate. His mother, Beverly, was a lawyer and real estate agent as well. At one time, she was a member of the Wilmette Board of Trustees. He did not grow up in a particularly religious household, as his family had never been churchgoers. His father, an agnostic, however, later converted to Christianity.[15] The curious Ben launched his own search for God, and for a brief period of time, declared himself a Muslim.[16] According to Smith's account, he became "racially aware" in the eighth grade after he was forced to learn about the Holocaust in school. His racialism further crystallized during the 1992 riot in Los Angeles. To the young Smith, the event presaged a larger race war on the horizon.[17]

As a teenager, Smith attended the New Trier High School, a wealthy and highly competitive public institution. His principal described him as an unremarkable student with average grades and no disciplinary problems. While in high school, Smith did not openly exhibit racist tendencies. In fact, for a while, he had a Korean girlfriend and his best friend, Scott Durbin, was a Jew. His former Korean girlfriend told interviewers that there was nothing in his previous history to indicate that he would become racist and anti-Semitic, let alone set out on a murderous rampage.[18] Although quiet, he seemed like a normal adolescent. Nevertheless, he began showing something of a rebellious streak by his senior year in high school. In his school yearbook, his entry carried the slogan *"Sic semper tyrannis*—or Thus is always [the end] of tyrants," the same words that John Wilkes Booth shouted after shooting Abraham Lincoln and that were printed on the T-shirt that Timothy McVeigh wore on April 19, 1995.[19] A slightly built man, six feet tall and weighing 135 pounds, Smith had the message "Sabbath Breaker" tattooed on his chest.[20]

In the autumn of 1996, Smith began attending the University of Illinois in Champaign-Urbana. In an interview he gave the previous year, Smith said that he felt uncomfortable around so many foreign students and professors. As a result, he started to read neo-Nazi literature and founded an organization called the Odin Saves Ministry.[21] He began immersing himself in the netherworld of the white racialist movement, spending hours visiting related Web sites and reading books, such as William Pierce's *The Turner Diaries* and Hitler's *Mein Kampf*.[22] Nevertheless, he actually joined a left-leaning group called the Student Environmental Action Coalition. However, Smith seemed more concerned with rightist grievances, such as the incidents at Ruby Ridge and Waco. He later dropped out of the student group saying that he "couldn't trust those people." His days at the university were stormy and his racist views were well known to his fellow students. Increasingly, his behavior became impulsive and brash. In one incident while he was standing in a cafeteria line with his girlfriend Elizabeth Sahr, a male student insulted her for being overweight. Enraged by the slight to his girlfriend, Smith grabbed a plate and smashed it over the offensive man's head.[23] In October 1997, he was accused of beating Sahr in his dorm room after seeing her with another man.[24]

While in college, he had numerous brushes with the law. University officials once disciplined him for putting up racist posters in his dormitory.[25] In another incident, he allegedly peeped in dorm windows and carried unspecified weapons.[26] When the police responded, they spotted Smith running and arrested him. Smith produced a false identification with the name Erwin Rommel—the name of the famed German Field Marshal who commanded the Afrika Korps. When Smith failed to appear for his court date in October of 1996, the judge issued a warrant for the arrest of Erwin Rommel.[27] More complaints would follow. Because of his notoriety, university authorities searched his room and discovered a large knife and marijuana. Reporting this matter to the police, authorities decided to throw the book at Smith, but his father hired an attorney to work out a deal in which Smith would avoid prosecution in exchange for leaving the university with a promise never to return.[28]

Soon afterward, Smith moved to Bloomington, and, in the fall of 1998, he enrolled in Indiana University where he rented a room in an apartment in a predominantly African American housing complex across from Hoosier Stadium.[29] Almost immediately, he set about creating another racialist organization on campus, the White Nationalist Party of Indiana University. While on campus, he was not shy about espousing his racial views.[30] His activities gained him notoriety and the student newspaper carried an article on him. Originally, a computer science major, he switched to criminal justice hoping to pursue a legal career like his mentor Matt Hale. As time went by, he became increasingly estranged from earlier acquaintances to whom he referred as "race traitors."[31]

Smith first became acquainted with Hale in the spring of 1998 when he noticed a WCOTC flyer tucked under the wiper blade of his car. Shortly thereafter, Hale received an e-mail from Smith, who was curious about the WCOTC. Hale arranged to meet with Smith at a Bob Evans restaurant in Champaign, Illinois. They quickly established a good rapport, as they both agreed on ideology and opposition to Christianity. At the meeting, Hale handed Smith a copy of the Creator pamphlet "Facts that the Government and Media Don't Want You to Know." Impressed with the pamphlet, Smith purchased 5,000 copies with his own money ($5,000) for distribution.[32] After the meeting, Smith decided to devote himself to Hale's group.[33]

Interviews with Smith's former associates reveal a man who increasingly came under the ideological sway of Matt Hale.[34] In the January 1999 issue of *The Struggle*, Hale even designated Smith "Creator of the Year" for 1998 for his efforts in bringing new recruits into the church and distributing literature. Moreover, he commended Smith for bringing more media attention to the church than any other member.[35] Identifying more and more with the Creativity creed, Smith assumed the name "August" presumably out of respect for the Roman Emperor Augustus Caesar, who, in Smith's words, "brought *Pax Romana* to his people."[36] Gaining more local recognition, Smith was featured in an article titled "To Be Young, White and Racist" in the *Bloomington Independent* on August 28, 1998, in which he declared his intention to establish a WCOTC chapter on the campus of Indiana University.[37] As he continued to distribute WCOTC fliers and pamphlets in the area, some local residents were annoyed by his activities. Consequently, on November 10, 1998, 500 Bloomington residents staged a rally against hate. Becoming even more audacious, Smith publicly debated John Fernandez, the mayor of Bloomington, who characterized the WCOTC as a violent and criminal organization and revealed that he had contacted the FBI for help. Increasingly, Smith's behavior isolated him from conventional society. He lost friends, and family members stopped talking to him. Because of his public notoriety, he was the object of death threats and harassment from the antiracist Skinheads against Racial Prejudice and other assorted groups and individuals. His ostracism, though, only seemed to deepen his commitment to Hale and Creativity.[38] In the March 1999 issue of *The Struggle* Smith proclaimed, "Whether people love me or hate me, I will be a Creator regardless."[39]

On April 30, 1999, Smith met with an old acquaintance, Christine Weiss, and together they drove to Smith's old home town of Wilmette, where they distributed racist literature in residents' doors and yards. The police arrested them for littering and Smith was charged with driving under the influence of alcohol as well. During their confinement in separate holding cells in the Wilmette police station, the two carried on a very loud conversation, the vehemence of which caused the arresting officer to go beyond normal procedure. As a result, he took several photographs of Smith, Weiss, and the blue Ford Taurus that Smith drove during the incident. These photos were later used by police in identifying Smith during his rampage in July of that year.[40] Just prior to his literature blitz in Wilmette, Smith had withdrawn $6,795 from the Harris Bank in that town, presumably to pay for the literature. On May 17, 1999, he withdrew another $10,275.[41]

Not long after the incident, Smith dropped out of college and moved into a small apartment in Morton, Illinois, with Weiss, who had recently left her husband.[42] She did not stay long with Smith, however, and moved out at the end of May. Nevertheless, she joined him at the Cook County Circuit Court House in Skokie, Illinois, to face littering charges stemming from their literature distribution in Wilmette. In court, Smith invoked the First Amendment and received a continuance to prepare for his defense.[43] Ominously, around this same time, in a conversation on racial issues with an old acquaintance, Patrick Langballe, Smith commented that "the shooting [would] begin in Rogers Park."[44] Still, at this time, Smith followed a nonviolent course of racial activism and recommended this position to his fellow Creators in an article he wrote for *The Struggle*:

> At this stage, it is important to remember that we are fighting the Propaganda War. A few dead jigs in the street will not save our people. The muds can breed faster than individuals acting alone can kill them. Our main priority is straightening out White people's thinking. Once we do that, the Jews and the muds will not even be an issue. So, remember that legal street actions are the only offense we need right now. We cannot allow the media to portray us as violent and/or murderers.[45]

When Smith heard that Hale's first bid for a law license was rejected, he supposedly asked him if it "was time to start RAHOWA?" Hale replied that he planned on making the affair a "national spectacle" but insisted that violence was not appropriate at that particular time.[46] In a conversation with Smith, Hale once explained, "we can accomplish a lot more peacefully, you know, straddling the system, one foot on the inside, one foot on the outside. . . . We're legal. We're peaceful. We're non-violent but we, you know, try to undermine the system every chance we can, you know."[47]

On Friday, July 2, not long after Hale had discovered that his application to the bar had once again been rejected, Smith began his rampage. At dusk, he shot at a group of Jews congregating outside a synagogue in Rogers Park, Illinois, and injured six in the process. Next, he traveled north in his light blue Ford Taurus to Skokie, Illinois, where he fired shots into the back of Ricky Byrdsong, an African American who once coached basketball at Northwestern University. Byrdsong had recently begun a new career as vice president of community affairs at Aon Corporation—the world's second largest insurance holding company. Actively involved in his community, he operated a program for youths called "Not-Just-Basketball" camps.[48] At about 1:00 a.m. the next morning, Byrdsong succumbed to his injuries.

Next, Smith drove downstate to Springfield where he shot at two black men, but missed. While in Decatur, he wounded a black pastor, the Reverend Stephen Anderson, and an Asian-American university student, Steven Kuo. He then made his way to Bloomington, Indiana, where he fatally shot Won-Joon Yoon, a 26-year-old Korean doctoral student who was studying music at Indiana University. All of those killed or wounded in the spree were Orthodox Jews, African Americans, or Asians.[49]

Exactly one year earlier to the day, Smith had been arrested for distributing WCOTC flyers in Bloomington. Not long after the first reports of Smith's shooting spree came in, NORTAF (North Regional Major Crimes Task Force)—a consortium of north suburban communities—and the Chicago police began putting together a profile of the perpetrator. Upon hearing the description, the Wilmette police officer who had photographed Smith and Weiss after their arrest on April 30 retrieved the photos and noticed that they matched the description of the driver and the car. Thus by 2:00 a.m. on Saturday morning, the police had a good idea that they were searching for Smith. Moreover, using the previous arrest information, the police also knew the license number of the blue Ford Taurus.[50]

Finally, a police chase caught up with Smith on an Illinois highway, but he refused to be taken alive. According to the police version of events, officers Todd Garten and David Hiltibidal stopped Smith driving a van north on Highway 37 toward Salem around 9:30 p.m. Earlier, Smith had stolen the van from a woman and her child at gunpoint at a gas station in the small town of Ina, Illinois, about forty miles from where he was finally stopped.⁵¹ With their guns drawn, the officers approached the van and shouted for Smith to raise his hands. At this point, Smith's neck was covered with blood, the result of a gunshot to his chin, presumably self-inflicted at the time the van ran off the highway. When Smith did not comply with their orders, Officer Hiltibidal entered the van through the passenger door, at which point Smith reached for a duffel bag on the floor by the passenger seat. The officer shoved Smith into a space between the two seats. As they struggled, two muffled gun shots could be heard from a small caliber weapon. It was later ascertained that Smith had fired two more self-inflicted shots: one to his right thigh and one to his chest. The officer claimed that he did not see the weapon during the struggle. Smith was rushed to a Salem hospital where emergency room doctors worked for forty minutes to save him, but he died due to massive bleeding. Hiltibidal, whose face bore scratches from his struggle with Smith, said the man put up strong resistance. In a subsequent interview, Hale cast doubt on the police account, noting that it was "kind of strange to shoot one's self three times to commit suicide." He speculated that the police might have killed him.⁵²

Just days after the shootings, federal agents arrested Donald Fiessinger, a former elementary school janitor and an unlicensed gun dealer in Peoria, who had allegedly sold Smith the weapons he used, including a .22 caliber pistol and a .380 semiautomatic.⁵³ Prior to the sale to Smith, the Bureau of Alcohol, Tobacco, and Firearms had been investigating Fiessinger for possible firearms violations.⁵⁴

Evidence suggests that Smith may have planned his rampage for some time before it occurred. On June 27, 1999, he visited John McLaughlin in Cerro Gordo, near Decatur. McLaughlin, who testified on behalf of Hale at his law license hearing, had been convicted in 1995 of amassing weapons for an impending race war.⁵⁵ Just a few days after the incident, Hale showed reporters a registered letter he received the day the spree began, in which Smith formally resigned from the organization.⁵⁶ Before embarking on his mission, Smith entered the Wilmette post office and purchased a certified letter card on the back of which he wrote:

> Although I have not been a member of the World Church of the Creator since April 1999, due to my past public support of that legal religious organization run by Matt Hale, I find it necessary to

formerly [sic] break with the World Church of the Creator because I am unable and unwilling to follow a legal Revolution of Values—Benjamin N. Smith.[57]

Viewed in retrospect, the letter appears as an attempt to absolve the church from any civil liability it might have incurred from Smith's actions. According to the Simon Wiesenthal Center, Hale had significant contact with Smith in the weeks leading up to the shooting spree; he spoke on the phone with Smith for more than thirteen hours in the three weeks prior to the attacks, and some authorities believe that Smith immediately packed his bags, loaded his guns, and commenced his spree just after ending his final phone conversation with Hale.[58] The two met for the last time on June 28, 1999, at the same Bob Evans restaurant where they had met for the first time. That same evening, they went to a storage locker that the WCOTC rented. Smith paid Hale $150 for 3,000 copies of the *Facts* pamphlet stored in the locker and loaded them into his Taurus. According to phone records, on June 30, the two talked for thirty minutes.[59]

Near the end of Smith's life, some of his associates described him as an angry man. His ex-girlfriend did not seem surprised at Smith's actions when she first heard of them and commented, "He wanted to make a name for himself, to show people that this could be done if you wanted to do it." Further she added, "This is Independence Day from the government, from everything. He's not going to give up until he leaves this world."[60]

Despite his contempt for nonwhites, Hale has consistently favored a nonviolent approach on practical grounds. As he once explained, even if "someone goes out and kills ten blacks" there [would still be] millions more.[61] Although he had no moral problem with violence, tactically, he believed that it was counterproductive as it "arouse[d] sympathy in the masses against our cause."[62] At first, Hale commented after the spree that it was "a sad day for a lot of people" and that it "wasn't the correct way to promote our cause." Further, he stated, "If I had any inkling of this I would have, of course, taken him and said, 'Ben, brother, this isn't the way. We need you free, we need you alive, we need you amongst the public to pass the word, to spread the message of truly the greatest idea the world has ever known, and that is our religion, [C]reativity.'"[63]

As the national media focused attention on Hale, he was always prepared to offer an acerbic sound bite. Looking back on the episode, he once commented, "I wish [Smith] hadn't done it in a sense . . . but he made us a household name. That's why I'll always remember him, respect him and appreciate him."[64] Reflecting on all of the attention in the aftermath of the tragedy, church membership was reported to have increased from 200 to 300 members. Furthermore, Hale refused to condemn the actions of Smith and went so far as to characterize him as a "martyr of free speech."[65] He eulogized him as a well-meaning racialist, who "snapped" when apprised of the Illinois Bar's decision not to grant Hale a law license. Hale conjectured that his failure to be granted a law license had so angered Smith that it set him on his destructive course. After the Smith affair, Hale issued a press statement warning of potential violence if the Illinois Supreme Court decided to deny him a law license.[66] Callously, Hale refused to apologize to the families of the victims. He did, however, mourn the death of Smith, commenting, "As far as we're concerned, the loss is one white man."[67] It is this uncompromising approach on the part of the young leader that has ensnared him in so many legal problems. In an interview with the author, Hale categorically denied any responsibility for Smith's actions:

> GM: Your critics point to some of the rhetoric emanating from your theology, such as RAHOWA, or Racial Holy War, and argue that this contributes to violence and mayhem. How do you respond to charges that your church is some how responsible—directly or indirectly—for these acts?
> MH: Well you know, one analogy that comes to mind is that certainly no one will hold the Pope in Rome responsible when an abortion clinic is bombed. Even though the Pope certainly has very strong language concerning abortion. . . . Well, it does not mean that the Pope is responsible. People are responsible for their own actions. That's just a simple reality. Also one idea or phrase in the Christian bible and the Old Testament comes to mind. There is a passage in the Old Testament that says, "he shall slay the Ethiopians."[68] Well if an Ethiopian is slain tomorrow, do I believe that the Christian Church and every Christian is responsible, or every Jew is responsible for that message? I just do not think so. I just do not think that we can impute liability or responsibility to an organization for the acts of its members even if it uses strong language. It

would be a much [clearer]case, true, if I were to say, or the church were to say, that the other races should be killed or we advocate extermination or something like that. But we never advocate those things.[69]

The reaction to Smith's spree within the extreme right was mixed. For instance, Alex Curtis, an advocate of the leaderless resistance approach to right-wing terrorism, lauded Smith in a newsletter as an "Aryan kamikaze."[70] Conversely, although William Pierce of the National Alliance expressed some sympathy for Smith, he counseled his followers that he was not a model for emulation. Instead, Pierce advised that "knowledge and discipline" were the keys to white survival rather than "foolish and undisciplined acts of premature violence."[71]

Considerable attention was brought to the area in the wake of the shootings and the displays of public condolence that followed. Shortly after the episode, the U.S. Department of Justice commenced an investigation into WCOTC. In Illinois, Governor George Ryan announced the creation of the Commission on Discrimination and Hate Crimes to develop strategies to combat bias crimes.[72] On July 12, 1999, Bloomington United against Hate, along with other civic organizations, sponsored a service for Won-Joon Yoon, which U.S. Attorney General Janet Reno attended. At the event, a participant read a letter from President Clinton who pledged to work with Congress to pass federal hate crime legislation. Bloomington United succeeded in persuading local lawmakers to proscribe the distribution of hate literature. At another Bloomington United–sponsored event held in October of that year, Morris Dees gave the keynote speech.[73] Dees instructed members of the community on how they could fight hate and form a broad-based coalition on race issues. He recommended to authorities that they work closely with the Reverend David Ostendorf, the leader of the Chicago-based Center for New Community.[74] In September 1999, the Ricky Byrdsong Foundation was established, which offers career counseling to inner-city youths.[75]

A former member of Bloomington United, Dru Clark, lamented after the tragedy that their efforts might have unwittingly contributed to Smith's alienation and set him on the destructive course that he ultimately took. As Clark recounted, local antiracist activists once organized a trip to Smith's house to harass him. By doing so, Clark believed that they might have pushed him further away from the community. In retrospect, Clark believed that a better approach would be to seek out the alienated "before they commit random acts of misdirected hostility" and allow them back into the community.[76]

Several civil suits were filed against Hale and the church following the spree. In March 2000, Michael Bender, an attorney for two teenagers who were shot by Smith, filed a lawsuit against Hale and Smith's parents. The suit charged that Hale had ordered Smith to carry out the shootings; however, it declined to state what evidence there was to support the contention. On April 4, 2000, the Center for Constitutional Rights filed a civil rights suit on behalf of the Reverend Stephen Anderson, a pastor of the Greater Faith Temple Church who was wounded by Smith. The suit, which was filed under the federal Ku Klux Klan Act and the Illinois Hate Crimes Act, charged that Hale conspired with Smith to violate the civil rights of Anderson on the basis of race. Hale's attorney, Glenn Greenwald, responded that the suit was misguided in that it targeted Hale on the grounds of "guilt by association." A similar suit was filed by Chicago attorney Michael Ian Bender on behalf of two Orthodox Jewish teens—Ephraim Wolfe and Nosson Cohen—who were injured in Rogers Park. The suit claimed that Hale was liable for Smith, who allegedly acted as his agent.[77] Despite these civil suits, earlier in 2000, the FBI all but closed the door on the case, saying that it found no incriminating information on Smith's computer, which was stored in a shed shared by Hale and Smith.[78]

More Violence

Still other sporadic incidents involving WCOTC members followed. In August 2000, two members of a Connecticut WCOTC chapter were arrested in upstate New York when guns and ammunition were discovered in their car. The two, Bruce Silvernail and Brian Davis, had allegedly traveled to an illegal firearms training session in Washington County, New York. Davis was one of three members who were named "Creator of the Year" in 2000.[79] In August of 2002, a leader of the WCOTC in Australia, Patrick John O'Sullivan, was convicted of stabbing a man in the abdomen.[80] O'Sullivan had previously been involved in other extremist groups, including National Action and a Klan organization. He once claimed to have over 100 members in his local Klan group in Victoria alone, but according to an Australian newspaper, that figure was probably fewer than ten.[81]

Several other WCOTC members were implicated in a variety of crimes. Jody Lee Mathis of Davie, Florida, was arrested for selling a stolen shotgun to another church member. Jimmy Barnhill of Sunrise, Florida, who previously served several years in prison for burglary, admitted to participating in the assault but was not charged.[82] Still other "lone wolves" have left traces that they were familiar with Creativity. For example, in September 2001, a 20-year-old Sacramento security guard, Joseph Ferguson, killed five people and wounded a California Highway Patrol officer before killing himself. When police searched his home, they discovered literature from WCOTC and other racist organizations.[83] In light of these incidents, it is not surprising that the WCOTC occasioned considerable opposition, which is the subject of the next chapter.

12

Opposition

As a consequence of the aforementioned episodes of violence, the Creativity movement has come under close attention by both the government and private monitoring groups. When compared to other Western democracies, the American system is unique. Other democracies have much more legal latitude in responding to political extremism and violence. By contrast, the United States has a strong civil liberties tradition, and because of First Amendment protections, the government does not officially have the authority to disband extremist groups or proscribe speech that espouses unpopular ideas. A robust civil society and long tradition of democracy are thought to militate against political extremism in America.[1] Finally, since the mid-1970s, federal authorities have been hampered in their efforts to monitor political extremism due to the legacy of COINTELPRO, a secret program in which the FBI disrupted both far-left and far-right groups.[2] When details of COINTELPRO emerged, they provoked both a legislative and public backlash. The negative publicity surrounding the program pressured the Justice Department to make changes to the law enforcement and investigative policies of the FBI. Hence, the Levi Guidelines were adopted on April 5, 1976, in an attempt to de-politicize the FBI. According to the new guidelines, in order to commence an investigation of a dissident group, evidence of a criminal predicate was required.[3] The overall results of these changes were dramatic, as the number of domestic intelligence cases initiated dropped from 1,454 in 1975 to only 95 in 1977.[4] Significantly, however, there was nothing in the guidelines that precluded the FBI from opening an investigation based on information received from private groups.

Some private nongovernmental organizations (NGOs) have interjected themselves into this area of public policy and have done much to fill the void. For example, several NGOs, such as the Anti-Defamation League and the Southern Poverty Law Center, have persuaded the government to take a strong position vis-à-vis the extreme right. In essence, the response to the extreme right in the United States is a joint effort by both the government and private watchdog groups.[5] This seemingly backdoor relationship with law enforcement, however, is not without critics, as some believe that it raises serious civil liberties issues.[6] Further, some critics charge that the intelligence sharing between the FBI and the watchdog groups constitutes a circumvention of the Attorney General's Guidelines in that the FBI can receive access to the watchdogs' files when it sees fit to do so. Finally, watchdog groups do not have to concern themselves with strict civil liberties restrictions to which the FBI must adhere when gathering information on its subjects of investigation. Nevertheless these organizations have done much to stymie political extremism in the United States, most notably on the political right.

The Anti-Defamation League (ADL) has been in the forefront in confronting right-wing extremism in the United States. The ADL first publicly took notice of Ben Klassen in 1967 when he was mentioned in a book written by Benjamin R. Epstein and Arnold Forster on the influence of the John Birch Society.[7] Over the years, the ADL has released several reports and press releases on the Creativity movement.[8] In 1999, the ADL persuaded the Justice Department to open an investigation of the church following the Ben Smith shooting spree.[9] Neil Herman, a retired high-ranking FBI official who once led the agency's Joint Terrorist Task Force, became the head of the ADL's Fact-Finding Division upon his retirement from the bureau in 1999.[10] Not long after assuming this position, he lobbied senior Justice Department officials to relax the constraints that inhibit the FBI from investigating extremist groups, including the WCOTC.[11]

After 9/11, the federal government returned to a more proactive approach to countering right-wing extremism. Many in the movement feared that the government's war on international terrorism could spill over into a witch hunt against domestic extremists and dissidents as well. Several arrests in the months following 9/11 have given credence to such concerns, as federal authorities adopted a more aggressive posture toward domestic extremist groups. The federal government has demonstrated increased vigilance as suggested by the remarks of Department of Justice (DOJ) spokesman, Bryan Sierra: "[We are] making every effort to shut down hate groups and homegrown terrorists before they too, can act violently on their hatred."[12]

The World Church of the Creator came under particular scrutiny by the federal government. In testimony before the U.S. Senate Select

Committee on Intelligence on May 10, 2001, FBI director Louis Freeh announced that the WCOTC and the Aryan Nations "represent[ed] a continuing terrorist threat."[13] For his part, Hale rejected that characterization, explaining that he was "one of the most watched people in Illinois." Furthermore, he acknowledged that he had been in contact with the FBI for some time and said that he had a "good working relationship" with the agency.[14] Be that as it may, in 2004, the FBI released a critical report on Hale titled, "A Different Breed of Terrorist."[15] In the aftermath of 9/11, law enforcement authorities are increasingly prosecuting any known illegal activity by extremists while at the same time infiltrating the potentially more dangerous groups to guard against future attacks. As one law enforcement source commented, "You prosecute what you can prosecute."[16] Several key activists have been arrested, including Chester Doles and Shaun Walker, both of the National Alliance; Kevin Alfred Strom; Ernst Zündel; and David Duke. Perhaps the most threatening, William Krar, a lone wolf who stockpiled a large cache of guns and ammunition as well as sodium cyanide, was discovered by chance.[17] Several of these arrests suggested a high degree of political motivation on the part of the government.[18]

The Southern Poverty Law Center (SPLC) of Montgomery, Alabama, targeted the WCOTC as well. In 1994, the SPLC filed a civil suit on behalf of Harold Mansfield's family, claiming that the COTC was vicariously liable for the actions of George Loeb (see chapter 6).[19] The leader of COTC at that time, Dr. Rick McCarty, chose not to contest the suit and duly divested himself of responsibility. As a result, the SPLC received a default judgment of $1,000,000 for the family of Harold Mansfield.[20] Immediately thereafter, SPLC set its sights on William Pierce, who had recently purchased the church's property in Otto, North Carolina, at an ostensibly below-market price. Klassen was believed to have anticipated the suit and made a frantic attempt to "unload COTC assets and divest himself of responsibility for the organization."[21] Pierce purchased the property from Klassen for $100,000 and sold it soon after for $185,000, thus making a profit of $85,000. He recalled the events leading up to the transaction in an interview with this author:

> When [Klassen] decided to retire, he called me up and offered to sell to me his property in North Carolina. I was surprised. I said, "how much do you want for it?" He told me $100,000. . . . I had

working in my office at that time a fellow named Will Williams, who had formerly worked with Klassen. I discussed the thing with Will. And he said, "It's a good buy. . . . If you subdivide the thing you could sell it for twice that." Well, I wasn't particularly interested in the real estate speculation. But anyway, I decided to go down there and take a look at what he had. . . . I agreed to buy his property down there for a $100,000. . . . It was bigger hassle than I had intended for it to be. . . . I advertised it in Atlanta newspapers as a corporate retreat. But, nobody made an appointment to see it, so I turned it over to a realtor in Franklin [North Carolina]. Eventually he got an offer from a woman who wanted to make it a bed and breakfast. She would pay $200,000 if I would finance half of it. I ended up with less money than I started with.

Another thing Klassen told me was that he wanted to sell the property to somebody he knew and trusted, because if he just put it on the market the Jews would buy it and then they would make a retirement home for black crack dealers or something. And Klassen lived right next door to this property. He had his own house next to it. So, he was concerned about who was going to take over this property. And, he tended to be a little bit paranoid and conspiratorial in his approach to things. I didn't really mislead him, but he thought that I would use this property that he had built up there as sort of an extension of the National Alliance. But that wasn't my intention at all. I immediately put it on the market.[22]

According to Pierce, Dees met with McCarty prior to filing the suit. He took McCarty out to lunch and told him his plans. McCarty had no desire to get involved in the litigation, and therefore did not contest the suit. Pierce described McCarty as a "crook" and a "conman" who was not really interested in the church but just wanted to sell off Klassen's assets.[23] Dees claimed that Klassen's transaction with Pierce was a subterfuge to hide the money. On May 20, 1996, a federal court in Bryson City, North Carolina, ruled that the COTC had sold its property to avoid paying damages connected to the civil suit involving Loeb. As a result, the court ordered Pierce to turn over the $85,000 profit he had made from the sale to Mansfield's family.[24] Pierce appealed all the way to the U.S. Supreme Court, but the high court did not hear the case.

Not long after Benjamin Smith's shooting spree, the SPLC again set its sights on the WCOTC for a possible civil suit. In September 1999, Morris Dees told a Chicago audience the SPLC might eventually own the assets of the WCOTC.[25] However, as of yet, the suit has not been filed. The WCOTC has often been the topic in the SPLC's *Intelligence Report* magazine. In July 2006, the SPLC released a story about right-wing extremists in the ranks of the U.S. military. The story focused on Matt Buschbacher, a Navy SEAL, who was ordained as a minister in the WCOTC back in 1998. For a while, he was the leader of the organization's Cincinnati chapter. Around 2000, he joined the Navy and advanced quickly, completing the rigorous 26-week SEAL training program at the Naval Special Warfare Center in Coronado, California, and went on to serve in Operation Iraqi Freedom. He later left the WCOTC and joined the National Alliance for which he designed flyers and graphics on the organization's Web site. Now out of the military, Buschbacher received an honorable discharge and claims to have severed his connections to the white power movement.[26] He now runs seminars instructing men on how they can pick up women and even wrote a popular book on the subject titled *Date the Women of Your Dreams*.[27]

Smaller watchdog groups have also monitored the WCOTC. For example, the Center for New Community is a watchdog group based in Chicago, Illinois, whose primary focus is on regional far-right activity, such as Matt Hale's WCOTC and Midwestern Christian Identity groups. The center conducts workshops and public presentations to educate the public on issues such as racism, bias crime, and right-wing extremism. On occasion it collaborates with some of the other watchdog groups. For example, it prepared a special report on the WCOTC for the American Jewish Committee.[28]

For his part, in an interview with this author, Hale was dismissive of the various watchdog groups that have monitored his church:

> These watchdog groups, as they call themselves, are really amusing. I actually get a kick out of the various things that they say about me. They can lie about me, they can distort things, but all they do is bring more people into our ranks. The more people read Hatewatch,[29] for example, on the Internet, the more people come to our website. These people are desperate people in our view. They like to pretend that they are some kind of defenders of America from us nasty racists. In reality, we are winning. We may not be taking the

country tomorrow, or next week, or next year, but we are winning. And the white racial cause is much further along than it was ten years ago when I first began. Ten years ago, I could burn an Israeli flag and people would be outraged. Now, if I burn it, people are cheering and I know that. I walk down the street and have people waving at me. When I go to grocery store people want to shake my hand. This is just simple reality. As much as these watchdog groups want to attack and slander [me] . . . it's really not worth it. They are doing us a favor.[30]

In addition to surveillance from the federal government and watchdog groups, Hale faced still more opposition from Illinois state authorities. In July 1999, the Illinois Department of Revenue began an investigation into the WCOTC to determine whether the group violated any tax laws. Previously, in August 1995, the department had denied an application for a sales tax-exempt status filed by Hale in East Peoria.[31] Hale argued that his organization did not present itself as a charity; rather, he maintained it was a church and thus exempt from any registration requirement insofar as churches were not required to register under the law.[32] The Illinois state attorney general Jim Ryan sued the WCOTC for failing to register as a charity and disclose its finances. The Illinois state law required charities to register and report their finances to the government. For his part, Hale claimed that Ryan's suit was politically motivated in that Ryan sought to score points for his gubernatorial campaign by targeting him. Although Ryan denied that he was pursuing the suit because of Hale's newfound notoriety, the timing suggested otherwise; he commenced the investigation not long after the shooting spree of Benjamin Smith. In his defense, Hale contended that the Illinois solicitation law was so vague that one could not tell which groups the statute required to register as charitable organizations. A Cook County judge agreed and overturned the law. The judge found that the law was so vague that it threatened freedom of speech.[33] Not to be deterred, Ryan took the case to the Illinois Supreme Court.

In November 2001, the Illinois Supreme Court reversed the Illinois Circuit Court's decision, finding that the original statute was constitutionally valid. According to the Court, the Solicitation Act was tailored narrowly enough that it served the state's interest in protecting its citizens from fraud in such a way that the law did not unduly burden First

Amendment protection of free speech. Ryan cited as evidence a church receipt, which was found after the shooting spree, for $6,190 for printing services that was found in Benjamin Smith's car with the sales tax removed.[34] Hale decided to petition a U.S. Circuit Court of Appeals to hear the case, but a decision has yet to be rendered.[35]

Critics of Creativity often dismiss it as nothing more than hatred and bigotry cloaked in a theological garb. Moreover, by its own admission Creativity is atheist. Nevertheless, Hale defended Creativity as a legitimate religion in an interview with this author:

> Certainly if [our critics] can try to successfully undermine the legitimacy of our religion, as we definitely believe it is, they gained in their respective causes. But the fact of the matter is that we do have a religion. . . . We do not have to believe in their gods in order to be a religion. We do not have to believe in Jesus to have a religion. We do not have to believe in Yahweh to have a religion. In fact, religion itself doesn't dictate that you have a Supreme Being. Buddhism, for example, doesn't have a Supreme Being, yet it is recognized as religion. A religion is a philosophy of life that is all encompassing. That's exactly what we have in Creativity. And certainly, I think that everyone in our church believes very strongly in Creativity as a religion. The idea of hatred and bigotry, well, it's another self-serving comment. Certainly, the Jewish religion hates its enemies. Certainly, the Christians historically have hated those who opposed Christianity. There is bigotry in all religions. In fact, religion itself dictates bigotry. If you were tolerant of everything, why even have a religion? If you are tolerant of this and that which you consider evil, you might as well, you know, just throw in the towel.[36]

In the meantime, Hale still pursued his law license, but was unsuccessful in his bid. The notoriety stemming from Benjamin Smith's criminal activity made this issue all the more contentious. Although the ADL originally supported Hale's petition for a license, after Smith's shooting spree, the Jewish defense organization reversed its position; Harlan Loeb, the ADL general counsel, commented: "Matt Hale has lit the match and he must accept responsibility for the ensuing fire."[37] Still, others feared that denying Hale a law license set a dangerous precedent and amounted to a form of McCarthyism—in this case, against the political right. His case was discussed extensively in law journals.

On July 29, 1999, not long after the Illinois Bar rejected Hale's law license application, Hale petitioned the Illinois State Supreme Court for review of the fitness committee's decision. Robert Herman, a Jewish attorney based in St. Louis, agreed to take Hale's case to the Illinois Supreme Court on a pro bono basis.[38] The American Civil Liberties Union of Illinois filed an amicus curiae (friend of the court) brief in support of Hale's petition.[39] On November 12, 1999, the Illinois Supreme Court denied Hale's petition for review. Justice James D. Heiple dissented with the court's majority opinion. He argued that Hale's case raised a very serious question—that is, if a petitioner's controversial statements had been identified by the bar after the petitioner had obtained a license, would that be grounds for disbarment? If not, then it follows that there would be one standard for the admission to practice and another standard for continuing to practice. On the other hand, if the standard were the same for both, then conceivably, someone who had already obtained a license could be disbarred for obnoxious speech.[40] Refusing to capitulate, in February 2000, attorneys for Hale filed for a petition for a writ of certiorari with the U.S. Supreme Court.[41] However, when his case reached the high court in June 2000, the court declined to hear the case.[42]

Next, Hale set his sights on Montana, a state with a Creator presence. In September 2000, he applied for membership in the State Bar of Montana. He expressed an interest in specializing in constitutional law and criminal defense work. Paul Shively of the Montana Human Rights Network organized a petition drive to discourage Hale from moving to the state.[43] Not unlike his predicament in Illinois, various bar committees rejected his application.[44] Although he was denied a law license, Hale listed himself as an attorney in Peoria-area phone books.[45]

In retaliation for denying his application, Hale brought a suit against the Illinois Bar's Committee on Character and Fitness. In a suit filed in the U.S. District Court for the Northern District of Illinois Eastern Division in June 2001, Hale's lawyer, Glen Greenwald, argued that the members of the Committee on Character and Fitness, acting under the color of law, had violated Hale's constitutional rights of free statement, free association, due process, and equal protection by denying him a law license. As a consequence, they sought both compensatory and punitive damages along with declaratory and injunctive relief. Hale's lawyers argued that the committee was punishing Hale for no other reason than his political views, and this action thus amounted to a patent violation of the First Amendment. In their estimation, there was nothing objectionable about his actual conduct that should preclude him from receiving a law license.[46] Still seeking judicial relief, Hale filed suit in a lower federal court.

Next, Hale turned to the U.S. Seventh Circuit Court of Appeals for relief. In his petition, Hale claimed that his First Amendment rights had been abridged. Finally, on July 14, 2003, that court rejected his appeal and concluded that his case had already received adequate adjudication and thus allowed the Illinois State Supreme Court's decision to stand.[47] Nevertheless, Appellate Judge Diane Wood noted that there was a "disturbing lack of transparency" in the deliberations concerning Hale.[48]

Still other legal problems continued to mount for Hale. In particular, he and his organization became embroiled in a trademark suit with another entity over the Church of the Creator name. The controversy set in motion a series of events that may have sounded the death knell for his movement.

13

Denouement?

After 9/11, Matt Hale claimed that his organization experienced new growth. He attributed this development to the fact that people came to realize that his group "had been right all along" concerning the circumstances that led to the terrorist attacks.[1] Characteristic of the extreme right, Hale blamed the U.S. government for the tragedy, claiming that it was the "inevitable and ultimate result of a foreign policy that has been slavishly pro-Israel." Apparently not too upset over the attacks, some Creators pointed out that the proportion of Jews, "muds," and "lackeys of Jews" who perished in the WTC "undoubtedly approached 100 percent."[2]

To capitalize on heightened fears related to Islamic terrorism, in the fall of 2001, the World Church of the Creator (WCOTC) began an aggressive leafleting campaign in scattered cities throughout the United States. The flyers—which included quotes from a 1998 ABC News interview with Osama bin Laden—charged that the 9/11 attacks were perpetrated due to the U.S. government's unstinting support for Israel.[3] On that note, in July 2002, Hale released a booklet titled *The Truth about 9–11: How Jewish Manipulation Killed Thousands*, which examined the influence of Jewish lobbying groups, such as the American Israel Public Affairs Committee, over the U.S. government. The booklet also chronicled the history of numerous Jewish terrorist groups, including the Stern Gang, which perpetrated violence to usher in the creation of the state of Israel and pointed out alleged instances of Israeli perfidy, such as the Lavon Affair of 1954, in which some elements of the Israeli Mossad bombed American targets in Egypt, blaming the incident on the Egyptians, and the attack on the U.S.S. *Liberty* in 1967.[4] Previous espionage cases were cited, including those involving Elliot and Ethel Rosenberg and Jonathan Pollard. More recently, Hale accused the Israeli Mossad of orchestrating 9/11 as a political windfall for Israel. Such speculations have become legion in the aftermath of the tragedy.[5] While these theories usually only accuse the Mossad of having advance knowledge of the impending attack and failing to warn the Americans, Hale took it a step further and suggested that the Mossad actually placed devices in the twin towers that were set to explode upon impact from the airliners. Alleged Jewish control of the media prevented the conspiracy from being revealed to the public.[6]

Initial boldness later gave way to consternation, as many in the extreme right fear that the American government's war on international terror could spill over into a witch hunt against domestic extremists and dissidents as well. In the aftermath of 9/11, Hale expressed concern that the government would seek to curtail controversial speech.[7] Nevertheless, he was often quick to exploit racial tensions in various communities in the country. In November 2002, Hale spoke at Lewiston, Maine, which had experienced a large and rapid influx of indigent Somali immigrants that strained the social welfare system in the city.[8] The mayor, Larry Raymond, actually urged Somali elders not to encourage their fellow countrymen to settle in Lewiston insofar as it was a tremendous burden on local resources. Previously, Hale had sparked a free speech controversy at Northwestern University in January 2000 when he appeared on campus in an effort to obtain recognition of a student chapter of the WCOTC. In his provocative style, he challenged campus intellectuals to debate him in a public forum.[9] This move was all the more controversial as this was the same university for which Ricky Byrdsong—a victim of Benjamin's rampage—had once coached basketball.[10] Hale frequently sought out college campuses as a venue through which to disseminate his ideas, and his presence often generated much controversy. In July 2000, the Illinois Fourth District Appellate Court upheld a McLean County judge's decision that dismissed a suit by Hale, which claimed that Illinois State University had unlawfully denied him the right to speak to a campus group. At first, an Illinois State University student had invited Hale to speak on campus. However, the student later reneged on the offer, commenting that Hale's philosophy and goals were incompatible with purposes of the lecture series. Despite the legal defeat, Hale expressed satisfaction that he had "made it clear to ISU and other universities that they will not tread upon the liberties of white racists with impunity."[11] Through his audacity, by the early 2000s Hale had become one of the most visible leaders of the American extreme right. His leadership, however, was not without dispute even in the radical milieu of the Creativity movement.

Despite his media attention, there were challenges to Hale's leadership from within the WCOTC. For example, Guy Lombardi, a Florida Creator and the former head of the White Berets, complained: "Hale, in my opinion, is selling out. He's money hungry and recruiting anybody without doing criminal background checks and mental health checks. That's how we ended up with Benjamin Smith."[12]

The Montana chapter became restless as well. In 2002, a WCOTC Committee, which included Slim Deardorff, Dan Hassett, Dane Hall, and Claud Umphenour, was said to have forced Hale to resign as Pontifex Maximus by an impeachment vote.[13] During the attempted coup, Deardorff contacted the National Alliance and was supposed to have asked William Pierce to suggest a replacement. Once Hale discovered their treachery, he kicked Deardorff out of the group.[14] In February of that same year, Hale sent an e-mail to his followers indicating that Hassett had been banned from the group as well. Dismissing their impeachment decision, he claimed that he had ousted the "three stooges" from his organization. Hasset's activism in WCOTC actually preceded Hale's leadership. Both he and Deardorff had been members of the church for over ten years.[15] Hassett was once listed as the WCOTC's Northwest Regional Director. For his efforts, he was once named "Creator of the Year" and presented with the "Award of Honor." His falling out with Hale was all the more unsettling insofar as he was also one of the Creators who helped organize the 1996 meeting in Missoula, Montana, at which the Guardians of the Faith confirmed Hale as the Pontifex Maximus. Back in the 1970s, Deardorf had been involved in the Posse Comitatus—a far-right tax protest group. On occasion, he visited the Aryan Nations compound in Hayden Lake, Idaho. While there in 1984, he met Robert Jay Matthews and David Lane, both members of the Order. Hassett once described Hale as a "megalomaniac" who issued death threats to members who challenged his authority. Further, he accused Hale of harassing members and treating women horribly.

By the end of February 2002, the close relationship between Hale, Hassett, and Deardorff had finally come to an end, presumably, in large part over finances. According to Hale, Hassett stole over $8,000 in WCOTC funds. Supposedly, the money was in the form of gold bars that were buried on Deardorff's property. Hassett claimed that the gold bars were destroyed in a fire. Hale rejected this claim insofar as the gold bars were supposedly buried and thus should not have been damaged. Even worse, Hale charged that Hassett threatened to give damaging information concerning the WCTOC to the FBI.[16] In late 2002, Hassett finally left the church, publicly exclaiming that he was disappointed with some members and the leadership of Hale. He complained that the WCOTC "attracted a low caliber of people" for membership and he didn't want to be associated with them.[17] In addition to challenges to his leadership, Hale faced still more legal problems in both civil and criminal courts.

The Trademark Case

For much of 2002, the WCOTC was embroiled in a civil suit with the TE-TA-MA Truth Foundation over the foundation's trademarked "Church of the Creator" name. On its Web site, the Oregon-based religious group appears to blend new age spirituality with Christianity.[18] In 2000, the foundation filed the suit in the federal court in the Northern District of Illinois and was represented by the law firm Kirkland & Ellis LLP of Chicago. Hale argued that his church had existed prior to the TE-TA-MA Truth's trademark, and further, the "Church of the Creator" name was too generic to be exclusively held by only one organization. Upon assuming leadership over the church in 1995, Hale quickly changed the name, supposedly, to make the organization "judgment-proof" from the burden of the Southern Poverty Law Center (SPLC) civil lawsuit. First, he christened the reconstituted organization the "New Church of the Creator," then later the "World Church of the Creator."[19] Ben Klassen had actually incorporated the Church of the Creator on August 16, 1973, a fact that was barely mentioned in the court transcripts.[20] The foundation did not begin using the disputed name until 1982. However, in 1987, it registered its symbol (a radiant dove centered on six-pointed star) and the disputed name with the federal trademark registration system. And in 1988, the Patent and Trademark Office granted the foundation a trademark. Five years passed during which Klassen's church did not protest the registration. As a result, the Patent and Trademark Office accepted and filed a declaration that the foundation's trademark had become "incontestable."[21] During civil proceedings, neither Hale nor his attorneys used the "prior use" as a defense in the case.[22] Originally, U.S. District Judge Joan Humphrey Lefkow ruled in Hale's favor, agreeing that the Church of the Creator name was too generic to restrict its use to one entity.

In July 2002, however, the Seventh U.S. Circuit Court of Appeals reversed Lefkow's original decision and ordered Hale's organization to refrain from using the "Church of the Creator" name.²³ The court reasoned that there were significant and qualitative differences between the two entities and took notice that the foundation had received negative publicity as a result of its name's close association with Hale's group. Once again, Hale argued that the disputed name was too generic to be trademarked. The appellate court concluded, however, that the name was descriptive rather than generic. Although Klassen may have incorporated his organization under that name in 1973, the court determined that that entity no longer existed and, as a consequence, there was no formal continuity between that organization and Hale's group.²⁴ According to records, Rick McCarty had formally taken over the organization on February 9, 1993 and had voluntarily dissolved it on February 22, 1994.²⁵

Compelled to enforce the appellate court's decision, on November 19, 2002, Judge Lefkow ordered—among other things—that Hale's group permanently desist from using the "Church of the Creator" name; cease using Internet domain names that used infringing marks; and most controversially—"deliver up for destruction (or, where feasible, removal or obliteration of any infringing mark from) all printed and other materials bearing the infringing marks."²⁶ To Hale, this order amounted to an act of war insofar as WCOTC members considered the organization's books to be holy texts. To avoid complying with this provision, Hale transferred the church's materials to Wyoming in the hope that they would be out of the reach of Judge Lefkow's order.

In December 2002, Hale filed suit against Lefkow, claiming that she was wrong in ordering the WCOTC to desist from using the "Church of the Creator" label.²⁷ After Lefkow had issued her judicial order, her home address appeared on numerous white supremacist Web sites along with messages that she was a "probable jew" and a "kike-and nigger-loving traitor."²⁸ Hale had repeatedly told his followers that the U.S. government was illegitimate and that it was appropriate to take whatever actions were deemed necessary to resist it.²⁹ Not taking the order lightly, Hale was defiant. In a message to his followers he stated:

> Any court order ordering the confiscation and burning of a church's bibles is an obvious violation of the Constitution of the United States and should be opposed by every American citizen by whatever means. After all, no federal judge has the power to order a free people to "dutifully" turn over their Bibles so that they may be

destroyed by those who oppose their religious beliefs. This court order places our Church in a state of war with this federal judge and any acting on authority from her kangaroo court.[30]

The Plot to Kill Judge Lefkow

Despite the formidable opposition arrayed against it, the church continued to attract new followers in large measure because of its nihilistic appeal to rebellious youth. However, this has left the organization vulnerable to agents provocateur and disruption. It later transpired that a trusted member of Hale's security legion had also been working as an informant for the federal government. Tony Evola claimed that he first went to authorities after he met Hale for the first time in the summer of 1999, when Hale solicited him to distribute racist literature at a Chicago public school where Evola worked. Evola remarked that he believed the racist material "was not safe for children to read"; consequently, he approached the Chicago police about the matter and was referred to a sergeant who was working with the FBI. In March 2000, Evola joined the WCOTC in his undercover role after he attended a public speech by Hale. At the event, Hale was impressed by Evola, who warded off a protestor wielding an object wrapped in a sock. The two met afterward at the church headquarters in East Peoria. As Evola was a security guard by trade, Hale requested that he join his security detail—the White Berets—and eventually, Evola was appointed its chief.[31] At that time, Hale feared that Ken Dippold, who once led the White Berets, could no longer be trusted. He was thus glad to replace him with Tony Evola, a solidly built man with receding dark hair and a moustache, who, as one observer put it, "could pass for a cast member of 'The Sopranos.'"[32] Approaching middle age, Evola was living on his Social Security payments, delivering pizzas, and doing volunteer work for Chicago public schools. Evola traveled across the country with Hale and accompanied him during public speeches, regularly reporting his activities to the FBI. For his undercover work, Evola was paid $52,000 and an additional $20,000 to cover expenses.[33]

According to the indictment against Hale, he had solicited Tony Evola to murder Judge Lefkow in the period from November 29 to December 17, 2002.[34] On December 4, 2002, Evola sent an e-mail to Hale requesting

Lefkow's address.³⁵ During a visit to Hale's residence in Peoria, Illinois, on December 5, 2002, Evola wore a concealed wire, which recorded Hale requesting the address of Judge Lefkow. Evola implied that she should be killed, and although Hale did not directly endorse the plan, he never instructed the informant not to carry it out. The recorded conversation suggests that Evola sought to suborn Hale:

> *AE*: Are we gonna exterminate that rat [Judge Lefkow]?
> *MH*: Well, whatever you want to do, basically. . . . My position has always been that, you know, I'm going to fight within the law and, but, ah [Judge Lefkow's home address has] been provided if you wish to ah, do anything yourself, you can. . . . So that makes it clear.
> *AE*: Consider it done.
> *MH*: Good.³⁶

Although Hale did not explicitly request that Lefkow be killed, under subsequent cross-examination, Evola testified that Hale nodded yes in agreement when he broached the topic with Hale.³⁷ A few days later, on December 9, 2002, Evola sent yet another e-mail to Hale in which he wrote:

> I called the exterminator. I know about the rat problem we talked about. The guy is good and does a good quiet job. You have to know where rats hide and he think [*sic*] he located her. He is working to get rid of the femala [*sic*] rat right now.³⁸

Hale did not reply to the message, but an electronic reply confirmed that someone had opened it.³⁹ Inasmuch as Hale received but did not reply to the message, the prosecution argued that he tacitly approved of the plot.⁴⁰ On December 17, Evola still pressed Hale on the issue, appearing unannounced at the Hale's home. Hale did not want to discuss the matter because he assumed that he was being monitored. Once again, Evola mentioned "exterminating the rat," to which Hale replied, "I can't be a party to such a thing."⁴¹ During the conversation, Hale complained that Evola was putting him "in an impossible situation." As he explained, "there's a federal statute that makes it . . . an imprisonable offense to know that a crime that's to be occurred . . . without telling anybody." Evola responded that the plan had already been set in motion and that it was costing more than what he had originally planned. He asked Hale if there were "two trusted brothers that could help out," to which Hale responded, "I can't take any steps to further anything illegal ever." At that point, Evola asked if he could stay with Hale "when this stuff comes to happen." Hale refused, explaining that he did not want to be an accessory to such an incident, but added that "whatever a person does is according to the dictates of their own conscience." Further, he conceded that he might "have a smile on his face" if he were to read in a newspaper that "something happens to certain creepy people." Nevertheless, once again, he was adamant that he could not "be any kind of party" to such plan. At the end of the exchange, Hale instructed Evola not to turn up unannounced at his home again.[42] Despite Evola's numerous suggestions to kill Lefkow, surprisingly, Hale, a lawyer, did not suspect entrapment. From early on, when he first started his association with Hale, Evola made numerous suggestions of killing "the rat" (i.e., Judge Lefkow).

Finally, on January 8, 2003, at the Dirksen Federal Courthouse in Chicago just before he was to appear at a contempt of court hearing at 1:30 p.m. regarding his refusal to comply with Judge Lefkow's judicial order, Hale was arrested by the FBI-led Joint Terrorism Task Force on charges that he solicited someone to kill a federal judge. The United States Attorney's Office for the District of Illinois also assisted in the investigation.[43] Commenting on Hale's arrest, Mark Potok of the Southern Poverty Law Center did not think the WCOTC would survive its current crisis. Rabbi Abraham Cooper of the Simon Wiesenthal Center noted that if the charges against Hale stuck it would result in "the removal of the most dangerous American racist of [Hale's] generation."[44] Likewise, the ADL applauded Hale's arrest and subsequent conviction as well.[45]

The WCOTC launched a Web site titled "Free Matt Hale Legal Defense Fund," which alleged that the government's prosecution was instigated by Michael Chertoff, chief of the Department of Justice Criminal Division. In January of 2003, President George W. Bush nominated Chertoff for a seat on the U.S. Court of Appeals for the Third Circuit.[46] Adding to the suspicion was Chertoff's association with the Anti-Defamation League, which in 1992, bestowed its Distinguished Public Service Award on him.[47] Furthermore, Chertoff's wife was once a co-chairwoman of an ADL regional civil rights committee in New Jersey.[48] Interestingly, it was the Latham & Watkins law firm, of which Chertoff is a partner, that brought suit against the WCOTC over the Benjamin Smith shooting rampage of 1999. In a broadcast on the National Alliance's *American*

Dissident Voices radio program, Kevin Alfred Strom accused Michael Chertoff of deliberately seeking to persecute white racist dissidents, such as Hale.[49]

Two militant groups—the Jewish Defense League (JDL) and the Jewish Defense Organization (JDO)—also had their sights on Hale. Both groups had a history of violence. According to a WCOTC Web site, Ian Sigel, the leader of the Chicago chapter of the Jewish Defense League, threatened and coerced WCOTC member, Ken Dippold, into making false statements under oath in a civil lawsuit against the WCOTC, which implicated Hale in Smith's shooting rampage.[50] In one instance, Tony Evola suggested that someone should kill Dippold. In response to Evola's entreaties in an e-mail, Hale replied: "You are very persuasive and obviously I think extremely well of you for your idea," but he concluded, "I must instruct you not to proceed."[51]

Still more legal problems continued for Hale. In June 2003, he was charged under a new indictment with obstruction of justice. Allegedly, he lied to Lefkow in a letter he had written to the judge in December 2002 concerning the copyright lawsuit. In the letter, Hale claimed that he possessed no materials that were in violation of the judicial order concerning the disputed copyright.[52] Still another indictment followed. In August 2003, it was announced that a federal grand jury was investigating him for additional obstruction of justice violations. According to the indictment, Hale instructed his father to lie to a grand jury about Benjamin Smith's death. Allegedly, in April 2003, Hale called his father and told him to tell the grand jury that Hale had stopped a television interview when he started to cry over Smith's death, thus suggesting that he was surprised to hear about the incident and had no advance knowledge of Smith's plans.[53]

On top of all of this, Hale's civil litigation was not turning out well. At the end of April 2003, a $1,000-a-day fine levied on the WCOTC went into effect for the organization's failure to comply with the order to desist using the Church of the Creator name. Todd Reardon, an attorney working on behalf of Hale, explained that it was difficult to comply with the order insofar as no member wanted to come forward as its leader while Hale was incarcerated.[54] By October 2003, Judge Lefkow had levied a $200,000 fine on the church for ignoring the court order.[55]

In December 2004, the Seventh U.S. Circuit Court of Appeals once again weighed in on the trademark controversy. The TE-TA-MA Truth

Foundation appealed a lower court's decision to recover attorney's fees. This time, the appeals court ruled in favor of the foundation, reasoning that the circumstances surrounding the case were exceptional and thus the plaintiff was entitled to compensation. During the litigation process, the court pointed out that the foundation was subjected to harassment and numerous threats from Hale's supporters, who sent a barrage of e-mails and phone calls to the foundation's counsel. Because of this action, the foundation had consumed time and money dealing with the annoying messages. Moreover, the court determined that the intent of the harassment was to drive up the cost of litigating the case and thus pressure the foundation to drop the trademark claim. As evidence, the court cited Hale's instructions to his followers to "take matters into their own hands," following the district court's order and injunction in the foundation's favor.[56] Finally, in May 2005, U.S. District Court judge Samuel Der-Yeghiayan ordered Hale's group to pay more than $450,000 plus interest and attorney's fees after losing the lawsuit that was initiated by the Te-Ta-Ma Foundation. For his part, Hale called the ruling a "travesty."[57]

The criminal charges, though, were even more serious and preoccupied Hale. Awaiting his criminal trial, Hale penned a poem in his jail cell titled "The Great Trial Nears"

> The Great Trial Nears, excitement does grow,
> Soon my innocence all will know
> And yet no matter what the outcome may be
> Our Cause will never be brought to its knee
> Our wings for freedom will not be clipped,
> Our budding flowers will not be nipped,
> Our children's future, secure will be
> As eternal as the roaring sea
> I may wince before their blows, 'tis true
> But others have done so before me too
> And the trial will prove to all what's right
> The brightest of day will follow the darkest of night
> Lies will succumb and the truth will shine
> Our foes will squirm, our enemies whine
> Their twilight—our dawn—approaches
> For them the heart of our people reproaches
> Our people awakened to the evil we fight,

Those who say it's a crime to be White
Will one day ask for forgiveness, yea
As through our pain we will have our day.[58]

Hale's defense attorneys, Thomas Anthony Durkin and Patrick W. Blegan, requested that the trial be moved to a venue outside of the Chicago area because of the notoriety that their client had acquired. Furthermore, they argued that insofar as Hale's alleged offenses occurred in East Peoria, and not Chicago, the trial should be held elsewhere. Federal prosecutors argued against moving the trial to downstate Illinois. Assistant U.S. attorney David Weisman submitted a nineteen-page response to the defense team's request arguing that the defendant had not cited any legal authority to support moving the venue.[59] Court officials appointed James T. Moody, a U.S. district court judge from Hammond, Indiana, to preside over the case.[60] Moody refused to grant bail to Hale, despite the fact that Hale's father offered to post real estate worth as much as $175,000. Federal prosecutors objected to the notion of granting Hale bail. They cited an intercepted phone call Hale made from prison in which he asked his father how many marshals would escort him to court and how many guns they had. Hale exhausted his personal savings on his defense. As a result, the state had to pay for the rest.[61]

Apparently, the Hale case was taken quite seriously by the government. Then attorney general John Ashcroft even signed a memorandum invoking Special Administrative Measures (SAMs), which placed severe restrictions on Hale's defense team, thus hindering their ability to communicate with their client. First implemented in 1996, SAMs were used by U.S. attorney Patrick Fitzgerald as a measure to prevent terrorism suspects from sending coded messages to their followers.[62] Coincidentally, Fitzgerald was involved in the prosecution of Hale as well.

Prosecutors explicitly sought to link Hale with the July 1999 shooting spree of Benjamin Smith. U.S. attorneys in Chicago contended that Hale had likely known of Smith's plans in advance, yet did nothing to prevent him from carrying them out. To bolster their assertion, prosecutors claimed that Hale and Smith had had significant phone contact in the days leading up to the incident. Moreover, many of Smith's personal items were found in a storage locker of Hale's after the incident, thus suggesting a close relationship between the two. Finally, they cited the fact that Hale had given Smith a blank business check, implying that

Hale had great trust in him.[63] At the trial, the prosecution argued that Hale's favorable comments about Smith after the shooting spree undermined his claim that he encouraged his followers to act within the law.[64] On recordings that Evola secretly taped, Hale was heard laughing as he recounted the shooting spree, commenting that Smith was a poor marksman whose "aim got better as he went along."[65] In a controversial decision, the judge allowed the prosecution to interject comments about Smith during the trial. Hale objected, arguing that such references prejudiced the jury against him.[66] Initially, the district court ruled in his favor. However, the prosecution agued that such evidence was outweighed by the prejudice insofar as it had high probative value.[67]

During the trial, things did not go well for Hale, who eschewed a standard suit and tie for his orange prison jumpsuit in an effort to present the image of a "political prisoner." His organization appeared to unravel, as a leader in the church, Jon Fox, turned state's evidence and testified against him.[68] In his testimony, Fox said that Hale wanted the leader of the TE-TA-MA Truth Foundation and his attorneys dead.[69] Hale had first met Fox at a Ku Klux Klan rally in West Virginia in October 2002. At the time, Fox was a member of a Kentucky chapter of the WCOTC. Although Fox was a high school dropout and suffers from severe bipolar disorder, Hale was nevertheless impressed with him and asked him to become the state leader of the Illinois chapter, an important position in the organization. Hale told Fox that he wanted "someone he could trust" and "someone older and mature." He even offered to pay his moving expenses out of the church's coffers. Fox, who, at that time was living in a homeless shelter in Kentucky with his two daughters, thought it was a good offer. However, upon arriving in East Peoria, Fox immediately found the church in a state of internal turmoil, as Hale was fending off challenges to his leadership from two disgruntled chapters. Furthermore, the legal battle with the TE-TA-MA Foundation was just getting under way as well.[70]

Seeking to discredit Fox, Hale's defense attorney, Durkin, claimed that he testified against Hale because he wanted to take over his position as Pontifex Maximus. Fox denied this accusation but acknowledged that he wanted to start a new Creativity group under a different name. Durkin added that Fox held a grudge against Hale because he considered him responsible for that fact that his daughter had become pregnant by Scott Gulbranson, another group member who had moved to Illinois from Kentucky with Fox.[71] During his testimony, Fox admitted that he felt betrayed by Hale because he failed to help him and his family during a crisis.[72] Finally, Durkin sought to dismiss Fox as a credible witness, claiming that Fox suffered from a manic depressive disorder and experienced memory problems. Previously, Fox had told representatives of the media that the charges against Hale were false.[73] However, another church member, James Burnett, testified against Hale as well.[74]

To make matters worse, as the trial progressed the relationship between Hale and his defense team appeared strained. Glen Greenwald, a lawyer for Hale, claimed that Hale's mother asked Greenwald to relay a cryptic message from Hale to one of his supporters. Greenwald declined to deliver it and later told federal investigators about the conversation he had had with Hale's mother, Evelyn Hutcheson. For her part, Hutcheson said that the reason the message was coded was to prevent federal agents from figuring out Hale's legal strategy.[75] Not long thereafter, an official from the Chicago Metropolitan Correctional Center, where Hale was being held, ordered that he would no longer be allowed to visit or speak with his parents.[76] Greenwald, who is Jewish, received criticism from some quarters, most notably, the Jewish Defense League, for representing Hale.[77]

In his closing statements, Durkin was said to have given a fiery two-hour speech that kept the courtroom riveted. He argued that the case was not about Hale and his "ugly, hateful, vile ideas." Rather, it was a chilling example of "how dangerous it is when the government . . . infiltrates and attempts to capture people for what they think they might have done."[78]

On April 27, 2004, a federal jury in Chicago found Hale guilty of one of two counts of soliciting crimes of violence and all three counts of obstructing justice.[79] Reportedly, Hale showed no emotion as the verdict was announced. Sitting with his hands clasped on the table, he dipped his head slightly but showed no other reaction.[80]

After the trial, Timothy Murphy took over as Hale's counsel. Dissatisfied with his counsel, Hale fired his defense attorney and represented himself at the sentencing phase, a maneuver that U.S. magistrate Andrew Rodovich allowed.[81] Later, Hale sued his attorney, Thomas Durkin, claiming that Durkin did not properly defend him. He pointed out that Durkin failed to mount a defense during the trial. Moreover, in a seemingly poor tactical maneuver, Durkin worked to exclude whites from the jury in favor of blacks because the latter were supposedly more likely to be "anti-system" and thus be more inclined to acquit Hale. The jury included five blacks, a Latino, and six whites, one of whom was a college dean with a black partner.[82] Some critics from the extreme right went so far as to conjecture that Durkin had been bribed by the government to deliberately sabotage Hale's case, for which he was paid $50,000.[83]

The story took a tragically odd twist on February 28, 2005, when Judge Lefkow's husband, Michael, sixty-four, and mother, Donna Humphrey, eighty-nine, were found murdered execution style in her home. At first, authorities suspected a WCOTC connection to the crime. On the Internet, some Hale sympathizers cheered the slayings, even as they criticized the rush to implicate his group in the incident. As one supporter exclaimed, "While I certainly understand that we are not supposed to be advocating illegal activities, there is nothing illegal or harmful in being happy about this incident. I can barely contain my glee."[84]

Inasmuch as the murders occurred just before Hale was about to be sentenced, he was understandably upset over the news. Categorically denying any involvement, he described the killings as a "heinous crime." Further, he explained, "only an idiot" would think that he had ordered the murders in light of his legal situation. In rare conciliatory style, he went so far as to condemn the act and expressed his desire to see "the perpetrator caught and prosecuted."[85] Hale's father, Russell Hale, offered his condolences to Lefkow's family after the killings but was adamant that his son was not involved in any way.[86]

It soon transpired that the perpetrator was not a member of the WCOTC, but rather, Bart Allan Ross, a fifty-seven-year-old Polish immigrant and self-employed electrician, whose medical malpractice lawsuit had been dismissed by Lefkow as "delusional."[87] On March 9, 2005, police stopped Ross for a minor traffic violation as he drove in West Allis, Wisconsin, whereupon Ross shot himself in the head. The bullet nearly struck the police officer who pulled him over. Notes Ross left, along with his DNA, tied him to the murders. Apparently, Ross had no connection to Hale or his group.[88]

Hale had to wait a year for his sentence. Seeking leniency, Hale told Judge Moody, "I have to go back to a solitary cell—I have to go back to hell. They want me to die in a hole." Acting as his own attorney during the sentencing hearing, Hale delivered a two-hour statement in which he maintained his innocence. In his speech before the court, he compared himself to Lefkow, despite Judge Moody's efforts to stop him. Finally, on April 6, 2005, U.S. district judge James Moody sentenced Hale to forty years in prison for his offense.[89] He received twenty years for the solicitation count and ten years for each of the obstruction of justice counts. One church member, "Kathy," who was present at the sentencing, recounted the courtroom scene:

> The whole morning was theatrics at its finest. Every FBI agent in the Chicago area was in the courtroom. Rows and rows of them, several surrounding Matt as he spoke. You had seasoned, gray-haired agents, down to rookies looking to climb the kosher ladder, they were all there.
>
> Our local media weren't as brutal as I expected. Some called Matt's speech impassioned; others said it was a tirade.
>
> All I know is we were very proud of him, he told the world how the FBI lied and set him up. He turned and pointed at the stuttering prosecutor Weisman and called him a shameful liar. One of the news stations reported that Matt made some very good points during his speech and the judge listened intently. Of course the judge did not listen intently.
>
> I would like to get Judge Moody in a poker game sometime; he has quite a story to tell. When Matt pointed out certain errors the judge had made, he developed this very visible twitching from his right cheek down to his chin. Matt told him how he instructed Weisman he was not to bring up Ben Smith in closing, Weisman defied the court and Judge Moody sat there and did nothing. Matt told Judge Moody he could not add on the terrorist enhancement because nowhere was that written in any government filings or was that brought out at trial that he was a terrorist. Again, Moody twitched up a storm.
>
> Matt pointed to different FBI agents, named them by name and told the world what they did to convict him, such as threatening Jon Fox with taking away his kids, he pointed to the hispanic female agent who made the threat to Fox. He pointed to agents that took one of his members in handcuffs from Central Illinois to Chicago and threatened him and told him what to testify at trial. . . .
>
> Matt pointed out how the "jew rat" all of a sudden two e-mails later became "female jew rat," and he suggested that Tony Evola screwed up and the FBI told him to use the word "female." Matt

said jew rat has always been the jew attorney in the trademark case. Matt said besides, nobody ever refers to females as rats. Well, I don't know, the JDL has called me worse.

Matt pointed to the fact that there was no American flag in the courtroom. He quoted from the Star Spangled Banner. He talked about loving his country and being a patriot and how he was taught by his police sergeant father to respect the badge. . . .

Matt's mother cried through most of the two hour speech and his father was visibly nervous. I feel that it didn't matter if it was four years or 40 years, it was still on to the appeal process. I personally am not angry at the sentence, I expected it, I'm angry that he even had to be in a position to be sentenced, that flimsy, cheap-ass evidence that convicted him and he gets 40 years, all because of a terrorist enhancement.

I am furious with the Chicago press, they are 90% responsible for his conviction, they tried and convicted him and tainted the jury. I am angry at his attorney Durkin who should have fought a change of venue all the way to the Supreme Court. I hounded them endlessly to fight that change of venue but one denied motion and they moved on. I pleaded with Durkin to object, to do something to get the Ben Smith angle out of the trial; it's the single most important factor in that conviction. I told Durkin to put an FBI agent on the witness stand and ask him if it were not true that Matt Hale was exonerated of any wrongdoing in 1999. Durkin didn't do it, Ben Smith dominated the trial and they got their conviction. . . .

At least Matt got his day in court; he got to say all the things he's had a chance to think about for over two years. He looked his enemies right in the face and called them liars as they hung their heads, refusing to look at him.[90]

After the sentencing, U.S. attorney Patrick Fitzgerald dismissed Hale, remarking that he "put no stock in his claims, the crocodile tears that he didn't do anything wrong." Judge Lefkow seemed glad to have the ordeal behind her, commenting that the "story would be out of the news now so that [she] could go back to [her] obscurity."[91] After the sentencing, Hale was sent to the nation's highest security prison—the Administrative Maximum United States Penitentiary—in Florence, Colorado, an institution that housed, at one time or another, the Unabomber Theodore

Kaczynski, Olympics bomber Eric Rudolph, the mastermind of the 1993 WTC bombing Ramzi Yousef, and Oklahoma City bomber Timothy McVeigh.[92]

Within the extreme right, the reaction to Hale's conviction was mixed. Some believed that Hale's approach was imprudent, as he did not adequately grasp the opposition arrayed against him, and as a result, was an easy target for the federal government, which was hell-bent on prosecuting the more radical elements of the extreme right.[93] Richard Barrett, the leader of the Nationalist Movement, publicly rebuked Hale for his conduct and said that he should be found guilty if the evidence indicated that he arranged for the murder of Lefkow. Further, he referred to Hale's conduct as "repugnant and repulsive." Previously, Ben Klassen had considered Barrett for the Pontifex Maximus position. Barrett claimed that Klassen even offered to donate the church's assets to the Nationalist Movement because he anticipated that they would be subject to seizure as a result of an impending civil suit initiated by the SPLC on behalf of Harold Mansfield's family. However, Barrett declined the offer. Presenting himself as a traditional American conservative, albeit with a racialist bent, Barrett, not surprisingly, counseled Hale and his group to pursue a more tempered approach to their activism. On occasion, the two exchanged barbs on their respective Web sites.[94]

Others, however, came forward to defend Hale. Edgar J. Steele, an attorney who had previously represented the leader of the Aryan Nations, the Reverend Richard Butler, in a civil suit filed by the Southern Poverty Law Center, charged that Hale was railroaded by the federal government. As he saw it, Hale was the victim of a systematic frameup that culminated in a sham trial. He maintained that Hale was innocent and had pursued a nonviolent course of activism. According to Steele, the ADL had instigated the trademark suit initiated by the TE-TA-MA Foundation. Supposedly, an ADL regional director, Richard Hirshhaut, had applied for and received a trademark for the "Church of the Creator" name. Shortly thereafter, with the supposed connivance of the ADL, the foundation filed a suit against Hale for trademark infringement. Steele claimed that he was actually serving as an attorney for Hale and provided him with legal advice. Previously, he refrained from speaking out on the trial because of the Special Administrative Measures, which did not permit him to publicly comment on the case. Adding a conspiratorial twist, before it transpired that Ross was the likely culprit of the murders of Judge Lefkow's family members, Steele speculated that an Israeli Mossad hit squad may have been responsible for the crimes.[95]

In May 2006, a U.S. Court of Appeals upheld Hale's conviction. The court rejected his appeal, concluding that there was sufficient evidence for the jury's finding that Hale had solicited the murder plot. In support of this decision, the court noted that Hale had provided Evola with Judge Lefkow's address, which was interpreted as a preliminary step in the process. Furthermore, Hale did not explicitly veto Evola's plan for the murder. Rather, he responded with silence when Evola sent an e-mail regarding the plot. As far as Hale's repeated assertions that he could not be a party to such a plot, the court interpreted these statements as an attempt by Hale to insulate himself from blame.[96] On the issue of entrapment, the court ruled that in order to adequately demonstrate this defense, the defendant had to establish that he was not predisposed to commit the offense with which he was charged. In response to that legal point, the court maintained that the best way to "manifest one's unwillingness to participate in criminal activity, and avoid the attendant penalties, is to 'say no and walk away.'"[97]

Still another feature in Hale's saga occurred in October 2008, when Bill White, an outspoken neo-Nazi from Roanoke, Virginia, was arrested after a federal grand jury in Chicago accused him of soliciting others to commit bodily harm to the foreperson of the federal jury that convicted Hale. According to Patrick J. Fitzgerald, the U.S. attorney for the Northern District of Illinois who was also involved in the prosecution of Hale, White was indicted on one count of solicitation. Allegedly, White used his Web site, Overthrow.com, to persuade someone to injure "Juror A" because of the juror's role in the conviction and subsequent sentencing of Hale, a sentence that White described as "criminally long." The Web site also published the name and home address of the jury foreman for the Hale trial. In March 2005, White lauded the assassinations of Judge Lefkow's husband and mother, commenting in an Internet essay that "everyone associated with the Matt Hale Trial [had] deserved assassination for a long time." He further added that he laughed when he first heard of the killings.[98] A former anarchist, White was affiliated with the National Socialist Movement, one of the most active and notorious neo-Nazi groups in America during the 2000s. At the time of White's arrest, another federal grand jury in Roanoke was investigating him for allegedly threatening members of the *Roanoke Times* newsroom and African American residents in that city.[99]

In light of Hale's conviction, the future of the World Church of the Creator is uncertain. Nonetheless, the Creativity ideology resonates with some of the more radical elements in the extreme right in both the United States and overseas. Despite all of the setbacks, there are signs that the movement is reconstituting albeit with considerable fragmentation.

14

Conclusion

Fragmentation and Beyond

After Hale's arrest, the WCOTC began a steady decline and process of fragmentation. The resulting fallout shook the foundation of the church. According to Mark Potok of the Southern Poverty Law Center, the number of chapters soon fell from eighty-eight to five. Although that number later rebounded to sixteen, he added that the organization was in disarray and that some chapters did not recognize the other chapters.[1] Potok believes that for all intents and purposes the formal organization of the WCOTC is now defunct and many of its former activists have gone on to affiliate with other neo-Nazi type organizations.[2]

Not long after Hale's arrest, Thomas Kroenke, a former Wyoming corrections officer, announced that he had assumed leadership of the church and had moved the headquarters to Riverton, Wyoming.[3] According to Kroenke, he first heard of Creativity from an inmate when he worked as a prison guard and he soon became a member.[4] Kroenke and the WCOTC were not well received in Riverton, a small community of 9,000 with a population that is 87 percent white but surrounded by an Indian reservation.[5] The local chamber of commerce sponsored workshops on diversity in response to the presence of the WCOTC. Kroenke, for his part, reported receiving numerous death threats and being ignored by local businesses, which refused to serve him.[6]

Without Hale's leadership, the Creativity movement in Montana began to disintegrate. A disgruntled member known only as "Carl" left the church in 2003 and absconded with $41,000 worth of Creativity books, along with boxes of church documents and e-mails. According to those who had reviewed the documents, they painted a picture of paranoia and organizational chaos. Carl later sold the books to the Montana Human Rights Network for $300. The books were used as a public art exhibit and later removed from circulation. A Creator newsletter castigated Carl as a thief who had delivered a "devastating setback" to their movement. By

March 2004, it was reported that the Montana chapter consisted only of Slim Deardorff and Dane Hall who led the small group.[7]

Several new organizations claiming the Creativity mantle have emerged. The Creativity Movement appears to be the heir to Hale's group. Based in East Peoria, Illinois, its Web site also lists contacts in Virginia, Florida, Mississippi, New Jersey, Ohio, Australia, Italy, Norway, and Ukraine. The Missouri chapter of the Creativity Movement suffered a setback in March 2005 when its leader Adam Daniel Jacobs was arrested in Springfield for the alleged beating of Anthony L. Williams. Jacobs, who previously led the Florida chapter, was charged with first-degree assault, kidnapping, and armed criminal action. Jacobs accused Williams of helping federal investigators in the murders of U.S. District judge Joan Lefkow's husband and mother.[8] In late April 2005, members of the Seminole, Florida, chapter of the Creativity Movement announced that James Logsdon, head of the White Berets, would assume the Pontifex Maximus title and replace Matt Hale.[9]

Some Creator chapters were unhappy with Logsdon's leadership. Consequently, in 2004, "The Church of the RaHoWa" broke off from the Creativity movement yet still adheres to the teachings of Ben Klassen and publicly supports Matt Hale. The founder, an Australian named Colin Campbell, once served in the Australian Regular Army and was a member of the far-right organization called Australian National Action. Campbell feared the government was infiltrating the Church of the RaHoWa and consequently terminated the membership of many of its recruits, an action that alienated some members. Dissatisfied with Campbell, the Reverend James Halen took over the leadership of the Church of the RaHoWa and officially chartered the organization in March of 2006.[10]

Another splinter group called The White Crusaders of RaHoWa! is based on the original precepts of Creativity. Organized hierarchically, according to its constitution, it is led by a World Council of Elders. Supposedly, below that body in descending order are national councils, state or territory councils, district councils, and chapter councils.[11] Given the organization's small size, it is unlikely that all of these subdivisions are actually extant. In October 2006, its leader Joel Nathan Dufrense was sentenced to fifty to seventy years in prison for a sexual assault that he allegedly committed against his former lover in Michigan. Defiant at his sentencing, Dufrense claimed that he was being persecuted for his political beliefs. Emmet County Circuit Court judge Charles W. Johnson described Dufrense as a "crude, vulgar, sub-human, individual who has no regard for the rights or feelings of others."[12] Patrick O'Sullivan currently leads an organization by the same name (The White Crusaders of RaHoWa) in Australia. In January 2006, the attorney general of South Australia, Michael Atkinson, called on the police to open an investigation into the group because he asserted that its Web site potentially violated the state's racial vilification laws.[13]

In March 2005, the Ohio chapter rechristened itself The Church of Creativity and split from the Creativity Movement.[14] However, the organization no longer has a presence on the Internet and is probably defunct. Nevertheless, an Ohio Creativity Movement chapter is still led by the Reverend Mitchell Irwin.

Still another Creativity organization emerged in 2007 in the area of Pittsburgh, Pennsylvania. The organization's Web site identified "Reverend Lloyd" as the Pontifex Maximus. Previously, Hardy Lloyd led the Pittsburgh chapter of the World Church of the Creator from April 2001 until April 2003 at which time the chapter broke off from the parent organization and was later renamed the Church of Creativity. A close friend of Hale, Lloyd was ordained as a Creator minister in December 2003. The new congregation selected Lloyd to be the Pontifex Maximus. From April 1999 to June 2007, Lloyd was also the chairman of the Order of National Socialism, which the Web site described as a "think tank of racialism." In 2004, Lloyd shot to death a former associate who attempted to kill him and his family. In November 2006, a jury ruled that the action was in self-defense. He was convicted, however, on a misdemeanor weapons charge and received three years probation in addition to the time he had served.[15] While the Reverend Lloyd was in prison from August 2004 to November 2006, G. W. Hayduke served as the acting chairman; Lloyd and Hayduke founded the White Pittsburgh Front (WPF) in 2003, which was described as a "non-membership association of like minded White Power people who live[d] in the region of Southwest [Pennsylvania]." The WPF included assorted Creators, neopagans, and even Satanists. In the summer of 2007, Lloyd effectively merged all of his organizations into the Church of Creativity. According to his brief biography, he was raised as a Mormon but later renounced Christianity. Previously, he supposedly worked as a stage actor but was blacklisted for being openly racist. He claims to be a "voracious reader" with an

IQ of over 150. Lloyd produces a newsletter called *Racial Loyalty* that is co-edited by "Sister Lisa," who is identified as the coordinator of the Women's Division. Together, the two co-authored a new fifty-one-page *Creator's Manual*.[16]

With Hale in prison, the Creativity movement began to adopt a more "leaderless resistance" organizational approach.[17] Scattered Web sites still keep the Creativity creed alive. One Web site—SolarGeneral.com—seeks to syncretize Creativity with the Cosmotheist creed founded by the late Dr. William L. Pierce of the National Alliance. Various Creator Web sites indicate that there are still other chapters in Germany, Ukraine, Belarus, and Russia, although the number of members belonging to these chapters is probably small. Nevertheless, the Creativity creed continues to resonate with elements of the extreme right over which it has exerted a significant influence.

The Influence of the Church of the Creator on the Far Right

Although the Creativity movement has always been a relatively modest operation, arguably it has had a disproportionate influence on the broader racialist movement of which it is only a small part. First, the Creativity movement was instrumental in spearheading the anti-Christian orientation that is increasingly popular among the younger racialist activists. There is also evidence to suggest that Creativity influenced the development of Odinism and steered it in a more radical direction.[18] Although Odinism is clearly more popular and has more followers than Creativity, Creativity certainly facilitated the growth of Odinism in the 1990s by introducing a strident critique of Christianity into the discourse of the extreme right. Their differences notwithstanding, Creators and racist pagans often cooperate locally in the opposition to ZOG—the Zionist Occupation Government.[19] Its seemingly atheistic theology notwithstanding, Creativity shares the chiliastic ethos of other radical religions that are popular with the extreme right, all of which look forward to a day when whites will establish a monoracial society, free from the nefarious influence of Jews, in which their full potential can be realized.[20] In several ways, Creativity is reminiscent of fascism in that it seeks to destroy the "old order" to make way for a utopian "new order."[21] Observers have noted that the fear of social marginalization can serve as a powerful motive for participation in terrorist organizations. Religion can provide a renewed sense of honor and empowerment as well as a framework for political mobilization.[22]

Second, the nihilistic tone of Creativity resonated with the more radical elements of the extreme right. Much of Creativity's rhetoric, such as RAHOWA, gained currency in the vernacular of the extreme right all over the world. The now defunct, skinhead musical band, RAHOWA, had a very strong influence on the genre of white power music. And on some occasions, the exhortatory tone of Creativity's rhetoric has contributed to sporadic episodes of right-wing violence.

Finally, the WCOTC contributed to the convergence of the white power movement scattered around the world. As Jeffrey Kaplan and Leonard Weinberg observed in their study *The Emergence of a Euro-American Radical Right*, scattered elements of the extreme right in the West, faced with declining white birth rates, sweeping third-world immigration, diminishing life opportunities for working-class youths, and perceived cultural decadence, have come to feel like strangers in their lands. Communicating through chat rooms and other Internet media, they have found solace in the slogan "white power" and sought to develop a new pan-Aryan identity based on race and civilization that transcends national borders.[23] The Creativity movement was in the forefront of this development and contributed to the popularity of the ZOG discourse both in the United States and abroad.[24] The church's theology rejected nationalism as divisive. In its stead, Creativity sought to instill a pan-white racialism, or "racial socialism," which sought to unite all white ethnic groups into a larger racial community based on a common religion.

Despite some setbacks over the past few years, the revolutionary racialist right continues to endure. Perhaps the principal reason is that the issues and trends that give rise to the movement have become more pronounced over time. As Nicholas Goodrick-Clarke pointed out, multicultural societies in the West face a significant challenge in that they are absorbing ever-larger levels of immigration while their political commitment to multiracialism has become an article of faith.[25] Globalization has greatly transformed Western societies, as it has unleashed a massive flow of capital, information, skills, and personnel across national borders. Fears of economic marginalization and racial inundation have fueled the resurgence of the extreme right in North America and Western Europe. Therefore, according to Goodrick-Clarke, it is no coincidence that the "Aryan cult of White identity" is now most marked in the United States, the country in which the challenges of multiculturalism and third-world immigration are most pronounced. Such a development is open-ended to say the least; as Goodrick-Clarke observed, the conversion of the United States into a "colony of the world" or a "universal nation" is without precedent in the modern world.[26] The ascendancy of liberal elites in the societies of the West and the concomitant ideological programs of multiculturalism, affirmative action, and antiracism have narrowed the political space through which openly racist activists can participate in the political system. Confronted by the entrenchment of these trends in contemporary liberal society, as Goodrick-Clarke noted, "certain white nationalists feel so embattled and disinherited that they can express their ideology only in terms of sacred, absolute affirmations": hence their flight into sectarian "churches" underpinned with racial theologies of white identity and supremacy.[27] The Creativity movement exemplifies this trend.

Although the American extreme right is currently marginalized, it nevertheless addresses issues of vital importance that are often ignored in mainstream discourse. Representatives of the extreme right are willing to speak frankly on some of the pressing issues of the day that are often ignored by mainstream commentators. Thus, examining their analysis could serve as a kind of canary in the mine and alert us to controversies on the horizon.[28] Quite possibly, race, immigration, diversity, and multiculturalism will be the most important issues facing the United States in the twenty-first century, as it undergoes a rapid demographic transformation. Although the extreme right is scorned for its endemic racism and ethnocentrism, recent social science research suggests that many Americans do not look upon diversity with equanimity.

The African American scholar Carol M. Swain observed that demographic changes in the country have affected the strategic calculations of all major racial and ethnic groups. She found that Americans continue to ground their identity in race and ancestry. Moreover, census figures show that whites are moving away from high immigration metropolitan areas. Those states that have undergone an immigration inflow have also experienced a native outflow. Self-segregation is evident, as whites tend to flee those areas that become more diverse.[29]

In a study of psychology and white attitudes on race, the highly controversial scholar, Kevin MacDonald, argued that severe social sanctions inhibit the expression of white ethnocentrism in America. Nevertheless, white ethnocentrism persists but in "a sort of underground world of unconscious, automatic processing."[30] In fact, a recent representative sample of 2,000 households found that 74 percent of those whites surveyed believed that racial identity was very important (37 percent) or somewhat important (37 percent). Furthermore, 77 percent of whites thought that they had a culture worth preserving.[31] MacDonald also cites research indicating that there is a significant gap between whites' explicit and implicit attitudes on race. Surprisingly, the gap is actually larger for white liberals than white conservatives. Although highly educated whites usually have liberal explicit attitudes on race, they are actually more likely to seek out racially segregated schools for their children and reside in racially segregated neighborhoods.[32]

In 2007, the esteemed Harvard political scientist Robert Putnam released a study indicating that ethnic and racial diversity, at least initially, greatly reduces community solidarity and cohesion. According to his analysis, residents in diverse neighborhoods evince lower trust, have fewer friends, and are less likely to be civically engaged. Diversity tends to have an atomizing effect, as people retreat or "hunker down" and a sense of anomie results. Not only are people less likely to trust the "other" but they are also less likely to trust those like themselves. Despite these dismal findings, Putnam holds out hope that these baleful effects can be mitigated by public policy.[33] Previous studies have demonstrated the importance of social trust on political and economic development.[34]

What do these trends presage for the future? Swain identified seven conditions that could fuel the growth of what she referred to as the "new white nationalism" in the years ahead. First, the increasing presence of nonwhite immigrants in certain areas could reduce whites to minority status. Second, structural changes in the global economy have reduced the proportion of high-wage production jobs for low-skill workers who must now compete with legal and illegal immigrants for low-paying employment opportunities. Third, white resentment and grievance persists over the perceived unfairness of race-based programs, such as affirmative action. Fourth, the continuing high rate of black-on-white crime has occasioned white fear of blacks. Fifth, the growing acceptance of multiculturalism with its emphasis on group rights, solidarity, and identity politics could engender a similar movement for disgruntled whites. In this sense, white nationalism would be a logical conclusion of the multicultural paradigm. Sixth, the rising expectations of racial and ethnic minorities could lead to increased interracial competition for resources and political power. And finally, the expansion of the Internet presents opportunities for like-minded people to share information and ideas, thus consolidating their strength and enabling them to mobilize their resources for political action.[35] The extreme right has enthusiastically taken advantage of the new medium and sees it as a powerful vehicle through which to spread its message. According to some estimates, there are somewhere between 600 to 2,100 such Web sites worldwide.[36]

One could add another condition to Swain's list, which could bolster the strength of the extreme right—that is, the growing salience of the Middle East conflict in American foreign policy in the future. If the situation in Iraq and the rest of the Middle East continues to fester, it is conceivable that the extreme right's critique of American foreign policy in that region and its focus on Israeli influence on it could become more mainstream. In March 2006, two prominent academics—John J. Mearsheimer, a professor of political science at the University of Chicago, and Stephen Walt, a dean at Harvard University's John F. Kennedy School of Government—released a working paper titled "The Israel Lobby and U.S. Foreign Policy." In it, they asserted that the various interest groups lobbying on behalf of Israel have subverted foreign policy in the Middle East to the detriment of the national interests of the United States.[37] The report occasioned considerable controversy. Critics like Harvard Law School's Alan M. Dershowitz were quick to point out the stylistic parallels between the study and traditional anti-Semitic canards of Jewish dual loyalty and malfeasance. Dershowitz, according to *The Harvard Crimson*, went so far as to claim that the authors culled information for their report from "hate sites" on the Internet. Although such allegations appear spurious, the paper did contain motifs—about, for example, the power of Jews in the news media and Jewish manipulation of the political system—that have formed the basis of classic anti-Semitic narratives. The report, indeed, has been enthusiastically received by representatives of the extreme right, including David Duke, who expressed satisfaction that his criticism of Israel has been vindicated by such esteemed academics. Representatives of Hamas and the Muslim Brotherhood praised the report as well.[38]

In contemporary American society, in which whites are rapidly losing majority status, the revolutionary racialist right does not hold the electoral route to power to be viable. According to U.S. Census Bureau projections, by the year 2050, whites will no longer comprise a majority of the American population due in large part to huge increases in both the Hispanic and Asian segments of the population.[39] Furthermore, those in the movement generally believe in an overarching conspiracy in which Jews will use whatever means are available to retain power and suppress dissidents to their assumed rule. Therefore revolutionary resistance is seen as the only feasible solution. Over the past few years the revolutionary racialist right has experienced several setbacks, as groups such as the Aryan Nations, National Alliance, and the World Church of the Creator have all lost important leaders either to death or imprisonment. Whether the Creativity movement can survive is uncertain. As the history of the church has demonstrated, the Creativity message has reached countries in many parts of the globe. What is more, the medium of the Internet has kept the Creativity idea alive. Although, the Creativity movement may currently be in retreat, it is likely that its ideology will continue to inspire racialist activists in the future.

Notes

Introduction

1. See, for example, Jeffrey Kaplan, *Radical Religion in America: Millenarian Movements from the Far Right to the Children of Noah* (Syracuse, NY: Syracuse University Press, 1997); Nicholas Goodrick-Clarke, *The Black Sun: Aryan Cults, Esoteric Nazism and the Politics of Identity* (New York: New York University Press, 2002); and Mattias Gardell, *Gods of the Blood: The Pagan Revival and White Separatism* (Durham, NC: Duke University Press, 2003).

Chapter 1. The Early Life of Ben Klassen

1. Dave Jackson and Neta Jackson, *No Random Act: Behind the Murder of Ricky Birdsong* (Colorado Springs, CO: Waterbrook Press, 2002), p. 9.
2. Jackson and Jackson, *No Random Act*, p. 9.
3. Makhno and Trotsky differed over tactics. While Makhno employed guerilla tactics against White Russian forces, Trotsky preferred a disciplined army and looked with distaste upon partisan activities. For more on Makhno, see Michael Malet, *Nestor Makhno in the Russian Civil War* (London: Macmillan, 1982).
4. Ben Klassen, *The Klassen Letters Volume One: 1969–1976* (Otto, NC: Church of the Creator, 1988), p. 5.
5. Jackson and Jackson, *No Random Act*, p. 11.
6. Jackson and Jackson, *No Random Act*, p. 11.
7. Klassen, *The Klassen Letters Volume One*, p. 5.
8. Letter to Mr. H. L. Snider from Ben Klassen, January 9, 1978, in Ben Klassen, *The Klassen Letters Volume Two: 1976–1981* (Otto, NC: Church of the Creator, 1989), pp. 123–27.
9. Jackson and Jackson, *No Random Act*, p. 21.
10. Jackson and Jackson, *No Random Act*, p. 21.
11. Klassen, *The Klassen Letters Volume One*, p. 6.
12. Ben Klassen, *Against the Evil Tide: An Autobiography.* (Otto, NC: Church of the Creator, 1991), p. 95.
13. Klassen, *Against the Evil Tide*, p. 95.
14. Klassen, *Against the Evil Tide*, p. 97.
15. Klassen, *Against the Evil Tide*, p. 121.
16. Klassen, *Against the Evil Tide*, pp. 174–84.
17. Klassen, *Against the Evil Tide*, pp. 186–87.
18. Klassen, *Against the Evil Tide*, p. 194.
19. Klassen, *Against the Evil Tide*, p. 301.
20. Klassen, *Against the Evil Tide*, pp. 209–15.

21. Klassen, *Against the Evil Tide*, p. 225.

22. Klassen, *Against the Evil Tide*, p. 241.

23. Klassen, *Against the Evil Tide*, pp. 293–94.

24. George John and Laird Wilcox, *Nazis, Communists, Klansmen, and Others on the Fringe* (Buffalo, NY: Prometheus Books, 1992), p. 214.

25. Birch was doing both missionary and intelligence work in China during the war. At war's end he stumbled upon a communist force with which he became embroiled in a heated argument. Eventually, the communist troops executed him. Welch considered Birch the first casualty in the Western world's war with communism and thus named his organization after him. For more on the life of John Birch see Welch's hagiographic *The Life of John Birch* (Chicago: Henry Regnery, 1954).

26. In addition to this figure, John George and Laird Wilcox estimate that perhaps as many as 250,000 Americans had once been John Birch Society members, most for only a few years. George and Wilcox, *Nazis, Communists*, p. 220.

27. Svonkin notes that the "Studies in Prejudice" research underwritten by the American Jewish Committee in the 1940s found that those people who exhibited authoritarian tendencies, such as right-wing anticommunists, were also susceptible to anti-Semitic appeals. See Stuart Svonkin, *Jews against Prejudice: American Jews and the Fight for Civil Liberties* (New York: Columbia University Press, 1997), p. 115.

28. Some leading anti-Semites at one time or another were JBS members including Revilo P. Oliver, George Lincoln Rockwell, Ben Klassen, Tom Metzger, and Robert Jay Matthews. Virtually to a man, these disgruntled former members have renounced the JBS as a Zionist-led operation that confuses well-meaning patriots. See, for example, George Lincoln Rockwell's criticism of the JBS in his book *White Power* (Reedy, WV: Liberty Bell, 1983), pp. 358–407.

29. John Stormer, *None Dare Call It Treason* (Florissant, MO: Liberty Bell, 1964).

30. Letter to Mr. John A. Stormer from Ben Klassen, October 11, 1976, in Klassen, *The Klassen Letters Volume Two*, p. 5.

31. Klassen, *Against the Evil Tide*, p. 303.

32. Kathy Marks, *Faces of Right Wing Extremism* (Boston, MA: Branden, 1996), p. 95.

33. Benjamin R. Epstein and Arnold Forster, *The Radical Right: Report on the John Birch Society and Its Allies* (New York: Random House, 1967), p. 150.

34. Ben Klassen's letter to Robert Welch, November 4, 1969, in Klassen, *The Klassen Letters Volume One*, pp. 16–18.

35. Linor Langer, *A Hundred Little Hitlers: The Death of a Black Man, the Trial of a White Racist, and the Rise of the Neo-Nazi Movement in America* (New York: Picador, 2004), p. 115.

36. Letter to Mr. George Lukick from Ben Klassen, February 13, 1976, in Klassen, *The Klassen Letters Volume One*, pp. 132–34.

37. Jackson and Jackson, *No Random Act*, p. 63.

38. Jackson and Jackson, *No Random Act*, pp. 18–26.

39. Dan T. Carter, *The Politics of Rage: George Wallace, the Origins of the New Conservatism, and the Transformation of American Politics* (New York: Simon and Schuster, 1995), pp. 139, 296–97.

40. For more on the Columbians, see Steven Weisenburger, "The Columbians, Inc: A Chapter of Racial Hatred from Post-World War II South," *Journal of Southern History*, 69, no. 4 (November 2003), pp. 821–60. For more on the National Renaissance Party, see Jeffrey Kaplan and Leonard Weinberg, *The Emergence of a Euro-American Radical Right* (New Brunswick, NJ: Rutgers University Press, 1998), pp. 106–18. The National Renaissance Party was founded by James Madole in 1948 and lasted until his death in 1978. The now-defunct U.S. House Committee on Un-American Activities actually issued a report on Madole's group in 1954. See Committee on Un-American Activities, *Preliminary Report on Neo-Fascist and Hate Groups* (Washington, DC: Committee on Un-American Activities, 1954).

41. Frederick J. Simonelli, *American Fuehrer: George Lincoln Rockwell and the American Nazi Party* (Chicago: University of Illinois Press, 1999), pp. 35–36.

42. The World Union of National Socialists (WUNS) was one of the first major postwar efforts to create a united "Neo-Fascist International." Representatives included Colin Jordan and John Tyndall from Great Britain, Savitri Devi from France, Bruno Ludtke from Germany, Franz Pfeiffer from Chile, Horst Eichmann (son of Adolf Eichmann) from Argentina, and Rockwell from the United States, among others. For more on WUNS see Simonelli, *American Fuehrer*, pp. 81–95.

43. In 1959, a Washington, DC, representative of the Anti-Defamation League (ADL) forwarded information that Rockwell had been sending wires and registered letters to then president Gamal Abdel Nasser of the United Arab Republic. Upon receipt of the information, the FBI opened an investigation. See FBI Internal Memorandum, File Number 97–3835–33, July 13, 1959.

44. Letter to Prof. R. Ben Kreigh from Ben Klassen, February, 20, 1975, in Klassen, *The Klassen Letters Volume One*, pp. 192–95.

45. Ben Klassen's letter to Mr. David Rust, September 17, 1976, in Klassen, *The Klassen Letters Volume Two*, pp. 18–19.

46. Klassen claimed that for every dollar that had been raised by Nazi parties, Jewish organizations had probably taken in $100 because of their efforts. Ben Klassen's letter to Matt Koehl, September 18, 1973, in Klassen, *The Klassen Letters Volume One*, pp. 123–25.

47. Ben Klassen's letter to Bonnie Parker, May 22, 1973, in Klassen, *The Klassen Letters Volume One*, pp. 109–10.

48. Ben Klassen's letter to Mr. David Rust, September 1, 1976, in Klassen, *The Klassen Letters Volume Two*, pp. 12–14. Joseph Tomassi, a member of Rockwell's successor organization, eventually departed and founded the National Socialist Liberation Front, a neo-Nazi organization that patterned itself on the new left models of the Weatherman and the Symbionese Liberation Army. Tomassi correctly saw that in the early 1970s, the idea of creating a Nazi-style party that would win support of a majority of the population was futile. Still, he believed that it was possible to strike

blows against "the system" provided that revolutionaries were prepared to act resolutely and alone. Whereas the state demonstrated over and over again that it could infiltrate and effectively neutralize any right-wing organization, it had yet to develop the capability of thwarting the actions of individuals or small groups acting alone. However, the NSLF campaign was reckless and its revolutionary arm was quickly crushed. Like Rockwell, Tomassi was also killed by a disgruntled member. See Jeffrey Kaplan, "Leaderless Resistance," *Terrorism and Political Violence*, 9, no. 3 (1997), pp. 81–82.

49. Letter to Mr. Paul Englert from Ben Klassen, January 13, 1975, in Klassen, *The Klassen Letters Volume One*, pp. 132–34.

50. In 1983, J. B. Stoner was a fugitive after he was convicted of bombing a church in Alabama in the 1960s. At the first trial, Stoner was acquitted. However, a district attorney later reopened the case and managed to convict Stoner. While Stoner was on the run, there was suspicion that he was hiding out at Klassen's headquarters in Otto, but there was no evidence for this supposition. Klassen vehemently denied the allegation. See Ben Klassen, *Trials, Tribulations and Triumphs* (Niceville, FL: Church of the Creator, 1993), p. 15.

51. Ben Klassen's letter to Omar C. Miller, March 20, 1970, in Klassen, *The Klassen Letters Volume One*, pp. 28–29.

52. Letter to Mr. E. Walter Carr from Ben Klassen, November 5, 1978, in Klassen, *The Klassen Letters Volume Two*, pp. 223–24.

53. Klassen, *The Klassen Letters Volume One*, pp. 61–67.

54. "'Third Party Gets Charter,'" in Klassen, *The Klassen Letters Volume One*, p. 34.

55. Klassen, *The Klassen Letters Volume One*, p. 34.

56. Klassen, *The Klassen Letters Volume One*, pp. 35–41.

57. As Klassen explained, the "W" signified the white race. The crown over the letter "W" signified the "aristocratic" nature of the white race. Finally, the halo above the crown signified what Klassen saw as the "divine mission" of his organization to carry on the "sacred heritage" of the white race into the future. See Klassen, *The Klassen Letters Volume One*, p. 41.

58. Letter to the *Sun Sentinel*, July 14, 1970, in Klassen, *The Klassen Letters Volume One*, p. 5.

59. Letter to Mr. John R. Adams, Ph.D., from Ben Klassen, January 10, 1972, in Klassen, *The Klassen Letters Volume One*, pp. 73–84.

60. Letter to Mrs. Eleanor Kramer from Ben Klassen, August 5, 1971, in Klassen, *The Klassen Letters Volume One*, pp. 69–73.

61. Klassen expressed these ideas in a letter to Eleanor Kramer, August 5, 1971. See Klassen, *The Klassen Letters Volume One*, pp. 69–73.

Chapter 2. The Theology and Ideology of Creativity

1. Accordingly, Creators consider 1973 the starting point, or the first year, of their church calendar. Rejecting a chronology based on Christianity, Creators designate

1973 as year 0. The years prior to this date are designated *Prius Creativitat* (Before Creativity). Likewise, the years 1974 and forward are designated *Anno de Creativitat* (Years of Creativity). There appears to have been some disagreement as far as the proper start of the COTC chronology. The Milwaukee chapter designated March 10, 1982—the day that ground was broken on the first headquarters in Otto, North Carolina—as the official start date of the church. As such, March 10 was designated as "RAHOWA Day." Klassen had originally designated that date as "Foundation Day." See Ben Klassen, *Trials, Tribulations and Triumphs* (Niceville, FL: Church of the Creator, 1993), p. 1. Such chronology was at play in other rightist ideologies as well. For example, 1922 became year 1 of the Fascist era in Italy after Mussolini's March on Rome in that same year. Likewise, the date on which Hitler attained power in Germany—January 30, 1933—was viewed as the day of national liberation. See Roger Griffin, "I Am No Longer Human. I Am a Titan. A God! The Fascist Quest to Regenerate Time," unpublished paper.

2. Ben Klassen, *Expanding Creativity: An Idea Whose Time Has Come* (Otto, NC: Church of the Creator, 1985), p. 173.

3. Ben Klassen, *Nature's Eternal Religion* (Niceville, FL: Church of the Creator, 1992), pp. 58–59.

4. Klassen, *Expanding Creativity*, pp. 89–96.

5. Klassen, *Expanding Creativity*, p. 96.

6. Norman Cameron and R. H. Stevens (trans.), *Hitler's Table Talk 1941–1944: His Private Conversations* (New York: Enigma Books, 2000), p. 419.

7. Richard Dawkins, *The God Delusion* (Boston, MA: Houghton Mifflin, 2006).

8. Letter to Mr. John R. Adams, Ph.D., from Ben Klassen, January 10, 1972, in Klassen, *The Klassen Letters Volume One*, pp. 73–84.

9. Klassen, *Nature's Eternal Religion*, p. 171.

10. Klassen, *Nature's Eternal Religion*, p. 172.

11. It is worth noting that some scholars have impugned the historicity of Jesus as well. See, for example, Robert M. Price, *Incredible Shrinking Son of Man: How Reliable Is the Gospel Tradition?* (Amherst, NY: Prometheus Books, 2003); and Nicholas Carter, *The Christ Myth* (Sussex, UK: Historical Review Press, 1993).

12. Klassen expressed these ideas in a letter to Eleanor Kramer, August 5, 1971. See Klassen, *The Klassen Letters Volume One*, pp. 69–73.

13. Ben Klassen, *On the Brink of a Bloody Racial War* (Otto, NC: Church of the Creator, 1993), pp. 354–59.

14. Letter to E. V. Johnson from Ben Klassen, December 8, 1976, in Ben Klassen, *The Klassen Letters Volume Two: 1976–1981* (Otto, NC: Church of the Creator, 1989), pp. 36–37.

15. To make his case, Voskuilen asked, Why did Saul stop persecuting Christians? Vokskulien discusses the possibility that rather than undergoing a life-changing conversion on the road to Damascus, Paul faked his conversion of faith. His secret mission was to undermine the Jewish messianist movement by introducing a radically new concept of a crucified "King of the Jews." In its original Jewish historical context,

"messianist" implied a temporal longing for a Messiah who would reinstall Jewish sovereignty over Palestine. In Palestine at that time, the political situation was tense to say the least. Consequently, the Roman authorities took measures deemed necessary to thwart any Jewish resistance to their rule. The nascent Christian movement was seen as potentially dangerous in Roman eyes. By transforming the movement into a project more concerned about the afterlife than temporal affairs, Christianity would be politically less subversive. Thus, Paul's efforts amounted to an early type of "psychological warfare" against the Jews of Palestine. Vokskulien pointed out that Paul, a Roman-born citizen, was allowed to spread his message for twenty years with little molestation from Roman authorities. Why was Jesus executed for spreading his message, but Paul was allowed to go about his life with little interference? Although Roman authorities took him into custody in King Herod's palace in Caesarea, Vokskulien argues that this measure was taken for his protection rather than confinement. According to his thesis, numerous Christians were highly suspicious of the sincerity of Paul's conversion and sought to eliminate him. Furthermore, when time for his trial arrived, he requested to be sent to Rome rather than be tried by his Jewish enemies. While he was in Rome, the regimen to which he was subjected was very lax, thus suggesting the move was made for strategic purposes seeking to protect Paul from potential Jewish assassins. It is recognized by both his detractors and admirers alike that it was he who first spread the gospel of the Messiah Jesus. See Thijs Voskuilen, "Operation Messiah: Did Christianity Start as a Roman Psychological Counterinsurgency Operation?" *Small Wars and Insurgencies*, 16, no. 2 (June 2005), pp. 192–215.

16. Kevin MacDonald, *Separation and Its Discontents: Toward an Evolutionary Theory of Anti-Semitism* (Westport, CT: Praeger, 1998), p. 108.

17. Robert S. Wistrich, *Anti-Semitism: The Longest Hatred* (New York: Pantheon Books, 1991), pp. 29–42.

18. Ben Klassen, *Building a Whiter and Brighter World.* (Otto, NC: Church of the Creator, 1986), pp. 100–101.

19. Klassen, *On the Brink of a Bloody Racial War*, pp. 364–65.

20. Ben Klassen, *A Revolution of Values through Religion* (Otto, NC: Church of the Creator, 1991), p. 6.

21. Klassen, *A Revolution of Values through Religion*, pp. 2–3.

22. Kevin MacDonald, *A People that Shall Dwell Alone: An Evolutionary Theory of Judaism* (Westport, CT: Praeger, 1994), p. 7.

23. Klassen, *Nature's Eternal Religion*, pp. 4–20.

24. Marcus Eli Ravage, "A Real Case against the Jews," in Ben Klassen, *The White Man's Bible* (2nd ed.) (Otto, NC: Church of the Creator, 1992), pp. 305–314.

25. Letter to Mr. John R. Adams, Ph.D. from Ben Klassen, January 10, 1972, in Klassen, *The Klassen Letters Volume One*, pp. 73–84.

26. Klassen, *Nature's Eternal Religion*, pp. 96–97.

27. MacDonald, *A People that Shall Dwell Alone*, p. 143.

28. MacDonald, *A People that Shall Dwell Alone*, p. 36.

29. A popular tract in extreme right circles is *The Talmud Unmasked* by I. B. Pranaitis, which seeks to uncover the supposed misanthropic nature of the Jewish holy text (Kessinger Publishing). For a rebuttal from the Anti-Defamation League, see *The Talmud in Anti-Semitic Politics* (New York: Anti-Defamation League, 2003), http://www.adl.org/presrele/asus_12/the_talmud.pdf.

30. *The Protocols of the Learned Elders of Zion* is believed to be a revision of an 1858 French novel titled *Dialogues of Hell* by Maurice Jolly, which parodied a Masonic plot to take over Europe. Some historians believed that agents of the Okhrana, the Czar's secret police, appropriated the document and switched Jews for Masons as the culprits for the purpose of fomenting anger against Russian Jews because of the role some of their members played in revolutionary activities. The principal author is thought to have been Serge Nilus. The Baltic German and Nazi philosopher, Alfred Rosenberg, brought the *Protocols* from Russia to Germany. From there the document spread to America and the rest of the world. The *Protocols* obviously inspired the myth of the "International Jew" popularized by the American industrialist and automobile magnate Henry Ford. In 1922, he began a fiercely anti-Semitic campaign in his newspaper the *Dearborn Independent,* which featured a series of articles titled the "International Jew: The World's Foremost Problem." Some historians suspect that Ford hired William Cameron, an obscure Canadian, to write the series. The series accused Jews of subverting the Christian underpinnings of American society and included reprinted sections from the notorious *Protocols of the Learned Elders of Zion*. A compilation of the series was published as a four-volume set of books also titled *The International Jew*. There was much cross-fertilization as *The International Jew* influenced rightists in Europe including the Nazis and Hitler who in turn inspired American far rightists. Adolf Hitler was an admirer of Ford and in 1938 awarded him a high honor from the German state, the Grand Order of the German Eagle. Moreover, Hitler was rumored to have had a portrait of Ford on his desk at his Nazi headquarters, the Brown House, and Ford was the only American mentioned by name in his tome, *Mein Kampf.* See James Pool and Suzanne Pool, *Who Financed Hitler?* (New York: Dial Press, 1978), pp. 85–130. For its part the ADL has sought to counter publications such as the *Protocols* and *The International Jew* with special reports of its own. See, for example, Anti-Defamation League, "The International Jew: Anti-Semitism from the Roaring Twenties Is Revived on the Web," 1999, and "The Protocols of the Learned Elders of Zion: A Hoax of Hate," 1999.

31. For more on the history of the Protocols, see Norman Cohn, *Warrant for Genocide: The Myth of the Jewish World Conspiracy and the Protocols of the Elders of Zion* (London: Serif, 1996). For its influence in the Islamic world, see George Michael, *The Enemy of My Enemy: The Alarming Convergence of Militant Islam and the Extreme Right* (Lawrence: University Press of Kansas, 2006).

32. Klassen, *Nature's Eternal Religion*, pp. 220–34.

33. For more on the role of Schiff in financially assisting the Bolsheviks, see E. L. Goldstein, *The Politics of Ethnic Pressure: The American Jewish Committee Fight against Immigration Restriction, 1906–1917* (New York: Garland, 1990); and Z. Sza-

jkowski, "Paul Nathan, Lucien Wolf, Jacob H. Schiff and the Jewish Revolutionary Movements in Eastern Europe," *Jewish Social Studies*, 29, no. 1 (1967), pp. 1–15.

34. Klassen, *The White Man's Bible*, pp. 232–45.

35. Stoddard's book, *The Rising Tide of Color*, is still sold by far-right book dealers to this day. Lothrop Stoddard, *The Rising Tide of Color* (Torrance, CA: Noontide Press, 1981).

36. Klassen, *The White Man's Bible*, pp. 185–92.

37. Mattias Gardell, *Gods of the Blood: The Pagan Revival and White Separatism* (Durham, NC: Duke University Press, 2003), p. 130.

38. Arthur de Gobineau, *The Inequality of Human Races* (New York: Howard Fertig, 1967).

39. Klassen, *The White Man's Bible*, pp. 320–31.

40. Klassen, *Nature's Eternal Religion*, pp. 29–34.

41. This is all the more surprising given the fact that former Nazi scientists, most notably Werhner von Braun, led the Apollo 11 effort that resulted in man's first landing on the moon.

42. Ben Klassen, *RAHOWA! This Planet Is All Ours* (Otto, NC: Church of the Creator, 1987), p. 141.

43. Klassen, *Building a Whiter and Brighter World*, pp. 210–220.

44. Arnold DeVries and Ben Klassen, *Salubrious Living* (Otto, NC: Church of the Creator, 1983), p. 244.

45. Ian Robertson, *Sociology* (3rd ed.) (New York: Worth, 1988), p. 401.

46. Klassen, *The White Man's Bible*, pp. 39–43.

47. Klassen, *The White Man's Bible*, pp. 35–89.

48. Klassen, *The White Man's Bible*, pp. 18–21.

49. Klassen, *The White Man's Bible*, pp. 410–413.

50. Klassen, *A Revolution of Values through Religion*, pp. 8–15.

51. MacDonald's highly controversial trilogy on the study of Judaism and anti-Semitism has gained him tremendous prestige among admirers in the far right; at an award ceremony on October 31, 2004, he discussed the applicability of the "Jewish Model" as an approach to ensure the survival of the West. MacDonald presented the lecture during a ceremony at which he was awarded the Jack London Literary prize for his trilogy. The event was sponsored by the Charles Martel Society. See "Can the Jewish Model Help the West Survive?" http://theoccidentalquarterlycom/jllp1/jllpkm.html.

52. In a trilogy of books, MacDonald advances an evolutionary theory to explain both Jewish and anti-Semitic collective behavior. As he argues in the first book of the trilogy, *A People That Shall Dwell Alone: An Evolutionary Theory of Judaism*, Judaism can best be explained as an evolutionary group strategy that features such characteristics as endogamy, ethnic exclusivity, in-group altruism, eugenics, and "crypsis." Even more controversial, he argues in his second book, *Separation and Its Discontents*, that the various anti-Semitic mass movements that have bedeviled the history of the West have been largely reactive in the sense that they were Gentile group

strategies as part of a competition over resources with Jews. According to MacDonald, ethnic separatism tends to lead to resource competition and, in doing so, to exacerbate intergroup tensions. What is perhaps most controversial according to his theory is the assertion that the group interests of Jews on the one hand and those of Gentiles on the other have occasionally been at cross-purposes, at least in the history of the West. Consequently, anti-Semitism is reactive and arises out of legitimate conflicts of interest. In order to survive as a precarious minority over the years, Jews have developed and promoted numerous intellectual movements to further their group interests and combat anti-Semitism. In that vein, the third book, and perhaps most popular in his trilogy, *The Culture of Critique*, argues that there is considerable Jewish hostility to traditional Western culture, which is manifested in various intellectual movements including Freudian psychology, the Frankfurt School, and Boazian anthropology. The desire is to undermine the European-derived civilization of America and replace it with a society more congenial to Jews. According to his analysis, Jewish organizations have promoted policies and ideologies that have undermined the cultural cohesion of the West while practicing just the opposite for themselves. Specifically, Jewish organizations are chided for extolling multiculturalism in the West while insisting upon ethnic exclusivity in Israel. See Kevin MacDonald, *A People that Shall Dwell Alone: An Evolutionary Theory of Judaism* (Westport, CT: Praeger, 1994); Kevin MacDonald, *Separation and Its Discontents: Toward an Evolutionary Theory of Anti-Semitism* (Westport, CT: Praeger, 1998); Kevin MacDonald, *The Culture of Critique: An Evolutionary Analysis of Jewish Involvement in Twentieth-Century Intellectual and Political Movements*. (Westport, CT: Praeger, 1998). For a review and synopsis of his research, see George Michael, "Professor Kevin MacDonald's Critique of Judaism: Legitimate Scholarship or the Intellectualization of Anti-Semitism?" *Journal of Church and State*, 48 (Autumn 2006), pp. 779–806.

53. Klassen, *On the Brink of a Bloody Racial War*, pp. 202–212.

54. Klassen, *On the Brink of a Bloody Racial War*, pp. 352–53.

55. For example, William L. Pierce, founder of the National Alliance, made the same point, arguing that whites should not judge people as individuals but as representatives of hostile groups. See Andrew Macdonald (pseudonym for William Pierce), *Hunter* (Hillsboro, WV: National Vanguard Books, 1989), pp. 72–73.

56. Klassen, *Nature's Eternal Religion*, pp. 256–76.

57. Klassen, *The White Man's Bible*, pp. 122–29.

58. Klassen, *Nature's Eternal Religion*, p. 75.

59. "Mud people" or "muds" is a pejorative used in the vernacular of the racialist right to denote nonwhites.

60. Klassen, *Expanding Creativity*, pp. 56–67.

61. Letter to Mr. Clifford D. Herrington from Ben Klassen, March 14, 1977, in Ben Klassen, *The Klassen Letters Volume Two: 1976–1981* (Otto, NC: Church of the Creator, 1989), pp. 51–54.

62. Adolf Hitler (trans. Ralph Manheim), *Mein Kampf* (Boston, MA: Houghton Mifflin, 1971), p. 42.

63. Hitler, *Mein Kampf*, p. 88.

64. Klassen, *The White Man's Bible*, pp. 444–47.

65. Hitler, *Mein Kampf*, p. 114.

66. Hitler, *Mein Kampf*, p. 135.

67. Hitler, *Mein Kampf*, p. 184.

68. Hitler, *Mein Kampf*, p. 249.

69. Gilmer W. Blackburn, *Education in the Third Reich: Race and History in Nazi Textbooks* (Albany: State University of New York Press, 1985), pp. 73–79.

70. Hitler, *Mein Kampf*, p. 255.

71. Hitler, *Mein Kampf*, p. 308.

72. Hitler, *Mein Kampf*, pp. 496–97.

73. Klassen, *RAHOWA!*, p.10.

74. According to Klassen, there was an inordinate emphasis on the Civil War in American history. He saw the period as a fratricidal conflict that led to the decimation of much of the country's male population and as such was not worth celebrating. According to his analysis, the war was orchestrated by the Rothschild banking family for the very purpose of destroying the country's white males. Klassen pointed out that President Lincoln expressed a desire to repatriate black slaves to Africa. To that end, the American Colonization Society, which was founded in 1817, sought to repatriate American blacks to Africa. The organization and its program received support from several prominent Americans including Thomas Jefferson, James Monroe, Abraham Lincoln, and Marcus Garvey. Klassen claimed that Lincoln's assassin—John Wilkes Booth—was a member of the Jewish family of Botha. During the war, Lincoln issued millions of dollars in U.S. government "greenbacks," which was supposed to have drawn the ire of Jewish bankers who saw this as a circumvention of their banking monopoly. With the war over, leaving scores of white men dead, Klassen argued that Lincoln had served his purpose as far as his putative Jewish masters were concerned. As a result, he was assassinated, which scuttled any plans for the repatriation of blacks. See Ben Klassen, "The Rothschilds, the Civil War and the Lincoln Assassination," *Racial Loyalty*, 47 (February 1989), pp. 1–3, 9.

75. Some white separatists advocate the creation of a separate white republic to be carved out of the Pacific Northwest, which would include the states of Oregon, Washington, Montana, Wyoming, and Colorado.

76. Klassen, "Introduction," Klassen, *On the Brink of a Bloody Racial War*.

77. Letter to Mr. Terry Oaks from Ben Klassen, June 16, 1978, in Klassen, *The Klassen Letters Volume Two*, pp. 161–63.

78. Klassen, *RAHOWA!*, p. 9.

79. Klassen, *Expanding Creativity*, p. 152.

80. Klassen, *A Revolution of Values through Religion*, p. 99.

81. Klassen admired the *Truth Seeker* magazine, which had some rightist leanings. Published since 1873 by the American Association for the Advancement of Atheism,

the organization that was once led by Charles Lee Smith from 1937 to 1964. Smith was an associate of Willis Carto, the central figure of the postwar American far right. For more on Smith and his association with Carto, see George Michael, *Willis Carto and the American Far Right* (Gainesville, FL: University Press of Florida, 2008).

82. Klassen, *On the Brink of a Bloody Racial War*, p. 164.

Chapter 3. The Far Right and the Critique of Christianity

1. For a short but excellent exegesis on the religion of nature, see Jeffrey Kaplan, "Religion of Nature," in *The Encyclopedia of White Power: A Sourcebook on the Radical Racist Right* (New York: AltaMira Press, 2000), pp. 253–58.

2. August Kubizek (trans. E. V. Anderson), *The Young Hitler I Knew* (Cambridge, MA: Houghton Mifflin, 1955), p. 101

3. H. P. Blavatsky, *The Secret Doctrine: The Synthesis of Science, Religion, and Philosophy* (Pasadena, CA: Theosophical University Press, 1988).

4. Nicholas Goodrick-Clarke, *The Occult Roots of Nazism: Secret Aryan Cults and Their Influence on Nazi Ideology* (Washington Square, NY: New York University Press, 1992), p. 34.

5. Wotan is the German name for Odin. The two are interchangeable and refer to the same deity.

6. Goodrick-Clarke, *The Occult Roots of Nazism*, p. 64.

7. Jorg Lanz Liebenfels was another important figure in the neopagan movement; however, his brand of paganism was not really Odinist but instead a hodgepodge of racial mysticism and the Nordic Atlantis myth. He published an occult journal, *Ostara*, which was popular with racial nationalists and anti-Semites. There is some evidence that Hitler was an avid reader of *Ostara* during his Vienna years and allegedly on one occasion he even visited Liebenfels in order to secure back issues of the journal. Just how much if any influence Liebenfels had on Nazi policy is difficult to determine. Be that as it may, there are striking parallels between the two. For example, Liebenfels advocated a eugenics program, sterilization of the unfit and racially undesirable, enslavement of non-Aryans, deportation of non-Aryans to Madagascar, and if all else failed, extermination. Such prescriptions prefigured much of Nazi racial policy. Soon after the Anschluss with Austria in 1938, the Nazis forbade Liebenfels from continuing his publishing activities. Some historians cite this as evidence that Hitler wanted to obscure any occult connections to the Nazi *Weltanschauung*. For more on Liebenfels, see Goodrick-Clarke, *The Occult Roots of Nazism*.

8. For more on the Thule Gesellschaft, see Goodrick-Clarke, *The Occult Roots of Nazism*; and Reginald Phelps, "'Before Hitler Came': Thule Society and the Germanen Orden." *Journal of Modern History*, 25, (1963), pp. 245–61.

9. Gilmer W. Blackburn, *Education in the Third Reich: Race and History in Nazi Textbooks* (Albany: State University of New York Press, 1985), pp. 182–83.

10. Adolf Hitler (trans. Ralph Manheim), *Mein Kampf* (Boston, MA: Houghton Mifflin, 1971), p. 475.

11. Blackburn, *Education in the Third Reich*, p. 88.

12. Richard Steigmann-Gall, "Nazism and the Revival of Political Religion Theory," *Totalitarian Movements and Political Religions*, 5, no. 3 (Winter 2004), p. 387.

13. Robert A. Pois, *National Socialism and the Religion of Nature* (London: Croom Helm, 1986), p. 3.

14. Pois, *National Socialism and the Religion of Nature*, p. 11.

15. Hitler, *Mein Kampf*, p. 288.

16. Peter Viereck, *Meta-Politics: The Roots of the Nazi Mind* (New York: Capricorn Books, 1961).

17. For a good exegesis of the German Christian movement, see Doris L. Bergen, *Twisted Cross: The German Christian Movement in the Third Reich* (Chapel Hill: University of North Carolina Press, 1996).

18. Alfred Rosenberg, *The Myth of the Twentieth Century: An Evaluation of the Spiritual-Intellectual Confrontations of Our Age* (Newport Beach, CA: Noontide Press, 1993). For a very readable summation of Rosenberg's philosophy, see James B. Whisker, *The Philosophy of Alfred Rosenberg: Origins of the National Socialist Myth* (Costa Mesa, CA: Noontide Press), p. 23

19. Norman Cameron and R. H. Stevens (trans.), *Hitler's Table Talk 1941-1944: His Private Conversations* (New York: Enigma Books, 2000), p. 422.

20. Ben Klassen, *A Revolution of Values through Religion* (Otto, NC: Church of the Creator, 1991), pp. 55–67.

21. See, for example, Gerald Suster, *Hitler: Black Magician* (London: Skoob Books, 1996). Trevor Ravenscroft asserted that as a young man, Hitler longed to obtain the so-called "spear of destiny"—that is, the putative spear used by the Roman centurion Gaius Cassius Longinus to pierce the chest of Jesus during the crucifixion. For centuries, more than one relic has survived in Europe purporting to be the original spear. According to Ravenscroft, during his years in Vienna, the young Hitler would visit the Hofburg Treasure House in Vienna and gaze at the relic with awe. After the Anschluss between Germany and Austria in 1936, Hitler sought to harness the supposed occult power of the spear toward his political goals. See Trevor Ravenscroft, *The Spear of Destiny* (York Beach, ME: Samuel Weiser, 1991). Although there is a genre of literature linking Hitler to the occult, these assertions appear spurious and are not taken seriously by most historians. For a refutation of Ravenscroft's thesis, see Ken Anderson, *Hitler and the Occult* (Amherst, NY: Prometheus Books, 1995).

22. Cameron and Stevens, *Hitler's Table Talk 1941-1944*, p. 143.

23. Cameron and Stevens, *Hitler's Table Talk 1941-1944*, p. 145.

24. Cameron and Stevens, *Hitler's Table Talk 1941-1944*, pp. 51 and 325.

25. Cameron and Stevens, *Hitler's Table Talk 1941-1944*, p. 7.

26. Cameron and Stevens, *Hitler's Table Talk 1941-1944*, p. 722.

27. Cameron and Stevens, *Hitler's Table Talk 1941-1944*, p. 75.

28. Cameron and Stevens, *Hitler's Table Talk 1941-1944*, p. 253.

29. Hitler, *Mein Kampf*, pp. 55–60.

30. Hitler, *Mein Kampf*, p. 150.

31. Hitler, *Mein Kampf*, p. 306.

32. Hitler, *Mein Kampf*, p. 65.

33. Hitler, *Mein Kampf*, pp. 201–206. For more on Hitler's epiphany, see Blackburn, *Education in the Third Reich*, pp. 80–81.

34. Quoted in Blackburn, *Education in the Third Reich*, p. 154.

35. Quoted in Blackburn, *Education in the Third Reich*, p. 77.

36. In the postwar neofascist Internationale, Degrelle was an iconic figure. In Belgium, during the interwar years, he was the leader of the fascistic Rexist movement. During World War II, he organized a Waffen-SS Division—"the Wallonian Legion"— which was composed primarily of French-speaking Belgian volunteers. The division was involved in numerous ferocious battles on the Eastern Front. For his valor, Degrelle became the most highly decorated foreigner in the service of the Third Reich. When Hitler bestowed a prestigious medal on Degrelle—the Knight's Cross with oak leaves—the German führer was quoted as saying "If I had had a son . . . I would want him to be like you." After receiving asylum in Franco's Spain at the end of the war, Degrelle remained unrepentant and wrote several books on his wartime exploits and hagiographic accounts of Hitler that were published by Willis Carto. For more on Degrelle, see Leon Degrelle, *Campaign in Russia*. (Newport Beach, CA: Institute for Historical Review, 1993); Leon Degrelle, *Epic: The Story of the Waffen SS* (Torrance, CA: Institute for Historical Review, 1985); Leon Degrelle, *Hitler: Born at Versailles* (Torrance, CA: Institute for Historical Review, 1992).

37. Degrelle, Leon, "The Enigma of Hitler," n.d., http://www.historiography-project.com/jhrchives/v14/v14n3p22_Degrelle.html, downloaded August 1, 2007.

38. Hitler, *Mein Kampf*, p. 361.

39. Cameron and Stevens, *Hitler's Table Talk 1941–1944*, p. 418.

40. Robert Waite discusses some of Hitler's esoteric interests in Robert G. I. Waite, *The Psychopathic God: Adolf Hitler* (New York: Basic Books, 1977).

41. In his memoirs, Himmler's physician, Dr. Kersten, mentioned that Himmler confided to him his desire to make paganism the official religion of Europe and hang the pope after German victory in World War II. See Herma Briffault (ed.), *The Memoirs of Doctor Felix Kersten* (Garden City, NY: Doubleday, 1947).

42. Steigmann-Gall, "Nazism and the Revival of Political Religion Theory," p. 387.

43. Heather Pringle, *The Master Plan: Himmler's Scholars and the Holocaust* (New York: Hyperion, 2006), p. 146. Himmler came under the influence of Karl Maria Wiligut, an important figure in the Ahnerbe, the Ancestral Division of the SS. Wiligut designed much of the paraphernalia of the SS including the SS dagger and rings. His efforts earned him the appellation, "Himmler's Rasputin." For more on Wiligut, see Goodrick-Clarke, *The Occult Roots of Nazism*, and Michael Moynihan (ed.), *The Secret King: Karl Maria Wiligut: Himmler's Lord of the Runes* (Waterbury, VT: Dominion Press, 2001).

44. The primary purpose of the Ahnerbe division was to investigate German prehistory. For more on the organization, see Pringle, *The Master Plan*.

45. Quoted in Horst von Malitz, *The Evolution of Hitler's Germany: The Ideology, the Personality, the Movement* (New York: Macmillan, 1973), p. 191.

46. Hess was reported to have been an occultist and avid follower of astrology. Some historians believe that British Intelligence, MI5, infiltrated Hess's inner circle of occultists and goaded Hess into making the journey to Scotland. The British government has not been forthcoming on the details of Hess's trip; disclosure on the incident is not planned until far into the next century. See Peter Levenda, *Unholy Alliance: A History of Nazi Involvement with the Occult* (New York: Avon Books, 1995), pp. 226–34; and James Douglas-Hamilton, *Motive for a Mission: The Story behind Hess's Flight to Britain* (New York: St. Martin's Press, 1971).

47. Cameron and Stevens, *Hitler's Table Talk 1941–1944*, pp. 59–60.

48. Pois, *National Socialism and the Religion of Nature*, p. 39.

49. Blackburn, *Education in the Third Reich*, p. 23.

50. Blackburn, *Education in the Third Reich*, p. 24.

51. Pois, *National Socialism and the Religion of Nature*, p. 47.

52. Julius Evola, *Revolt against the Modern World* (Rochester, VT: Inner Traditions, 1995).

53. Julius Evola, *Race as a Revolutionary Idea* (London: Rising Press, 2001).

54. Julius Evola, *Men among the Ruins: War Reflections of a Radical Traditionalist* (Rochester, VT: Inner Traditions, 2002).

55. Julius Evola, *Ride the Tiger: A Survival Manual for Aristocrats of the Soul* (Rochester, VT: Inner Traditions, 2003).

56. For more on Evola, see Nicholas Goodrick-Clarke, *The Black Sun: Aryan Cults, Esoteric Nazism and the Politics of Identity* (New York: New York University Press, 2002), pp. 52–71; Kevin Coogan, *Dreamer of the Day: Francis Parker Yockey and the Postwar Fascist International* (New York: Autonomedia, 1999), pp. 304–314; and Joscelyn Godwin, "Julius Evola: A Philosopher for the Age of the Titans," in *Tyr*, 1 (2002), pp. 127–42.

57. The Know Nothing movement of the 1850s was in large part a reaction among native Protestants against the influx of Catholic immigrants. See Carleton Beals, *Brass-Knuckle Crusade: The Great Know-Nothing Conspiracy: 1820–1860* (New York: Hastings House, 1960). The Second Ku Klux Klan, which was revived in 1915, had many fundamentalist ministers in its ranks. See Nancy MacLean, *Behind the Mask of Chivalry: The Making of the Second Ku Klux Klan* (New York: Oxford University Press, 1994). Eventually anti-Catholicism waned, allowing Father Charles Coughlin to gain a mass following during the Great Depression. And another Depression-era demagogue, the Reverend Gerald K. Smith, was very influential in the far right and active up until his death in 1976. Geoffrey S. Smith, *To Save a Nation: American 'Extremism,' the New Deal, and the Coming of World War II* (Chicago: Elephant Paperbacks, 1992). More recently, a new sect, Christian Identity, has gained a following among a large portion of the far right. An anti-Semitic mutation of British Israelism, Christian Identity posits that the various peoples of Northern Europe are the ten lost tribes of Israel and that contemporary Jews are impostors who are actually the spawn

of Satan or remnants of a Eurasian tribe, the Khazars. See Michael Barkun, *Religion and the Racist Right: The Origins of the Christian Identity Movement* (Chapel Hill: University of North Carolina Press, 1994).

58. Robert N. Bellah, "Civil Religion in America," in Robert A. Bellah, *Beyond Belief: Essays on Religion in a Post Traditional World* (New York: Harper and Row, 1970), pp. 168–99.

59. Leonard Dinnerstein, *Anti-Semitism in America* (New York: Oxford University Press, 1994), p. 239.

60. George Michael, *Confronting Right-Wing Extremism and Terrorism in the USA* (New York: Routledge, 2003).

61. The late Herbert Armstrong's Church of Christ, which publishes the periodical *The Plain Truth*, is one prominent exception. Others include the Church of Israel and the National Message Ministry. For more on the Christian Identity sect, see Barkun, *Religion and The Racist Right*; and Jeffrey Kaplan, *Radical Religion in America: Millenarian Movements from the Far Right to the Children of Noah* (Syracuse, NY: Syracuse University Press, 1997).

62. According to this theory, in the eighth century, a Eurasian tribe known as the Khazars converted to Judaism and their descendents comprise the vast majority of contemporary Jews. Anti-Semites and occasionally some anti-Zionists invoke this theory to reject contemporary Jewish ancestral claims to Palestine. Ironically, the esteemed Hungarian-Jewish author Arthur Koestler unwittingly did much to popularize this theory in his book *The Thirteenth Tribe* (New York: Random House, 1976). Far rightists have arrogated this book, as it has become a staple in their literature. Many far-right book distributors sell the title.

63. At first thought this might sound a little paradoxical but according to this theory those terrorists who believe God is on their side are more self-assured in their mission and hence have less compunction about using violence. In recent years several terrorism scholars have propounded similar theories; see Bruce Hoffman, *Inside Terrorism* (New York: Columbia University Press, 1998); and Bruce Hoffman, *Holy Terror: The Implications of Terrorism Motivated by a Religious Imperative* (Santa Monica, CA: Rand Corporation, 1993); Thomas Flanagan, "The Politics of the Millennium," *Terrorism and Political Violence*, 7, no. 3 (1995), pp. 164–75; and Michael Barkun, "Religion, Militias and Oklahoma City: The Mind of Conspiratorialists," *Terrorism and Political Violence*, 8, no. 1 (1996), pp. 50–64.

64. For example, Brent Smith found that of the seventy-five persons indicted for right-wing terrorism during the 1980s were all closely allied with the Christian Identity movement. See Brent L. Smith, *Terrorism in America: Pipe Bombs and Pipe Dreams* (Albany: State University of New York Press, 1994), p. 8.

65. As John George, a longtime observer of political extremism in America, noted, "The majority probably comprehend little about Identity theology, except that it makes 'whites' God's chosen people, and that is enough for them." John George, "Emergence of a Euro-American Radical Right Book Review," *Menasha*, 93, no. 3 (September 1999), pp. 714–15.

66. This observation is made in Eugene V. Gallagher, "God and Country: Revolution as a Religious Imperative on the Radical Right," *Terrorism and Political Violence*, 9, no. 3 (1997), pp. 63–64.

67. See James Aho, *The Politics of Righteousness: Idaho Christian Patriotism* (Seattle: University of Washington Press, 1990); Morris Dees and James Corcoran, *Gathering Storm: America's Militia Threat* (New York: HarperCollins, 1996); Howard L. Bushard, John R. Craig, and Myra Barnes, *Soldiers of God: White Supremacists and Their Holy War for America* (New York: Kensington Books, 1998); and David Niewart, *In God's Country: The Patriot Movement and the Pacific Northwest* (Pullman: Washington State University Press, 1999).

68. There seems to be a generational shift in religious preferences taking place among the more radical elements of the far right. Younger activists are increasingly adopting Odinism, a form of neopaganism, as their religion of choice. See the article "The New Romantics" in the Spring 2001 issue of the Southern Poverty Law Center's *Intelligence Report* for more on this development.

69. One such claim of an unbroken tradition can be found in Mark L. Mirabello, *The Odin Brotherhood* (Edmonds, WA: Sure Fire Press, 1992).

70. During the 1960s, at least one member of George Lincoln Rockwell's American Nazi Party, Dan Buros, was a practicing Odinist. See A. M. Rosenthal and Arthur Gelb, *One More Victim: The Life and Death of a Jewish Nazi* (New York: New American Library, 1967).

71. Jeffrey Kaplan observed that story books containing Norse myths became popular with boys in the 1950s and 1960s. Moreover, the movie, *The Vikings*, starring Kirk Douglas, also gave the old religion some exposure. See Kaplan, *Radical Religion in America*. Finally, in 1963, Marvel Comics introduced one of its most popular heroes, Thor. The series continues to this day.

72. A. Rud Mills, "Our Ancient Religion," *Right*, 50 (November, 1959), p. 3.

73. According to her side of the story, she agreed to drive a car from Texas to Florida for a young couple in her neighborhood. Unbeknownst to her, the trunk contained large amounts of marijuana and synthetic heroin. After her release from prison, she was deported to Canada. See Mattias Gardell, *Gods of the Blood: The Pagan Revival and White Separatism* (Durham, NC: Duke University Press, 2003), p. 176.

74. Carl G. Jung, "Wotan," in *C. G. Jung, The Collected Works*, Vol. 10, Bollingen Series XX (New York: Pantheon, 1990), pp. 179–93.

75. Kaplan, *Radical Religion in America*, pp. 69–99.

76. The Asatru Alliance avoids explicit connections to National Socialism yet it still holds that Asatru should be open only to those of European descent. By contrast, the Ring of Troth is open to all and includes among its members a few gays and lesbians, ethnic Jews, and even interracial couples! See Kaplan, *Radical Religion in America*, pp. 30–32.

77. George Michael, *Confronting Right-Wing Extremism and Terrorism in the USA* (London: Routledge, 2003), pp. 118–19.

78. Jeffrey Kaplan, *The Encyclopedia of White Power: A Sourcebook on the Radical Racist Right* (New York: AltaMira Press, 2000), p. 201.

79. Robert S. Griffin, *The Fame of a Dead Man's Deeds: An Up-Close Portrait of White Nationalist William Pierce* (Bloomington, IN: 1st Books, 2001), pp. 114–15.

80. For more on Cosmotheism, see Griffin, *The Fame of a Dead Man's Deeds*, pp. 178–97; George Michael, "The Revolutionary Model of Dr. William L. Pierce," *Terrorism and Political Violence*, 15, no.3 (Autumn, 2003), pp. 62–80; and Martin Durham, "The Upward Path: Palengenisis, Political Religion and the National Alliance," *Totalitarian Movements and Political Religions*, 5, no. 3 (Winter 2004), pp. 454–68. Pierce wrote three unpublished small tracts on Cosmotheism—"The Path," "On Society," and "On Living Things." Also, he outlined his philosophy in a 1976 speech to members of the National Alliance. See William L. Pierce, "Our Cause," *Free Speech*, 8, no. 8 (July 2002), http://www.natall.com/free-speech/fs0208c.html.

81. Savitri Devi, *The Lighting and the Sun* (Hillsboro, WV: National Vanguard Books, 2000).

82. For more on Devi and her influence in the far right subculture, see Nicholas Goodrick-Clarke, *Hitler's Priestess: Savitri Devi, the Hindu-Aryan Myth, and Neo-Nazism* (New York: New York University Press, 1998).

83. James Larratt Battersby, *The Holy Book of Adolf Hitler* (Southport England: German World Church in Europe, 1952). For more on Battersby, see Richard Thurlow, *Fascism in Britain: From Oswald Mosley's Blackshirts to the National Front* (London: I. B. Tauris, 1998), pp. 178, 196, 199.

84. George Lincoln Rockwell, *This Time the World* (6th ed.) (Reedy, WV: Liberty Bell, 1993), p. 28.

85. Rockwell, *This Time the World*, p. 29.

86. Rockwell, *This Time the World*, p. 29.

87. Rockwell, *This Time the World*, pp. 175–76.

88. George Lincoln Rockwell, *White Power* (publisher unknown, 1983), pp. 455–56.

89. Matt Koehl, *Faith of the Future* (Milwaukee, WI: New Order, 1995).

90. Research indicates that Christian Identity draws very few members from the Catholic Church, the Church of Latter Day Saints, or the more established Protestant denominations. Identity believers tend to come from fundamentalist backgrounds. See Aho, *The Politics of Righteousness*.

91. Gardell, *Gods of the Blood*.

92. Gardell, *Gods of the Blood*.

Chapter 4. Reaching Out to the Right

1. Dave Jackson and Neta Jackson, *No Random Act: Behind the Murder of Ricky Birdsong* (Colorado Springs, CO: Waterbrook Press, 2002), p. 102.

2. Letter to P. Charles Labbe, U. L. from Ben Klassen, December 1, 1977, in Ben Klassen, *The Klassen Letters Volume Two: 1976–1981* (Otto, NC: Church of the Creator, 1989), pp. 115–16.

3. Peter Scharff Smith, Niels Bo Poulsen, and Claus Bundgard Christensen, "The Danish Volunteers in the Waffen SS and German Warfare at the Eastern Front," *Contemporary European History*, 8, no. 1 (1999), p. 73.

4. William Pfaff, *The Wrath of Nations: Civilization and the Furies of Nationalism* (New York: Simon and Schuster, 1993), p. 66.

5. As mentioned earlier, the late Dr. William L. Pierce led the National Alliance. Matt Koehl leads New Order, which is the successor organization to George Lincoln Rockwell's American Nazi Party. The late James H. Madole led the National Renaissance Party, which was based in New York City. Tom Metzger is leader of White Aryan Resistance (WAR). Frank Collin led the National Socialist Party of America, which would gain nationwide notoriety in the U.S. Supreme Court's Skokie case in 1978. His former colleague, Harold Covington, has sojourned through numerous neo-Nazi organizations.

6. Letter to Mr. Lewis Moore, February 9, 1977, in Klassen, *The Klassen Letters Volume Two*, p. 44.

7. Ben Klassen's letter to William Pierce, November 2, 1976, in Klassen, *The Klassen Letters Volume Two*, p. 32.

8. Interview with Dr. William Pierce, July 12, 2000. When I broached the topic of Christianity with Pierce, like Klassen, he recognized that it was derived from Judaism. However, Pierce said that he respected many members of his organization who were Christians and thus saw no compelling reason to provoke a war with Christianity.

9. Robert S. Griffin, *The Fame of a Dead Man's Deeds: An Up-Close Portrait of White Nationalist William Pierce* (Bloomington, IN: 1st Books, 2001), pp. 254–55.

10. David Segal, "The Pied Piper of Racism," *Washington Post* (January 12, 2000), C1, p. 8.

11. Andrew Macdonald (pseudonym for William Pierce), *The Turner Diaries* (Hillsboro, WV: National Vanguard Books, 1978).

12. Ben Klassen, *On the Brink of a Bloody Racial War* (Otto, NC: Church of the Creator, 1993), p. 13.

13. Letter to Dr. William L. Pierce from Ben Klassen, June 30, 1976, in Ben Klassen, *The Klassen Letters Volume One: 1969–1976* (Otto, NC: Church of the Creator, 1988), pp. 286–88.

14. Letter to Dr. William L. Pierce from Ben Klassen, June 20, 1976, in Klassen, *The Klassen Letters Volume Two*, pp. 8–9.

15. Ben Klassen's letter to Dan Gayman, January 10, 1978, in Klassen, *The Klassen Letters Volume Two*, pp. 130–31.

16. Ben Klassen, *A Revolution of Values through Religion*. (Otto, NC: Church of the Creator, 1991), p. 69.

17. Ben Klassen, *Building a Whiter and Brighter World*. (Otto, NC: Church of the Creator, 1986), p. 90.

18. Ben Klassen's letter to Stephen A. McNallen, March 17, 1975, in Klassen, *The Klassen Letters Volume One*, pp. 202–203.

19. Klassen, *A Revolution of Values through Religion*, p. 110.

20. Letter to Mrs. E. Christensen from Ben Klassen, November 5, 1973, in Klassen, *The Klassen Letters Volume One*, pp. 10–13.

21. Letter to Mr. M. Montgomery from Ben Klassen, February 16, 1976, in Ben Klassen, *The Klassen Letters Volume One*, pp. 272–74.

22. Anti-Defamation League, *Church of the Creator: Creed of Hate* (New York: Anti-Defamation League, 1993), p. 4.

23. Jeffrey Kaplan, *Radical Religion in America: Millenarian Movements from the Far Right to the Children of Noah* (Syracuse, NY: Syracuse University Press, 1997), p. 97.

24. "Brickbats and Bouquets," *Racial Loyalty*, 47 (February 1989), p. 8.

25. Ben Klassen, *Trials, Tribulations and Triumphs*. (Niceville, FL: Church of the Creator, 1993), p. 83.

26. John George and Laird Wilcox, *Nazis, Communists, Klansmen, and Others on the Fringe* (Buffalo, NY: Prometheus Books, 1992), p. 278.

27. George and Wilcox, *Nazis, Communists, Klansmen*, p. 275.

28. Some members, however, were responsible for blowing up a police station in Redmond, Washington, and also attempted to rob three banks in Seattle. See John and Wilcox, *Nazis, Communists, Klansmen*, p. 275. Another member, Keith Gilbert, was implicated in the theft of 1,400 pounds of TNT, which he allegedly planned to use to bomb an ADL convention. See J. Harry Jones Jr., *The Minutemen* (Garden City, NY: Doubleday, 1968), pp. 397–399. Not surprisingly, the ADL paid close attention to the Minutemen and in 1968 sponsored a critical 1968 study of the group by Richard P. Albares titled *Nativist Paramilitarism in the United States: The Minutemen* (Chicago, IL: Center for Social Studies, 1968).

29. Ben Klassen, *Against the Evil Tide: An Autobiography* (Otto, NC: Church of the Creator, 1991), pp. 436–50.

30. Letter to Mr. Robert B. De Pugh from Ben Klassen, June 13, 1977, in Ben Klassen, *The Klassen Letters Volume Two*, pp. 77–81.

31. Letter to Mr. Robert B. De Pugh from Ben Klassen, July 3, 1977, in Ben Klassen, *The Klassen Letters Volume Two*, pp. 81–86.

32. Ben Klassen's letters to Robert De Pugh in Klassen, *The Klassen Letters Volume Two*, pp. 76–88.

33. Klassen, *Trials, Tribulations and Triumphs*, p. 163.

34. Ben Klassen, *Building a Whiter and Brighter World* (Otto, NC: Church of the Creator, 1986), p. 172.

35. The Liberty Lobby was forced to dissolve itself as a result of a civil judgment brought against the Institute for Historical Review (IHR), which was once a subsidiary. In the early 1990s, Jean Farrel Edison, an heiress to the Thomas Edison estate, bequeathed a $15 million dollar inheritance to the IHR. Carto claimed to have had control over the IHR when the will was consummated and was thus entitled to the money. However, in December 2000, California Superior Court Judge Runston G. Maino ruled otherwise and ordered the Liberty Lobby to surrender its assets to the

IHR. See *Spotlight*, December 31, 2000, Emergency Edition. Despite this apparent setback, the Liberty Lobby reconstituted itself and its *Spotlight* publication as *American Free Press* later that year. See George Michael, *Willis Carto and the American Far Right* (Gainesville, FL: University Press of Florida, 2008).

36. Willis Carto's letter to Ben Klassen, May 13, 1973, in Klassen, *The Klassen Letters Volume One*, p. 109.

37. Letter to Mr. John Tiffany from Ben Klassen, October 30, 1978, in Klassen, *The Klassen Letters Volume Two*, pp. 176–78.

38. Klassen, *Building a Whiter and Brighter World*, pp. 43–44.

39. Revilo Oliver, *Christianity and the Survival of the West* (Sterling, VA: Sterling Enterprises, 1973).

40. Ben Klassen's letter to Revilo P. Oliver, June 19, 1973, in Klassen, *The Klassen Letters Volume One*, pp. 91–93.

41. Ralph Perrier (Revilo P. Oliver), *The Jews Love Christianity* (Reedy, WV: Liberty Bell, 1980).

42. Wilmont Robertson lamented the obstacles he faced in distributing his book, *The Dispossessed Majority*, perhaps the most eloquent and sophisticated work of American far-right literature. Although there was a strong demand (90,000 copies were sold as of 1981), Robertson could find no outlets to sell his book—even on a consignment basis. He next tried advertising, but even conservative publications like *The National Review*, the John Birch Society's *American Opinion*, *The Retired Officers Magazine*, or *The American Rifleman* would not touch it. Robertson alluded to Justice Wendell Holmes's marketplace of ideas dictum, "the rights defined in the First Amendment must apply to the dissemination of ideas as well as their expression." See Wilmont Robertson, *Ventillations* (Cape Caneveral, FL: Howard Allen, 1982), pp. 22–25.

43. Wilmont Robertson, *The Dispossessed Majority* (Cape Canaveral, FL: Howard Allen, 1981).

44. Ben Klassen's letter to Wilmont Robertson, December 11, 1974, in Klassen, *The Klassen Letters Volume One*, pp. 177–79.

45. William Gayley Simpson, *Which Way Western Man?* (Washington, DC: National Alliance, 1978). For a good synopsis of the book, see Robert S. Griffin, *The Fame of a Dead Man's Deeds: An Up-Close Portrait of White Nationalist William Pierce.* (Bloomington, IN: 1st Books, 2001), pp. 245–85.

46. Letter to Mr. Henry Madeksho from Ben Klassen, September 18, 1973, in Klassen, *The Klassen Letters Volume One*, pp. 216–217.

47. Ben Klassen, *Building a Whiter and Brighter World*, p. 45.

48. Klassen, *The Klassen Letters Volume Two*, p. 5.

Chapter 5. Groundbreaking in North Carolina

1. Klassen, *Trials, Tribulations and Triumphs*, p. 2.

2. Ben Klassen's letter to Emory Burke, April 7, 1975, in Klassen, *The Klassen Letters Volume One*, p. 215.

3. Klassen, *Trials, Tribulations and Triumphs*, p. 21.

4. Nicholas Goodrick-Clarke, *The Black Sun: Aryan Cults, Esoteric Nazism and the Politics of Identity* (New York: New York University Press, 2002), p. 253.

5. Anti-Defamation League, *Extremism on the Right: A Handbook* (New York: Anti-Defamation League, 1988), p. 108.

6. Klassen, *Trials, Tribulations and Triumphs*, p. 87.

7. Ben Klassen, *Expanding Creativity: An Idea Whose Time Has Come* (Otto, NC: Church of the Creator, 1985), p. 45.

8. Klassen, *Trials, Tribulations and Triumphs*, p. 13.

9. Ben Klassen, *The Little White Book: Fundamentals of the White Racial Religion of Creativity* (Otto, NC: Church of the Creator, 1991), p. 3.

10. Dave Jackson and Neta Jackson, *No Random Act: Behind the Murder of Ricky Birdsong*. (Colorado Springs, CO: Waterbrook Press, 2002), pp. 126–27.

11. Letter to Mr. E. P. Thornton from Ben Klassen, September 29, 1976, in Klassen, *The Klassen Letters Volume Two*, pp. 19–21.

12. The Creativity books published during this period include the following:
    Salubrious Living, by Arnold DeVires and Ben Klassen, published in 1982.
    Expanding Creativity, by Ben Klassen, published in 1985.
    Building a Whiter and Brighter World, by Ben Klassen, published in 1986.
    RAHOWA! This Planet Is All Ours, by Ben Klassen, published in 1987.
    The Klassen Letters Vol. One (1969–1976), by Ben Klassen, published in 1988.
    The Klassen Letters Vol. Two (1976–1981), by Ben Klassen, published in 1989.
    A Revolution of Values through Religion, by Ben Klassen, published in 1991.
    Against the Evil Tide, by Ben Klassen, published in 1991.
    On the Brink of a Bloody Racial War, by Ben Klassen, published in 1993.
    Trials, Tribulations, and Triumphs, by Ben Klassen, published in 1993.
    The Little White Book, compiled by the Reverend Victor Wolf, published in 1991.

13. For more on the Universal Church of the Master, see its Web site at http://www.u-c-m.org/new/.

14. For a short biographical sketch of DeVries, see his obituary on the PAF-WAYS Web site at http://www.pafways.org/obituaries/mcgg/1996/feb4.htm, February 19, 1996.

15. Arnold DeVries and Ben Klassen, *Salubrious Living* (Otto, NC: Church of the Creator, 1983).

16. Harold Covington, "Enough Is Enough!" Circular Letter #2, July 20, 1989.

17. Klassen, *The Little White Book*.

18. Klassen, *The Little White Book*, pp. 10–11.

19. Klassen, *Building a Whiter and Brighter World*, p. 25.

20. Letter from Ben Klassen to Tom Metzger, January 25, 1985, reprinted in Klassen, *Trials, Tribulations and Triumphs*, pp. 204–206.

21. Klassen, *Building a Whiter and Brighter World*, pp. 106–119.

22. Letter to Mr. W. J. Guillaume from Ben Klassen, December 12, 1977, in Ben Klassen, *The Klassen Letters Volume Two*, pp. 120–22.

23. Letter to Mr. Art Stinnett from Ben Klassen, May 17, 1978, in Klassen, *The Klassen Letters Volume Two*, pp. 154–56.

24. Letter to Mr. G. Edward Griffin, October 31, 1977, in Klassen, *The Klassen Letters Volume Two*, p. 104–12.

25. Klassen, *Expanding Creativity*, p. 24.

26. For many years, Kaldenberg has worked with Metzger and contributes articles and cartoons to his newspaper *WAR*, which was renamed *The Insurgent*. Gallo led a small organization called the National Democratic Front and published a paper called *The Nationalist*, which was a left-leaning rightist organ that, among other things, championed ecology. See Michael Novick, *White Lies White Power: The Fight against White Supremacy and Reactionary Violence* (Monroe, ME: Common Courage Press, 1995), p. 206.

27. Ben Klassen, "Bashing the Rich," *Racial Loyalty*, 45 (December 1988), pp. 1–3, 9.

28. Klassen, *On the Brink of a Bloody Racial War*, pp. 67–80.

29. Mike German, *Thinking Like a Terrorist: Insights of a Former FBI Undercover Agent* (Dulles, VA: Potomac Books, 2007), p. 12.

30. For more on Gordon Kahl, see James Corcoran, *Bitter Harvest: Gordon Kahl and the Posse Comitatus: Murder in the Heartland* (New York: Penguin Books, 1990).

31. The organization used several names including the Silent Brotherhood and a German version of that same title, the *Brüder Schweigen*.

32. James Aho, *The Politics of Righteousness: Idaho Christian Patriotism* (Seattle: University of Washington Press, 1990), p. 7.

33. Danny O. Coulson and Elaine Shannon, *No Heroes: Inside the FBI's Secret Counter-Terror Force* (New York: Pocket Books, 1999), p. 194.

34. This is according to the statements of Danny O. Coulson, the founder of the FBI's Hostage Rescue Team, who was involved in the Order investigation. See Coulson and Shannon, *No Heroes*, p. 195. According to one estimate, the investigation is said to have involved one-quarter of the total manpower resources of the FBI. See Aho, *The Politics of Righteousness*, p. 61.

35. Several books have been written on the campaign of the Order, the most comprehensive of which is Kevin Flynn and Gary Gerhardt, *The Silent Brotherhood* (New York: Signet, 1990). Also, see William E. Barker, *Aryan America: Race, Revolution and the Hitler Legacy* (St. Maries, ID: Falcon Ridge, 1993); Stephen Singular, *Talked to Death: The Life and Murder of Alan Berg* (New York: Beech Tree Books/William Morrow, 1987); and Thomas Martinez with John Guinther, *Brotherhood of Murder* (New York: Pocket Books, 1988).

36. The prison addresses of the "POWs" are occasionally listed in the far-right literature and readers are encouraged to write and provide material and moral support to them and their families.

37. George Eric Hawthorne, "The Brüders Schweigen: Men against Time," in David Lane, *Deceived, Damned, and Defiant: The Revolutionary Writings of David Lane* (St. Maries, ID: 14 Word Press, 1999), p. 157.

38. George Eric Hawthorne, "History in the Making," in Lane, *Deceived, Damned, and Defiant*, p. 229.

39. This observation is made in Betty A. Dobratz and Stephanie L. Shanks-Meile, *White Power, White Pride! The White Separatist Movement in the United States* (New York: Twayne, 1997), p. 193.

40. For more on the Order's donations to the White Patriot Party and WAR, see Glen Miller, *A White Man Speaks Out* (self-published, 1999), pp. 149–56. The White Patriot Party dissolved under pressure from federal prosecutors and Morris Dees of the Southern Poverty Law Center. WAR continues operations to this day; however, it has lost strength due to a civil suit initiated by Dees.

41. According to an account of Matthew's former lover, Zillah Craig, Matthews stuffed a large amount of money in a paper bag. Later she saw Matthews hand the paper bag to Pierce. See Flynn and Gerhardt, *The Silent Brotherhood*, pp. 321–22. Soon after the meeting Pierce paid $95,000 in cash for a 346-acre plot in Hillsboro, West Virginia, on which the National Alliance encampment is headquartered. See Kathy Marks, *Faces of Right Wing Extremism* (Boston, MA: Branden, 1996), p. 59. The encampment has accorded the organization a good deal of privacy to go about its business unmolested and away from the watchful eyes of its opponents. A 1987 FBI memorandum on the activities of the National Alliance lamented that due to the remoteness of the West Virginia National Alliance encampment, "physical surveillance [was] nearly impossible." FBI Internal Memorandum, File Number: 100–487473–53X.

42. Actually, 241 servicemen died in the attack, which took place on October 23, 1983, at the Marine Corps barracks in Beirut, Lebanon. The Lebanese organization, Hezbollah, was believed to have been responsible for the attack. For more on the attack, see Amir Taheri, *Holy Terror: Inside the World of Islamic Terrorism* (Bethesda, MD: Adler and Adler, 1987).

43. Ben Klassen, *On the Brink of a Bloody Racial War* (Niceville, FL: Church of the Creator, 1992), pp. 14–15.

44. Ben Klassen, "Best E.T.E.F. Award," *Racial Loyalty*, 47, (February 1989).

45. Quoted in Jeffrey Kaplan and Leonard Weinberg, *The Emergence of a Euro-American Radical Right* (New Brunswick, NJ: Rutgers University Press, 1998), p. 182.

46. Kaplan and Weinberg, *The Emergence of a Euro-American Radical Right*, p. 180.

47. Kaplan and Weinberg, *The Emergence of a Euro-American Radical Right*, p. 186.

48. Arnold DeVries was the co-author of Klassen's book *Salubrious Living*.

49. Heléne Lööw, "Racist Violence and Criminal Behaviour in Sweden: Myths and

Reality," in Tore Bjorgo (ed.), *Terror from the Extreme Right* (London: Frank Cass, 1995), pp. 123–24.

50. Jeffrey Kaplan, *The Encyclopedia of White Power: A Sourcebook on the Radical Racist Right* (New York: AltaMira Press, 2000), p. 270.

51. Kaplan and Weinberg, *The Emergence of a Euro-American Radical Right*, p. 190.

52. Kaplan, *The Encyclopedia of White Power*, p. 271.

53. Heléne Lööw, "The Idea of Purity," in Jeffrey Kaplan and Heléne Lööw, *The Cultic Milieu: Oppositional Subcultures in an Age of Globalization* (New York: Alta Mira Press, 2002), pp. 204–205.

54. For a good biographical sketch of Rydén, see Kaplan and Weinberg, *The Emergence of a Euro-American Radical Right*, pp. 169–93.

55. Kaplan and Weinberg, *The Emergence of a Euro-American Radical Right*, p. 192.

56. Anti-Defamation League, "Extremism in America: Creativity Movement," http://www.adl.org/Learn/Ext_US/WCOTC.asp?LEARN_Cat=Extremism&LEARN_SubCat=Extremism_in_America&xpicked=3&i tem+cm, accessed October 14, 2004.

57. Anti-Defamation League, *Church of the Creator: Creed of Hate* (New York: Anti-Defamation League, 1993), p. 15.

58. Those books are *The Little White Book* and *Trials, Tribulations and Triumphs*. The eldest son of a minister, Horst Wessel was a member of the SA (*Sturmabteilung*), or "brownshirts," that supported Hitler in his seizure of power. The events surrounding Wessel's death are not entirely clear. On January 14, 1930, he was shot in his apartment. He died on February 23, 1930, from the injuries he sustained in the attack. Wessel had a conflict with his landlady over rent. A group of five persons, who were either members or sympathizers of the Communist Party, carried out the attack. Thus Wessel seems to have been killed for a mixture of private and political interests. Joseph Goebbels seized upon the incident to elevate Wessel to the status of a martyr. Before his death, Wessel wrote a song—"The Flag on High"—which was subsequently renamed "The Horst Wessel Song" and became a quasi-anthem of the Nazi regime. For more on Wessel, see Heiko Luckey, "Believers Writing for Believers: Traces of Political Religion in National Socialist Pulp Fiction," *Totalitarian Movements and Political Religions*, 8, No. 1 (March 2007), pp. 77–92; and Jay W. Baird, *To Die for Germany: Heroes in the Nazi Pantheon* (Bloomington: Indiana University Press, 1992).

59. Crocker Stephenson, "Missionaries of Hate," *Milwaukee Journal Sentinel*, March 19, 2000.

60. Klassen, *Trials, Tribulations and Triumphs*, pp. 5–6.

61. Klassen, *Trials, Tribulations and Triumphs*, pp. 1–18.

62. Klassen, *Trials, Tribulations and Triumphs*, pp. 8–9.

63. Klassen, *Trials, Tribulations and Triumphs*, pp. 10–11.

64. Klassen, *Trials, Tribulations and Triumphs*, p. 12.

65. Klassen, *Trials, Tribulations and Triumphs*, pp. 17–18.
66. Klassen, *Trials, Tribulations and Triumphs*, p. 19.
67. Klassen, *Trials, Tribulations and Triumphs*, p. 60.
68. Klassen, *Trials, Tribulations and Triumphs*, p. 65.
69. Jackson and Jackson, *No Random Act*, pp. 114–15.
70. Jackson and Jackson, *No Random Act*, p. 115.
71. Klassen, *Trials, Tribulations and Triumphs*, pp. 132–40.
72. Klassen, *Trials, Tribulations and Triumphs*, p. 162.
73. Klassen, *Trials, Tribulations and Triumphs*, pp. 187–96.
74. Jackson and Jackson, *No Random Act*, p. 116.
75. Jackson and Jackson, *No Random Act*, p. 123.
76. Klassen, *Trials, Tribulations and Triumphs*, p. 196.
77. Klassen, *Trials, Tribulations and Triumphs*, pp. 200–202.
78. Klassen, *Trials, Tribulations and Triumphs*, p. 213.
79. Jackson and Jackson, *No Random Act*, p. 125.
80. Victor Wolf, "The Basis of Organization," reprinted in Klassen, *Trials, Tribulations and Triumphs*, pp. 226–33.
81. Klassen, *Trials, Tribulations and Triumphs*, pp. 242–43.
82. For a brief biographical sketch of DeWest Hooker, see Michael Collins Piper, *The Judas Goats: The Enemy Within* (Washington, DC: American Free Press, 2006), pp. 159–71.
83. Klassen, *Trials, Tribulations and Triumphs*, pp. 249–54; Letter to Mr. Paul Englert, January 23, 1978, in Klassen, *The Klassen Letters Volume Two*, pp. 134–35.

Chapter 6. Disintegration and Collapse

1. Ben Klassen, *Expanding Creativity: An Idea Whose Time Has Come* (Otto, NC: Church of the Creator, 1985), p. 106.
2. Ben Klassen, *Trials, Tribulations and Triumphs*, pp. 1–128.
3. Jeffrey Kaplan, "Religiosity and the Radical Right: Toward a Creation of a New Ethnic Identity," in Jeffrey Kaplan and Tore Bjorgo, *Nation and Race: The Developing Euro-American Racist Subculture* (Boston, MA: Northeastern University Press, 1998), p. 104.
4. See Richard Barrett, *The Commission* (Jackson, MS: Barrett, 1982).
5. Klassen, *Trials, Tribulations and Triumphs*, pp. 128–31.
6. Tyler Bridges, *The Rise of David Duke* (Jackson: University of Mississippi Press, 1994), pp. 127, 129.
7. For more on the political career of Metzger, see Jack Carter, *In the Eye of the Storm: The True Story of Tom Metzger* (self-published, 1992/93); Linor Langer, *A Hundred Little Hitlers: The Death of a Black Man, the Trial of a White Racist, and the Rise of the Neo-Nazi Movement in America* (New York: Picador, 2004); and Morris Dees, *Hate on Trial: The Case against America's Most Dangerous Neo-Nazi* (New York: Villard Books, 1993).

8. Dave Jackson and Neta Jackson, *No Random Act: Behind the Murder of Ricky Birdsong*. (Colorado Springs, CO: Waterbrook Press, 2002), p. 125.

9. Klassen, *Trials, Tribulations and Triumphs*, p. 83; Search Warrant for Willis Carto and Henry Fischer, March 17, 1995, http://homepage.mac.com/lsf/personal/950317warrant.html, accessed February 5, 2005.

10. For more on the civil suit against WAR, see Morris, *Hate on Trial*.

11. Interview with Dr. William L. Pierce, July 12, 2000.

12. Interview with Dr. William L. Pierce, July 12, 2000.

13. Rudy "Butch" Stanko, *The Score* (Gering, NE: Institute for Christian Bankers, 1986), pp. 2–5.

14. Center for New Community, *Creating a Commotion: Matt Hale and the "World Church of the Creator"* (Chicago, IL: Center for New Community, January 7, 2003), p. 13.

15. Stanko, *The Score*, pp. 5–7.

16. Klassen occasionally invoked the Kehilla in his writings. This may have contributed to Stanko's attraction to Klassen's creed.

17. According to Stanko, the most egregious company that indulged in this practice was UNICOR, or Federal Prisons, Inc., a wholly owned federal government corporation that was established by Congress in 1934, ostensibly to provide job skills to prison inmates. Beneath this high-sounding veneer, wrote Stanko, are the machinations of the "Jewish Money Barons." See Rudy "Butch" Stanko, *Slavery! Survives in America!* (self-published, n.d.).

18. Klassen, *Trials, Tribulations and Triumphs*, pp. 255–63.

19. Center for New Community, *Creating a Commotion*, p. 13.

20. Montana Human Rights Network, "Law Enforcement, Community and Press Briefing Paper, March 10, 2003, www.mhrn.org.

21. Deborah Frazier, "Church of the Creator Born in Florida," *Rocky Mountain News*, December 26, 2002.

22. Klassen, *Trials, Tribulations and Triumphs*, pp. 287–89.

23. Anti-Defamation League, *Church of the Creator: Creed of Hate* (New York: Anti-Defamation League, 1993), p. 9.

24. Jackson and Jackson, *No Random Act*, p. 141.

25. Jackson and Jackson, *No Random Act*, pp. 137–38; and Klassen, *Trials, Tribulations and Triumphs*, pp. 278–86.

26. Ben Klassen, "Transfer of Leadership," in Klassen, *Trials, Tribulations and Triumphs*, pp. 289–93.

27. Jackson and Jackson, *No Random Act*, p. 142.

28. Jackson and Jackson, *No Random Act*, p. 143; and Klassen, *Trials, Tribulations and Triumphs*, p. 309.

29. Klassen, *Trials, Tribulations and Triumphs*, p. 309.

30. Anti-Defamation League, *Church of the Creator*, p. 10; and Jackson and Jackson, *No Random Act*, p. 143.

31. Jackson and Jackson, *No Random Act*, p. 143

32. Jackson and Jackson, *No Random Act*, p. 155.

33. Ben Klassen, "Transfer of Leadership," in Klassen, *Trials, Tribulations and Triumphs*, p. 316.

34. Letter to Ben Klassen from Dr. Rick McCarty in Klassen, *Trials, Tribulations and Triumphs*, p. 317.

35. Despite her love and affection for her father, Kim abandoned his ideas in 1979 and joined the Mormon Church. Nevertheless, in this instance, she agreed to help him. See Jackson and Jackson, *No Random Act*, p. 145. Incidentally, of all the Christian denominations, Klassen had the most respect for Mormonism. He admired the discipline of the members of the Church of Jesus Christ of Latter Day Saints. In fact, he sought to use the denomination as a model for his own church's proselytizing efforts. Similarly, in March 2002, after he made news in Utah, Matt Hale criticized the Mormon Church for its hypocrisy after its leadership condemned him for racism. Hale was quick to point out that at one time, racism was integral to Mormonism. He cited a stricture by Brigham Young in which the early church leader espoused the death penalty for race mixers. See "Mormon Religion Is Inherently Racist, Reverend Matt Hale Says," March 23, 2002, http://creativity1973.org/Creativity-Writings/MormonismIsRacist.html.

36. Ben Klassen, "Transfer of Leadership," in Klassen, *Trials, Tribulations and Triumphs*, pp. 288–89.

37. Klassen, *Trials, Tribulations and Triumphs*, pp. 305–310.

38. Klassen, *Trials, Tribulations and Triumphs*, pp. 317–18.

39. Anti-Defamation League, *Church of the Creator*, p. 114.

40. Anti-Defamation League, *Church of the Creator*, p. 13.

41. Jackson and Jackson, *No Random Act*, p. 158.

42. Kathy Marks, *Faces of Right Wing Extremism* (Boston, MA: Branden, 1996), p. 132.

43. See Sally Ann Stewart, "FBI: LA Race War Plot 'Despicable,'" *USA Today* (July 16–18, 1993), p. A-1; Christopher John Farley, "Today Los Angeles, Tomorrow . . . ," *Time*, July 26, 1993; and Jim Newton and Ann W. O'Neill, "Alleged White Supremacists Seized in Assassination Plot," *Los Angeles Times*, July 16, 1993.

44. "Murder Target Cecil Murray Praises the Lord and Continues His Ministry," *People*, August 2, 1993, pp. 83–84.

45. Anti-Defamation League, *Church of the Creator*, p. 7.

46. Farley, "Today Los Angeles, Tomorrow . . . "

47. Farley, "Today Los Angeles, Tomorrow . . . "

48. "Going under Cover," *Intelligence Report*, 121, (Spring 2006), http://www.splcenter.org/intel/intelreport/article.jsp?aid=616.

49. See David Niewart, *In God's Country: The Patriot Movement and the Pacific Northwest* (Pullman: Washington State University Press, 1999), pp. 288–96; and David Niewart, "Playing Politics with Terrors," *Orcinus*, August 4, 2004, http://dneiwert.blogspot.com/2004/08/playing-politics-with-terror.html.

50. His superiors responded by stripping him of his security clearance, which

precluded him from conducting undercover operations. The Justice Department conducted a whistleblower's investigation and substantiated German's claims that the case in Orlando, Florida, was mishandled and mismanaged. In 2002, he was involved in an investigation in northern Florida in which he explored links between a domestic extremist group and an international terrorist organization. See "Going under Cover," *Intelligence Report*, 121 (Spring 2006), http://www.splcenter.org/intel/intelreport/article.jsp?aid=616. German recorded a conversation between a domestic white supremacist and an Islamic extremist. There was a meeting of the minds between the two on the basis of a shared anti-Semitism. According to a transcript of the recorded conversation, the two discussed, among other things, shooting Jews; their shared admiration of Adolf Hitler; arms shipments from Iran; their desire for a civil war in the United States; their approval of suicide bombings; and assassinating pro-Israeli journalists in the United States. For its part, the FBI downplayed the significance of the meeting and publicly went on television announcing that German was essentially full of hot air. Commenting on the putative connection between the extremist groups, an FBI spokeswoman stated that "it did not exist, there was no coming together of those two separate groups." German proposed that the FBI should infiltrate the group. However, according to German, the FBI sat on his request and botched the investigation. Furthermore, the FBI supposedly falsified documents in an effort to discredit German. The FBI inspector general later found that the agency effectively retaliated against German and falsified records related to the case. German found an influential supporter in U.S. Senator Chuck Grassley (R-IA), who publicly defended German in his testimony before an FBI oversight hearing held in March 2007 by the Senate Committee on the Judiciary. Grassley criticized the FBI for its treatment of German and ignoring the significance of his undercover work in that particular investigation. See "Grassley Statement at the FBI Oversight Hearing," March 27, 2007, http://grassley.senate.gov/index.cfm?FuseAction=PressReleases.Detail&PressRelease_id=5332&Month=3&Year=2007. German's last assignment was as a counterterrorism instructor at the FBI National Academy. He is now a recognized authority on counterterrorism and has appeared on numerous news programs and networks, including *Dateline NBC, Paula Zahn Now*, CNN, and MSNBC. In a June 2005 op-ed in the *Washington Post*, German argued that leaders of extremist groups should be held responsible for their rhetoric that inspires so-called lone wolves to commit acts of violence. See Mike German, "Behind the Lone Terrorist, a Pack Mentality," *Washington Post*, June 5, 2005, p. B01.

51. Anti-Defamation League, *Danger: Extremism. The Major Vehicles and Voices on America's Far-Right Fringe* (New York: Anti-Defamation League, 1996), p. 200.

52. Jackson and Jackson, *No Random Act*, p. 157.

53. Jackson and Jackson, *No Random Act*, p. 159.

54. See, for example, Harold Covington, *The March Up Country* (Reedy, WV: Liberty Bell, 1987).

55. For more on the Greensboro Massacre, see Elizabeth Wheaton, *Codename Greenkil: The 1979 Greensboro Killings* (Athens: University of Georgia Press, 1987).

56. Covington claimed that these allegations stemmed from Elizabeth Wheaton's book, *Codename Greenkil: The 1979 Greensboro Killings*. According to Covington, Wheaton was affiliated with a left-leaning organization called the Institute for Southern Studies and thus had an axe to grind. Interview with Harold Covington, July 24, 2000.

57. Ben Klassen's letter to Harold Covington, July 23, 1973 in Klassen, *The Klassen Letters Volume One*, pp. 122–23.

58. Harold Covington, "South Rising," *Racial Loyalty*, 47 (February 1989), pp. 5 and 8.

59. See Harold A. Covington, *The Hill of the Ravens* (Bloomington, IN: 1st Books, 2003); Harold A. Covington, *A Distant Thunder* (Bloomington, IN: authorHouse, 2004); and Harold A. Covington, *A Mighty Fortress* (New York: iUniverse, 2005).

60. Harold Covington, "Enough Is Enough!" Circular Letter #2, July 20, 1989.

61. Jeffrey Kaplan, *The Encyclopedia of White Power: A Sourcebook on the Radical Racist Right* (New York: AltaMira Press, 2000), p. 84. According to Covington, Williams telephoned his supervisor and posed as an FBI agent. He then supposedly claimed that the Jewish Defense League was planning to attack the office where Covington worked to assassinate him. See Covington, "Enough Is Enough!"

62. Covington, "Enough is Enough!"

63. Harold Covington, "Disaster for the National Alliance," e-mail message from Covington, September 9, 2000.

64. Jeffrey Kaplan, *Radical Religion in America: Millenarian Movements from the Far Right to the Children of Noah* (Syracuse, NY: Syracuse University Press, 1997), p. 41.

65. E-mail from the Miami-Dade Police Department to Adam Baugess, April 17, 2008.

66. Interview with George Burdi, August 2, 2007.

67. Warren Kinsella, *Web of Hate: Inside Canada's Far Right Network* (Toronto: Harper Perennial, 1995), p. 270.

68. Jeffrey Kaplan, "Right Wing Violence in North America," in Tore Bjorgo (ed.), *Terror from the Extreme Right* (London: Frank Cass, 1995), p. 66.

69. Klassen, *The White Man's Bible*, pp. 386–87.

70. Jackson and Jackson, *No Random Act*, p. 145

71. Winston Smith [Harold Covington], "Sayonara to a Sodomite," e-text file obtained from Minuteman BBS, n.d., in Kaplan, *Radical Religion in America*, pp. 41–42.

72. William L. Pierce, "The Perils of Hobbyism," *National Alliance Bulletin*, November–December 1992, pp. 4–6.

73. Quoted in Kaplan, *Radical Religion in America*, p. 41.

74. "White Supremacist Movement Reels from Severe Setbacks in 1993," *Intelligence Report*, March 1994, p. 12.

75. Jackson and Jackson, *No Random Act*, p. 155.

76. Jackson and Jackson, *No Random Act*, p. 157.

77. Jackson and Jackson, *No Random Act*, p. 159.

Chapter 7. George Hawthorne and RAHOWA

1. Ben Klassen, *RAHOWA! This Planet Is All Ours* (Otto, NC: Church of the Creator, 1987), p. 123.
2. Jeffrey Kaplan, *The Encyclopedia of White Power: A Sourcebook on the Radical Racist Right* (New York: AltaMira Press, 2000), p. 123.
3. Anthony Parsonno, "I Am Not My DNA!" *Acid Logic*, n.d. http://www.forbisthemighty.com/acidlogic/georgeburdi.htm.
4. Warren Kinsella, *Web of Hate: Inside Canada's Far Right Network* (Toronto: Harper Perennial, 1995), p. 264.
5. Nicholas Goodrick-Clarke, *The Black Sun: Aryan Cults, Esoteric Nazism and the Politics of Identity* (New York: New York University Press, 2002), p. 202.
6. Michael Moynihan, "RAHOWA," *The Black Flame*, 6, nos. 1 and 2 (1997), p. 40.
7. "Hate Rock to Spiritual Revelation—The Transformation of George Burdi," http://www.engaged-zen.org, accessed June 27, 2006.
8. "Present at the Creation," *Intelligence Report*, Fall 2001, http://www.splcenter.org/intel/intelreport/ article. jsp?aid=179.
9. "Present at the Creation."
10. Interview with George Burdi, August 14, 2007.
11. Interview with George Burdi, August 14, 2007.
12. For more on the Zündel legal controversies, see Stanley R. Barrett, *Is God a Racist?: The Right Wing in Canada* (Toronto: University of Toronto Press, 1987); Michael A. Hoffman, *The Great Holocaust Trial* (Torrance, CA: Institute for Historical Review, 1985); Warren Kinsella, *Web of Hate*; Manuel Prutschi, "The Zündel Affair," in Alan Davies, *Anti-Semitism in Canada: History and Interpretation* (Waterloo, Ontario: Wilfrid University Press, 1992), pp. 249–77; and Gabriel Weimann and Conrad Winn, *Hate on Trial: The Zündel Affair, the Media, Public Opinion in Canada* (New York: Mosaic Press, 1986).
13. Kinsella, *Web of Hate*, p. 267; and Goodrick-Clarke, *The Black Sun*, p. 201.
14. Irving is probably the most sophisticated of the so-called revisionist historians whose books, although controversial, have gained critical acclaim. His works include *Hitler's War, Churchill's War, Göring, The Desert Fox*, and *The Destruction of Dresden*. Irving is unique in that he is the only revisionist historian whose books are sold in regular bookstores. They are often used in military academies and senior officer schools such as the various war colleges. He attained widespread notoriety in 2000 when he initiated a libel suit in England against Deborah Lipstadt whom he claimed had libeled him in her book *Denying the Holocaust: The Growing Assault on Truth and Memory*. In the book, Lipstadt referred to Irving as a "Holocaust denier," a characterization he charged was libelous, despite the fact that Irving questions certain details concerning the mainstream historiography of the Holocaust. For more on the controversy, see D. D. Guttenplan, *The Holocaust on Trial* (New York: Norton,

2001); and Deborah E. Lipstadt, *History on Trial: My Day in Court with David Irving* (New York: HarperCollins, 2005).

15. Moynihan, "RAHOWA," p. 41.
16. Moynihan, "RAHOWA," p. 42. "Black metal" is informed greatly by Satanism and Norse neopaganism. See Michael Moynihan and Didrik Soderlind, *Lords of Chaos: The Bloody Rise of the Satanic Metal Underground* (Venice, CA: Feral House, 1998). Burdi was not the first representative of the extreme right who sought to build bridges with Satanists. James Madole, leader of the National Renaissance Party, maintained an amicable correspondence with Anton LaVey, founder of the Church of Satan. See Jeffrey Kaplan, "The Postwar Paths of Occult National Socialism: From Rockwell and Madole to Manson," in Jeffrey Kaplan and Heléne Lööw, *The Cultic Milieu: Oppositional Subcultures in an Age of Globalization* (New York: Alta Mira Press, 2002), p. 235; and Blanche Barton, *The Secret Life of a Satanist: The Authorized Biography of Anton LaVey* (Los Angeles: Feral House, 1992). As mentioned earlier, for a while, Madole had a correspondence with Creativity founder Ben Klassen. Although LaVey was of Jewish descent, he was attracted to the Nazi aesthetics but not so much the ideology. In particular, LaVey was intrigued by Dietrich Eckart, a close confidant of Hitler during the early years of his seizure of power. Also, LaVey presumably named his daughter (Karla Maritza) after Karl Maria Wiligut, a Nazi occultist and confidant of Heinrich Himmler. LaVey included elements of Nazism in his Satanic rituals. See Anton LaVey, *The Satanic Rituals* (New York: Avon Books, 1972). Further, inasmuch as LaVey counseled his followers to flout the conventions of mainstream society, it is not surprising that he would champion some aspects of Nazism—the most reviled ideology in the postwar era.
17. George Eric Hawthorne, "Reasons for Hope," *Resistance*, 7 (1996), p. 4.
18. Parsonno, "I Am Not My DNA!"
19. "Hate Rock to Spiritual Revelation."
20. Parsonno, "I Am Not My DNA!"
21. "Present at the Creation."
22. Kaplan, *The Encyclopedia of White Power*, p. 127.
23. Ian Stuart Donaldson was born in 1958 in Pourlton-leFylde near Blackpool in Lancashire, England. In 1975, he formed a band called Tumbling Dice, which played cover versions of popular hard rock bands. In 1979, it was transformed into a skinhead band and rechristened Skrewdriver. The band popularized the white power musical genre and established links with rightist organizations, such as the British National Front and Combat 18. Increasingly, the band took on the trappings of National Socialism as its songs featured lyrics praising Hitler. Along with Nicky Crane, Donaldson founded Blood and Honour, a network that distributed CDs and organized concerts. He died in a car accident in Derbyshire in 1993. See Heléne Lööw, "White-Per Rock 'n' Roll: A Growing Industry," in Jeffrey Kaplan and Tore Bjorgo (eds.), *Nation and Race: The Developing Euro-American Racist Subculture* (Boston, MA: Northeastern University Press, 1998), pp. 138–47.
24. Kaplan, *The Encyclopedia of White Power*, p. 124.

25. "Present at the Creation."

26. "Present at the Creation."

27. George Eric Hawthorne, "We Must Heed the Call," *Resistance*, 2 (Summer 1994), p. 4.

28. George Eric Hawthorne, "The Essence of Timing," *Resistance*, 4 (Spring 1995), p. 4.

29. George Eric Hawthorne, "Guitars or Guns?" *Resistance*, 8 (1997), p. 4.

30. In a 1990 report, the Anti-Defamation League estimated that there were approximately 3,000 skinheads in the United States. See Anti-Defamation League, "Neo-Nazi Skinheads: A 1990 Status Report" (1990), p. 3. A 1995 publication reported that the figure had risen to about 3,500 and has held steady at that figure. See Anti-Defamation League, *The Skinhead International: A Worldwide Survey of Neo-Nazi Skinheads* (New York: Anti-Defamation League, 1995), p. 1.

31. "Sheeple" is derived from the combination of the words "sheep" and "people." In the extreme right subculture, it is basically meant to denote apathetic whites, who "blindly" follow the "system."

32. Hawthorne, "Reasons for Hope," p. 4.

33. Quoted in Kaplan, *The Encyclopedia of White Power*, pp. 125–26.

34. George Eric Hawthorne, "The Blood of Our Martyrs," *Resistance*, 3 (Winter 1995), p. 4.

35. Goodrick-Clarke, *The Black Sun*, p. 201.

36. Anti-Defamation League, *High-tech Hate: Extremist Use of the Internet* (New York: Anti-Defamation League, 1996), p. 69.

37. Anti-Defamation League, *Church of the Creator*, p. 14.

38. Kinsella, *Web of Hate*, p. 261.

39. Kinsella, *Web of Hate*, p. 272.

40. "The Making of a Neo-Nazi Mogul," *The New York Times Magazine*, Sunday, February 25, 1996, in Anti-Defamation League, *High-tech Hate*, p. 69.

41. Carol M. Swain, *The New White Nationalism in America: Its Challenge to Integration* (New York: Cambridge University Press, 2002), p. 333.

42. Quoted in Anti-Defamation League, *High-tech Hate*, p. 70.

43. Goodrick-Clarke, *The Black Sun*, p. 211.

44. Anti-Defamation League, *High-tech Hate*, p. 70.

45. "Resisting Arrest: Racist Resistance Records Isn't Slowing Down," *Intelligence Report*, Winter 1998, http://www.splcenter.org/intel/intelreport/article.jsp?aid=452.

46. "Resisting Arrest."

47. "Hate Rock to Spiritual Revelation."

48. "Carto Sells the Liberty Lobby List to Todd Blodgett," http://homepage.mac.com/lsf/personal/business_tb.html,accessed February 5, 2005.

49. An ADL report estimates that currently Resistance Records has the potential to draw in $1 million in sales annually. See Anti-Defamation League, "Deafening Hate: The Revival of Resistance Records," 2000.

50. Parsonno, "I Am Not My DNA!"

51. "Present at the Creation."
52. John Murdoch, "Bye-Bye Burdi," *Resistance*, 12 (Summer 2000), p. 13.
53. Murdoch, "Bye-Bye Burdi," p. 13.
54. Interview with George Burdi, August 14, 2007.
55. "Hate Rock to Spiritual Revelation."
56. Parsonno, "I Am Not My DNA!"
57. Parsonno, "I Am Not My DNA!"
58. "Hate Rock to Spiritual Revelation."
59. Parsonno, "I Am Not My DNA!"
60. Interview with George Burdi, August 14, 2007.

Chapter 8. Resurrection: Matt Hale and the World Church of the Creator

1. "Creative News," *RaHoWA News*, 10 (January 1995), p. 2.
2. Center for New Community, *Creating a Commotion: Matt Hale and the "World Church of the Creator"* (Chicago, IL: Center for New Community, January 7, 2003), p. 11.
3. Matt Hale, *The Creator Membership Manual* (East Peoria, IL: World Church of the Creator, 2002), p. XX.
4. Hale, *The Creator Membership Manual*, p. XX.
5. Anti-Defamation League, "Recurring Hate: Matt Hale and the World Church of the Creator," March 1998, http://www.adl.org/special_reports/wcotc/wcotc-intro.asp.
6. "Church of the Creator: A History," *Intelligence Report*, 95 (Summer 1999), http://www.splcenter.org/intel/intelreport/article.jsp?sid=219.
7. Hale, *The Creator Membership Manual*, p. XX.
8. Nick Ryan, *Into a World of Hate: A Journey among the Extreme Right* (New York: Routledge, 2003), p. 230.
9. Dale Burghart, *"Creating" a Killer: A Background Report on Benjamin "August" Smith and the World Church of the Creator* (Oak Park, IL: Center for New Community, 1999).
10. Donald J. Devine, "Taught to Think for Himself," *Washington Times*, July 28, 1999.
11. Anti-Defamation League, "Extremism in America: Matt Hale," http://www.adl.org/learn/Ext_US/Hale.asp?xpicked=2&item=6, accessed December 26, 2004.
12. Terry Bibo, "Matt Hale," *Illinois Issues*, July/August 1999, http://131.156.59.13/ipo/1999/ii990730.html.
13. Dave Jackson and Neta Jackson, *No Random Act: Behind the Murder of Ricky Birdsong* (Colorado Springs, CO: Waterbrook Press, 2002), p. 170.
14. Jackson and Jackson, *No Random Act*, p. 3.
15. Jackson and Jackson, *No Random Act*, p. 171.
16. Nicholas D. Kristof, "Hate, American Style," *New York Times*, August 30, 2002.
17. Jackson and Jackson, *No Random Act*, p. 172.

18. Interview with Matt Hale, July 30, 2000.
19. Interview with Matt Hale, July 30, 2000.
20. Tom Leyland, "Remembering Our Youth," *G21*, n.d., http://g21.net/amdream9a.html.
21. Jackson and Jackson, *No Random Act*, pp. 173–74.
22. Jackson and Jackson, *No Random Act*, p. 175.
23. "The Following is an Interview with the Controversial Rev. Matthew Hale, Pontifex Maximus of the World Church of the Creator Based in East Peoria, Illinois with a Membership Worldwide," http://www.whitestruggle.net/Hale_Interview.html, Accessed August 6, 2006.
24. Terry Bibo, "Matt Hale," *Illinois Issues*, July/August 1999, http://131.156.59.13/ipo/1999/ii990730.html.
25. Hale received 546 votes. See Betty A. Dobratz and Stephanie L. Shanks-Meile, *White Power, White Pride! The White Separatist Movement in the United States* (New York: Twayne, 1997), p. 222; and Bibo, "Matt Hale."
26. Dobratz and Shanks-Meile, *White Power, White Pride!* p. 242.
27. Carol M. Swain and Russ Nieli (eds.), *Contemporary Voices of White Nationalism in America* (Cambridge: Cambridge University Press, 2003), p. 245.
28. Jackson and Jackson, *No Random Act*, p. 175.
29. Jackson and Jackson, *No Random Act*, p. 178.
30. Bibo, "Matt Hale,"
31. Richard Hirschault, the Midwestern director of the ADL gave the figure of 300 in the article. See Jay Hughes, "Racist Group Growing a Year after Member's Killing Spree," *USA Today*, July 3–4, 2000, A-2. In 2002 the organization moved its headquarters to Riverton, Wyoming.
32. Hale, *The Creator Membership Manual*.
33. Klassen referred to this body as the "College of Electors," which would consist of approximately 300 men. Ben Klassen, *Expanding Creativity: An Idea Whose Time Has Come* (Otto, NC: Church of the Creator, 1985), p. 76.
34. Hale, *The Creator Membership Manual*, p. XII.
35. Matt Hale, *Festum Album* (East Peoria, IL: World Church of the Creator), 2002.
36. Hale, *The Creator Membership Manual*, p. XXI.
37. Kenneth Molyneaux, *White Empire* (self-published, n.d.).
38. Kenneth Molyneaux, *Klassen* (self-published, n.d.).
39. "Trash Talk Not Covered by Litter Statute," Ohio Department of Natural Resources, http://www.dnr.state.oh.us/recycling/pages/lawnewsarchive1.htm, accessed July 23, 2007.
40. Hale, *The Creator Membership Manual*, p. XV.
41. Matt Hale, *Facts that the Government and Media Don't Want You to Know!*
42. Jeffrey Kaplan, Leonard Weinberg, and Ted Oleson, "Dreams and Realities in Cyberspace: The White Aryan Resistance and World Church of the Creator on the Internet," *Patterns of Prejudice*, 37, no. 2 (2003), pp. 139–56

43. Tasha Robertson, "Extreme TV: Hate Groups Exploit Cable," *Boston Globe*, September 30, 2000.

44. Michael Greenwood, "With the Web, Midwest Minister of Hate Gains Global Reach," *Hartford Courant*, December 4, 2000.

45. Interview with Matt Hale, July 30, 2000.

46. Interview with Matt Hale, July 30, 2000.

47. Bibo, "Matt Hale."

48. "Church of the Creator: A History," *Intelligence Report*, 95 (Summer 1999), http://www.splcenter.org/intel/intelreport/article.jsp?sid=219.

49. Swain and Nieli, *Contemporary Voices of White Nationalism in America*, pp. 240–41.

50. Swain and Niel, *Contemporary Voices of White Nationalism in America*, p. 241.

51. Swain and Nieli, *Contemporary Voices of White Nationalism in America*, pp. 239–44.

52. In May 2006, Hale's brother David was arrested for possessing a dozen stolen firearms, including an AK-47 rifle. Earlier, in 1995, David M. Hale was convicted on charges stemming from threats to kill his wife. For that offense, he was sentenced to six years in prison. In 2002, he was sentenced to two years in prison for violating an order of protection. See Karen McDonald, "Brother of Matt Hale Allegedly Stole, Sold 12 Firearms from Father," *Peoria Journal Star*, May 27, 2006.

53. "The Great Creator," *Intelligence Report*, Summer, 1999, www.splcenter.org.

54. Matt Hale, "Battleground: Courtroom," *Resistance*, 14 (Winter 2001), p. 13.

55. Jeffrey Kaplan, "Religiosity and the Radical Right: Toward a Creation of a New Ethnic Identity," in Jeffrey Kaplan and Tore Bjorgo, *Nation and Race: The Developing Euro-American Racist Subculture* (Boston, MA: Northeastern University Press, 1998), p. 104.

56. Kristof, "Hate, American Style."

57. Daniel Kurtzman, "Chicago Gunman's Hate Group among Fastest Growing," Jewish Telegraphic Agency, July 9, 1999, http://www.jewishsf.com/content/2-0-/module/displaystory/story_id/11565/edition_id/222/format/html/displaystory.html.

58. Allison Farrell, "World Church of Creator Founded in 1973," *Independent Record*, March 28, 2004. In 2000, Mark Potok said that 203 copies of the WCOTC's newsletter, *The Struggle*, were mailed to members, thus suggesting that the membership was 203. See Michael Greenwood, "With the Web, Midwest Minister of Hate Gains Global Reach," *Hartford Courant*, December 4, 2000.

59. Carol M. Swain, *The New White Nationalism in America: Its Challenge to Integration* (New York: Cambridge University Press, 2002), p. 309.

60. Anti-Defamation League, "Extremism in America: Creativity Movement."

61. Mary Jo Hill, "'Creativity' Is a Name for Racism," *Worcester Telegram and Gazette*, July 18, 2002.

62. "The Great Creator."

63. Jeffrey Kaplan and Leonard Weinberg, *The Emergence of a Euro-American Radical Right* (New Brunswick, NJ: Rutgers University Press, 1998).

64. Swain, *The New White Nationalism in America*, p. 336.

65. Nicholas Goodrick-Clarke, *The Black Sun: Aryan Cults, Esoteric Nazism and the Politics of Identity* (New York: New York University Press, 2002), pp. 249–50.

66. Goodrick-Clarke, *The Black Sun*, p. 254.

67. Dobratz and Shanks-Meile, *White Power, White Pride!*, p. 26.

68. James Bandler, "Racist Group's Fliers Seen in the Boston Area," *Boston Globe*, July 6, 1999, in Swain, *The New White Nationalism in America*, p. 335.

69. Mark Potok, "Divided Alliance," *Intelligence Report*, Winter 2002, http://www.splcenter.org/intel/ intelreport/article.jsp?aid=75.

70. Ryan, *Into a World of Hate*, p. 77.

71. Ryan, *Into a World of Hate*, p. 229.

72. Anti-Defamation League, *Dangerous Convictions: An Introduction to Extremist Activities in Prisons* (New York: Anti-Defamation League, 2002), pp. 40–41.

73. Swain and Nieli, *Contemporary Voices of White Nationalism in America*, p. 237.

Chapter 9. The WCTOC's Women's Frontier

1. Martin Durham, *White Rage: The Extreme Right and American Politics* (London: Routledge, 2007), pp. 83–98.

2. Jeffrey Kaplan and Leonard Weinberg, *The Emergence of a Euro-American Radical Right* (New Brunswick, NJ: Rutgers University Press, 1998), p. 188.

3. Carol M. Swain and Russ Nieli (eds.), *Contemporary Voices of White Nationalism in America* (Cambridge: Cambridge University Press, 2003), p. 247.

4. Swain and Nieli, *Contemporary Voices of White Nationalism in America*, p. 252. Representatives of the American far right often criticize the government and media for ignoring black-on-white crime while over-dramatizing the obverse. To make their case, they often cite a 1999 study by the New Century Foundation, which found that for the year 1994, of the approximately 1.7 million crimes of interracial violence involving blacks and whites, roughly 90 percent were committed by blacks against whites. Although the report received criticism because the New Century Foundation is a part of the racialist organization, American Renaissance, the report used reliable data from the Federal Bureau of Investigation and the Bureau of Justice Statistics. See *The Color of Crime* (Oakton, VA: New Century Foundation, 1999).

5. Carol M. Swain, *The New White Nationalism in America: Its Challenge to Integration* (New York: Cambridge University Press, 2002), p. 332.

6. Swain and Nieli, *Contemporary Voices of White Nationalism in America*, p. 255.

7. Swain and Nieli, *Contemporary Voices of White Nationalism in America*, p. 248.

8. "The Role of Women," n.d., http://creativity1973.org/Creativity-Writings/TheRoleOfWomen.html.

9. Swain and Nieli, *Contemporary Voices of White Nationalism in America*, p. 251.

10. Dennis McCafferty, "Desperately Seeking Angry White Females," *Salon.com*, October 14, 1999, http://www.salon.com/news/feature/1999/10/14/hate/index.html.

11. Swain and Nieli, *Contemporary Voices of White Nationalism in America*, p. 250.

12. Swain and Nieli, *Contemporary Voices of White Nationalism in America*, p. 251.

13. Swain and Nieli, *Contemporary Voices of White Nationalism in America*, p. 251.

14. Center for New Community, *World Church of the Creator: One Year Later* (Chicago, IL: Center for New Community, June 26, 2000), p. 3; and Mattias Gardell, *Gods of the Blood: The Pagan Revival and White Separatism* (Durham, NC: Duke University Press, 2003), p. 133.

15. Lisa Turner, "The Co-optation of White Women," http://www.wcotc.com/wcotccwf/copt.html, accessed September 6, 2001.

16. Gardell, *Gods of the Blood*, p. 133.

17. Gardell, *Gods of the Blood*, p. 133.

18. Anti-Defamation League, "Feminism Perverted: Extremist Women on the World Wide Web, http://www.adl.org/main_Extremism/feminism_perverted.htm, January 2000.

19. For Klassen's praise of Queen Isabella, see Ben Klassen, "Queen Isabella—the Inspired Crusader," in Ben Klassen, *Nature's Eternal Religion* (Niceville, FL: Church of the Creator, 1992), pp. 342–56.

20. Swain and Nieli, *Contemporary Voices of White Nationalism in America*, pp. 250–51.

21. Lisa Turner, "Our Stand on Abortion," 2001, in Jackson and Jackson, *No Random Act*, p. 91.

22. Swain and Nieli, *Contemporary Voices of White Nationalism in America*, p. 252.

23. Martin Durham, *White Rage*, pp. 83–86.

24. Felton is the son of a white mother and a black father who, ironically, were both civil rights activists. See "'White Supremacists' on Trial in Boston," BBC News, http://news.bbc.co.uk/1/hi/world/americas /2116623.stm, July 8, 2002; and Anti-Defamation League, "World Church of the Creator, The Women's Frontier, the Sisterhood," ADL Law Enforcement Agency Resource Network, http://www.adl.org/learn/felton/wcotc.asp, accessed July 1, 2001.

25. Denise Lavoie, "Woman Gets Nearly 5 Years in Racist Plot," Associated Press, March 13, 2003.

26. Center for New Community, *Creating a Commotion: Matt Hale and the "World Church of the Creator"* (Chicago, IL: Center for New Community, January 7, 2003), p. 8.

Chapter 10. The Controversy over a Law License

1. Pam Belluck, "Avowed Racist Barred from Practicing Law," *New York Times*, February 10, 1999.

2. Avi Brisman, "Rethinking the Case of Matthew F. Hale: Fear and Loathing on the Part of the Illinois Bar Committee on Character and Fitness," *Connecticut Law Review*, 35, no. 3 (2003), p. 1403.

3. See *In re Stolar* (1971) and *Baird v. State Bar of Arizona* (1971).

4. Emelie E. East, "The Case of Matthew F. Hale: Implications for First Amendment Rights, Social Mores and the Direction of Bar Examiners in an Era of Intolerance and Hatred," *Georgetown Journal of Legal Ethics*, Summer 2000, http://findarticles.com/p/articles/mi_qa3975/is_200007/ai_n8912301.

5. East, "The Case of Matthew F. Hale."

6. Quoted in Brisman, "Rethinking the Case of Matthew F. Hale," p. 1407.

7. Mathew Stevenson, "Hate vs. Hypocrisy: Matt Hale and the New Politics of Bar Admissions," *Montana Law Review*, 63, no. 2 (Summer 2002), pp. 431–34.

8. Afterward, Hale thanked Smith for his testimony, stating that he did a fine job and stood in solidarity with him. see Matt Hayhow, "A Creator Profile: Brother Ben 'August' Smith," *The Struggle*, March 1999, p. 3.

9. Brisman, "Rethinking the Case of Matthew F. Hale," pp. 1407–1408.

10. W. Bradley Wendel, "Hate and the Bar: Is the Hale Case McCarthyism Redux or a Victory for Racial Equality?" *The Bar Examiner*, May 2001, p. 39.

11. Stevenson, "Hate vs. Hypocrisy," p. 426.

12. Stevenson, "Hate vs. Hypocrisy," pp. 426–27.

13. Stevenson, "Hate vs. Hypocrisy," p. 429.

14. Richard L. Sloan, "Barbarians at the Gates: Revisiting the Case of Matthew F. Hale to Reaffirm that Character and Fitness Evaluations Appropriately Preclude Racists from the Practice of Law," *Georgetown Journal of Legal Ethics*, Winter 2002, http://findarticles.com/p/articles/mi_qa3975/is_200201/ai_n9066915.

15. Brisman, "Rethinking The Case of Matthew F. Hale," pp. 1399–1425.

16. Sloan, "Barbarians at the Gates."

17. Quoted in Stevenson, "Hate vs. Hypocrisy," p. 422.

18. Stevenson, "Hate vs. Hypocrisy," p. 424.

19. Stevenson, "Hate vs. Hypocrisy," p. 424.

20. Elizabeth Wright, "Free Speech for Some, but Not All," *Issues and Views*, November 2000, http://www.issues-views.com/index.php/sect/1001/article/1030.

21. See *In re Elmers*, 358 So. 2d, 7 10 (Fla. 1978) in Carla D. Pratt, "Should Klansmen Be Lawyers? Racism as an Ethical Barrier to the Legal Profession," *Florida State University Law Review*, 30, no. 4 (Summer 2003), p. 865.

22. Carol M. Swain and Russ Nieli (eds.), *Contemporary Voices of White Nationalism in America* (Cambridge: Cambridge University Press, 2003), p. 236.

23. Pratt, "Should Klansmen Be Lawyers?" p. 865.

24. Wendel, "Hate and the Bar," p. 28

25. See *Wadmond*, 401 U.S. 154, cited in Wendel, "Hate and the Bar," p. 29.

26. Wendel, "Hate and the Bar," pp. 33–36.
27. Stevenson, "Hate vs. Hypocrisy," p. 430.
28. East, "The Case of Matthew F. Hale."
29. Michael, *Confronting Right-Wing Extremism in the USA*, pp. 162–67.
30. See, for example, Blain, "Group Defamation and the Holocaust," pp. 45–68. Analogously, Laurence Hauptman argues that the group defamation of Native Americans created an environment that led to their dehumanization and oppression. See Hauptman, "Group Defamation and the Genocide of American Indians," pp. 9–22. More recently the genocidal violence in Rwanda has been ascribed to provocative "hate radio" that urged violence against the Tutsi tribe. ABC News, *Nightline*, November 21, 1996.
31. Walker, *Hate Speech*, p. 15.
32. Walker, *Hate Speech*, pp. 99–105.
33. Walker, *Hate Speech*, pp. 15–16.
34. Walker, *Hate Speech*, pp. 160.
35. Mike Steele, "Interview with Matt Hale," *Resistance*, 10 (Winter 2000), pp. 25–27.
36. Although the ADL condemned Hale's beliefs, the organization expressed concern over the decision and argued that it should be based on an applicant's "individual conduct" and not "moral views." See Anti-Defamation League, "ADL Reacts to Illinois Bar Panel's Rejection of Extremist Matt Hale: Well-Intentioned Yet Sets a Dangerous Precedent," February 4, 1999. The ADL later switched its position after the Ben Smith shooting spree in July 1999.
37. Interview with Matt Hale, July 30, 2000.
38. Quoted in "Good Morning from the Zundelsite," September 18, 1999, http://www.zundelsite.org/english/zgrams/zg1999/zg9909/990918.html.
39. Belluck, "Avowed Racist Barred from Practicing Law."

Chapter 11. Benjamin Smith

1. Ben Klassen, *Expanding Creativity: An Idea Whose Time Has Come* (Otto, NC: Church of the Creator, 1985), p. 16.
2. Ben Klassen, *The White Man's Bible* (2nd ed.) (Otto, NC: Church of the Creator, 1992), pp. 429–30.
3. Jeffrey Kaplan, "Right Wing Violence in North America," in Tore Bjorgo (ed.), *Terror from the Extreme Right* (London: Frank Cass, 1995), p. 80.
4. Ramon Coronado, "Man Receives Life for Hate Attacks: The Fair Oaks Resident Committed Two Racially Motivated Attacks," *Sacramento Bee*, September 22, 2001.
5. Anti-Defamation League, "Extremism in America: Creativity Movement," http://www.adl.org/Learn/Ext _US/WCOTC.asp? LEARN_Cat=Extremism&LEARN_SubCat=Extremism_in_America &xpicked =3&i tem + cm, accessed October 14, 2004.
6. Anti-Defamation League, "ADL Backgrounder: World Church of the Creator," July 6, 1999, http://www.adl.org/ backgrounders/wcotc.asp.

7. Anti-Defamation League, "ADL Backgrounder: World Church of the Creator."
8. "Church of Creator Hate Group Weakened, Divided after Arrests," *Miami Herald*, August 3, 1999.
9. Sam Stanton and Gary Delsohn, "Poster Boys for the Summer of Hate," *Salon.com*, October 6, 1999, http://archive.salon.com/news/feature/1999/10/06/redding/index.html.
10. Gary Delsohn and Sam Stanton, "White Separatist Groups Targeted in Arson Probe," *Contra Cosa Times*, June 24, 1999.
11. Anti-Defamation League, "Extremism in America: Creativity Movement"; and "Sacramento Authorities Question Members of World Church of the Creator," *CNN*, July 13, 1999.
12. Stanton and Delsohn, "Poster Boys for the Summer of Hate."
13. Stacy Finz, "White Power's New Face," *SFGate*, March 6, 2005.
14. Edward Walsh, "'Appalled' Reno Pledges Review of Midwest Shootings," *Washington Post*, July 9, 1999, p. A12.
15. Matt Hayhow, "A Creator Profile: Brother Ben 'August' Smith," *The Struggle*, March 1999, p. 3.
16. Dave Jackson and Neta Jackson, *No Random Act: Behind the Murder of Ricky Birdsong* (Colorado Springs, CO: Waterbrook Press, 2002), p. 205.
17. Dale Burghart, *"Creating" a Killer: A Background Report on Benjamin "August" Smith and the World Church of the Creator* (Oak Park, IL: Center for New Community, 1999), p. 5.
18. Carol M. Swain, *The New White Nationalism in America: Its Challenge to Integration* (New York: Cambridge University Press, 2002), p. 306.
19. Swain, *The New White Nationalism in America*, p. 304.
20. "What Triggered White Supremacist to Violence?" CNN, July 5, 1999.
21. Bill Dedman, "Midwest Gunman Who Shot 11 Had Engaged in Acts of Racism at 2 Universities," *New York Times*, July 5, 1999.
22. In a conversation with Hale, Smith claimed that it was actually his father, a staunch anticommunist, who recommended that his son read *The Turner Diaries*. See Jackson and Jackson, *No Random Act*, pp. 194, 207.
23. Jackson and Jackson, *No Random Act*, p. 193.
24. Dedman, "Midwest Gunman Who Shot 11 Had Engaged in Acts of Racism at 2 Universities."
25. Burghart, *"Creating" a Killer*, p. 5.
26. Martha Irvine, "Gunman 'Seemed Mad at the World,'" *Miami Herald*, July 6, 1999.
27. Jackson and Jackson, *No Random Act*, pp. 193.
28. Jackson and Jackson, *No Random Act*, pp. 202–203.
29. Jackson and Jackson, *No Random Act*, p. 203.
30. Dedman, "Midwest Gunman Who Shot 11 Had Engaged in Acts of Racism at 2 Universities."

31. Dedman, "Midwest Gunman Who Shot 11 Had Engaged in Acts of Racism at 2 Universities."
32. Jackson and Jackson, *No Random Act*, pp. 188–91.
33. Anti-Defamation League, "Extremism in America: Creativity Movement."
34. Swain, *The New White Nationalism in America*, p. 307.
35. Stephanie Simon, "Leader of Hate's Church Mourns 'One White Man,'" *Los Angeles Times*, July 6, 1999; and "The Great Creator," *Intelligence Report*, Summer, 1999, www.splcenter.org. Smith passed out more than 5,000 copies of the Creator pamphlet, "Facts That the Government and Media Don't Want You to Know" in a single month. See Swain, *The New White Nationalism in America*, p. 305.
36. Burghart, *"Creating" a Killer*, p. 5. As mentioned earlier, Klassen was an admirer of Augustus Caesar and credited him with consolidating the Roman Empire.
37. Jackson and Jackson, *No Random Act*, p. 205.
38. Jackson and Jackson, *No Random Act*, pp. 204–205.
39. Matt Hayhow, "A Creator Profile: Brother Ben 'August' Smith," *The Struggle*, March 1999, p. 2.
40. Jackson and Jackson, *No Random Act*, p. 206.
41. "Cops Probe Hate Writing Found in Smith's Car," *Chicago Tribune*, July 10, 1999.
42. Jackson and Jackson, *No Random Act*, p. 206.
43. Jackson and Jackson, *No Random Act*, p. 218.
44. Quoted in Andy Kravetz, "Hale Changing His Story on Smith," *Peoria Star Journal*, July 15, 1999.
45. Burghart, *"Creating" a Killer*, pp. 6–7.
46. Jackson and Jackson, *No Random Act*, pp. 204–205.
47. Quoted in *United States of America v. Matthew Hale*, in the United States Court of Appeals for the Seventh Circuit, May 30, 2006.
48. Jackson and Jackson, *No Random Act*, p. 1.
49. Richard L. Sloan, "Barbarians at the Gates.
50. Jackson and Jackson, *No Random Act*, p. 230.
51. Edward Walsh, "Racial Slayer Killed Himself in Struggle," *Washington Post*, July 6, 1999.
52. Matt Sharkey, "The Matt Hale Interview," *G21*, 1999, http://g21.net/amdream9.html.
53. "Alleged Gun Dealer Arrested in Racial Killings Case," *CNN*, July 7, 1999, http://www.cnn.com/US/9907/07/illinois.shootings.01/index.html.
54. Jackson and Jackson, *No Random Act*, p. 220.
55. Andy Kravetz, "Hale Changing His Story on Smith," *Peoria Star Journal*, July 15, 1999. At the hearing, McLaughlin testified that Hale should be certified "because there [was] a need for lawyers to defend white supremacists." See Emelie E. East, "The Case of Matthew F. Hale: Implications for First Amendment Rights, Social Mores and the Direction of Bar Examiners in an Era of Intolerance and Hatred," *Georgetown*

Journal of Legal Ethics, Summer 2000, http://findarticles.com/p/articles/mi_qa3975/is_200007/ai_n8912301.

56. "The Great Creator."

57. Kirsten Scharnberg, "FBI Agents Quiz Church Leader over Rampage," *Chicago Tribune*, July 8, 1999, p. 20, in Jackson and Jackson, *No Random Act*, p. 4.

58. "Behind the World Church of the Creator: Youthful Haters Who Call for Holy War against Jews and Blacks," *Response*, 20, no. 2 (Summer/Fall 1999), p. 7.

59. Jackson and Jackson, *No Random Act*, pp. 222–23.

60. Susan Skiles Luke, "Gunman Said Wanted to Be Famous," Associated Press, July 6, 1999.

61. Nicholas D. Kristof, "Hate, American Style," *New York Times*, August 30, 2002.

62. Quoted in Julia Scheeres, "Will the Hatemongers Survive?" *Wired*, January 30, 2001, http://www.wired.com/culture/lifestyle/news/2001/01/41460.

63. Quoted in "White Supremacist Leader Says His Law Battle Set Off Shooter," *CNN*, July 5, 1999.

64. Quoted in Ramsey, "Hale Held without Bond," Associated Press, January 24, 2003.

65. Matt Sharkey, "The Matt Hale Interview," *G21*, 1999, http://g21.net/amdream9.html.

66. East, "The Case of Matthew F. Hale."

67. Quoted in Simon, "Leader of Hate's Church Mourns 'One White Man.'"

68. Hale was alluding to Second Chronicles 14:8–14.

69. Interview with Matt Hale, July 30, 2000.

70. Alex Curtis, "Aryan Kamikaze Terrorizes Midwest," *Nationalist Observer*, 15, July 1999.

71. William L. Pierce, "Knowledge and Discipline," *American Dissident Voices*, 5, no. 7 (July 1999).

72. Terry H. Burns, "Top Prosecutor Seeks Status of World Church of the Creator," Copley News Service, July 15, 1999.

73. For more on Bloomington United Campaign against Hate Speech and Hate Crimes, see the Bloomington United Web site, http://www.bloomington.in.us/~bu/history.htm, accessed August 6, 2006.

74. Jo Thomas, "In East Peoria, an Intolerance for Hate," *New York Times*, September 21, 1999.

75. Jackson and Jackson, *No Random Act*, p. 258.

76. Dru Clark, "Killer's alienation Shows Need for Vision of a New America," *People's Tribune*, August 1999.

77. See Molly McDonough, "Civil Right Group Sues White Supremacist," *American Lawyer Media*, April 6, 2000; and "Docket: *Anderson v. Hale and the World Church of the Creator*," http://www.ccr-ny.org/v2/legal/justice/justiceArticle.asp?ObjID=yEPjrfpAMX&Content=78, accessed August 5, 2006; and East, "The Case of Matthew F. Hale."

78. Lorraine Forte, "Suit Alleges Hale Ordered Shootings," *Chicago Sun-Times*, March 15, 2000.

79. Anti-Defamation League, "Extremism in America: Creativity Movement."

80. "The Creativity Movement (TCM): A History of Violence, http://www.religioustolerance.org/wcotc2.htm, accessed November 27, 2004.

81. Matthew Collins, "Creative Hate," *The Review*, October 2002, http://www.aijac.org.au/review/2002/2710/wtotc2710.html.

82. "Church Members Serving Time or Awaiting Trial," *Miami Herald*, August 3, 1999.

83. Cindy Clayton, "White-power Church Causes Stir in New York," *Virginian-Pilot*, April 25, 2002.

Chapter 12. Opposition

1. As Lipset and Raab point out, several characteristics endemic to the American political system seem to inhibit far right movements from sustaining any kind of enduring significant support. First, owing to the nature of the American political party system, the mainstream political parties are able to co-opt the issues that fuel right-wing extremism. Second, the first-past-the-post or plurality electoral system militates against the development of both fringe right and left political parties. What's more, in plurality systems, the larger the constituency, the less likely it is for minor parties to compete successfully in elections. Third, the two-party system in a nation as large and diverse as the United States encourages political moderation. Finally, the wide availability and the character of education in America has fostered a high level of "democratic restraint." See Seymour Martin Lipset and Earl Raab, *The Politics of Unreason: Right Wing Extremism in America, 1790–1970* (New York: Harper and Row, 1970), pp. 499–506.

2. James Kirkpatrick Davis, *Spying on America: The FBI's Domestic Counterintelligence Program* (Westport, CT: Praeger, 1992).

3. The evidentiary criterion for a criminal predicate is slightly below the threshold of "probable cause," which is less than absolute certainty but greater than mere suspicion or "hunch."

4. Davis, *Spying on America*, p. 176.

5. George Michael, *Confronting Right-Wing Extremism and Terrorism in the USA* (London: Routledge, 2003).

6. Laird Wilcox, *The Watchdogs: A Close Look at Anti-Racist "Watchdog" Groups* (Olathe, KS: Laird Wilcox Editorial Research Center, 1999); and Michael, *Confronting Right-Wing Extremism and Terrorism in the USA*, pp. 192–93.

7. Benjamin R. Epstein and Arnold Forster, *The Radical Right: Report on the John Birch Society and Its Allies* (New York: Random House, 1967), p. 150.

8. See, for example, Anti-Defamation League, "Pulpit of Bigotry: Ben Klassen and His Anti-Semitic 'Church,'" June 1990.

9. See Rebecca Rosenlum, "Justice Dept. Investigating World Church of the Creator," *Jewish Bulletin News*, August 20, 1999; Anti-Defamation League, "ADL Press

Release: In Shooting Aftermath, ADL Calls for Full-Scale Federal Probe into Violent Hate Group World Church of the Creator," July 6, 1999; and Anti-Defamation League, "Press Release: ADL Pleased with Reno's Response to Its Request for an Investigation of Violent Hate Group World Church of the Creator," July 8, 1999.

10. The Joint Terrorist Task Force is a joint program created in 1980 to pool the resources of the FBI and the New York City Police Department to combat terrorism in New York. Herman was involved in several high-profile terrorist cases and led the investigation into the 1993 World Trade Center bombing. For more on the Joint Terrorist Task Force and Herman, see Simon Reeve, *The New Jackals: Ramzi Yousef, Osama bin Laden, and the Future of Terrorism* (Boston, MA: Northeastern University Press, 1999).

11. Rebecca Rosenlum, "FBI Surveillance of Hate Groups Critical, Jewish Leaders Assert," *Jewish Bulletin of Northern California*, September 3, 1999. Herman resigned from this position in 2000.

12. Maria Glod and Jerry Markon, "Tracking Hate Groups Aids Terrorism Fight," *Washington Post*, May 19, 2003, p. B01.

13. This is according to a statement by Dale L. Watson, the executive assistant director for counterterrorism and counterintelligence for the FBI to the Senate Select Committee on Intelligence. See Dale L. Watson, "The Terrorist Threat Confronting the United States: Statement for the Record of Dale L. Watson, Executive Assistant Director for Counterterrorism and Counterintelligence for the FBI before the Senate Select Committee on Intelligence," February 6, 2002.

14. DeWayne Bartels, "Hale's Group a Terrorist threat?" *Peoria Times-Observer*, November 10, 2001.

15. "A Different Breed of Terrorist: Hate Group Leader Convicted of Plotting Federal Judge's Murder," June 9, 2004. http://www.fbi.gov/page2/june04/hale060904.htm.

16. Glod and Markon, "Tracking Hate Groups Aids Terrorism Fight," p. B01.

17. For more on the Krar case, see "Feds: What Did Texas Couple Plan to Do with Cyanide?" *USA TODAY*, January 30, 2004. http://www.usatoday.com; "Prison Sentence for Possessing Chemical Weapons," *ATF News*, May 4, 2004. http://www.atf.org; and Camille Jackson, "Terror, American Style," *Intelligence Report*, 113 (Spring 2004), http://www.splcenter.org.

18. For more on these various arrests, see George Michael, *The Enemy of My Enemy: The Alarming Convergence of Militant Islam and the Extreme Right* (Lawrence: University Press of Kansas, 2006), pp. 179–92.

19. "National Alliance Leader William Pierce Sued in Connection with Church of the Creator Case," *Klanwatch Intelligence Report*, 77 (March 1995), p. 9.

20. "Church of the Creator: A History," *Intelligence Report*, 95 (Summer 1999), http://www.splcenter.org/intel/intelreport/article.jsp?sid=219.

21. Anti-Defamation League, *Danger: Extremism. The Major Vehicles and Voices on America's Far-Right Fringe* (New York: Anti-Defamation League, 1996), p. 199.

22. Interview with Dr. William L. Pierce, July 12, 2000.

23. Interview with Dr. William L. Pierce, July 12, 2000.

24. Anti-Defamation League, *Danger: Extremism*, p. 201.

25. Stephen Anderson, "Morris Dees Battles Hatred with Legal System's Weapons," *Bar News*, 40, no. 7 (January 18, 2000).

26. David Holthouse, "A Few Bad Men," *Intelligence Report*, Summer 2006, http://www.splcenter.org/intel/news/item.jsp?aid=66; and John Kifner, Hate Groups Are Infiltrating the Military, Group Asserts, *New York Times*, July 7, 2006.

27. In his book, Buschbacher advances a number of strategies to meet, approach, talk to, and seduce women. He never mentions his racist past in the book. See Matthew R. Buschbacher, *Date the Women of Your Dreams* (Montgomery, AL: E-BookTime, LLC, 2005).

28. See Dale Burghart, *"Creating" a Killer: A Background Report on Benjamin "August" Smith and the World Church of the Creator* (Oak Park, IL: Center for New Community, 1999).

29. David Goldman founded Hatewatch in 1995 as a Web site to counter the proliferation of right-wing extremist sites on the World Wide Web. The now defunct site examined issues involving online right-wing extremists and even contained direct links to some of their Web sites. For more on Hatewatch, see Michael, *Confronting Right-Wing Extremism and Terrorism in the USA*, p. 35.

30. Interview with Matt Hale, July 30, 2000.

31. "Two More State Agencies Investigate Racist Group," Associated Press, July 12, 1999.

32. Matt Sharkey, "The Matt Hale Interview," G21, 1999, http://g21.net/amdream9.html.

33. "Racist Church Keeps Tax-exempt Status," *Daily Southtown*, February 9, 2000.

34. *The People ex rel. James E. Ryan, Attorney General of Illinois, Appellant, v. The World Church of the Creator et al., Apelles*. Filed November 21, 2001.

35. Associated Press, "Illinois High Court Rejects Challenge of Charities Law," November 26, 1001.

36. Interview with Matt Hale, July 30, 2000.

37. Quoted in Richard L. Sloan, "Barbarians at the Gates."

38. Previously, Herman had taken the Missouri Department of Transportation to court and won for a local Klan group the right to participate in Missouri's Adopt-a-Highway cleanup program. See Crocker Stephenson, "Missionaries of Hate," *Milwaukee Journal Sentinel*, March 19, 2000.

39. See Amicus Brief of American Civil Liberties Union of Illinois cited in Avi Brisman, "Rethinking the Case of Matthew F. Hale: Fear and Loathing on the Part of the Illinois Bar Committee on Character and Fitness," *Connecticut Law Review*, 35, no. 3 (2003), p. 1421.

40. Sloan, "Barbarians at the Gates."

41. Molly McDonough, "White Supremacist Takes Law License Fight to D.C." *Law News*, February 11, 2000.

42. Mike Ramsey, "Hale Continues Bid for Law License," *State Journal-Record*, October 31, 2002.

43. Ron Selden, "Supremacist Matt Hale Wants Montana Practice," *Indian Country Today*, December 20, 2000, http://www.indiancountry.com/content.cfm?id=489.

44. Avi Brisman, "Rethinking the Case of Matthew F. Hale," p. 1409.

45. Andy Kravetz and John Sharp, "Matt Hale Listed as Attorney," *Journal Star*, August 31, 2002.

46. *Matthew F. Hale v. Committee on Character and Fitness for the State of Illinois; Board of Admissions: To the Bar: Committee on Character and Fitness, State of Illinois, Third Judicial District; Gordon L. Lustfeldt; Thomas Dunn, Clark Erickson; Charles Marshall;: L. Lee Perrington and the Supreme Court of Illinois*, June 27, 2001.

47. *Matthew F. Hale v. Committee on Character and Fitness for the State of Illinois, et al.*, In the United States Court of Appeals for the Seventh Circuit, July 14, 2003; Matt O'Connor, "Court Again Thwarts Hale," *Chicago Tribune*, July 15, 2003.

48. Mike Ramsey, "Hale Continues Bid for Law License," *State Journal-Record*, October 31, 2002.

Chapter 13. Denouement?

1. DeWayne Bartels, "Hale's Group a Terrorist Threat?" *Peoria Times-Observer*, November 10, 2001.

2. Quoted in Mattias Gardell, *Gods of the Blood: The Pagan Revival and White Separatism* (Durham, NC: Duke University Press, 2003), pp. 325–26.

3. "Literature of Hate Hits South Hill," October 19, 2001, http://www.wiesenthal.com/social/press.

4. The USS *Liberty* was a U.S. Navy vessel that was attacked on June 8, 1967, during the Six-Day War between Israel and her Arab neighbors. The USS *Liberty*, an intelligence ship, was sailing in the Eastern Mediterranean Sea when it came under attack by Israeli aircraft and Israeli motorboats for 75 minutes. Thirty-four U.S. sailors were killed and 173 others were wounded. The Israeli government insists that the Israeli armed forces had mistaken the ship for an Egyptian vessel whose country was at war with Israel. Survivors of the attack maintain that American flags were prominently displayed on the vessel, rendering the Israeli explanation untenable. Far right literature often cites the case of the USS *Liberty* as an example of Israeli malfeasance and mendacity. For more on the USS *Liberty*, see James Ennes, *Assault on the Liberty: The True Story of the Attack by Israel on an American Intelligence Ship* (New York: Random House, 1970); and John Crewdson, "New Revelations in Attack on American Spy Ship," *Chicago Tribune*, October 2, 2007; and the USS *Liberty* Memorial Web site at http://www.ussliberty.org/.

5. For more on 9/11 conspiracy theories from the perspective of the extreme right, see George Michael, *The Enemy of My Enemy: The Alarming Convergence of Militant Islam and the Extreme Right* (Lawrence: University Press of Kansas, 2006).

6. Matt Hale, *The Truth about 9–11: How Jewish Manipulation Killed Thousands* (East Peoria, IL: Creativity).

7. Robert Nelson, "Peacenik Nazis," *Phoenix New Times*, November 29, 2001.

8. Ann S. Kim, "Second White Supremacist Group Targets Lewiston," Associated Press, November 29, 2002.

9. Carol M. Swain, *The New White Nationalism in America: Its Challenge to Integration* (New York: Cambridge University Press, 2002), p. 323.

10. Martha Irvine, "Supremacist's Campus Cause," *Washington Post*, January 23, 2000.

11. Quoted in Adriana Colinders, "Court Upholds Dismissal of Hale's Suit," Peoria Journal-Star, July 29, 2000.

12. Quoted in "Church of Creator Hate Group Weakened, Divided after Arrests," *Miami Herald*, August 3, 1999.

13. "Matt Hale Ousted," http://www.liesexposed.net/nfp/issue0205/hale.htm, accessed August 5, 2006.

14. Allison Farrell, "Down to Two," *Independent Record*, March 28, 2004.

15. "Matt Hale Responds," http://www.liesexposed.net/nfp/issue0207/hale.htm, accessed July 12, 2007.

16. Montana Human Rights Network, "Law Enforcement, Community and Press Briefing Paper," March 10, 2003, www.mhrn.org.

17. Allison Farrell, "Moving On: Former Member Nearly Bankrupts 'Creativity Movement,'" *Billings Gazette*, March 28, 2004.

18. See the TE-TA-MA Truth Foundation Web site at http://www.churchofthecreator.org/TM/TMindex.html.

19. Center for New Community, *Creating a Commotion: Matt Hale and the "World Church of the Creator"* (Chicago, IL: Center for New Community, January 7, 2003), pp. 4–5.

20. Klassen's incorporation information can be found at the Web site for the Florida Department of Corporations at http://www.sunbiz.org/. Document Number: 727195; FEI Number: 237320644.

21. Center for New Community, *Creating a Commotion*, p. 3.

22. Center for New Community, *Creating a Commotion*, p. 5.

23. "Supremacist Church Name Change," Associated Press, July 26, 2002.

24. *TE-TA-MA Truth Foundation—Family of URI, Inc., v. World Church of the Creator*, in the United States Court of Appeals for the Seventh Court, July 25, 2002.

25. Document Number: 727195; FEI Number: 237320644, Florida Department of State Division of Corporations.

26. United States District Court Northeastern District of Illinois Eastern Division, *United States of America v. Matthew Hale, Count One*.

27. "Supremacist Disagrees with Ruling, Sues Judge," *Peoria Journal-Star*, December 27, 2002.

28. Stacy Finz, "White Power's New Face," *SFGate*, March 6, 2005.

29. *United States of America v. Matthew Hale*.

30. "An American Judge Orders the Destruction of Bibles," December 4, 2002, http://www.whitestruggle.net/Under_Attack.html.

31. "Pontifex Ex," *Intelligence Report*, 114 (Summer 2004), http://www.splcenter.org/intel/intelreport/article.jsp?aid=476

32. "Pontifex Ex."

33. Matt O'Connor, "Hale Guard Went to Cops over Supremacist Material," *Chicago Tribune*, April 15, 2004.

34. United States District Court Northeastern District of Illinois Eastern Division, "White-Supremacist Church Leader Arrested on Charges of Soliciting Murder of U.S. Judge Presiding over Trademark Case," January 8, 2003, http://www.usdoj.gov/usao/iln/pr/chicago/2003/pr010803_01.pdf.

35. Rudolph Bush, "Hale's Security Boss Was FBI Informer, E-mails, Tapes Led to Arrest, U.S. Says," *Chicago Tribune*, January 24, 2003.

36. John Beckham and P. J. Huffstutter, "Supremacist Guilty in Plot to Kill Judge," *Los Angeles Times*, April 27, 2004, latimes.com.

37. Mike Ramsey, "Informant: Hale Smiled, Nodded to Kill," *Peoria Star Journal*, April 17, 2004.

38. Quoted in *United States of America v. Matthew Hale*, in the United States Court of Appeals for the Seventh Circuit, May 30, 2006, p. 11.

39. *United States of America v. Matthew Hale*, p. 10

40. Mike Ramsey, "Prosecutors Counter Hale Defense," *Peoria Star Journal*, January 1, 2004, downloaded from http://www.rickross.com/reference/hale/hale85.html.

41. Beckham and Huffstutter, "Supremacist Guilty in Plot to Kill Judge."

42. *United States of America v. Matthew Hale*, pp. 10–11.

43. United States Attorney District of Illinois, "White Supremacist Church Leader Arrested on Charges of Soliciting Murder of U.S. Judge Presiding over Trademark Case."

44. Karen McDonald and Andy Kravetz, "Some Feel the World Church Will Falter, and Hale Is Capable of Crime," *Peoria Journal Star Online*, January 9, 2003, http://www.pjstar.com/news/topnews/hold/ g135498a.html.

45. Anti-Defamation League, "ADL Press Release: ADL Lauds Law Enforcement for Preventing Extremist Violence with Arrest of Matt Hale," January 8, 2003; Anti-Defamation League, "ADL Press Release: "ADL Lauds Sentencing of White Supremacist Matt Hale," April 6, 2005.

46. Susan Schmidt, "Bush to Name Chertoff to Court," *Washington Post*, January 18, 2003, p. A14.

47. "Michael Chertoff, J.D., Assistant Attorney General in the Department of Justice, to Deliver Keynote Address at Seton Hall University School of Law Commencement," May 24, 2002, http://domapp01shu.edu/depts/special%20programs/pressrelease.nsf/f7b9c5bae1fc659852569d.

48. "Michael Chertoff," Jewish Virtual Library, http://www.jewishvirtuallibrary.org/jsource/biography/Chertoff.html, accessed September 27, 2007.

49. Kevin Alfred Strom, "Terror in Chicago," *American Dissident Voices*, January 18, 2003, https://www.natall.com/pub/2003/011803.txt. Strom, along with other far-right commentators, accused Chertoff of releasing members of an extensive Israeli spy ring that was apprehended around the time of 9/11. See, for example, Michael Collins Piper, "Proposed New Homeland Security Czar Gave Free Pass to Foreign Spies in America," *American Free Press*, January 24, 2005, p. 18.

50. "Free Matt Hale Legal Defense Fund, http://www.matthale.org/, accessed November 16, 2003.

51. Quoted in *United States of America v. Matthew Hale*, p. 7.

52. Mike Robinson, "White Supremacist Charged with Lying to Federal Judge," Associated Press, June 26, 2003.

53. "White Supremacist Group Founder Probed," Associated Press, August 30, 2003.

54. Steve Warmbir, "Hale's Church Sued over Use of Name on Web Site," *Chicago Sun-Times*, May 22, 2003.

55. Steve Warmbir, "Hale 'Church' Dealt $200,000 Defeat," *Chicago Sun-Times*, October 25, 2003.

56. *TE-TA-MA Truth Foundation-Family of URI, Inc., v. The World Church of the Creator*.

57. Natasha Korecki, "Judge Orders Hale's Group to Pay Up," *Chicago Sun-Times*, May 24, 2005.

58. "Matt Hale's Poem: Written in Prison," October 19, 2003, http:www.nationalvanguard.org.

59. Mike Ramsey, "Prosecutors Don't Want Hale Trial Moved," Copley News Service, June 18, 2003, http://www.rickross.com/reference/hale/hale74.html.

60. "Lawyers Want Hale Trial Moved," Associated Press, May 26, 2003.

61. Mike Robinson, "Judge: Hale Must Stay in Custody; Trial Delayed," Associated Press, October 31, 2003.

62. Carol Marin, "How the War on Terrorism Has Gone Way Too Far," *Chicago Tribune*, May 7, 2003.

63. Andy Kravetz and Mike Ramsey, "Prosecutors Link Hale to 1999 Killings," *Peoria Star Journal*, October 4, 2003.

64. *United States of America v. Matthew Hale*, p. 12.

65. O'Connor, "Hale Guard Went to Cops over Supremacist Material."

66. *United States of America v. Matthew Hale*, p. 13

67. *United States of America v. Matthew Hale*, pp. 13–14.

68. Tony Willow, "'Creativity' Movement Leader, Jon Fox to Turn States Evidence!" October 21, 2003, http://citizensagainsthate.com/home/modules.php?op=modload&name=News&file=article&sid=129&mode=thread.

69. Mike Robinson, "Former Follower Says Hale Urged Killing of Federal Judge," Associated Press, April 14, 2004.

70. "Pontifex Ex."

71. "Pontifex Ex."

72. O'Connor, "Hale Guard Went to Cops over Supremacist Material."
73. "Church Leader to Testify against Hale," *WEEK TV News*, October 22, 2003.
74. Natasha Korecki, "Hale Loyalist Turns on Him at Trial," *Chicago Sun-Times*, April 14, 2004.
75. "Lawyer: Hale Passed Message to Supporter," Associated Press, March 9, 2005, http://www.foxnews.com/story/0,2933,149853,00.html.
76. "Hale Not Allowed to See, Talk to Parents," Associated Press, March 8, 2005, http://www.foxnews.com/story/0,2933,149771,00.html.
77. "Nazi Alert: Jewish Attorney Represents Jew-hater," June 1, 2001, http://www.jdl.org/enemies/nazi/greenwald.shtml.
78. Quoted in "Pontifex Ex."
79. *United States of America v. Matthew Hale*, p. 14.
80. "White Supremacist Guilty of Plotting to Kill Judge," *CNN*, April 26, 2004.
81. Matt O'Connor, "Hale Asks to Handle His Own Defense," *Chicago Tribune*, July 16, 2004; and "Judge Rules Matthew Hale Can Represent Himself," *NWITimes.com*, August 11, 2004.
82. Mike Colias, "Supremacist on Tape Says Murder of Basketball Coach 'Must Have Been Fun,'" Associated Press, April 15, 2004; and "Pontifex Ex."
83. "Matt Hale Sues Durkin," *Libertarian Socialist News*, August 4, 2006, http://www.overthrow.com/lsn/news.asp?articleID=9671; and Beckham and Huffstutter, "Supremacist Guilty in Plot to Kill Judge."
84. Quoted in Oscar Avila, "On the Web, Allies of Hale Cheer Slayings," *Chicago Tribune*, March 2, 2005.
85. Finz, "White Power's New Face."
86. Tara Burghart, "Hale's Group Linked to Violence in the Past," *New York Times*, March 2, 2005.
87. Jeff Coen and David Heinzmann, "Police: DNA Matches," *Chicago Tribune*, March 11, 2005, http://www.chicagotribune.com/news/local/na/chi-0503110284 mar11,1,4896586.story?coll=chi-news-hed.
88. Clarence Page, "It's the White Supremacist Who Owes *Us* the Apology," *Jewish World Review*, March 16, 2005, http://www.jewishworldreview.com/0305/page_2005_03_16.php3.
89. Natasha Korecki and Frank Main, "Hale Sentenced to 40 Years," *Chicago-Sun Times*, April 6, 2005, http://www.suntimes.com/output/news/hale06.html.
90. "The Revenge of Matt Hale," 2005, http://www.solargeneral.com/news/revenge.htm.
91. Mike Robinson, "White Supremacist Sentenced to 40 Years," *Sun-Sentinel*, April 7, 2005.
92. Natasha Korecki, "Hale Held with the Worst of the Worst," *Chicago Sun-Times*, April 28, 2005.
93. See, for example, Keith Vanlandingham, "Matt Hale: Understanding What Went Wrong," http://www.nationalist.org/alt/2003/jan/understanding.html, accessed August 5, 2007.

94. "Repulsive and Repugnant Conduct Repudiated," January 8, 2003, http://www.nationalist.org/news/flashes/2003/hale.html.
95. Edgar J. Steele, "The Railroading of Matt Hale," March 4, 2005, http://www.conspiracypenpal.com/columns/hale.htm.
96. *United States of America v. Matthew Hale*, p. 20.
97. *United States of America v. Matthew Hale*, p. 29.
98. Judi Wilgoren, "Haunted by Threats, U.S. Judge Finds New Horror," *New York Times*, March 2, 2005.
99. See U.S. Department of Justice, "Self-Proclaimed White Supremacist William White Indicted for Allegedly Soliciting Violence against Hale Jury Foreperson," October 22, 2008, http://chicago.fbi.gov/dojpressrel/pressrel08/oct22_08.htm, and "Bill White Will Stay behind Bars in Roanoke," WBDJ7.com October 23, 2008, http://www.wdbj7.com/global/story.asp?s=9199698.

Chapter 14. Conclusion: Fragmentation and Beyond

1. Judy L. Thomas, "Ten Years after Oklahoma City Bombing, Militia Movements Are Rudderless and in Disarray—Which Makes Them Deadlier," *Jewish World Review*, April 19, 2005.
2. Interview with Mark Potok, August 1, 2007.
3. Stacy Finz, "White Power's New Face," *SFGate*, March 6, 2005.
4. "Kroenke no Longer with Corrections Department," Associated Press, March 27, 2003.
5. "Supremacist Church Leaving Midwest for Riverton, Wyo.," Associated Press, December 10, 2002.
6. Howard Berkes, "A White Supremacist Church and a Small Town," *All Things Considered*, February 10, 2003, http://www.npr.org/templates/story/story.php?storyId=992253; and Sarah Cooke, "Experts Say World Church Struggling," Associated Press, June 23, 2003.
7. An inveterate drifter, Carl was said to have had a lengthy rap sheet that included convictions for drug and property crimes and bounced in and out of prisons across the Northwest until settling in Idaho. Married three times, he had two daughters with a woman who later died of a heroin overdose. While working there at a cedar mill in Idaho, he met members of the organization. Later, he moved to Montana, where, in 1999, he heard of an annual WCOTC meeting that was to be held at Deardorff's place and decided to attend. Carl stayed on with Deardorff and did various odd jobs for him. See Allison Farrell, "Moving On: Former Member Nearly Bankrupts 'Creativity Movement,'" *Billings Gazette*, March 28, 2004; and Allison Farrell, "Down to Two," *Independent Record*, March 28, 2004.
8. Mark Potok, "The Year in Hate, 2004," *Intelligence Report*, 117 (Spring 2005), http://www.splcenter.org/intel/intelreport/article.jsp?aid=529.
9. Anti-Defamation League, *Extremism in Florida: The Dark Side of the Sunshine State* (New York: Anti-Defamation League, 2007), p. 9.

10. For more on the Church of the RaHoWa see its Web site at http://official rahowa.com/index1.htm.

11. "The Constitution of the White Crusaders of the RaHoWa!" http://www.solargeneral.com/creator/constitution.pdf.

12. Steve Zucker, "50–75 Years in Prison for Rapist," *Petoskey News-Review*, October 12, 2006.

13. Nance Haxton, "SA Attorney-General Wants Racist Web site Closed Down," *The World Today*, January 31, 2006, http://www.abc.net.au/worldtoday/content/2006/s1559149.htm.

14. "The Revenge of Matt Hale," 2005, http://www.solargeneral.com/news/revenge.htm.

15. "The Blotter," *Intelligence Report*, 125 (Spring 2007), http://www.splcenter.org/intel/intelreport/article.jsp?aid=738.

16. Reverend Lloyd with Sister Lisa, *The Creator's Manual*. (n.p.: 2007).

17. Finz, "White Power's New Face."

18. Take, for example, the case of Ron McVan, who worked at the COTC headquarters in North Carolina in the early 1990s. Eventually, he left the church because he found it "spiritually shallow." However, a few years later he joined David and Katja Lane's Wotansvolk, which is stridently anti-Christian and anti-Semitic in orientation. See Nicholas Goodrick-Clarke, *The Black Sun: Aryan Cults, Esoteric Nazism and the Politics of Identity* (New York: New York University Press, 2002), p. 274. Despite his departure from the COTC, members occasionally seek out McVan's advice on internal matter. For example, McVan was invited to attend the August 1996 meeting of the Guardians of the Faith, at which Hale was appointed Pontifex Maximus. See Mattias Gardell, *Gods of the Blood: The Pagan Revival and White Separatism* (Durham, NC: Duke University Press, 2003), pp. 205–223.

19. Furthermore, some activists actually share both faiths. In 1999, Hale sought a rapprochement between the two creeds, explaining that both were essentially moving in the same direction: "We are both anti-Christian. We both have a lot of respect and honor of our ancestry. We both believe in nature's laws." The white power bands and fanzines have no problem accommodating both creeds as nature based and militantly racist. See Gardell, *Gods of the Blood*, pp. 222–23.

20. Jeffrey Kaplan, "Right Wing Violence in North America," in Tore Bjorgo (ed.), *Terror from the Extreme Right* (London: Frank Cass, 1995), p. 867.

21. Roger Griffin, borrowing from the terminology of biology, succinctly captured the essence of one variant of right-wing extremism—fascism—by defining it as an ideology that has at its core an ultra-nationalist palingenetic myth (i.e., process of death and rebirth). This definition has a great deal of merit insofar as many variants of fascism and right-wing extremism espouse the creation of a "New Order" built on the ruins of a perceived decadent and decrepit "Old Order." Thus, he sees a strong revolutionary element in right-wing extremism and fascism. See Roger Griffin, *The Nature of Fascism* (New York: Routledge, 1993). He later buttressed his theory using

the palingenetic myth as the leitmotif of an anthology of essays, which he edited, with contributions from both fascists and observers of fascism. See Roger Griffin, *Fascism, Oxford Readers* (Oxford: Oxford University Press, 1995).

22. See, for example, Mark Jurgensmeyer, *Terror in the Mind of God: The Global Rise of Religious Violence* (Berkeley: University of California Press, 2000); Jessica Stern, *Terror in the Name of God: Why Religious Militant Kill* (New York: Harper-Collins, 2003); and Oliver McTernan, *Violence in God's Name: Religion in an Age of Conflict* (Maryknoll, NY: Orbis Books, 2003).

23. Jeffrey Kaplan and Leonard Weinberg, *The Emergence of a Euro-American Radical Right* (New Brunswick, NJ: Rutgers University Press, 1998)

24. Jeffrey Kaplan and Tore Bjorgo, *Nation and Race: The Developing Euro-American Racist Subculture* (Boston, MA: Northeastern University Press, 1998), p. ix. Actually, the WCOTC used a close facsimile, JOG, which stands for Jewish Occupation Government. Ben Klassen adamantly emphasized that his church attacked Jews qua Jews, not Jews as Zionists, communists, and so on.

25. Goodrick-Clarke, *The Black Sun*, p. 2.

26. Goodrick-Clarke, *The Black Sun*, pp. 305–306.

27. Goodrick-Clarke, *The Black Sun*, pp. 255–56.

28. This observation is made in Kaplan and Weinberg, *The Emergence of a Euro-American Radical Right*, pp. 109–110. Likewise Wilcox and George opined that extremist groups sometimes fulfill a "watchdog" function in society insofar as they are especially sensitive to issues concerning their particular interests. See John George and Laird Wilcox, *Nazis, Communists, Klansmen, and Others on the Fringe* (Buffalo, NY: Prometheus Books, 1992), p. 61.

29. Carol M. Swain, *The New White Nationalism in America: Its Challenge to Integration* (New York: Cambridge University Press, 2002), pp. 84–108.

30. Kevin MacDonald, "Psychology and White Ethnocentrism," *Occidental Quarterly*, 6, no. 4 (Winter 2006–2007), pp. 7–46.

31. P. C. Croll, D. Hartman, and J. Gerteis, *Putting Whiteness Theory to the Test: An Empirical Assessment of Core Theoretical Propositions* (Minneapolis, MN: Department of Sociology, University of Minnesota, 2006) in MacDonald, "Psychology and White Ethnocentrism," p. 16.

32. M. O. Emerson and D. Sikkink, "Does Education Help Breed Segregation?" *Rice* [University] *Sallyport* 61 (Fall 2006). www.rice.edu/sallyport/2006/fall/sallyport/segregation.html in MacDonald, "Psychology and White Ethnocentrism," pp. 17–18.

33. Robert Putnam, *"E Pluribus Unum*: Diversity and Community in the Twenty-first Century. The 2006 Johan Skytte Prize Lecture," *Scandinavian Political Studies*, 30, no. 2 (2007), pp. 137–74.

34. See, for example, Robert D. Putnam, *Making Democracy Work: Civic Traditions in Modern Italy* (Princeton, NJ: Princeton University Press, 1994); and Francis

Fukuyama, *Trust: The Social Virtues and the Creation of Prosperity* (New York: Free Press, 1996).

35. Swain, *The New White Nationalism in America*, p. 2.

36. Kenneth Stern (1999) from the American Jewish Committee cites two studies on this issue. *The Ottawa Citizen* estimated approximately 600, while Gina Smith estimated 800. The Simon Wiesenthal Center puts the number at 2,100. For more, see the SWC's site at www.wiesenthal.com.

37. John J. Mearsheimer and Stephen M. Walt, "The Israel Lobby and U.S. Foreign Policy" (Harvard University, March 2006), http://ksgnotes1.harvard.edu/Research/wpaper.nsf/rwp/RWP06–011/$File/rwp_06_011_walt.pdf.

38. George Michael, "Strange Bedfellows," *Chronicle of Higher Education*, 52, no. 33 (April 21, 2006), p. B9.

39. Susan Miller, "Census Predicts Decline of Whites," *Washington Times*, March 18, 2004.

Bibliography

Aho, James. *The Politics of Righteousness: Idaho Christian Patriotism.* Seattle: University of Washington Press, 1990.

"Alleged Gun Dealer Arrested in Racial Killings Case." CNN, July 7, 1999. http://www.cnn.com/US/9907/07/illinois.shootings.01/index.html.

"An American Judge Orders the Destruction of Bibles." December 4, 2002. http://www.whitestruggle.net/Under_Attack.html.

Anderson, Ken. *Hitler and the Occult.* Amherst, NY: Prometheus Books, 1995.

Anderson, Stephen. "Morris Dees Battles Hatred with Legal System's Weapons." *Bar News*, 40, no. 7 (January 18, 2000).

Anti-Defamation League. "ADL Backgrounder: World Church of the Creator." July 6, 1999. http://www.adl.org/ backgrounders/wcotc.asp.

Anti-Defamation League. "ADL Press Release: ADL Lauds Law Enforcement for Preventing Extremist Violence with Arrest of Matt Hale." January 8, 2003.

Anti-Defamation League. "ADL Press Release: "ADL Lauds Sentencing of White Supremacist Matt Hale." April 6, 2005.

Anti-Defamation League. "Press Release: ADL Pleased with Reno's Response to Its Request for an Investigation of Violent Hate Group World Church of the Creator." July 8, 1999.

Anti-Defamation League. "ADL Press Release: In Shooting Aftermath, ADL Calls for Full-Scale Federal Probe into Violent Hate Group World Church of the Creator." July 6, 1999.

Anti-Defamation League. "ADL Reacts to Illinois Bar Panel's Rejection of Extremist Matt Hale: Well-Intentioned Yet 'Sets a Dangerous Precedent.'" February 4, 1999. http://www.adl.org/presrele/DiRaB_41/matt_hale_41.asp

Anti-Defamation League. *Church of the Creator: Creed of Hate.* New York: Anti-Defamation League, 1993.

Anti-Defamation League. *Danger: Extremism. The Major Vehicles and Voices on America's Far-Right Fringe.* New York: Anti-Defamation League, 1996.

Anti-Defamation League. *Dangerous Convictions: An Introduction to Extremist Activities in Prisons.* New York: Anti-Defamation League, 2002.

Anti-Defamation League. "Deafening Hate: The Revival of Resistance Records." 2000. http://www.adl.org/resistance%20records/introduction.asp

Anti-Defamation League. "Extremism in America: Creativity Movement." http://www.adl.org/Learn/Ext _US/WCOTC.asp? LEARN_Cat=Extremism&LEARN_SubCat=Extremism_in_America &xpicked =3&i tem + cm, accessed October 14, 2004.

Anti-Defamation League. "Extremism in America: Matt Hale." http://www.adl.org/learn/Ext_US/Hale.asp?xpicked=2&item=6, accessed December 26, 2004.

Anti-Defamation League. *Extremism in Florida: The Dark Side of the Sunshine State.* New York: Anti-Defamation League, 2007.

Anti-Defamation League. *Extremism on the Right: A Handbook.* New York: Anti-Defamation League, 1988

Anti-Defamation League. "Feminism Perverted: Extremist Women on the World Wide Web. January 2000. http://www.adl.org/main_Extremism/feminism_perverted.htm.

Anti-Defamation League. *High-tech Hate: Extremist Use of the Internet.* New York: Anti-Defamation League, 1996.

Anti-Defamation League. "Pulpit of Bigotry: Ben Klassen and His Anti-Semitic "Church." New York: Anti-Defamation League, June 1990.

Anti-Defamation League. "Recurring Hate: Matt Hale and the World Church of the Creator." March 1998. http://www.adl.org/special_reports/wcotc/wcotc-intro.asp.

Anti-Defamation League. *The Skinhead International: A Worldwide Survey of Neo-Nazi Skinheads.* New York: Anti-Defamation League, 1995.

Anti-Defamation League. "The Talmud in Anti-Semitic Politics." New York: Anti-Defamation League, 2003. http://www.adl.org/presrele/asus_12/the_talmud.pdf.

Anti-Defamation League. "World Church of the Creator, the Women's Frontier, the Sisterhood." ADL Law Enforcement Agency Resource Network. http://www.adl.org/learn/felton/wcotc.asp, accessed July 1, 2001.

Avila, Oscar. "On the Web, Allies of Hale Cheer Slayings." *Chicago Tribune,* March 2, 2005.

Bandler, James. "Racist Group's Fliers Seen in the Boston Area." *Boston Globe,* July 6, 1999.

Barker, William E. *Aryan America: Race, Revolution and the Hitler Legacy.* St. Maries, ID: Falcon Ridge, 1993.

Barkun, Michael. "Religion, Militias and Oklahoma City: The Mind of Conspiratorialists." *Terrorism and Political Violence,* 8, no. 1 (1996), pp. 50–64.

Barkun, Michael. *Religion and the Racist Right: The Origins of the Christian Identity Movement.* Chapel Hill: University of North Carolina Press, 1994.

Barrett, Richard. *The Commission.* Jackson, MS: Barrett, 1982.

Barrett, Stanley R. *Is God a Racist?: The Right Wing in Canada.* Toronto: University of Toronto Press, 1987.

Bartels, DeWayne. "Hale's Group a Terrorist Threat?" *Peoria Times-Observer,* November 10, 2001.

Barton, Blanche. *The Secret Life of a Satanist: The Authorized Biography of Anton LaVey.* Los Angeles: Feral House, 1992.

Battersby, James Larratt. *The Holy Book of Adolf Hitler.* Southport, UK: German World Church in Europe, 1952.

Beals, Carleton. *Brass-Knuckle Crusade: The Great Know-Nothing Conspiracy: 1820–1860.* New York: Hastings House, 1960.

Beckham, John, and P. J. Huffstutter. "Supremacist Guilty in Plot to Kill Judge." Los Angeles Times, April 27, 2004. www.latimes.com.
Bellah, Robert A. *Beyond Belief: Essays on Religion in a Post Traditional World*. New York: Harper and Row, 1970.
Belluck, Pam. "Avowed Racist Barred from Practicing Law." *New York Times*, February 10, 1999.
Bergen, Doris L. *Twisted Cross: The German Christian Movement in the Third Reich*. Chapel Hill: University of North Carolina Press, 1996.
Berkes, Howard. "A White Supremacist Church and a Small Town." All Things Considered, February 10, 2003. http://www.npr.org/templates/story/story.php?storyId=992253.
Bibo, Terry. "Matt Hale." *Illinois Issues*, July/August 1999. http://131.156.59.13/ipo/1999/ii990730.html.
"Bill White Will Stay behind Bars in Roanoke." WBDJ7.com, October 23, 2008, http://www.wdbj7.com/global/story.asp?s=9199698.
Blackburn, Gilmer W. *Education in the Third Reich: Race and History in Nazi Textbooks*. Albany: State University of New York Press, 1985.
"The Blotter." *Intelligence Report*, 125 (Spring 2007). http://www.splcenter.org/intel/intelreport/article.jsp?aid=738.
Bridges, Tyler. *The Rise of David Duke*. Jackson, MS: University of Mississippi Press, 1994.
Briffault, Herma (ed.). *The Memoirs of Doctor Felix Kersten*. Garden City, NY: Doubleday, 1947.
Brisman, Avi. "Rethinking the Case of Matthew F. Hale: Fear and Loathing on the Part of the Illinois Bar Committee on Character and Fitness." *Connecticut Law Review*, 35, no. 3 (2003), pp. 1399-1425.
Burghart, Dale. *"Creating" a Killer: A Background Report on Benjamin "August" Smith and the World Church of the Creator*. Oak Park, IL: Center for New Community, 1999.
Burghart, Tara. "Hale's Group Linked to Violence in the Past." *New York Times*, March 2, 2005.
Burns, Terry H. "Top Prosecutor Seeks Status of World Church of the Creator." Copley News Service, July 15, 1999.
Buschbacher, Matthew R. *Date the Women of Your Dreams*. Montgomery, AL: E-BookTime, 2005.
Bush, Rudolph. "Hale's Security Boss Was FBI Informer, E-mails, Tapes Led to Arrest, U.S. Says." *Chicago Tribune*, January 24, 2003.
Bushard, Howard L., John R. Craig, and Myra Barnes. *Soldiers of God: White Supremacists and Their Holy War for America*. New York: Kensington Books, 1998.
Cameron, Norman, and R. H. Stevens (trans.). *Hitler's Table Talk 1941–1944: His Private Conversations*. New York: Enigma Books, 2000.
Carter, Dan T. *The Politics of Rage: George Wallace, the Origins of the New Con-*

servatism, and the Transformation of American Politics. New York: Simon and Schuster, 1995.

Carter, Jack. *In the Eye of the Storm: The True Story of Tom Metzger*. Self-published, 1992/93.

Carter, Nicholas. *The Christ Myth*. Sussex, UK: Historical Review Press, 1993.

"Carto Sells the Liberty Lobby List to Todd Blodgett." http://homepage.mac.com/lsf/personal/business_tb.html, accessed February 5, 2005.

Center for New Community. *Creating a Commotion: Matt Hale and the "World Church of the Creator."* Chicago, IL: Center for New Community, January 7, 2003.

Center for New Community. *World Church of the Creator: One Year Later*. Chicago, IL: Center for New Community, June 26, 2000.

"Church of Creator Hate Group Weakened, Divided after Arrests." *Miami Herald*, August 3, 1999.

"Church of the Creator: A History." *Intelligence Report*, 95 (Summer 1999). http://www.splcenter.org/intel/intelreport/article.jsp?sid=219.

"Church Leader to Testify against Hale." *WEEK TV News*, October 22, 2003.

"Church Members Serving Time or Awaiting Trial." *Miami Herald*, August 3, 1999.

Clark, Dru. "Killer's Alienation Shows Need for Vision of a New America." *People's Tribune*, August 1999.

Clayton, Cindy. "White-power Church Causes Stir in New York." *Virginian-Pilot*, April 25, 2002.

Coen, Jeff, and David Heinzmann. "Police: DNA Matches." *Chicago Tribune*, March 11, 2005. http://www.chicagotribune.com/news/local/na/chi-0503110284mar11,1,4896586.story?coll=chi-news-hed.

Cohn, Norman. *Warrant for Genocide: The Myth of the Jewish World Conspiracy and the Protocols of the Elders of Zion*. London: Serif, 1996.

Colias, Mike. "Supremacist on Tape Says Murder of Basketball Coach 'Must Have Been Fun.'" Associated Press, April 15, 2004.

Colinders, Adriana. "Court Upholds Dismissal of Hale's Suit." *Peoria Journal-Star*, July 29, 2000.

Collins, Matthew. "Creative Hate." *The Review*, October 2002. http://www.aijac.org.au/review/2002/2710/wtotc2710.html.

Committee on Un-American Activities. *Preliminary Report on Neo-Fascist and Hate Groups*. Washington, DC: Committee on Un-American Activities, 1954.

"The Constitution of the White Crusaders of the RaHoWa!" http://www.solargeneral.com/creator/constitution.pdf.

Coogan, Kevin. *Dreamer of the Day: Francis Parker Yockey and the Postwar Fascist International*. New York: Autonomedia, 1999.

Cooke, Sarah. "Experts Say World Church Struggling." Associated Press, June 23, 2003.

"Cops Probe Hate Writing Found in Smith's Car." *Chicago Tribune*, July 10, 1999.

Corcoran, James. *Bitter Harvest: Gordon Kahl and the Posse Comitatus: Murder in the Heartland.* New York: Penguin Books, 1990.

Coronado, Ramon. "Man Receives Life for Hate Attacks: The Fair Oaks Resident Committed Two Racially Motivated Attacks." *Sacramento Bee,* September 22, 2001.

Coulson, Danny O., and Elaine Shannon. *No Heroes: Inside the FBI's Secret Counter-Terror Force.* New York: Pocket Books, 1999.

Covington, Harold. "Disaster for the National Alliance." E-mail message from Harold Covington, September 9, 2000.

Covington, Harold. *The March Up Country.* Reedy, WV: Liberty Bell, 1987.

Covington, Harold A. *A Distant Thunder.* Bloomington, IN: authorHouse, 2004.

Covington, Harold A. *The Hill of the Ravens.* Bloomington, IN: 1st Books, 2003.

Covington, Harold A. *A Mighty Fortress.* New York: iUniverse, 2005.

"The Creativity Movement(TCM): A History of Violence." http://www.religioustolerance.org/wcotc2. htm, accessed November 27, 2004.

Crewdson, John. "New Revelations in Attack on American Spy Ship." *Chicago Tribune,* October 2, 2007.

Croll, P. C., D. Hartman, and J. Gerteis. *Putting Whiteness Theory to the Test: An Empirical Assessment of Core Theoretical Propositions.* Minneapolis, MN: Department of Sociology, University of Minnesota, 2006.

Curtis, Alex. "Aryan Kamikaze Terrorizes Midwest." *Nationalist Observer,* 15, July 1999.

Davies, Alan. *Anti-Semitism in Canada: History and Interpretation.* Waterloo, Ontario: Wilfrid University Press, 1992.

Davis, James Kirkpatrick. *Spying on America: The FBI's Domestic Counterintelligence Program.* Westport, CT: Praeger, 1992.

Dawkins, Richard. *The God Delusion.* Boston, MA: Houghton Mifflin, 2006.

Dedman, Bill. "Midwest Gunman Who Shot 11 Had Engaged in Acts of Racism at 2 Universities." *New York Times,* July 5, 1999.

Dees, Morris. *Hate on Trial: The Case against America's Most Dangerous Neo-Nazi.* New York: Villard Books, 1993.

Dees, Morris, and James Corcoran. *Gathering Storm: America's Militia Threat.* New York: HarperCollins, 1996.

de Gobineau, Arthur. *The Inequality of Human Races.* New York: Howard Fertig, 1967.

Degrelle, Leon. "The Enigma of Hitler." n.d. http://www.historiography-project.com/jhrchives/v14/v14n3p22_Degrelle.html, accessed August 1, 2007.

Degrelle, Leon. *Epic: The Story of the Waffen SS.* Torrance, CA: Institute for Historical Review, 1985.

Degrelle, Leon. *Hitler: Born at Versailles.* Torrance, CA: Institute for Historical Review, 1992.

Delsohn, Gary, and Sam Stanton. "White Separatist Groups Targeted in Arson Probe." *Contra Cosa Times,* June 24, 1999.

Devi, Savitri. *The Lighting and the Sun*. Hillsboro, WV: National Vanguard Books, 2000.

Devine, Donald J. "Taught to Think for Himself." *Washington Times*, July 28, 1999.

DeVries, Arnold, and Ben Klassen. *Salubrious Living*. Otto, NC: Church of the Creator, 1983.

"A Different Breed of Terrorist: Hate Group Leader Convicted of Plotting Federal Judge's Murder." June 9, 2004. http://www.fbi.gov/page2/june04/hale060904.htm.

Dinnerstein, Leonard. *Anti-Semitism in America*. New York: Oxford University Press, 1994.

Dobratz, Betty A., and Stephanie L. Shanks-Meile. *White Power, White Pride! The White Separatist Movement in the United States*. New York: Twayne, 1997.

"Docket: Anderson v. Hale and the World Church of the Creator." accessed August 5, 2006, http://www.ccr-ny.org/v2/legal/justice/justiceArticle.asp?ObjID=yEPjrfpAMX&Content=78.

Douglas-Hamilton, James. *Motive for a Mission: The Story behind Hess's Flight to Britain*. New York: St. Martin's Press, 1971.

Durham, Martin. "The Upward Path: Palingenesis, Political Religion and the National Alliance." *Totalitarian Movements and Political Religions*, 5, no. 3 (Winter 2004), pp. 454–68.

East, Emelie E. "The Case of Matthew F. Hale: Implications for First Amendment Rights, Social Mores and the Direction of Bar Examiners in an Era of Intolerance and Hatred." *Georgetown Journal of Legal Ethics*, Summer 2000. http://findarticles.com/p/articles/mi_qa3975/is_200007/ai_n8912301.

Emerson, M. O., and D. Sikkink. "Does Education Help Breed Segregation?" *Rice* [University] *Sallyport* 61 (Fall 2006). www.rice.edu/sallyport/2006/fall/sallyport/segregation.html.

Ennes, James. *Assault on the Liberty: The True Story of the Attack by Israel on an American Intelligence Ship*. New York: Random House, 1970.

Epstein, Benjamin R., and Arnold Forster. *The Radical Right: Report on the John Birch Society and Its Allies*. New York: Random House, 1967.

Evola, Julius. *Men among the Ruins: War Reflections of a Radical Traditionalist*. Rochester, VT: Inner Traditions, 2002.

Evola, Julius, "Race as a Revolutionary Idea." London: Rising Press 2001.

Evola, Julius. *Revolt against the Modern World*. Rochester, VT: Inner Traditions, 1995.

Evola, Julius. *Ride the Tiger: A Survival Manual for Aristocrats of the Soul*. Rochester, VT: Inner Traditions, 2003.

Farley, Christopher John. "Today Los Angeles, Tomorrow . . . " *Time*, July 26, 1993.

Farrell, Allison. "Down to Two." *Independent Record*, March 28, 2004.

Farrell, Allison, "Moving On: Former Member Nearly Bankrupts 'Creativity Movement.'" *Billings Gazette*, March 28, 2004.

Farrell, Allison. "World Church of Creator Founded in 1973." *Independent Record,* March 28, 2004.
"Feds: What Did Texas Couple Plan to Do with Cyanide?" *USA Today,* January 30, 2004. http://www.usatoday.com.
Finz, Stacy. "White Power's New Face." *SFGate,* March 6, 2005.
Flanagan, Thomas. "The Politics of the Millennium." *Terrorism and Political Violence,* 7, no. 3 (1995), pp. 164–75.
Flynn, Kevin, and Gary Gerhardt. *The Silent Brotherhood.* New York: Signet, 1990.
"The Following Is an Interview with the Controversial Rev. Matthew Hale, Pontifex Maximus of the World Church of the Creator Based in East Peoria, Illinois With a Membership Worldwide." http://www.whitestruggle.net/Hale_Interview.html, accessed August 6, 2006.
Forte, Lorraine. "Suit Alleges Hale Ordered Shootings." *Chicago Sun-Times,* March 15, 2000.
Frazier, Deborah. "Church of the Creator Born in Florida." *Rocky Mountain News,* December 26, 2002.
Fukuyama, Francis. *Trust: The Social Virtues and the Creation of Prosperity.* New York: Free Press, 1996.
Gallagher, Eugene V. "God and Country: Revolution as a Religious Imperative on the Radical Right." *Terrorism and Political Violence,* 9, no. 3 (1997), pp. 63–64.
Gardell, Mattias. *Gods of the Blood: The Pagan Revival and White Separatism.* Durham, NC: Duke University Press, 2003.
George, John. "Emergence of a Euro-American Radical Right Book Review." *Menasha,* 93, no. 3 (September 1999), pp. 714–15.
George, John, and Laird Wilcox. *Nazis, Communists, Klansmen, and Others on the Fringe.* Buffalo, NY: Prometheus Books, 1992.
German, Mike. "Behind the Lone Terrorist, a Pack Mentality." *Washington Post,* June 5, 2005.
German, Mike. *Thinking like a Terrorist: Insights of a Former FBI Undercover Agent.* Dulles, VA: Potomac Books, 2007.
Glod, Maria, and Jerry Markon. "Tracking Hate Groups Aids Terrorism Fight." *Washington Post,* May 19, 2003, p. B01.
Godwin, Joscelyn. "Julius Evola: A Philosopher for the Age of the Titans." *Tyr,* 1 (2002), pp. 127–42.
"Going under Cover." *Intelligence Report,* 121 (Spring 2006). http://www.splcenter.org/intel/intelreport/article.jsp?aid=616.
Goldstein, E. L. *The Politics of Ethnic Pressure: The American Jewish Committee Fight against Immigration Restriction, 1906–1917.* New York: Garland, 1990.
Goodrick-Clarke, Nicholas. *The Black Sun: Aryan Cults, Esoteric Nazism and the Politics of Identity.* New York: New York University Press, 2002
Goodrick-Clarke, Nicholas. *Hitler's Priestess: Savitri Devi, the Hindu-Aryan Myth, and Neo-Nazism.* New York: New York University Press, 1998.

Goodrick-Clarke. *The Occult Roots of Nazism: Secret Aryan Cults and Their Influence on Nazi Ideology*. Washington Square, NY: New York University Press, 1992.
"Grassley Statement at the FBI Oversight Hearing." March 27, 2007. http://grassley.senate.gov/index.cfm?FuseAction=PressReleases.Detail&PressRelease_id=5332&Month=3&Year=2007.
"The Great Creator." *Intelligence Report*, 95, (Summer, 1999). www.splcenter.org.
Greenwood, Michael. "With the Web, Midwest Minister of Hate Gains Global Reach." *Hartford Courant*, December 4, 2000.
Griffin, Robert S. *The Fame of a Dead Man's Deeds: An Up-Close Portrait of White Nationalist William Pierce*. Bloomington, IN: 1st Books, 2001.
Griffin, Roger. *Fascism, Oxford Readers*. Oxford: Oxford University Press, 1995.
Griffin, Roger. "I Am No Longer Human. I Am a Titan. A God! The Fascist Quest to Regenerate Time." Unpublished paper.
Griffin, Roger. *The Nature of Fascism*. New York: Routledge, 1993.
Guttenplan, D. D. *The Holocaust on Trial*. New York: Norton, 2001.
"Hale Not Allowed to See, Talk to Parents." Associated Press, March 8, 2005. http://www.foxnews.com/story/0,2933,149771,00.html.
Hale, Matt. "Battleground: Courtroom." *Resistance*, 14 (Winter, 2001), p. 13.
Hale, Matt. *The Creator Membership Manual*. East Peoria, IL: World Church of the Creator, 2002.
Hale, Matt. *Facts that the Government and Media Don't Want You to Know!*
Hale, Matt. *Festum Album*. East Peoria, IL: World Church of the Creator, 2002.
Hale, Matt. *The Truth about 9–11: How Jewish Manipulation Killed Thousands*. East Peoria, IL: Creativity.
"Hate Rock to Spiritual Revelation—The Transformation of George Burdi." http://www.engaged-zen.org, accessed June 27, 2006.
Hawthorne, George Eric. "The Blood of Our Martyrs." *Resistance*, 3 (Winter 1995), p. 4.
Hawthorne, George Eric. "The Brüders Schweigen: Men against Time." In David Lane. *Deceived, Damned, and Defiant: The Revolutionary Writings of David Lane*. St. Maries, ID: 14 Word Press, 1999.
Hawthorne, George Eric. "The Essence of Timing." *Resistance*, 4 (Spring 1995), p. 4.
Hawthorne, George Eric. "Guitars or Guns?" *Resistance*, 8 (1997), p. 4.
Hawthorne, George Eric. "History in the Making." In David Lane. *Deceived, Damned, and Defiant: The Revolutionary Writings of David Lane*. St. Maries, ID: 14 Word Press, 1999.
Hawthorne, George Eric. "We Must Heed the Call." *Resistance*, 2 (Summer 1994), p. 4.
Hayhow, Matt. "A Creator Profile: Brother Ben 'August' Smith." *The Struggle*, March 1999, p. 3.
Haxton, Nance. "SA Attorney-General Wants Racist Website Closed Down." *World Today*, January 31, 2006. http://www.abc.net.au/worldtoday/content/2006/s1559149.htm.

Hill, Mary Jo. "'Creativity' Is a Name for Racism." *Worcester Telegram and Gazette*, July 18, 2002.
Hitler, Adolf (trans. Ralph Manheim). *Mein Kampf.* Boston, MA: Houghton Mifflin, 1971.
Hoffman, Bruce. *Holy Terror: The Implications of Terrorism Motivated by a Religious Imperative.* Santa Monica, CA: Rand, 1993.
Hoffman, Bruce. *Inside Terrorism.* New York: Columbia University Press, 1998.
Hoffman, Michael A. II. *The Great Holocaust Trial.* Torrance, CA: Institute for Historical Review, 1985.
Holthouse, David. "A Few Bad Men." *Intelligence Report* 122, (Summer 2006). http://www.splcenter.org/intel/news/item.jsp?aid=66.
"Illinois High Court Rejects Challenge of Charities Law." Associated Press, November 26, 2001.
Irvine, Martha. "Gunman 'Seemed Mad at the World.'" *Miami Herald*, July 6, 1999.
Irvine, Martha. "Supremacist's Campus Cause." *Washington Post*, January 23, 2000.
Jackson, Camille. "Terror, American Style." *Intelligence Report*, 113 (Spring 2004). http://www.splcenter.org.
Jackson, Dave, and Neta Jackson. *No Random Act: Behind the Murder of Ricky Birdsong.* Colorado Springs, CO: Waterbrook Press, 2002.
Jones, J. Harry Jr. *The Minutemen.* Garden City, NY: Doubleday, 1968.
"Judge Rules Matthew Hale Can Represent Himself." *NWITimes.com*, August 11, 2004.
Jung, Carl G. 1964. "Wotan." In *C. G. Jung, the Collected Works*, Vol. 10. Bollingen Series XX. New York: Pantheon, 1970, pp. 179–93.
Jurgensmeyer, Mark. *Terror in the Mind of God: The Global Rise of Religious Violence.* Berkeley: University of California Press, 2000.
Kaplan, Jeffrey. *The Encyclopedia of White Power: A Sourcebook on the Radical Racist Right.* New York: AltaMira Press, 2000.
Kaplan, Jeffrey. "Leaderless Resistance." *Terrorism and Political Violence*, 9, no. 3 (1997), pp. 81–82.
Kaplan, Jeffrey. "The Postwar Paths of Occult National Socialism: From Rockwell and Madole to Manson." In Jeffrey Kaplan and Heléne Lööw. *The Cultic Milieu: Oppositional Subcultures in an Age of Globalization.* New York: Alta Mira Press, 2002.
Kaplan, Jeffrey. *Radical Religion in America: Millenarian Movements from the Far Right to the Children of Noah.* Syracuse, New York: Syracuse University Press, 1997.
Kaplan, Jeffrey. "Religiosity and the Radical Right: Toward a Creation of a New Ethnic Identity." In Jeffrey Kaplan and Tore Bjorgo. *Nation and Race: The Developing Euro-American Racist Subculture.* Boston, MA: Northeastern University Press, 1998.
Kaplan, Jeffrey. "Right Wing Violence in North America." In Tore Bjorgo (ed.). *Terror from the Extreme Right.* London: Frank Cass, 1995.

Kaplan, Jeffrey, and Tore Bjorgo. *Nation and Race: The Developing Euro-American Racist Subculture*. Boston, MA: Northeastern University Press, 1998.

Kaplan, Jeffrey, and Leonard Weinberg. *The Emergence of a Euro-American Radical Right*. New Brunswick, NJ: Rutgers University Press, 1998.

Kaplan, Jeffrey, Leonard Weinberg, and Ted Oleson. "Dreams and Realities in Cyberspace: The White Aryan Resistance and World Church of the Creator on the Internet." *Patterns of Prejudice*, 37, no. 2 (2003), pp. 139–56.

Kifner, John. Hate Groups Are Infiltrating the Military, Group Asserts. *New York Times*, July 7, 2006.

Kim, Ann S. "Second White Supremacist Group Targets Lewiston." Associated Press, November 29, 2002.

Kinsella, Warren. *Web of Hate: Inside Canada's Far Right Network*. Toronto: Harper Perennial, 1995.

Klassen, Ben. *Against the Evil Tide: An Autobiography*. Otto, NC: Church of the Creator, 1991.

Klassen, Ben. *Building a Whiter and Brighter World*. Otto, NC: Church of the Creator, 1986.

Klassen, Ben. *Expanding Creativity: An Idea Whose Time Has Come*. Otto, NC: Church of the Creator, 1985.

Klassen, Ben. *The Klassen Letters Volume One: 1969–1976*. Otto, NC: Church of the Creator, 1988.

Klassen, Ben. *The Klassen Letters Volume Two: 1976–1981*. Otto, NC: Church of the Creator, 1989.

Klassen, Ben. *The Little White Book: Fundamentals of the White Racial Religion of Creativity*. Otto, NC: Church of the Creator, 1991.

Klassen, Ben. *Nature's Eternal Religion*. Niceville, FL: Church of the Creator, 1992.

Klassen, Ben. *On the Brink of a Bloody Racial War*. Otto, NC: Church of the Creator, 1993.

Klassen, Ben. *RAHOWA! This Planet Is All Ours*. Otto, NC: Church of the Creator, 1987.

Klassen, Ben. *A Revolution of Values through Religion*. Otto, NC: Church of the Creator, 1991.

Klassen, Ben. *Trials, Tribulations and Triumphs*. Niceville, FL: Church of the Creator, 1993.

Klassen, Ben. *The White Man's Bible*. 2nd ed. Otto, NC: Church of the Creator, 1992.

Koehl, Matt. *Faith of the Future*. Milwaukee, WI: New Order, 1995.

Koestler, Arthur. *The Thirteenth Tribe*. New York: Random House, 1976.

Korecki, Natasha. "Hale Held with the Worst of the Worst." *Chicago Sun-Times*, April 28, 2005.

Korecki, Natasha. "Hale Loyalist Turns on Him at Trial." *Chicago Sun-Times*, April 14, 2004.

Korecki, Natasha. "Judge Orders Hale's Group to Pay Up." *Chicago Sun-Times*, May 24, 2005.
Korecki, Natasha, and Frank Main. "Hale Sentenced to 40 Years." *Chicago-Sun Times*, April 6, 2005. http://www.suntimes.com/output/news/hale06.html.
Kravetz, Andy. "Hale Changing His Story on Smith." *Peoria Star Journal*, July 15, 1999.
Kravetz, Andy, and Mike Ramsey. "Prosecutors Link Hale to 1999 Killings." *Peoria Star Journal*, October 4, 2003.
Kravetz, Andy, and John Sharp. "Matt Hale Listed as Attorney." *Journal Star*, August 31, 2002.
Kristof, Nicholas D. "Hate, American Style." *New York Times*, August 30, 2002.
"Kroenke no Longer with Corrections Department." Associated Press, March 27, 2003.
Kubizek, August (trans. E. V. Anderson). *The Young Hitler I Knew*. Cambridge, MA: Houghton Mifflin, 1955.
Kurtzman, Daniel. "Chicago Gunman's Hate Group among Fastest Growing." Jewish Telegraphic Agency, July 9, 1999. http://www.jewishsf.com/content/2-0-/module/displaystory/story_id/11565/edition_id/222/format/html/displaystory.html.
Langer, Linor. *A Hundred Little Hitlers: The Death of a Black Man, the Trial of a White Racist, and the Rise of the Neo-Nazi Movement in America*. New York: Picador, 2004.
LaVey, Anton. *The Satanic Rituals*. New York: Avon Books, 1972.
Lavoie, Denise. "Woman Gets Nearly 5 Years in Racist Plot." Associated Press, March 13, 2003.
"Lawyer: Hale Passed Message to Supporter." Associated Press, March 9, 2005. http://www.foxnews.com/story/0,2933,149853,00.html.
"Lawyers Want Hale Trial Moved." Associated Press, May 26, 2003.
Levenda, Peter. *Unholy Alliance: A History of Nazi Involvement with the Occult*. New York: Avon Books, 1995.
Leyland, Tom. "Remembering Our Youth." *G21*, n.d. http://g21.net/amdream9a.html.
Lipset, Seymour Martin, and Earl Raab. *The Politics of Unreason: Right Wing Extremism in America, 1790–1970*. New York: Harper and Row, 1970.
Lipstadt, Deborah E. *History on Trial: My Day in Court with David Irving*. New York: HarperCollins, 2005.
"Literature of Hate Hits South Hill." October 19, 2001. http://www.wiesenthal.com/social/press.
Lööw, Heléne. "The Idea of Purity." In Jeffrey Kaplan and Heléne Lööw. *The Cultic Milieu: Oppositional Subcultures in an Age of Globalization*. New York: Alta Mira Press, 2002.
Lööw Heléne. "Racist Violence and Criminal Behaviour in Sweden: Myths and Reality." In Tore Bjorgo (ed.). *Terror from the Extreme Right*. London: Frank Cass, 1995.

Lööw, Heléne. "White-Power Rock 'n' Roll: A Growing Industry." In Jeffrey Kaplan and Tore Bjorgo (eds.). *Nation and Race: The Developing Euro-American Racist Subculture*. Boston, MA: Northeastern University Press, 1998.

Luckey, Heiko. "'Believers Writing for Believers': Traces of Political Religion in National Socialist Pulp Fiction." *Totalitarian Movements and Political Religions*, 8, no. 1 (March 2007), pp. 77–92.

Macdonald, Andrew (pseudonym for William Pierce). *Hunter*. Hillsboro, WV: National Vanguard Books, 1989.

Macdonald, Andrew (pseudonym for William Pierce). *The Turner Diaries*. Hillsboro, WV: National Vanguard Books, 1993.

MacDonald, Kevin. *The Culture of Critique: An Evolutionary Analysis of Jewish Involvement in Twentieth-Century Intellectual and Political Movements*. Westport, CT: Praeger, 1998.

MacDonald, Kevin. *A People that Shall Dwell Alone: An Evolutionary Theory of Judaism*. Westport, CT: Praeger, 1994.

MacDonald, Kevin. "Psychology and White Ethnocentrism." *Occidental Quarterly*, 6, no. 4 (Winter 2006–2007), pp. 7–46.

MacDonald, Kevin. *Separation and Its Discontents: Toward an Evolutionary Theory of Anti-Semitism*. Westport, CT: Praeger, 1994.

MacLean, Nancy. *Behind the Mask of Chivalry: The Making of the Second Ku Klux Klan*. New York: Oxford University Press, 1994.

"The Making of a Neo-Nazi Mogul." *New York Times Magazine*, Sunday, February 25, 1996.

Marin, Carol. "How the War on Terrorism Has Gone Way Too Far." *Chicago Tribune*, May 7, 2003.

Marks, Kathy. *Faces of Right Wing Extremism*. Boston, MA: Branden, 1996.

Martinez, Thomas, with John Guinther. *Brotherhood of Murder*. New York: Pocket Books, 1988.

"Matt Hale Ousted." http://www.liesexposed.net/nfp/issue0205/hale.htm, accessed August 5, 2006.

"Matt Hale Responds." http://www.liesexposed.net/nfp/issue0207/hale.htm, accessed July 12, 2007,

"Matt Hale Sues Durkin." *Libertarian Socialist News*, August 4, 2006. http://www.overthrow.com/lsn/news.asp?articleID=9671.

"Matt Hale's Poem: Written in Prison." October 19, 2003, http:www.nationalvanguard.org.

Matthew F. Hale v. Committee on Character and Fitness for the State of Illinois; Board of Admissions: To the Bar: Committee on Character and Fitness, State of Illinois, Third Judicial District; Gordon L. Lustfeldt; Thomas Dunn, Clark Erickson; Charles Marshall;: L. Lee Perrington and the Supreme Court of Illinois, June 27, 2001.

McCafferty, Dennis. "Desperately Seeking Angry White Females." *Salon.com*, October 14, 1999. http://www.salon.com/news/feature/1999/10/14/hate/index.html.

McDonald, Karen. "Brother of Matt Hale Allegedly Stole, Sold 12 Firearms from Father." *Peoria Journal Star*, May 27, 2006.
McDonald, Karen, and Andy Kravetz. "Some Feel the World Church Will Falter, and Hale Is Capable of Crime." *Peoria Journal Star Online*, January 9, 2003. http://www.pjstar.com/news/topnews/hold/ g135498a.html.
McDonough, Molly. "Civil Right Group Sues White Supremacist." *American Lawyer Media*, April 6, 2000.
McDonough, Molly. "White Supremacist Takes Law License Fight to D.C." *Law News*, February 11, 2000.
McTernan, Oliver. *Violence in God's Name: Religion in an Age of Conflict*. Maryknoll, NY: Orbis Books, 2003.
Mearsheimer, John J., and Stephen M. Walt. "The Israel Lobby and U.S. Foreign Policy. Harvard University, March 2006. http://ksgnotes1.harvard.edu/Research/wpaper.nsf/rwp/RWP06–011/$File/rwp_06_011_walt.pdf.
"Michael Chertoff." Jewish Virtual Library. http://www.jewishvirtuallibrary.org/jsource/biography/Chertoff.html, accessed September 27, 2007.
"Michael Chertoff, J.D., Assistant Attorney General in the Department of Justice, to Deliver Keynote Address at Seton Hall University School of Law Commencement." May 24, 2002. http://domapp01shu.edu/depts/special%20programs/pressrelease.nsf/f7b9c5bae1fc659852569d.
Michael, George. *Confronting Right-Wing Extremism and Terrorism in the USA*. London: Routledge, 2003.
Michael, George. *The Enemy of My Enemy: The Alarming Convergence of Militant Islam and the Extreme Right*. Lawrence: University Press of Kansas, 2006.
Michael, George. "Professor of Kevin MacDonald's Critique of Judaism: Legitimate Scholarship or the Intellectualization of Anti-Semitism?" *Journal of Church and State*, 48 (Autumn 2006), pp. 779–806.
Michael, George. "Strange Bedfellows." *Chronicle of Higher Education*, 52, no. 33 (April 21, 2006), p. B9.
Michael, George. *Willis Carto and the American Far Right*. Gainesville, FL: University Press of Florida, 2008.
Miller, Susan. "Census Predicts Decline of Whites." *Washington Times*, March 18, 2004.
Mills, A. Rud. "Our Ancient Religion." *Right*, 50 (November 1959), p. 3.
Mirabello, Mark L. *The Odin Brotherhood*. Edmonds, WA: Sure Fire Press, 1992.
Molyneaux, Kenneth. *Klassen*. Self-published, n.d.
Molyneaux, Kenneth. *White Empire*. Self-published, n.d.
Montana Human Rights Network. "Law Enforcement, Community and Press Briefing Paper." March 10, 2003. www.mhrn.org.
Moynihan, Michael (ed.). *The Secret King: Karl Maria Wiligut: Himmler's Lord of the Runes*. Waterbury, VT: Dominion Press, 2001.
Moynihan, Michael, and Didrik Soderlind. *Lords of Chaos: The Bloody Rise of the Satanic Metal Underground*. Venice, CA: Feral House, 1998.

"Murder Target Cecil Murray Praises the Lord and Continues His Ministry." *People*, August 2, 1993, pp. 83–84.

Murdoch, John. "Bye-Bye Burdi." *Resistance*, 12 (Summer 2000), p. 13.

"National Alliance Leader William Pierce Sued in Connection with Church of the Creator Case." *Klanwatch Intelligence Report*, 77 (March 1995), p. 9.

"Nazi Alert: Jewish Attorney Represents Jew-hater." June 1, 2001. http://www.jdl.org/enemies/nazi/greenwald.shtml.

Nelson, Robert. "Peacenik Nazis." *Phoenix New Times*, November 29, 2001.

New Century Foundation. *The Color of Crime*. Oakton, VA: New Century Foundation, 1999.

Newton, Jim, and Ann W. O'Neill. "Alleged White Supremacists Seized in Assassination Plot." *Los Angeles Times*, July 16, 1993.

Niewart, David. *In God's Country: The Patriot Movement and the Pacific Northwest*. Pullman: Washington State University Press, 1999.

Niewart, David. "Playing Politics with Terror." *Orcinus*, August 4, 2004. http://dneiwert.blogspot.com/2004/08/playing-politics-with-terror.html.

Novick, Michael. *White Lies White Power: The Fight against White Supremacy and Reactionary Violence*. Monroe, ME: Common Courage Press, 1995.

O'Connor, Matt. "Hale Asks to Handle His Own Defense." *Chicago Tribune*, July 16, 2004.

O'Connor, Matt. "Hale Guard went to Cops over Supremacist Material." *Chicago Tribune*, April 15, 2004.

Oliver, Revilo. *Christianity and the Survival of the West*. Sterling, VA: Sterling Enterprises, 1973.

Page, Clarence. "It's the White Supremacist Who Owes *Us* the Apology." *Jewish World Review*, March 16, 2005. http://www.jewishworldreview.com/0305/page_2005_03_16.php3.

Parsonno, Anthony. "I Am Not My DNA!" *Acid Logic*, n.d. http://www.forbisthemighty.com/acidlogic/georgeburdi.htm.

The People ex rel. James E. Ryan, Attorney General of Illinois, Appellant, v. The World Church of the Creator et al., Apelles. Filed November 21, 2001.

Perrier, Ralph, and P. Oliver Revilo. *The Jews Love Christianity*. Reedy, WV: Liberty Bell, 1980.

Pfaff, William. *The Wrath of Nations: Civilization and the Furies of Nationalism*. New York: Simon and Schuster, 1993.

Phelps, Reginald. "'Before Hitler Came': Thule Society and the Germanen Orden." *Journal of Modern History*, 25 (1963), pp. 245–61.

Pierce, William. "Knowledge and Discipline." *American Dissident Voices*, 5, no. 7 (July 1999).

Pierce, William L. "The Perils of Hobbyism." *National Alliance Bulletin*, November-December 1992.

Piper, Michael Collins. *The Judas Goats: The Enemy Within*. Washington, DC: American Free Press 2006.

Piper, Michael Collins. "Proposed New Homeland Security Czar Gave Free Pass to Foreign Spies in America." *American Free Press*, January 24, 2005, p. 18.

Pois, Robert A. *National Socialism and the Religion of Nature*. London: Croom Helm, 1986.

"Pontifex Ex." *Intelligence Report*, 114 (Summer 2004). http://www.splcenter.org/intel/intelreport/article.jsp?aid=476.

Pool, James, and Suzanne Pool. *Who Financed Hitler?* New York: Dial Press, 1978.

Potok, Mark. "Divided Alliance." *Intelligence Report*,108 (Winter 2002). http://www.splcenter.org/intel/ intelreport/article.jsp?aid=75.

Potok, Mark. "The Year in Hate, 2004." *Intelligence Report*, 117 (Spring 2005). http://www.splcenter.org/intel/intelreport/article.jsp?aid=529.

Pranaitis, I. B. *The Talmud Unmasked*. Whitefish, MT: Kessinger Publishing, n.d.

Pratt, Carla D. "Should Klansmen Be Lawyers? Racism as an Ethical Barrier to the Legal Profession." *Florida State University Law Review*, 30, no. 4 (Summer 2003), p. 865.

"Present at the Creation." *Intelligence Report*,103 (Fall 2001). http://www.splcenter.org/intel/intelreport/ article. jsp?aid=179.

Price, Robert M. *Incredible Shrinking Son of Man: How Reliable Is the Gospel Tradition?* Amherst, NY: Prometheus Books, 2003.

Pringle, Heather. *The Master Plan: Himmler's Scholars and the Holocaust*. New York: Hyperion, 2006.

"Prison Sentence for Possessing Chemical Weapons." *ATF News*, May 4, 2004.

Putnam, Robert. "*E Pluribus Unum:* Diversity and Community in the Twenty-first Century. The 2006 Johan Skytte Prize Lecture." *Scandinavian Political Studies*, 30, no. 2 (2007), pp. 137–74.

Putnam, Robert D. *Making Democracy Work: Civic Traditions in Modern Italy*. Princeton, NJ: Princeton University Press, 1994.

"Racist Church Keeps Tax-exempt Status." *Daily Southtown*, February 9, 2000.

Ramsey, Mike. "Hale Continues Bid for Law License." *State Journal-Record*, October 31, 2002.

Ramsey, Mike. "Hale Held without Bond." Associated Press, January 24, 2003.

Ramsey, Mike. "Informant: Hale Smiled, Nodded to Kill." *Peoria Star Journal*, April 17, 2004.

Ramsey, Mike. "Prosecutors Counter Hale Defense." *Peoria Star Journal*, January 1, 2004. http://www.rickross.com/reference/hale/hale85.html.

Ramsey, Mike. "Prosecutors Don't Want Hale Trial Moved." Copley News Service, June 18, 2003. http://www.rickross.com/reference/hale/hale74.html.

Ravenscroft, Trevor. *The Spear of Destiny*. York Beach, ME: Samuel Weiser, 1991.

Reeve, Simon. *The New Jackals: Ramzi Yousef, Osama bin Laden, and the Future of Terrorism*. Boston, MA: Northeastern University Press, 1999.

"Repulsive and Repugnant Conduct Repudiated." January 8, 2003. http://www.nationalist.org/news/flashes/2003/hale.html.

"Resisting Arrest: Racist Resistance Records Isn't Slowing Down." *Intelligence Re-

port, 89 (Winter 1998). http://www.splcenter.org/intel/intelreport/article.jsp?aid=452.
"The Revenge of Matt Hale." 2005. http://www.solargeneral.com/news/revenge.htm.
Reverend Lloyd with Sister Lisa. *The Creator's Manual*. (2007).
Robertson, Tasha. "Extreme TV: Hate Groups Exploit Cable." *Boston Globe*, September 30, 2000.
Robertson, Wilmont. *The Dispossessed Majority*. Cape Canaveral, FL: Howard Allen, 1981.
Robinson, Mike. "Former Follower Says Hale Urged Killing of Federal Judge." Associated Press, April 14, 2004.
Robinson, Mike. "Judge: Hale Must Stay in Custody; Trial Delayed." Associated Press, October 31, 2003.
Robinson, Mike. "White Supremacist Charged with Lying to Federal Judge." Associated Press, June 26, 2003.
Robinson, Mike. "White Supremacist Sentenced to 40 Years." *Sun-Sentinel*, April 7, 2005.
Rockwell, George Lincoln. *This Time the World*. 6th ed. Reedy, WV: Liberty Bell, 1993.
Rockwell, George Lincoln. *White Power*. Reedy, WV: Liberty Bell, 1983).
"The Role of Women." n.d. http://creativity1973.org/Creativity-Writings/TheRoleOfWomen.html.
Rosenberg, Alfred. *The Myth of the Twentieth Century: An Evaluation of the Spiritual-Intellectual Confrontations of Our Age*. Newport Beach, CA: Noontide Press, 1993.
Rosenlum, Rebecca. "Justice Dept. Investigating World Church of the Creator." *Jewish Bulletin News*, August 20, 1999.
Rosenthal, A. M., and Arthur Gelb. *One More Victim: The Life and Death of a Jewish Nazi*. New York: New American Library, 1967.
Ryan, Nick. *Into a World of Hate: A Journey among the Extreme Right*. New York: Routledge, 2003.
"Sacramento Authorities Question Members of World Church of the Creator." CNN, July 13, 1999.
Scharnberg, Kirsten. "FBI Agents Quiz Church Leader over Rampage." *Chicago Tribune*, July 8, 1999.
Scheeres, Julia. "Will the Hatemongers Survive?" *Wired*, January 30, 2001. http://www.wired.com/culture/lifestyle/news/2001/01/41460.
Schmidt, Susan. "Bush to Name Chertoff to Court." *Washington Post*, January 18, 2003, p. A14.
Segal, David. "The Pied Piper of Racism." *Washington Post*, January 12, 2000.
Selden, Ron. "Supremacist Matt Hale Wants Montana Practice." *Indian Country Today*, December 20, 2000. http://www.indiancountry.com/content.cfm?id=489.

Sharkey, Matt. "The Matt Hale Interview." *G21*, 1999. http://g21.net/amdream9.html.
Simon, Stephanie. "Leader of Hate's Church Mourns 'One White Man.'" *Los Angeles Times*, July 6, 1999.
Simonelli, Frederick J. *American Fuehrer: George Lincoln Rockwell and the American Nazi Party.* Chicago: University of Illinois Press, 1999.
Simpson, William Gayley. *Which Way Western Man?* Washington, DC: National Alliance, 1978.
Singular, Stephen. *Talked to Death: The Life and Murder of Alan Berg.* New York: Beech Tree Books/William Morrow, 1987.
Sloan, Richard L. "Barbarians at the Gates: Revisiting the Case of Matthew F. Hale to Reaffirm that Character and Fitness Evaluations Appropriately Preclude Racists from the Practice of Law." *Georgetown Journal of Legal Ethics*, Winter 2002. http://findarticles.com/p/articles/mi_qa3975/is_200201/ai_n9066915.
Smith, Brent L. *Terrorism in America: Pipe Bombs and Pipe Dreams.* Albany: State University of New York Press, 1994.
Smith, Geoffrey S. *To Save a Nation: American "Extremism," the New Deal, and the Coming of World War II.* Chicago: Elephant Paperbacks, 1992.
Smith, Peter Scharff, Niels Bo Poulsen, and Claus Bundgard Christensen. "The Danish Volunteers in the Waffen SS and German Warfare at the Eastern Front." *Contemporary European History*, 8, no. 1 (1999).
Stanko, Rudy "Butch." *The Score.* Gering, NE: Institute for Christian Bankers, 1986.
Stanko, Rudy "Butch." "Slavery! Survives in America!" Self-published, n.d.
Stanton, Sam, and Gary Delsohn. "Poster Boys for the Summer of Hate." October 6, 1999. Salon.com. http://archive.salon.com/news/feature/1999/10/06/redding/index.html.
Steele, Edgar J. "The Railroading of Matt Hale." March 4, 2005. http://www.conspiracypenpal.com/columns/hale.htm.
Steigmann-Gall, Richard. "Nazism and the Revival of Political Religion Theory." *Totalitarian Movements and Political Religions*, 5, no. 3 (Winter 2004).
Stephenson, Crocker. "Missionaries of Hate." *Milwaukee Journal Sentinel*, March 19, 2000.
Stern, Jessica. *Terror in the Name of God: Why Religious Militants Kill.* New York: HarperCollins, 2003.
Stevenson, Mathew "Hate vs. Hypocrisy: Matt Hale and the New Politics of Bar Admissions." *Montana Law Review*, 63, no. 2 (Summer 2002), pp. 431–34.
Stewart, Sally Ann. "FBI: LA Race War Plot 'Despicable.'" *USA Today*, July 16–18, 1993, p. A-1.
Stoddard, Lothrop. *The Rising Tide of Color.* Torrance, CA: Noontide Press, 1981.
Stormer, John A. *None Dare Call It Treason.* Florissant, MO: Liberty Bell, 1964.
Strom, Kevin Alfred. "Terror in Chicago." *American Dissident Voices*, January 18, 2003. https://www.natall.com/pub/2003/011803.txt.

"Supremacist Church Leaving Midwest for Riverton, Wyo." Associated Press, December 10, 2002.

"Supremacist Church Name Change." Associated Press, July 26, 2002.

"Supremacist Disagrees with Ruling, Sues Judge." *Peoria Journal-Star*, December 27, 2002.

Suster, Gerald. *Hitler: Black Magician*. London: Skoob Books, 1996.

Svonkin, Stuart. *Jews against Prejudice: American Jews and the Fight for Civil Liberties*. New York: Columbia University Press, 1997.

Swain, Carol M. *The New White Nationalism in America: Its Challenge to Integration*. New York: Cambridge University Press, 2002.

Swain, Carol M., and Russ Nieli (eds.). *Contemporary Voices of White Nationalism in America*. Cambridge: Cambridge University Press, 2003.

Szajkowski, Z. "Paul Nathan, Lucien Wolf, Jacob H. Schiff, and the Jewish Revolutionary Movements in Eastern Europe." *Jewish Social Studies*, 29, no. 1 (1967), pp. 1–15.

Taheri, Amir. *Holy Terror: Inside the World of Islamic Terrorism*. Bethesda, MD: Adler and Adler, 1987.

TE-TA-MA Truth Foundation—Family of URI, Inc., v. World Church of the Creator. In the United States Court of Appeals for the Seventh Court, July 25, 2002.

Thomas, Jo. "In East Peoria, an Intolerance for Hate." *New York Times*, September 21, 1999.

Thomas, Judy L. "Ten Years after Oklahoma City Bombing, Militia Movements Are Rudderless and in Disarray—Which Makes Them Deadlier." *Jewish World Review*, April 19, 2005.

Thurlow, Richard. *Fascism in Britain: From Oswald Mosley's Blackshirts to the National Front*. London: I. B. Tauris, 1998.

"Trash Talk not Covered by Litter Statute." Ohio Department of Natural Resources. http://www.dnr.state.oh.us/recycling/pages/lawnewsarchive1.htm, accessed July 23, 2007.

Turner, Lisa. "The Co-optation of White Women." http://www.wcotc.com/wcotccwf/copt.html, accessed September 6, 2001.

Turner, Lisa. "Our Stand on Abortion." In Jackson and Jackson, *No Random Act*, p. 91.

"Two More State Agencies Investigate Racist Group." Associated Press, July 12, 1999.

United States of America v. Matthew Hale. In the United States Court of Appeals for the Seventh Circuit, May 30, 2006.

United States Attorney District of Illinois. "White Supremacist Church Leader Arrested on Charges of Soliciting Murder of U.S. Judge Presiding over Trademark Case."

United States District Court Northeastern District of Illinois Eastern Division. *United States of America v. Matthew Hale, Count One*.

United States District Court Northeastern District of Illinois Eastern Division. "White-Supremacist Church Leader Arrested on Charges of Soliciting Murder of U.S. Judge Presiding over Trademark Case." January 8, 2003. http://www.usdoj.gov/usao/iln/pr/chicago/2003/pr010803_01.pdf.

U.S. Department of Justice. "Self-Proclaimed White Supremacist William White Indicted for Allegedly Soliciting Violence against Hale Jury Foreperson." October 22, 2008, http://chicago.fbi.gov/dojpressrel/pressrel08/oct22_08.htm.

Vanlandingham, Keith. "Matt Hale: Understanding What Went Wrong." http://www.nationalist.org/alt/2003/jan/understanding.html, accessed August 5, 2007.

Viereck, Peter. *Meta-Politics: The Roots of the Nazi Mind.* New York: Capricorn Books, 1961.

von Malitz, Horst. *The Evolution of Hitler's Germany: The Ideology, the Personality, the Movement.* New York: Macmillan, 1973.

Voskuilen, Thijs. "Operation Messiah: Did Christianity Start as a Roman Psychological Counterinsurgency Operation?" *Small Wars and Insurgencies*, 16, no. 2 (June 2005), pp. 192–215.

Waite, Robert G. I. *The Psychopathic God: Adolf Hitler.* New York: Basic Books, 1977.

Walsh, Edward. "'Appalled' Reno Pledges Review of Midwest Shootings." *Washington Post*, July 9, 1999, p. A12.

Walsh, Edward. "Racial Slayer Killed Himself in Struggle." *Washington Post*, July 6, 1999.

Warmbir, Steve. "Hale 'Church' Dealt $200,000 Defeat." *Chicago Sun-Times*, October 25, 2003.

Warmbir, Steve. "Hale's Church Sued over Use of Name on Web site." *Chicago Sun-Times*, May 22, 2003.

Watson, Dale L. "The Terrorist Threat Confronting the United States: Statement for the Record of Dale L. Watson, Executive Assistant Director for Counterterrorism and Counterintelligence for the FBI before the Senate Select Committee on Intelligence." February 6, 2002.

Weimann, Gabriel, and Conrad Winn. *Hate on Trial: The Zündel Affair, the Media, Public Opinion in Canada.* New York: Mosaic Press, 1986.

Weisenburger, Steven. "The Columbians, Inc: A Chapter of Racial Hatred from Post–World War II South." *Journal of Southern History*, 69, no. 4 (November 2003).

Welch, Robert. *The Life of John Birch.* Chicago: Henry Regnery Company, 1954.

Wendel, W. Bradley. "Hate and the Bar: Is the Hale Case McCarthyism Redux or a Victory for Racial Equality?" *The Bar Examiner*, May 2001, p. 39.

Wheaton, Elizabeth. *Codename Greenkil: The 1979 Greensboro Killings.* Athens: University of Georgia Press, 1987.

Whisker, James B. *The Philosophy of Alfred Rosenberg: Origins of the National Socialist Myth.* Costa Mesa, CA: Noontide Press.

"White Supremacist Group Founder Probed." Associated Press, August 30, 2003.

"White Supremacist Guilty of Plotting to Kill Judge." CNN, April 26, 2004.

"White Supremacist Movement Reels from Severe Setbacks in 1993." Intelligence Report, (March 1994).

"'White Supremacists' on Trial in Boston." BBC News, July 8, 2002. http://news.bbc.co.uk/1/hi/world/americas /2116623.stm.

Wilcox, Laird. *The Watchdogs: A Close Look at Anti-Racist "Watchdog" Groups.* Olathe, KS: Laird Wilcox Editorial Research Center, 1999.

Willow, Tony. "'"Creativity" Movement Leader, Jon Fox to Turn States Evidence!" October 21, 2003. http://citizensagainsthate.com/home/modules.php?op=modload&name=News&file=article&sid=129&mode=thread.

Wistrich, Robert S. *Anti-Semitism: The Longest Hatred.* New York: Pantheon Books, 1991.

Wolf, Victor. "The Basis of Organization." Reprinted in Klassen, *Trials, Tribulations and Triumphs*, pp. 226–33.

Wright, Elizabeth. "Free Speech for Some, but Not All." *Issues and Views*, November 2000. http://www.issuesviews.com/index.php/sect/1001/article/1030.

Zucker, Steve. "50–75 Years in Prison for Rapist." *Petoskey News-Review*, October 12, 2006.

Index

Abortion issue, 137
Adams, John R., 11–12
ADL. *See* Anti-Defamation League
AFA. *See* Asatru Free Assembly
Africa, 82–83, 171; ANC, 84; First African Methodist Episcopal Church, Los Angeles, 100
African Americans, 101; Byrdsong, 154, 158; deportation of, 22, 208n74, 209n7; Mansfield, 99–100, 107, 186; racial separation for, 31, 102–3, 130–31, 208n75; as targets, 138, 148
African National Congress (ANC), 84
Afrikaner Resistance Movement (AWB), 83
Ahnerbe (division of Waffen-SS), 44, 211nn41–42
Albares, Richard P., 217n28
Almon, Jeff, 148
American Association for the Advancement of Atheism, 208n81
American Civil Liberties Union, 144
"American civil religion," 48
American Civil War, 48, 208n74
American Dissident Voices (radio program), 178
American Independent Party, 8
American Jewish Committee, 252n36
American Jewish Congress, 145
American Nazi Party, 52–54, 57, 216n5; Odinism and, 214nn68–70. *See also* Neo-Nazi groups
American Opinion Bookstore, 7
American Opinion Speakers Bureau, 6
American western frontier, 28, 30
American White Supremacist Party, 123
ANC. *See* African National Congress
Anticapitalism, 76–78
The Anti-Christ (Nietzsche), 13, 108
Anti-Defamation League (ADL), 7, 9–10, 48, 101, 161, 186, 237n36; on Matt Hale's law license, 145; monitoring Minutemen, 217n28; Resistance Records and, 116

Anti-Racist Action, 115
Anti-Semitism, 84, 200nn27–28, 205n29, 206nn51–52, 212n57, 225n50; Burdi's, 108; Ford's, 205n30; Ben Klassen, 2, 7, 8, 13–14, 16–17; Liebenfels,' 36, 209n7; post–WWII, 48; *The Thirteenth Tribe* used for, 213n62; ZOG, 80, 192, 193
Archetypes, 53
Armageddon, 49–50
Armstrong, Herbert, 213n61. *See also* British Israelism
Arson, 149. *See also* Bombing
Aryan(s): cults, 36, 44–45, 58, 59–60; White Aryan Resistance, 77, 92–93, 100, 134, 216n5, 221n40
Aryan Nations, 50, 78, 186, 197
Asatru Alliance, 53, 214n76
Asatru Free Assembly (AFA), 52–53
Ashcroft, John, 180
Atkinson, Michael, 191
Attack! (magazine), 64
Atwater, Lee, 116
Australia, 159, 190–91
Austria, 35, 36
AWB. *See* Afrikaner Resistance Movement

Bacon, Francis, 108
Baird v. Board of Bar Examiners, 142
Barnhill, Jimmy, 160
Barrett, Richard, 91
Baxter, Lawrence W., 139
Becker, Richard F., 84–86
Bee, Kathleen, 135
Bellah, Robert, 48
Bender, Michael Ian, 159
Berg, Alan, 79–81
Berwick, Christopher, 100–101
Bible, 12, 21, 49, 105; Paul (apostle), 16, 19–20, 39, 203n15. *See also The White Man's Bible*
Birch, John, 6–8, 77, 200nn25,26,28
Black metal music, 229n16

Blacks. *See* African Americans
Blavatsky, Helena, 35–36
Blegan, Patrick W., 180
Blodgett, Todd, 116
Bloomington United Campaign against Hate Speech and Hate Crimes, 129, 158
Bolshevism, 1–2, 41, 205n33
Bombing, 81–82, 101, 138, 185–86, 202n50, 217n28. *See also* World Trade Center
Bond v. Floyd, 144
Booth, John Wilkes, 150, 208n74
Bormann, Martin, 38, 44, 46
Bowers, Terree A., 101
Braun, Werhner von, 206n41
Brest-Litovsk Treaty of 1918, 1
British Intelligence (MI6), 212n46
British Israelism, 49, 212n57, 213n61
Brokaw, Tom, 130
Burdi, George Eric, ix, 104, 108–9, 229n16; on music, 110–15; in political arena, 115–19
Burke, Ben, 5
Buros, Dan, 214n70
Bush, George W., 177
Butler, Richard, 50, 186
Byrdsong, Ricky, 154, 158

Cameron, William, 205n30
Campbell, Colin, 190
Canada, 2–3; speech laws in, 116
Capitalism, 76–78
Carl (WCOTC member), 189–90, 249n7
Carto, Willis, 68, 116, 208n81, 211n36, 217n35
Caste system, 30
Casualties of War (De Palma), 97
Catholicism, 17, 40, 48, 212n57; Hitler raised in, 41. *See also* Christianity
Cattle King/Nebraska Beef Packer, 94–95
Chamberlain, Houston Stewart, 40, 42
Charles Martel Society, 206n51
Chase, Erica, 137
Chertoff, Michael, 177–78, 247n49
Chocolate Cake Club, 108
Christenson, Else, 52, 65, 66, 214n73
Christian Identity, 49–50, 212n57, 213nn61, 63–65, 215nn80,90. *See also* Ku Klux Klan

Christianity: Bible, 12, 16, 19–21, 39, 49, 105, 203n15; Catholic Church, 17, 40, 41, 48, 212n57; *Christianity and the Survival of the West*, 68–69; fascism *v.*, 37–38; Fundamentalist, 48, 212n57, 215n90; German Christian Movement, 38–39; Hitler and, 41–46, 210n21; as Jewish conspiracy, 19–21, 41–42; "Jewish-inspired," viii, 38, 41, 64; deconstruction of, by Ben Klassen, 13–20; *The Odinist Religion: Overcoming Judeo-Christianity*, 51–52; passivity engendered by, 2; Paul (apostle), 16, 19–20, 39, 203n15; Pierce on, 216n8; prominence in far right, vii–viii, 212n57, 215n90; "religion of nature" *v.*, 33–35. *See also* Jesus Christ
Christianity and the Survival of the West (Oliver), 68–69
Christian Patriot movement, 50
Christian-Patriots Defense League, 66
Church of Christ, 213n61
Church of Satan, 229n16
Church of the Creator (COTC), 202n1, 251n24; Burdi's cause célébre for, 115; divine mission of, 202n57; five fundamentals of, 74–75; flag and logo of, 73; headquarters, 72–73, 75; infrastructure, 73; international presence of, 83–84; *The Little White Book*, 88, 219n12, 222n58; Pontifex Maximus of, 73, 91–96, 186, 191; as racial religion, 74–75; South African, 84; trademark issue for, 173–75. *See also* Klassen, Bernhardt "Ben"; World Church of the Creator
Cicero, Marcus Tullius, 108
Civilization, race *v.*, 17, 22, 23–24, 29, 42, 206nn51–52
Clark, Dru, 158–59
Clinton, Bill, 158
CNN, 115, 123, 225n50
Cohen, Nosson, 159
COINTELPRO program, 9, 161
Collin, Frank, 62, 216n5
Columbians (neo-Nazi group), 9, 201n40
The Commission (Barrett), 91
Commission on Discrimination and Hate Crimes, Illinois, 129, 158

Communism, 20–21, 102; Bolshevism, 1–2, 41, 205n33
The Communist Manifesto (Marx), 20
Communist Workers Party, 102
Conspiracy, Jewish, 22, 170, 197, 205n30, 208n74; Christianity as, 19–21, 41–42; *Nature's Eternal Religion* on, 13–14, 16–17; Zionist Occupation Government, 80, 192, 193
Constitution. *See* United States
Cosmotheism, 54–55, 62, 83, 192, 215n80
COTC. *See* Church of the Creator
Coughlin, Charles, 212n57
Coulson, Danny O., 220n34
Covington, Harold, 62, 102–4, 216n5
Crane, Nicky, 229n23
Creativity movement: Creed, 24–25, 30–31, 124; far right influenced by, 192–97; FBI disruption of, 161; *Kreativistens Kyrka*, 83; names of, viii; Odinist cooperation with, 65; as religion, 32; sixteen commandments of, 26–28; theological justification behind, 59–60. *See also* Church of the Creator; World Church of the Creator; *specific books*
The Creator Membership Manual (Matt Hale), 124
Creator's Manual (Lloyd and Sister Lisa), 192
Creed, of Creativity movement, 24–25, 30–31, 124
Cult of the Holy War (RAHOWA), 110–11
The Culture of Critique (K. MacDonald), 206n52
Cupid's Corner, 73

DAP. *See* German Worker's Party
Darwin, Charles, 25, 34
Das Kapital (Marx), 20
Davis, Austin C., Jr., 9, 11
Davis, Brian, 159
Dawkins, Richard, 15
Deardof, Slim, 120, 172, 190, 249n7
Dees, Morris, 79, 93, 107, 158
Degrelle, Leon, 43, 211n36
"Delenda est Judaica," 26
Del Valle, P. A., 10

Denying the Holocaust: The Growing Assault on Truth and Memory (Lipstadt), 228n14
De Palma, Brian, 97
Depression era, 212n57
De Pugh, Robert, 66, 67
Dershowitz, Alan M., 145–46, 196
Der-Yeghiayan, Samuel, 179
Devi, Savitri, 201n42, 215n82
DeVries, Arnold, 73–74, 83
Dialogues of Hell (Jolly), 205n30
Dickson, Sam, 99
Dinnerstein, Leonard, 48
Dippold, Ken, 175
The Dispossessed Majority (Robertson), 69
Divide and conquer strategy, 19–21
Donaldson, Ian Stuart, 229n23
Dostoyevsky, Fyodor, 108
Dred Scott decision, 131
Droege, Wolfgang, 115
Dufrense, Joel Nathan, 190–91
Duke, David, 123–24, 134
Dunn, Thomas, 140
Durkheim, Emile, 24
Durkin, Thomas Anthony, 180–81; Matt Hale sues, 182–83

Eckart, Dietrich, 229n16
Edison, Jean Farrel, 217n35
Egalitarianism: Christianity's, 12; communism's, 21
Eichmann, Horst, 201n42
Elletson, Roger, 95
The Emergence of a Euro-American Radical Right (Kaplan and Weinberg), 193
Emotion, music's impact on, 112–13
Enemy Toll Effectiveness Factor (ETEF), 82
Erickson, Clark, 140
An Essay on the Inequality of Human Races (Gobineau), 22–23
Essene cult, 16
ETEF. *See* Enemy Toll Effectiveness Factor
"Eternal Laws of Nature," 32, 58–59
Eugenics, viii, 29, 36, 73, 209n7
Evola, Julius, 46–47
Evola, Tony, 175–88
Evolutionary strategy, K. MacDonald on, 19
Extreme right. *See* Far right

"Facts that the Government and Media Don't Want You to Know" (Matt Hale), 152, 239n35
Faith of the Future (Koehl), 58
Falwell, Jerry, 82
Fanzines, 250n19
Far left, FBI disruption of, 161
Farrakhan, Louis T., 89, 100
Far right: Christian Identity, 49–50, 212n57, 213nn61,63–65, 215nn80,90; Christianity prominent in, vii–viii, 212n57, 215n90; cosmotheism in, 54–55, 62, 83–84, 192, 215n80; critical of media attention, 234n4; *The Emergence of a Euro-American Radical Right*, 193; fascism *v*., 250n21; FBI disruption of, 161; generational shift in, 214n68; Matt Hale on, 170–73; Internet use by, 114, 129, 132, 134, 191, 196, 252n36; Ben Klassen reaching out to, 61–71; Ku Klux Klan, 8–9, 66, 77, 102, 159, 181, 212n57, 243n38; literature of, 125–28, 205nn29–30, 206nn35,51,52, 213n62, 218n42; in mid-1980s, 79–83; Odinism and, 50–54; post–WW II, 30, 48; POWS, 220n36; *The Protocols of the Elders of Zion*, 20–21, 30, 205n30; reaction to Benjamin Smith, 158–59; "religion of nature" roots of, 33–35; response to Matt Hale conviction, 186–88; since 9/11, 161–69; theological justification for, 59–60; "watchdog" function of, 251n28; WCOTC influence on, 192–97; Welch's contribution, 7; White Aryan Resistance, 77, 92–93, 100, 134, 216n5, 221n40; White Patriot Party, 81, 103, 221n40; White Pittsburgh Front, 191–92
Fascism: Christianity *v*., 37–38; far right *v*., 250n21. *See also* National Socialism; Nazism
Fasting, 74
Federal Bureau of Investigation (FBI), vii, 10, 100–101, 149, 152, 201n43, 221n41, 225n50, 234n4, 242n13; COINTELPRO program, 9, 161; Hostage Rescue Team, 220n34; Joint Terrorism Task Force, 177, 242n10
Felton, Leo, 137, 235n24

Ferguson, Joseph, 160
Festum Album (Matt Hale), 125
Fettu, Jules, 148
FICOTC. *See* First International Church of the Creator
Fields, Edward R., 10
Fiessinger, Donald, 155
First African Methodist Episcopal Church, Los Angeles, 100
First Amendment rights, 142–46, 218n42
First International Church of the Creator (FICOTC), 120. *See also* World Church of the Creator
Fischer, Christopher David, 100
Fisher, Elkar, 115
Fisher, Eric, 114–15
Fitzgerald, Patrick, 180, 187
Focus Fourteen (newsletter), 54
Ford, Henry, 205n30
Foundations of the Nineteenth Century (Chamberlain), 42
Fourteenth Amendment equal protection clause, 143
"14 Words" credo, 53–54
Fourth Reich Skinheads, 100
Fox, Jon, 181
Free-enterprise economy, 76
Friedan, Betty, 135
Fromm, Paul, 115
The Frontier. *See* World Church of the Creator's Women Frontier
Frugivorian diet, 24
Fuhrman, Mark, 143
Fundamentalist Christians, 48, 212n57, 215n90

Gaffney, Timothy J., 85
Gallo, Gary, 77, 220n26
Garten, Todd, 154–55
Garvey, Marcus, 208n74
Gayman, Dan, 50, 64
George, John, 213n65
Geraldo (TV show), 92, 130
German, Mike, 77–78, 101, 225n50
German Christian Movement, 38–39
German Worker's Party (DAP), 36
Germany, 38–39; German Christian Move-

ment, 38–39; German Worker's Party, 36; Ben Klassen's sympathies with, 4; national identity for, 33–35; National Socialism in, 28–29, 37–39, 121, 145, 222n58; Nazi, 28–29, 43, 126, 203n1, 211n36, 229n16; Romanticism period, 33–35; Weimar Republic, 144–45; Weimar Republic, Hitler and, 75–76. *See also* Hitler, Adolf

Gilbert, Keith, 217n28

Gilmore, Joshua Mark, 148

Gliebe, Eric, 116

Globalization, 59

Gobineau, Joseph Arthur Comte de, 22–23

God: American Association for the Advancement of Atheism, 208n81; cosmotheist, 54–55, 62, 83, 192, 215n80; *The God Delusion*, 15; Hitler as demigod, 56–59; Hitler's religiosity, 41–46, 210n21; "is on our side," 42, 202n57, 213nn63–64; Jews' covenant with, 20; Ben Klassen on, 2–3, 14–16; *Twilight of the Gods*, 13. *See also* Religion

The God Delusion (Dawkins), 15

Goebbels, Joseph, 222n58

Goenka, S. N., 118

Goldwater, Barry, 7

Goodrick-Clarke, Nicholas, 59–60, 193–94

Goth, 111

Grassley, Chuck, 225n50

Greensboro Massacre, 102

Greenwald, Glenn, 159, 182

Griffin, Roger, 250n21

Grobbelaar, Johannes Jurgens, 84

Guardian of the Faith Committee, 98, 125

Haeckel, Ernest, 34, 55

"Hail The New Dawn," 110

Hale, David M., 233n52

Hale, Evelyn Anderson, 121

Hale, Matt, 5, 120–25, 128–33, 152, 225n35, 233n58, 239n35, 250n19; criminal trial of, 179–88; Durkin sued by, 182–83; Fox's testimony on, 181; in law license controversy, 139–46, 178–79; contact with Benjamin Smith, 156–59; theory about 9/11, 170–73; WCOTC after arrest of, 189–92

Hale, Michael, vii

Hale, Russell, Jr., 121, 183

Hall, Dane, 172, 190

Hamas, 196

Hansard, Donald, 148

Hanson, Pauline, 137

Hard rock, 111

Hargis, Billy James, 10

Harrell, John R., 66

Harris, Andrew, 148

Hassett, Dan, 172–73

Hasta Primus, 85

Hatewatch Web sites, 145

Hatred, use of, 25, 116, 145, 158, 196; Bloomington United Campaign against Hate Speech and Hate Crimes, 129, 158; Canadian speech laws on, 116; "Delenda est Judaica," 26; Enemy Toll Effectiveness Factor, 82; Hatewatch Web sites, 145; law license *v.* belief in, 142–46; vitriol against Covington, 103–4; "Web of Hate," 130; white power music inciting, vii, 110–15, 229n23, 250n19

Hauptman, Laurence, 237n30

Hawthorne, George Eric, 80

Hayduke, G. W., 191

Heavy metal, 111

Heliotherapy, 74

Heritage Front, 115

Herron, Terra, 130

Hess, Carl, 120

Hess, Phillip, 5

Hess, Rudolf, 45, 212n46

Hezbollah, 221n42

Hierarchy, racial, 22–23, 35–36

Hiltibidal, David, 154–55

Himmler, Heinrich, 38, 44, 211n41

Hirshhaut, Richard, 186

Hispanic Americans, 197

Historicity, Jesus Christ's, 15–16, 25

Hitler, Adolf, 15, 22, 24, 37, 53, 55, 111, 203n1, 209n7, 222n58; appointed chancellor, 145; as demigod, 56–59; Ben Klassen influenced by, 28–30; *Mein Kamph*, 29, 42, 43–44, 121, 135, 150, 205n30; religiosity of, 41–46, 210n21; Waffen-SS, 43, 211nn36,41,42; white power music praising, 229n23

278 / Index

Holmes, Oliver Wendell, 144
Holocaust, denial of, 48, 68, 109, 228n14
Homosexuals, 101, 104, 148–49, 214n76
Hooker, DeWest, 89–90
Hoskins, Richard Kelly, 50
Humphrey, Donna, 183
Hutcheson, Evelyn, 182
Hypatia Publishing, 138

Illinois, 149–57, 159; Commission on Discrimination and Hate Crimes, 129, 158; State Bar Committee, 139–46
Immigration restriction, 30
Indiana, 149–59
Indian wars, 30
Individualism, 76
Institute for Historical Review, 217n35
The Insurgent (newspaper), 220n26
The International Jew (Cameron), 205n30
"International Jew: The World's Foremost Problem" (Cameron), 205n30
Internet, 114, 129, 132, 134, 145, 175–76, 191, 196, 252n36; Overthrow.com, 187; SolarGeneral.com, 192
Iran, 18
Irving, David, 109, 228n14
Irwin, Mitchell, 191
Isabella (queen of Spain), 137
Islam, 18, 74, 89, 108, 150, 205n31
Israel, 129, 131, 196, 212n57, 244n4, 247n49; British Israelism, 49, 212n57; Mossad, 104, 170, 187. *See also* Jew(s)
Italy, 47, 137, 203n1

Jackson, Dave, 102
Jackson, Neta, 102
Jackson, Paul, 95–96
Jacobs, Adam Daniel, 190
Jane Whitney Show (TV show), 130
Japanese, 28
JBS. *See* John Birch Society
Jefferson, Thomas, 208n74
Jerry Springer (TV show), 130
Jesus Christ, 95, 203n15, 210n21; *The Anti-Christ*, 13, 108; Church of Christ, 213n61; foisted upon Gentiles, 19–20; never existed, 15–16, 25, 123, 203n11; not a Jew,

11, 35, 39, 40; "suicidal advice" from, 12. *See also* Christianity
Jew(s): civilization destroyed by, 17, 22, 23–24, 29, 42, 206nn51–52; Jesus Christ is not a Jew, 11, 35, 39, 40; key books of, 20–21, 42, 205n29; media attention controlled by, 129; philo-Semitism, 48–49; racial separation for, 31, 102–3, 130–31, 208n75; as "real enemy," 6, 8, 27, 29, 34–35, 77; as targets, 159, 225n50, 251n24. *See also* Anti-Semitism; Conspiracy, Jewish; Israel; *specific persons*
Jewish Defense League, 178
Jewish Defense Organization, 178
"Jewish-inspired" Christianity, viii, 38, 41, 64
Jewish Kehilla, 21, 95, 224n16
Jewish organizations, 101, 201n46, 205n30; American Jewish Committee, 252n36; American Jewish Congress, 145; arson at, 149; Jewish Defense League, 178; Jewish Defense Organization, 178; Kehilla, 21, 95, 224n16; militant, 178, 182; National Jewish Community Relations Advisory Council, 145
Jihad, 108
JOG (Jewish Occupation Government), 85, 92, 120, 251n24
John Birch Society (JBS), 6–8, 77, 200nn25,26,28
Johnson, Charles W., 191
Johnson, Don, 87
Joint Terrorism Task Force: FBI, 177, 242n10; Los Angeles, 101
Jolly, Maurice, 205n30
Jordan, Colin, 201n42
Judaism: *The Odinist Religion: Overcoming Judeo-Christianity*, 51–52; *A People that Shall Dwell Alone: An Evolutionary Theory of Judaism*, 17, 19, 206nn51–52; as racial religion, 17, 18–19, 25, 26, 39–40, 42, 51–52, 59, 206nn51–52
Jung, Carl Gustav, 53

Kachikis, Brian, 120
Kaczynski, Theodore, 186
Kahl, Gordon, 78
Kaldenberg, Wyatt, 77, 220n26

Kaplan, Jeffrey, 147, 193, 214n71
Kathy (WCOTC member), 184–85
Kehilla, 21, 95, 224n16
Kennedy, Joseph P., 89
Khazars, 212n57, 213n62
Khomeini, Ayatollah, 18
King, Angela, 148
King, Rodney, 100
Kissinger, Henry, 79
Kjaersgaard, Pir, 137
Klassen, Bernhardt "Ben," viii, 18, 200n28; on American history, 208n74; in California, 4–6; deconstruction of Christianity, 13–20; entering politics, 6–12; family background, 1–3; Hitler's influence, 28–30; on Jewish conspiracy, 13–14, 16–17; *Klassen*, 127–28; *The Little White Book*, 88, 219n12, 222n58; *Nature's Eternal Religion*, viii, 7, 13–14, 16–17, 109, 124–25, 135, 147; neo-Nazi groups and, 9–10; Pierce on, 94, 106; reaching out to far right, 61–71; suicide of, 105, 120; sympathies with Germany, 4
Klassen (Molyneaux), 127–28
Klassen, Henrie Etta, 4, 97, 105
Klassen, Kim Anita, 5, 99, 105, 107, 225n35
Klassen Enterprises, Inc., 5–6
Knesal, Jeremiah Gordon, 101
Know Nothing movement, 212n57
Koch, Gerda, 66
Koehl, Matt, 9–10, 58–59, 62, 103, 216n5
Koestler, Arthur, 213n62
Kowaalski, Mark Frank, 102
Kozel, Brian, 84–85
Kreativistens Kyrka (Rydén), 83
Kreigh, R. Ben, 201n44
Kroenke, Thomas, 189
Kubizek, August, 35
Ku Klux Klan, 8–9, 66, 77, 102, 159, 181, 212n57, 243n38; White Patriot Party, 81, 103, 221n40

Lane, David, 53–54, 65–66, 250n18
Lane, Katja, 250n18
Langballe, Patrick, 153
La Rue, Jason, 138
La Rue, Melody, 138
Latin, 26, 28

Latvis, Jon, 110
LaVey, Anton, 229n16
Lavon Affair (1954), 170
Law license, Illinois, 139–46
Law Students Research Council v. Wadmond, 142
"Leaderless resistance," 54, 92
Lear, Norman, 79
Lebanon, 81, 221n42
Lee, Josh, 100
Lefkow, Joan Humphrey, 173–74, 190; plot to kill, 175–88
Lefkow, Michael, 183
Lefstein, Stuart R., 139
Lenin, Vladimir, 77
Leone, Raymond, 148
Lesbians, 101, 104, 214n76
Liberty Lobby, 68, 116, 217n35
Liebenfels, Jorg Lanz, 36, 209n7
Lincoln, Abraham, 150, 208n74
Lipset, Martin, 241n1
Lipstadt, Deborah, 228n14
List, Guido von, 36
The Little White Book (B. Klassen), 88, 219n12, 222n58
Lloyd, Hardy, 191–92
Loeb, Barbara, 99–100
Loeb, George, 99–100, 107, 147
Lombardi, Guy, 129, 172
London, Jack, 77
Lord of the Rings (Tolkien), 127
Los Angeles Joint Terrorism Task Force, 101
Loyalty, racial, viii, 51, 74–75, 137. *See also Racial Loyalty*
Ludendorff, Erich, 36
Ludtke, Bruno, 201n42
Lustfeldt, Gordon L., 140
Luther, Martin, 40

M16. *See* British Intelligence
Macdonald, Andrew, 63, 78, 125, 150, 216n11. *See also* Pierce, William L.
MacDonald, Kevin, 17, 19, 26, 194–95, 206nn51–52
Mack, John, 100
Maddox, Lester, 91

Madole, James H., 62, 201n40, 216n5, 229n16
Maino, Runston G., 217n35
Makhno, Nestor Ivanovich, 1–2, 199n3
Mansfield, Harold, Jr., 99–100, 107, 186
Marshall, Charles, 140
Martel, Charles, 206n51
Martin, Frank, 120
Martinez, Tom, 79
Marvel Comics, 214n71
Marx, Karl, 20, 21, 39
Mason, James, 62
Mathis, Jody Lee, 160
Matson, Gary, 148–49
Matthews, Jurgen, 84
Matthews, Robert Jay "Bob," 78–81, 115, 200n28, 221n41
Maynard, Drew, 115
Mazella, Daniel, 93
McCarthy, Joseph, 6
McCarty, Rick, 98, 106–7, 120
McClintock, Gregory K., 139
McCoy, Duke, 85
McLaughlin, John, 155, 239n55
McNallen, Stephen, 53, 65
McPheeters, Brian, 140
McVan, Ron, 54, 250n18
McVeigh, Timothy, 150
Mearsheimer, John J., 196
Media attention, 92–93, 95, 100, 115, 123, 225n50; Burdi's, 117; "Facts that the Government and Media Don't Want You to Know," 152, 239n35; far right criticism of, 234n4; Matt Hale's use of, 171–72, 178; Illinois Bar decision attracting, 146; WCOTC receiving, 129
Megret, Catherine, 137
Mein Kampf (Hitler), 29, 42, 43–44, 121, 135, 150, 205n30
Meister Eckhart, 39, 41
Men among the Ruins (J. Evola), 47
Mennonite community, 1–4
Messick, Carl, 86–87
Metagenetics theory, 53
Metzger, Tom, 62, 77, 92–93, 134, 200n28, 216n5, 220n26
Mexican-American War, 30
Mexico, 2

Miller, Glen, 80–81, 103. *See also* White Patriot Party
Mills, A. Rud, 51–52
Minutemen, 217n28
Miscegenation, 11, 22, 29, 30
Mohammed (prophet), 18
Molyneaux, Kenneth, 125–28
Mongrelization, 11, 22. *See also* Miscegenation
Monroe, James, 208n74
Montel Williams (TV show), 130
Moody, James T., 180–84
Mormonism, 5, 191, 225n35
Mossad, 104, 170, 187
Mowder, Winfield Scott, 148–49
MSNBC, 225n50
MTV, 115
"Mud race," 28, 49, 89, 114, 137, 207n59
Murphy, Timothy, 182
Murray, Cecil, 100
Music: black metal, 229n16; hard rock, 111; white power, vii, 110–15, 229n23, 250n19
Muslim Brotherhood, 196
Mussolini, Alessandra, 137
Mussolini, Benito, 47, 203n1
Mysticism, 36, 209n7; Rudolf Hess and, 45, 212n46
The Myth of the Twentieth Century (A. Rosenberg), 39–41

9/11, 161–69, 170–73, 237n49, 242n10
NAAWP. *See* National Association for the Advancement of White People
Nadal, Christian, 100–101
Nadal, Doris, 100
Nasser, Gamal Abdel, 201n43
National Alliance, 116, 172, 192, 197; FBI surveillance of, 221n41. *See also* Pierce, William L.
National Association for the Advancement of White People (NAAWP), 134
National Democratic Front, 220n26
Nationalism, beyond, 28, 59–60. *See also* National Socialism
The Nationalist (Gallo), 220n26
Nationalist White Party (NWP), 11, 202n57
National Jewish Community Relations Advisory Council, 145

National Renaissance Party (NRP), 9, 201n40, 216n5
National Socialism, 77; American, 9–10, 57–58, 61–62, 102, 124, 187, 216n5; German, 28–29, 37–39, 121, 145, 222n58. *See also* Nazism; Neo-Nazi groups; *specific groups*
National Socialist German Workers Party, 37, 145
National Socialist Liberation Front, 10, 201n48
National Socialist Movement, 187
National Socialist Party of America (NSPA), 102, 216n5
National Socialist White Americans Party, 124
National Socialist White People's Party, 9–10
National Socialist World (journal), 54
National States' Rights Party, 10
Nation of Islam, 89
Native Americans, 237n30
Nativist Paramilitarism in the United States: The Minutemen (Albares), 217n28
Natural laws, 32, 58–59
Natural selection, 34
Nature's Eternal Religion (B. Klassen), viii, 7, 109, 124–25, 135, 147; on Jewish conspiracy, 13–14, 16–17
Nazism: American Nazi Party, 52–54, 57, 214nn68–70, 216n5; German, 28–29, 43, 126, 203n1, 211n36, 229n16; Italian, 203n1; race theory behind, 33–35, 205n30, 209n7; *The Rise and Fall of the Third Reich*, 121; World Union of National Socialists, 9. *See also* Hitler, Adolf; National Socialism
Neo-Nazi groups, 50, 52–53, 59–60, 102, 124, 186, 201nn42, 46, 48; Columbians, 9, 201n40; Ben Klassen reaching out to, 9–10; National Socialist Movement, 187
Neopaganism, 36–37, 43, 45, 191, 209n7, 214nn68–71
"Never Again through the Serpent's Eyes," 24–25
New Age Spiritualism, 74
New Order, 216n5
New York City Police Department, 242n10

New York Times, 115
NGOs. *See* Nongovernmental organizations
Nietzsche, Friedrich, 13, 35, 46, 108
Niggaz with Attitude (NWA), 100
None Dare Call It Treason (Stormer), 7
Nongovernmental organizations (NGOs), 161–62
Norse religion, 35, 36, 51–54, 64–65
Novacosm, 118
NRP. *See* National Renaissance Party
NSDAP. *See* Nationalist Socialist German Workers Party
NSPA. *See* National Socialist Party of America
Nuremberg, Germany: Nazi rallies, 43; racial laws, 36
NWA. *See* Niggaz with Attitude
NWP. *See* Nationalist White Party

Odinism, 36, 59–60, 66, 192, 214nn68–71; Creativity movement and, 65; far right and, 50–54. *See also* Paganism, neo-; Wotan
Odinist Fellowship, 65, 66
The Odinist Religion: Overcoming Judeo-Christianity (Mills), 51–52
Oklahoma City bombing, 186
Oliver, Revilo P., 68, 200n28
"Operation Skinhead," 133
Oprah (TV show), 92
The Order, 78–81, 220n31, 220n34, 221n40
Order of National Racism, 191
Origin of Species (Darwin), 34
Ostara (journal), 209n7
Ostendorf, David, 158
O'Sullivan, Patrick John, 159, 191
Overthrow.com, 187

Padgett, Tom, 66
Paganism, neo-, 36–37, 43, 45, 191, 209n7, 214nn68–71. *See also* Odinism
Pahlavi, Mohammed Reza, 18
Palingenetic myth, 250n21
Pan-Germanism, 36
Pan-German Party, 35
Pantheism, 34–35
Paramilitary training, 114–15
Parasitism, 21–22, 25, 34–35

Parker, Bonnie, 201n47
Parsifal (Wagner), 35
Passivity, Christianity's, 2
Patler, John, 10
Paul (apostle), 16, 19–20, 39, 203n15
Peek, Merle Stanley, 5
A People that Shall Dwell Alone: An Evolutionary Theory of Judaism (K. MacDonald), 17, 19, 206nn51–52
Perrington, L. Lee, 140
Peters, Pete, 50
Pfaff, William, 62
Pfeiffer, Franz, 201n42
Philo-Semitism, 48–49
Pierce, William L., 54–55, 62, 93, 116, 172, 192, 197, 207n55, 215n80, 216n5; on Christianity, 216n8; on Ben Klassen, 94, 106; *The Turner Diaries*, 63, 78–79, 125, 150, 216n11
Pius XI (pope), 40
Plato, 46, 108
Poe, Edgar Allan, 108
Pois, Robert, 37–38
Politically Incorrect (TV show), 130
Polk, James, 30
Pollard, Jonathan, 170
Pontifex Maximus, 73, 91–96, 186, 191
Population growth, 27
Posse Comitatus, 78
Potok, Mark, 189, 233n58
Presbyterian Church, 5
Primitive Man and His Foods (DeVries), 73
Prisoners of war, 220n36
Prisoner Support Group, 137
The Protocols of the Elders of Zion, 20–21, 30, 205n30
Putnam, Robert, 195

Raab, Earl, 241n1
Race: civilization v., 17, 22, 23–24, 29, 42, 206nn51–52; *An Essay on the Inequality of Human Races*, 22–23; loyalty, viii, 51, 74–75, 137; "mud race," 28, 49, 89, 114, 137, 207n59; palingenetic myth about, 250n21; pre-Adamic, 49; theory behind Nazism, 33–35, 205n30, 209n7

Race war, 31–32, 134, 155, 157; South African, 82–84
Racial Loyalty, 54, 65, 88, 94, 99, 100, 124, 192; launching of, 72–73; vitriol against Covington, 103–4
Racial religion: COTC as, 74–75; Judaism as, 17, 18–19, 25, 26, 39–40, 42, 51–52, 59, 206nn51–52
Racial socialism, 76
Radical right. *See* Far right
RAHOWA, vii, 108, 112–15, 120, 126, 157, 193, 202n1; *Cult of the Holy War*, 110–11; *The White Crusaders of RaHoWa!*, 190–91
RaHoWa News (newsletter), 120
Rathborne, Prescott, 89
Ravage, Marcus Eli, 19–20
Raw food, 74
"A Real Case against the Jews" (Ravage), 19–20
Reckzin, Alicia, 115
Religion: American civil, 48; Creativity as, 32; Durkheim on, 24; Hitler's, 41–46, 210n21; Ben Klassen on, 3, 18, 32; of nature, 33–35; *Nature's Eternal Religion*, viii, 7, 13–14, 16–17, 109, 124–25, 135, 147; Norse, 35, 36, 51–54, 64–65; *The Odinist Religion: Overcoming Judeo-Christianity*, 51–52; pantheism, 34–35; "slave religion," 13–14, 35. *See also specific religions*
Reno, Janet, 158
Resistance (magazine), 114
Resistance Records, 111, 115–16, 118–19, 230n49
Resistlist (e-mail newsletter), 114
The Revolt against the Modern World (J. Evola), 46
Revolutionary Insurrectionary Army of Ukraine (RIAU), 1–2
RIAU. *See* Revolutionary Insurrectionary Army of Ukraine
Ricki Lake (TV show), 130
Ride the Tiger (J. Evola), 47
Rineman, Geremy C. Von, 100
Ring of the Nibelungs (Wagner), 35
Ring of Troth, 53, 214n76

The Rise and Fall of the Third Reich (Shire), 121
Robb, Thomm, 50, 98
Robertson, Wilmont, 69, 218n42
Rockefeller, David, 79
Rockwell, George Lincoln, 9–10, 57, 109, 200n28, 201nn42–43, 216n5
Rodovitch, Andrew, 182
Roe v. Wade, 144
Roman Empire, 28, 73; Jews' destruction of, 17, 22. *See also* Civilization, race *v.*
Romanov dynasty, 21
Romanticism, German, 33–35
Rosenberg, Alfred, 39–41, 205n30
Rosenberg, Elliot, 170
Rosenberg, Ethel, 170
Ross, Bart Allan, 183
Rothschild, Elie de, 79
Ruby Ridge, 150
Rudolph, Eric, 186
Runes, 36
Rust, David, 10, 201nn45, 48
Rydén, Tommy, 82–84, 98, 134

Salubrious living, 7, 24, 74, 84, 97, 126, 130, 219n12
Salubrious Living (DeVries), 74
San Domingo, 22
Saskatchewan, Canada, 2–3
Satan, 49, 191, 229n16
Scarborough, Jill, 100
Schiff, Jacob, 21, 205n33
Schoenerer, Georg Ritter von, 35
Second American Revolution, 81
Secret Doctrine (Blavatsky), 35–36
Separation: of church and state, 46; racial, 31, 82–84, 102–3, 130–31, 208n75; racist views *v.* law license, 140–46
Seraw, Mulageta, 93
Shakespeare, William, 108
Sharpton, Al, 100
Shaw, George Bernard, 108
Shelton, Robert K., 66
Shire, William, 121
Sigel, Ian, 178
Silvernail, Bruce, 159
Silver Spring Land Company, 5

Simpson, Orenthal James "O. J.," 143
Simpson, William Gayley, 69–70
Sister Lisa (WPF Women's Division coordinator), 192
Skinhead(s), 93, 97, 104, 148, 152; demographics, 230n30; movement, 100–101; "Operation Skinhead," 133; white power music of, vii, 110–15, 229n23, 250n19
Skinhead Army of Milwaukee, 97
Skinheads against Racial Prejudice, 152
Skrewdriver, 110, 113, 229n23
Slavery, 30–31, 209n7; "slave religion," 13–14, 35
Smith, Benjamin, ix, 129, 132, 140, 147–54, 160, 172, 178, 237n36; death of, 155; contact with Matt Hale, 156–59
Smith, Charles Lee, 208n81
Smith, Gerald K., 212n57
SolarGeneral.com, 192
Somali immigrants, 171
South Africa, 82–84
Southern Poverty Law Center, 48, 79, 93, 107, 145, 161, 186; on WCOTC membership, 132
Soviet Union, 1–2, 76
Spanish Inquisition, 17
"Spear of destiny," 210n21
Speer, Albert, 44
Spencer, Herbert, 34
Spengler, Oswald, 46
The Spotlight (newspaper), 68
Stanko, Rudy "Butch," 94–95, 224nn16–17
Steele, Edgar J., 186–87
Steigmann-Gall, Richard, 37
Steinem, Gloria, 135
Sterilization, of "defective" population, 29, 209n7
Stern Gang, 170
Stoddard, Lothrop, 22, 206n35
Stoner, J. B., 10, 202n50
Stormer, John, 7
The Struggle (Matt Hale), 124, 233n58
Stuart, Ian, 111
Suicide: of Ferguson, 160; Jesus' advice as racial, 12; of Ben Klassen, 105, 120; of Ross, 183

Supernatural elements, 24
"Survival of the fittest," 34
Swain, Carolyn, 132, 195–96
Sweden, 82–83
Swift, Wesley, 50
Symbionese Liberation Army, 201n48
Symbolism, 37

Talmud, 20–21, 42, 205n29
Technology, 23, 31, 206n41. *See also* Internet
Television stations, 101–2. *See also* Media attention
Terrorism, 78–81, 82–83, 99–100, 102, 180–84, 187–88, 192, 196, 221n42, 225n50; bombings, 81–82, 101, 138, 185–86, 202n50, 217n28; Christian Identity, 49–50, 212n57, 213nn61,63–65, 215nn80,90; "God is on our side," 42, 202n57, 213nn63–64; Hamas, 196; Hezbollah, 221n42; Joint Terrorism Task Forces, 101, 177, 242n10; "leaderless resistance," 54, 92; Muslim Brotherhood, 196; September 11, 161–69, 170–73, 237n49, 242n10; Symbionese Liberation Army, 201n48; Weathermen, 201n48
TE-TA-MA Truth Foundation, 173–75, 178–79, 186; Fox's testimony on, 181
Theosophical Society, 35–36
The Thirteenth Tribe (Koestler), 213n62
Thirty Years' War, 15
Thomas, Cal, 82
Thomas, Steve Cabott, 97, 99
Thompson, Tyler, 85
Thor, 51
Thucydides, 108
Thule, White Order of, 137
Thule Gesellschaft (study group), 36
"To Be Young, White, and Racist" (B. Smith), 152
Today (TV show), 130
Tolkien, J.R.R., 127
Tomassi, Joseph, 201n48
Trademark, 173–75
Troth, Ring of, 53, 214n76
Trotsky, Leon, 199n3
The Truth about 9-11: How Jewish Manipulation Killed Thousands (Matt Hale), 170

Truth Seeker (magazine), 208n81
Tucker, Bill, 86
Turner, Lisa, 134–35; message to white women, 136–37
The Turner Diaries (Pierce), 63, 78–79, 125, 150, 216n11
Twilight of the Gods (Nietzsche), 13
Two seeds doctrine, 49
Tyndall, John, 201n42

Ukraine, 1–2
Umphenour, Claud, 172
UNICOR, 224n17
United Klans of America, 66
United States: Civil War, 48, 208n74; constitution of, 48, 142–46, 161, 218n42; Court of Appeals, 187; Department of Justice, 158, 177, 225n50; foreign policy, 196; Mexican-American War, 30; political system of, 241n1; western frontier, 28, 30; 9/11 terrorist attack, 161–69, 170–73, 237n49, 242n10. *See also* Federal Bureau of Investigation; *specific ethnic groups*
Universal Church of the Master, 74
Urban League, 100
USS Liberty, 244n4
Utilitarianism, 18

Viereck, Peter, 38
Viktor, Jonathan, 130
Vincent, Allen, 62, 66
Völkisch movement, 35–37, 43–44
Volksgemeinschaft, 35

Waco, 150
Waffen-SS, 43, 211nn36,41,42
Wagner, Richard, 35, 40
Walker, Samuel, 145
Wallace, George, 8–9, 91
Walt, Stephen, 196
WAR. *See* White Aryan Resistance
Warrior elite, 47, 51, 59
Washington, George, 48
Washington State Militia, 101
WCOTC. *See* World Church of the Creator
Weathermen, 201n48
"Web of Hate" (Brokaw), 130

Weimar Republic, 76, 144–45
Weinberg, Leonard, 193
Weisman, Charles A., 50
Weiss, Christine, 152–53
Welch, Robert H. W., 6–8, 200n25
Weltanschauung (world view), 38, 45, 209n7
Wendel, W. Bradley, 144
Wessell, Horst, 84, 222n58
Which Way Western Man? (W. G. Simpson), 69–70
White, Bill, 187
White Aryan Resistance (WAR), 77, 92–93, 100, 134, 216n5, 221n40
White Berets, 54, 128–29, 148, 172, 175
The White Crusaders of RaHoWa!, 190–91
White Empire (Molyneaux), 125–27
The White Man's Bible (B. Klassen), 19–21, 105, 109, 125, 135
White Order of Thule, 137
White Patriot Party, 81, 103, 221n40
White Pittsburgh Front (WPF), 191–92
White Power (Rockwell), 109
White power music, vii, 110–15, 229n23, 250n19
White Rangers, 128–29
White Revolution (TV program), 130
Wiligut, Karl Maria, 211n41
Will, to hold power, 29, 45; Nietzsche on, 13, 35, 46, 108
Williams, Anthony L., 190
Williams, Benjamin Matthew, 146
Williams, James Tyler, 146
Williams, Keith, 86
Williams, Will White, 88, 103
Wilson, Mark, 97, 111, 117
Witherspoon, Dawn, 148
Witherspoon, Dennis, 104
Wolf, Ephraim, 159
Wolf, Victor, 88, 219n12
Women: Turner's message to, 136–37; WCOTC's Sisterhood, 137–38; WCOTC's Women Frontier, 134–38; WPF Women's Division, 192
Won-Joon Yoon, 158
Wood, Diane, 169
Wooten, Wayne Paul, 101
World Church of the Creator (WCOTC), 121–25, 129–31, 152, 160, 251n24; Carl, 189–90, 249n7; on court sentencing of Matt Hale, 184–85; far right influenced by, 192–97; after Matt Hale's arrest, 189–92; membership and demographics, 132–33; U.S. Justice Department investigation of, 158, 177, 225n50; Women Frontier, 134–38. *See also* Church of the Creator; Hale, Matt
World Church of the Creator's Sisterhood, 137–38
World Church of the Creator's Women Frontier, 134–38
World Trade Center, 161–69, 170–73, 242n10, 247n49
World Union of National Socialists (WUNS), 9, 201n42
World War I, 4, 46
World War II, 48, 59, 211nn36, 41. *See also* Germany
Wotan, 36, 40, 53, 209n5; wotansvolk, 54, 250n18. *See also* Odinism
WPF. *See* White Pittsburgh Front
The Wrath of Nations (Pfaff), 62
WUNS. *See* World Union of National Socialists

Yousef, Ramzi, 186

Zionist Occupation Government (ZOG), 80, 192, 193
ZOG. *See* Zionist Occupation Government
Zulu Inkatha Party, 84
Zündel, Ernst, 109–10, 228n12

George Michael, associate professor of political science at the University of Virginia's College at Wise, is the author of *Confronting Right-Wing Extremism and Terrorism in the USA*; *The Enemy of My Enemy: The Alarming Convergence of Militant Islam and the Extreme Right*; and *Willis Carto and the American Far Right*.